Giuseppe Frassinetti, William Hutch

The New Parish Priest's Practical Manual

A work useful also for other ecclesiastics, especially for confessors and for

preachers

Giuseppe Frassinetti, William Hutch

The New Parish Priest's Practical Manual
A work useful also for other ecclesiastics, especially for confessors and for preachers

ISBN/EAN: 9783742835840

Manufactured in Europe, USA, Canada, Australia, Japa

Cover: Foto ©Lupo / pixelio.de

Manufactured and distributed by brebook publishing software (www.brebook.com)

Giuseppe Frassinetti, William Hutch

The New Parish Priest's Practical Manual

THE NEW PARISH PRIEST'S
PRACTICAL MANUAL:

A WORK USEFUL ALSO FOR OTHER ECCLESIASTICS,
ESPECIALLY FOR CONFESSORS AND
FOR PREACHERS.

BY

JOSEPH FRASSINETTI,

PRIOR OF S. SABINA, GENOA.

Translated from the Italian by

WILLIAM HUTCH, D.D.,

PRESIDENT OF ST. COLMAN'S COLLEGE, FERMOY.
AUTHOR OF "NANO NAGLE: HER LIFE, HER LABOURS, AND THEIR FRUITS";
"MRS. BALL: A BIOGRAPHY"; TRANSLATOR OF BELLECIO'S
"SPIRITUAL EXERCISES ACCORDING TO THE
METHOD OF ST. IGNATIUS"; ETC., ETC.

LONDON: NEW YORK:
BURNS AND OATES.   CATHOLIC PUBLICATION
SOCIETY COMPANY.

1883.

Price Six Shillings.

CONTENTS.

	PAGE
TRANSLATOR'S PREFACE,	xi
AUTHOR'S PREFACE,	xv

PART I.

OF THE DUTIES OF A PARISH PRIEST.

CHAPTER I. : PRELIMINARY REMARKS.—Capacity for preaching the Word of God—Capacity for hearing Confessions—Spirit of Sacrifice—Type of the Pastoral Spirit—Purity of Intention—Whether one may seek for a parish without being invited to do so by the Bishop, ... 1

CHAPTER II. : ON TAKING POSSESSION OF THE PARISH.— The First Sermon—The Inaugural Dinner—The Furnishing of the Parochial House—Of the relations to be maintained with the Priests of the place, and with the neighbouring Parish Priests—On the Pastor's relations with the Authorities, and with the more distinguished persons in his Parish—Of the Respect which a Parish Priest ought to show towards his Predecessor—Of the information which a Parish Priest ought to seek concerning the Necessities of his Flock, 17

CHAPTER III. : ON ADMINISTERING CORRECTION.—On the Correction of Priests—On administering Correction to the more distinguished persons in the Parish—On administering Correction to persons of the Lower

Orders—On the various methods of Correction—Of the persons in particular to whom Correction must be administered—Two Counsels regarding Mildness in administering Correction. 32

CHAPTER IV.: OF THE SCANDALS TO BE PREVENTED.—Of Scandals ruinous to Faith—Of Scandals ruinous to Morals. 60

CHAPTER V.: ON THE CARE OF THE POOR.—On the Caution necessary in order to discover the really Poor—How a Parish Priest ought to act towards the pretended Poor—On giving alms to persons who lead bad lives—How a Parish Priest ought to act towards the really Poor—Of the Classes of poor persons to whom a Parish Priest must give a preference. . . 86

CHAPTER VI.: ON THE CARE WHICH A PASTOR OUGHT TO HAVE OF HIS CHURCH.—Of the Church Committee—Of the Assistants employed about the Church—Of the cleanliness of the Church—Of the Sacristy, . . 110

CHAPTER VII.: OF THE CURATE.—Of the qualities which a Curate ought to possess—Of the advantages of having a Curate—How advantageous it is that the Parish Priest and Curate should live together, . . 122

CHAPTER VIII.: OF RELIGIOUS FUNCTIONS AND PIOUS PRACTICES, ... 129

CHAPTER IX.: OF THE BLESSING OF THE HOUSES, . . 133

CHAPTER X.: OF THE EPISCOPAL VISITATION OF THE PARISH, ... 138

CHAPTER XI.: OF CONFRATERNITIES AND SODALITIES.—Of Adult Confraternities—Of Congregations of Young Persons—Of Charitable Societies—Of other Pious Sodalities, ... 143

CHAPTER XII.: OF THE SCHOOLS, ... 157

CHAPTER XIII.: OF PROVIDING WHOLESOME LITERATURE FOR THE PEOPLE, ... 162

CHAPTER XIV.: OF PREACHING.—Of Preparation for Preaching—Of Clearness and Intelligibility in Preaching—Of the Affability which should accompany Preaching—Of the Earnestness which should accompany Preaching—Of Assiduity in Preaching—Counsels regarding the Instruction of the Children—Of the Instruction of Adults—On Preaching in Chapels-of-ease—On the Moderation to be observed when treating of Moral Questions—Counsels regarding sermons on the Sixth Commandment—Of the fitness of instructing the People on the excellence and merit of Virginity and Perfect Continence—Of Lenten Courses, Missions, and Retreats, ... 168

CHAPTER XV.: OF VARIOUS DUTIES REGARDING THE TEMPORALITIES OF THE PARISH.—Of the Parochial Revenues—Of the Parochial Archives—Of the manner of keeping the Parochial Books, and of an Inventory, 243

PART II.

OF THE SACRAMENTS.

CHAPTER I.: OF THE SACRAMENTS OF BAPTISM AND CONFIRMATION.—Of the Baptistery—Of the Baptism of children in danger of Death—Of the care with which a Pastor ought to impress upon his People not to defer the Baptism of their children—Of the circumstances under which the Parish Priest ought to seek permission from the Bishop to baptise in private houses—Of the Sponsors—Of Confirmation, . . 251

CHAPTER II.: OF THE MOST HOLY EUCHARIST.—Of the Altar and the Sacred Vestments—Of the Tabernacle, the Lamp, and the Sacred Vessels—Of the Hosts and the Wine for the Most Holy Eucharist—Of the Devotion which a Parish Priest ought to show towards the Blessed Sacrament—Of the Holy Communion—Of the First Communion of the Children—Of administering Communion to the Sick, . . . 266

CONTENTS.

APPENDIX I. : ON ASSISTING THE SICK AND DYING.—How Vigilant a Parish Priest ought to be in order that the Sick may be fortified in due time by the Holy Sacraments—On the Integrity of Confession on the part of the Sick and Dying—Some Remarks regarding the Confessions of Women in private houses—Of the Time for administering the Holy Viaticum—Of the Time for administering Extreme Unction—Of various Difficulties which the Parish Priest may have to encounter in administering the Sacraments to the Sick—Of Assisting the Dying, ... 303

APPENDIX II. : OF REFUSING ECCLESIASTICAL BURIAL, . 345

CHAPTER III. : OF THE SACRAMENT OF PENANCE.—Of the Study of Moral Theology—Of the Choice of Authors and Opinions—Of Assiduity in hearing Confessions—Of the Confessions of Men—Of the Confessions of Women—Of the Confessions of Children—Of the Confessions of Pious Persons—Of the Direction of persons who receive Extraordinary Favours from God, ... 353

CHAPTER IV. : OF EXTREME UNCTION, ... 404

CHAPTER V. : OF THE SACRAMENT OF ORDERS.—Of the Training of Young Boys who show signs of an Ecclesiastical Vocation—Of the Vigilance to be observed with regard to Ecclesiastical Aspirants, and of their Training, ... 407

CHAPTER VI. : OF THE SACRAMENT OF MATRIMONY.—Of the Interference of the Parish Priest in arranging Marriages—Of the Publication of the Banns—Of Marriages of Conscience—Of the Religious Instruction necessary for those who are about to contract Marriage—Of the State of Grace necessary in those who are about to contract Marriage—Of the Jurisdiction necessary for the Validity of a Marriage—Of the

CONTENTS. ix

Consent of the Parents—Of Mistakes occurring in
the names of the contracting parties in Dispensations
obtained from Rome, and in the Publication of the
Banns—Of Invalid Marriages, ... 415

PART III.

ON THE PRACTICE OF SOME OF THE VIRTUES WHICH ARE
MOST NECESSARY TO A PARISH PRIEST.

CHAPTER I.: OF THE PURITY OF CONSCIENCE NECESSARY
TO A PARISH PRIEST.—Of Avoiding Mortal Sin—Of
Avoiding Venial Sin, ... 443

CHAPTER II.: OF THE DESIRE OF PERFECTION NECES-
SARY TO A PARISH PRIEST.—A Parish Priest ought
to be a Master of Perfection—How necessary it is
that a Parish Priest should have a good Director—
How a Parish Priest ought to regulate his Exterior
Life, ... 449

CHAPTER III.: OF THE PRACTICE OF HUMILITY, . . 455

CHAPTER IV.: OF THE PRACTICE OF FORTITUDE.—Of the
Fortitude required in a Parish Priest in order to
fulfil his duties and to prevent crimes—Of Fortitude in coming to the rescue of souls, . . . 459

CHAPTER V.: OF THE PRACTICE OF CHASTITY.—Of the
special Dangers which beset this Virtue—General
Precautions—Precautions to be observed in the Houses
of Seculars, especially when engaged in the Duties of
the Ministry with Sick Women—Precautions to be
adopted regarding Relatives who may be living with
the Parish Priest—Precautions to be observed regarding the Domestic and other Females connected with
the service of the Parochial House—Precautions
regarding Alms-giving in the case of poor women—
Precautions regarding the presence of dangerous
Objects of Art in the Parochial House or in the
Church—Precautions to be taken against Calumny—
Concluding Remarks on the Subject of Chastity, . 467

CONTENTS.

CHAPTER VI.: OF THE PRACTICE OF MORTIFICATION.—Of the Mortification of the Senses—Of the Mortification of the Appetite—Of Mortification in the matter of Luxuries—Of the Discretion to the observed in Corporal Mortifications, ... 492

CHAPTER VII.: OF THE PRACTICE OF DISINTERESTEDNESS, ... 505

CHAPTER VIII.: OF THE PRACTICE OF PRAYER, . . 514

CHAPTER IX.: OF THE PRACTICE OF ZEAL.—The zealous Parish Priest exerts himself to the utmost, and without sparing himself, to promote the Glory of God and the Salvation of Souls—A zealous Parish Priest will avail himself of the assistance of those Priests whom he has in his Parish, and will foster the proper spirit in them by means of Ecclesiastical Conferences—A zealous Parish Priest avails himself of the assistance of Pious Seculars—A zealous Parish Priest is very Moderate in his Recreations—A zealous Parish Priest promotes every good work of Christian Piety, . . 520

CHAPTER X.: OF THE PRACTICE OF OBEDIENCE, . . 534

CONCLUSION, ... 541

APPENDIX: *On the Perpetual Adoration of the Most Holy Sacrament, for the Exaltation of Holy Church*, . . 546

TRANSLATOR'S PREFACE.

ECCLESIASTICS, for whose exclusive use this work is intended, will ask no further guarantee of its merits than what is contained in the following extract from Father Ballerini's edition of Gury's Moral Theology. Writing "De obligationibus Parochorum," Father Ballerini says: "De hoc argumento dignissimum est quod legatur, imo quod diu noctuque manibus teratur opusculum, cui titulus '*Manuale pratico pel Parroco novello, per Giuseppe Frassinetti, Priore di S. Sabina in Genova: operetta utile anche agli altri Ecclesiastici, specialmente Confessori e Predicatori*'. Quidquid enim ad quœlibet Parochi munia pertinere quavis in re potest, in sacramentorum nimirum administratione, in functionibus sacris, in administrandis bonis tum quæ ad parochiale beneficium, tùm quæ ad fabricam Ecclesiæ spectant, in templi decore, ac domus etiam parochialis decentia servanda, in pauperum, infirmorum, scholarumque cura gerenda, in piis congregationibus instituendis aut fovendis, in divini verbi pabulo tum per prædicationem tum etiam per utilem librorum lectionem plebi suppeditando, in subditis, ubi opus sit, corrigendis, in scandalis, sive contra fidem sive contra bonos mores amovendis, etc., *id omne in egregio hoc opusculo attingitur.* Neque vero Auctor hæc exsequitur per prolixas, ac veluti concionatorias parænases, multoque minus per acerbiores, ut nonnulli assolent, expostulationes, quibus Ecclesiasticorum vitia carpere videatur, sed breviter ac sobrie per monita quædam, sapientiæ sane prudentiæque plena, quæ suavissima ac mitissima caritas, SOLIDA DOCTRINA, DIUTURNA EXPERIENTIA, AC TEMPERANTISSIMA JUDICII INDOLES (discretionem alii dixerint) suppeditare valet. Hinc autem illud existit summi profecto momenti commodum, quod ad cavendos errores, in quos impingere quidam, aut experientia nondum sat eruditi aut minus prudentia instructi, interdum solent, non quidem factis eum suo aliorumve damno subinde gravi experimentis, sed tutissima in antecessum via demonstrata præmuniantur" *(Ballerini's edition of Gury, Theol. Moral.*

Tract. de Stat. particular., Cap. II., Art. 2. De obligat. Parochorum, in Nota).

It would be impossible to add another word in commendation of Father Frassinetti's work. Indeed the praise bestowed upon it by the illustrious Jesuit Theologian, in the passage quoted above, might well seem extravagant, were not Ballerini's reputation for solid learning and sound judgment universally recognised in the Church.

Frassinetti's "Manual," which has already run through nine editions in Italy, appears now, for the first time, in an English dress. In executing my Translation of this valuable work, I have endeavoured throughout not only to reproduce faithfully the substance of the original, but also to adhere as closely as possible to the very letter of the text—a task which I have not always found easy, owing to the fact that the Author evinces a decided partiality for long and laboured sentences.

I have, now and again, omitted an occasional paragraph which, in my own judgment as well as in the judgment of others whom I consulted, would be entirely unsuited to the circumstances of English-speaking countries. These paragraphs, however, are very few, and if they were all put together, would not amount to more than seven or eight pages.

I have also added occasional foot-notes, whenever I thought that they might serve to explain or to confirm the doctrine laid down in the text.

With these few remarks, I now present this work to my brother priests in every English-speaking country, in the hope that it may contribute, even in a small degree, to promote God's glory and the salvation of souls.

WILLIAM HUTCH.

St. Colman's College, Fermoy,
Feast of St. Luke, *October 18, 1883.*

AUTHOR'S PREFACE.

BEING now thirty years a Parish Priest, although in many things, and even in all, I may be deficient in speculative science, I think I can no longer fail in matters of practical knowledge; and, moreover, having discharged the duties of this office for upwards of seven years in a suburban parish, which embraces both town and country, my experience may prove of some value for country, town, and city parishes.

Beyond this, I put forward no other claim to justify my project of publishing this "Practical Manual". I present it to new Parish Priests with the freedom of an elder brother, who can say to them: You, fresh from your studies, surpass me in theoretical science; but, in practical matters, I must, of necessity, have an advantage over you.

Nevertheless, I shall never rely on my own individual judgment. I promise to put forward nothing which has not the approval of persons more intelligent and more experienced than myself; and this resolution, which with God's help I will not change, gives me great ground for hoping that, even should I fail in accomplishing any considerable amount of good, at least there shall be no danger of my doing any harm.

I must not omit to mention that, some days after I had conceived the idea of composing this work, and had written barely a few pages of it, one of the brightest lights of our Episcopate was good enough to suggest to me the identical plan which I have followed in this Manual, exhorting me at the same time to commence it; and this fact, necessarily, encouraged me to complete the task which I had just begun.

I shall divide this Manual into Three Parts. In the First, I shall treat of the duties of a Parish Priest, with the exception of those which have reference to the administration of the Sacraments, which will form the subject-matter of the Second Part. In the Third Part, I shall speak of the practice of those virtues which are most necessary to a Parish Priest.

Part I.

OF THE DUTIES OF A PARISH PRIEST.

CHAPTER I.

PRELIMINARY REMARKS.

INASMUCH as this work of mine may excite the curiosity of some priest who is aspiring to a Parochial Benefice, it will not be irrelevant to make a few preliminary observations on the qualities and dispositions which are required in one who has in view the office of Parish Priest.

Now, in this matter, I prescind from those qualities which are required in any priest in order that he may be reputed good—that is to say, unblemished orthodoxy, irreproachable morals, a knowledge of Dogmatic and Moral Theology, and zeal for the glory of God. A priest who should be found wanting in any of these particulars would not be a good priest; much less would he be a good Parish Priest, which means a pastor of souls. He would be, instead, a wolf—that is, a dangerous guardian of the flock. In addition to the foregoing qualities, there are others requisite for a Parish Priest, in defect of which he would be unfit for his office. These are especially—

§ 1. Capacity for Preaching the Word of God.

A Parish Priest is bound, in the first place, to nourish his flock with the food of the word of God; and, therefore, it is necessary that he should have capacity for preaching. It is not required that he be endowed with extraordinary talent for the discharge of this duty, so as to be an accomplished orator in the usual acceptance of that term; but it *is* necessary that he be able to expound plainly, and clearly, the truths of Faith and of Christian morality, and to exhort his parishioners zealously to practise virtue, and to fly from vice. Now, this degree of capacity is ordinarily found in every priest possessed of intelligence and knowledge combined with discretion; unless, indeed, some weakness of the chest prevents him from speaking loudly, or a special nervousness restrains him from appearing before the public. But, if we except these two cases, every good priest could fit himself for the office of preaching, so far as it is required for the discharge of the pastoral ministry.

If, however, a priest be really defective in any quality necessary for announcing the divine word to the people *in a suitable manner*, he ought not to aspire to the office of Parish Priest. I say "*in a suitable manner*": because though a rare and finished style of oratory is not required, nevertheless, an ordinary and becoming fluency is indispensable; so that the preaching of the word of God may not become utterly disagreeable to the ears of the Faithful, whereby they would be induced to absent themselves from it altogether, to their serious loss. This does occur in some places, where the parishioners dispense themselves from hearing the word of God, because the parish priest wearies them, or delays them too long.

And let it not be said that the Parish Priest who is himself incapable of preaching may discharge his duty by deputy. This might be allowed where the incapacity arose subsequent to his appointment to the pastoral charge. In such case, certainly, he could not be required to renounce his benefice; although he would be bound to provide for the wants of his flock, by committing to another the duty of preaching in his stead. But when this incapacity exists previous to his appointment, we must conclude that, however worthy he may be as a priest, he is not called by God to the pastoral office. The opinion of St. Thomas of Aquin is well known—that God in electing a person to any office whatsoever, first confers upon him the qualities necessary to discharge its duties in a fitting manner.

§ 2. Capacity for Hearing Confessions.

A Parish Priest is bound, in the second place, to hear the confessions of his parishioners; and it is, therefore, necessary that he should possess the required aptitude for the exercise of this holy ministry.

Now, I shall say nothing of the knowledge requisite for the discharge of this duty; both because it is presupposed in a good priest, and, moreover, because without it he would not be approved in the concursus for obtaining the parish.[1] I shall merely observe that knowledge is not, of itself, sufficient; there being required, in addition, unvarying patience, and a prudent readiness of judgment, without which it would be impossible to exercise this ministry with that daily assiduity, and that attractive zeal, which the office of Parish Priest demands. Therefore, it cannot be doubted that a priest is unfitted for a parochial benefice, if long and constant attendance in the confessional would prove too irksome to him, or a task which he would be unable to discharge with sufficient despatch.

And, in truth, how could that priest endure weary hours in the confessional, who cannot put up with the coarse, vulgar manners of uneducated people, the obstinacy and whims of the capricious, and the inconstancy of relapsing sinners? How could he hold out under prolonged labours in the tribunal, if he were liable to give way to constant scruples regarding all the doubts and fancies that might come into his head—ever suspecting that his penitent is confessing badly, ever fearing that he is himself wanting in his duty in the matter of interrogation, and so forth?

---

[1] Here, and elsewhere throughout this work (see § 6 *infra*), the author supposes that parishes are conferred in accordance with the instructions of the Council of Trent (Sess. 24, cap. 18 *de reform*), which provide that the election of Parish Priest shall be made upon a competitive examination of candidates, or, as it is termed, *concursus*, the vacant parish being given to the candidate who shall be judged most worthy. It is scarcely necessary to remark that this method of conferring parishes is not followed in English-speaking countries.—*Trans.*

Nay, I will add, furthermore, how could such an one confess his penitents with fruit? And were he to suppose that he might discharge this portion of his pastoral duty by means of others, he would be labouring under a grave mistake; for, it is of far greater importance that a Parish Priest should himself direct the consciences of his parishioners, than that he should personally preach to them the word of God; since the former involves a spiritual culture much more delicate, affecting them far more intimately, and, therefore, to be less easily entrusted to others.

§ 3. Spirit of Sacrifice.

In the third place, there is required in a Parish Priest a spirit of sacrifice, so that he be ready to renounce his personal convenience, habits, tastes, and inclinations, whenever the good of his flock may demand it. And here I do not speak of those cases in which a pastor may be bound even to lay down his life for his flock, since such cases are extraordinary, and of rare occurrence. I speak of ordinary cases only, in which there is question, as has been said, of sacrificing merely one's convenience, habits, tastes and inclinations. The priest who does not feel himself daily disposed to submit to sacrifices and privations of this kind, ought not to aspire to the charge of a parish.

I have said "*daily disposed,*" because it may easily happen that a Parish Priest be called upon to make such sacrifices every day. Therefore, a priest who should think it too much to interrupt, even frequently, his night's rest, to deprive himself from time to time of his recreations and amusements, and who should wish to devote himself continually to the study of literature and the arts, would not be a good selection for a parochial benefice. But if such an one were to imagine that he might rid himself of the many troubles of his office, and avoid the many mortifications which it entails, by employing others to sacrifice themselves in his stead, I must repeat, for the third time, that he would be deceiving himself; for—it cannot be said too often—a Parish Priest must discharge the duties of his office *personally*. And on this subject it is well to remark that a Parish Priest is, *par excellence*, the "workman" mentioned in the Gospel. Now, a workman is one who works himself; and whosoever does not work in this manner, but contents himself with merely giving directions, and seeing that others work in his stead, is not a workman, but a superintendent of works.

§ 4. Type of the Pastoral Spirit.

If we duly reflect upon the matter, we cannot, perhaps, discover any more perfect type of the pastoral spirit, than that which animates a mother. It would appear that the spirit of divine charity infused into the heart of the priest whom God calls to the pastoral charge, to enable him to discharge his duties therein, cannot find a more fitting counterpart than the love implanted by nature in a mother's breast, to enable her to comply with a mother's duties.

Natural love employs a pleasing violence with a mother, compelling her to nourish her children with the fruit of her own blood. Afterwards, it imposes upon her a personal obligation to warm them, to clothe them, to keep them clean and neat, to amuse them, to guard and watch over them; to teach them to speak, to walk, to eat, to take repose, and whatever else is required by the usages or necessary laws of life. Yet, meanwhile, what surprises us is, that she finds pleasure and delight in all these occupations, which, of themselves, bring so much trouble and annoyance. Wherefore it is, that to these duties, in themselves so wearisome, but which maternal affection renders sweet and pleasant, she sacrifices the comforts belonging to her rank, her former habits of life, the entertainments and festivities most suitable to her age, and, frequently, the consideration due to her family, the demands of friendship, her legitimate recreations, and her night's repose. Such is the power of a mother's love! For this reason, a woman who has a presentiment that the duties imposed by maternity may prove too difficult or too burdensome for her, and who feels that she lacks the courage to subject herself to the privations and troubles which accompany them, ought not to aspire to become a mother, because she does not possess a mother's spirit.

Now, in the same manner, divine charity, diffused through the heart of a pastor of souls, does sweet violence to him in behalf of his spiritual children. Wherefore, he feels himself impelled to feed them, personally, with the fruit of the good spirit wherewith he nourishes himself interiorly; personally to excite in them a holy love of it; to clothe them with the robes of Christian virtues; to adorn them with merits for eternal life; to wash them from the stains of sin; to recreate their minds with the joys and delights of piety; and to be watchful of their wants and dangers, that he may guard and defend them. Wherefore, also, he personally instructs them in whatever appertains to faith and morals, and guides them in the path of perfection. In a word, he exerts himself to the utmost that they may attain eternal salvation.

Now, there is not the slightest doubt that cares of this kind would become unendurable, because of the many disgusts and annoyances which accompany them, if they were not rendered palatable by the supernatural relish of pastoral charity; but, once flavoured with this relish, it is astonishing how agreeable and pleasant they become, and how readily a good Parish Priest sacrifices to them his comforts, his convenience, his personal habits, his recreations, and the usages and requirements of society. Such is the power of a pastor's love for his flock! Wherefore, a priest who should foresee that the duties and cares of a pastor would prove too disagreeable to him, and who, wanting the courage to give them his personal attention, should be forced to discharge his duties by means of others, would not be endowed with the pastoral spirit, and ought not aspire to become a Parish Priest.

Nevertheless, I do not mean to say that a Parish Priest ought not to call in the assistance of others to aid him in the discharge of his duties; for this would be to lay down a doctrine no less foolish than injurious to souls. A good mother usefully employs the assistance of other women in the rearing of her children, and sometimes she has real need of such assistance. A workman, likewise, when occasion requires, procures help in his labours, nor does he thereby cease to be a good workman. So, too, a Parish Priest, who himself works, will usefully, and sometimes of necessity, seek for coadjutors to supply what he cannot personally perform, especially in large and populous parishes. Of these coadjutors we shall have to speak more particularly later on.

§ 5. OF PURITY OF INTENTION.

A priest who aspires to the care of souls must have in view the threefold end of the Glory of God, the Salvation of Souls, and his own Sanctification. Should he propose to himself other ignoble ends—such as to obtain authority or pre-eminence among the clergy, to enjoy a good revenue, &c.—he must be judged unworthy of a parochial benefice. Whosoever wishes to aspire worthily to this office, must seek the glory of God—that is, that God's name be sanctified amongst the members of the flock entrusted to him, by means of the exercise of all the works of Christian piety. He must seek the salvation of souls—that is, to extirpate from his parish deadly vices, and to plant therein life-giving virtues. He must seek his own sanctification—that is, he must aim at the attainment of that Christian perfection proper to the exalted state of the priesthood, and which is indispensable if a pastor wish to promote effectively the glory of God, and the salvation of souls.

Nevertheless, it is to be deplored that many aspire to a parochial benefice precisely as seculars seek for a situation; not looking to the good which it may be in their power to effect while discharging its duties, but solely to the advantages to be derived therefrom for themselves and for their families. In fact, many look exclusively to emolument. If a parish be poor, they decline it on this very score; if, on the other hand, it be rich, on this ground alone they strain every nerve to secure it. It is, moreover, somewhat astonishing to see them so incautious as not to conceal, or, at least, dissemble their views on this point. They do not call a parish good, unless it be rich, nor bad, unless it be poor; and they will tell you candidly that they do not care to get a parish at all, unless it be a good one.

But if sometimes, at the beginning of their career, they content themselves with a parish which affords but a small income, they do so merely through obedience to necessity; and meanwhile—even before they have entered into possession—they have already come to the resolution of resigning it, the moment that a richer parish offers. Thus, regarding themselves merely as Parish Priests *ad tempus*—and that for the very briefest period possible—they are like pilgrims or travellers in the parish, and do not entertain for their flock the affection of a true pastor. Parish Priests of this description ought to be compared, not to mothers, but to nurses, who care children for hire, and who are prepared to abandon the first entrusted to them, when another is offered that will bring better pay.

Woe to the people whose misfortune it is to have as Parish Priest one of these traffickers! They are the hirelings mentioned in the Gospel—whom the wolf fears not.

§ 6. Whether One may Seek for a Parish without being Commanded or Invited to do so by the Bishop.

Ecclesiastics ought not to forget that "the Holy Ghost hath placed Bishops to rule the Church of God" (Acts xx. 28); and there is no doubt that the collation of parochial benefices is a very special province of ecclesiastical government, because the sanctification of the people depends on having good Parish Priests, suited to their requirements. Wherefore it is that, to meet this want, Bishops receive special lights from God; and a priest invited by the Bishop to a concursus for a parish,[1] even though there be no express command, ought to accept the invitation, nor would it be commendable humility to refuse to present himself, under the pretext of his own unworthiness. On the other hand, he ought to doubt of his vocation to the pastoral office, or at least to the

---
[1] See note p. 4 *supra*.

government of a particular parish, should he be dissuaded by the Bishop from taking part in the concursus.

Prescinding, then, from those cases in which the Bishop may have manifested his wish, and supposing, on the other hand, that one is sufficiently prepared by prayer and study for the new burden which he proposes to assume, and that he has obtained the consent of his spiritual director, I reply in the affirmative to the question proposed above—that is, that with the simple permission of the Bishop, without his command or invitation, a priest may take part in a concursus for a parochial benefice. Indeed, this statement cannot be called in question: for, since the Council of Trent has ordained that parochial benefices should be conferred by concursus, it is manifestly supposed that a priest may present himself uninvited. Moreover, Bishops desire this; who, especially when they are strangers in a Diocese, do not know all the ecclesiastics who are capable of governing a parish, but become acquainted with the capacity of several by this very means of a free concursus.

Nevertheless, some persons who have an undue leaning towards the olden times, and yet, perhaps, are little acquainted with them, through a habit of generalising from some isolated facts, or interpreting too literally some emphatic saying of one of the Fathers, teach that no priest ought to aspire to a parochial benefice without the command, or at least the invitation, of the Bishop. They say that such was the ancient custom, and that the same ought to be observed at the present day, considering the great danger inseparable from the care of souls. Hence, they set down as rash, nay, presumptuous, those who voluntarily thrust themselves into an office from which the very saints shrank affrighted.

Such persons never reflect that, arguing from some particular facts of ecclesiastical history, they themselves, before aspiring to the priesthood, ought to have waited until the Bishops should have dragged them forcibly from their families, and led them into the sanctuary against their own inclination, as frequently happened in the early ages of the Church. Nay, in accordance with the example of some, not to say of many saints, they ought to have abandoned the world, and gone to dwell in the deserts, as those saints did, to avoid the dangers which surround those who live in the world.

Meanwhile, it seems to us that such persons are very imprudent. For when a practice is in accordance with the laws of the Church—as is the practice of a voluntary concursus—it never ought to be censured, but simply approved. Wherefore, an ecclesiastic will do well in aspiring to a parochial benefice, according to the provisions of the Council of Trent, if he can feel satisfied that he possesses the necessary qualifications, and is desirous of co-operating in the salvation of souls. For the rest, he may imitate the saints in their extraordinary practices, when he shall have had their extraordinary inspirations.

But what of the danger inseparable from the care of souls? The strength of divine grace is proportionate to it: for it is certain that to the hermit, who thinks only of himself, God gives grace sufficient for himself; and to the Parish Priest, who must think also of his parish, He gives grace sufficient for himself and for his parishioners; just as to the Pope, who has charge of the Universal Church, He gives as much grace as is sufficient for himself, and for the care of the entire Christian flock.

The remark of St. Peter Chrysologus on this subject is very consoling: namely, that the pastors of souls resemble nurses who rear the children of their sovereigns. Their masters do not consider these women entitled to any special treatment because of their own individual merit: yet, because they have been entrusted with the rearing of their offspring, they treat them like princesses, in order that the royal children may be fed upon more nutritious milk. God acts after the same manner with us, pastors of souls. Though we may merit nothing on our own account, yet, for the sake of the souls entrusted to us, among whom there are always some greatly beloved by Him, He shows Himself liberal in conferring blessings and graces upon us, and enriches our souls with His precious favours, in order that we may be enabled to supply proper nourishment to these His beloved daughters.[1] For this reason, the care of souls, far from being hurtful, will prove profitable to us.

This much I have said for the purpose of encouraging all good ecclesiastics, who possess the requisite capacity, to compete for parochial benefices, subject

[1] *Rodriguez*, Part III., Treatise I., chap. vi.

to due dependence on the Bishop, in accordance with the provisions of the Council of Trent; and such encouragement cannot fail to prove beneficial to the faithful. As a matter of fact, Parish Priests are necessary in the Church of God: they are necessary in great numbers; and these are they who can effect the greatest good. Nay more, it must be confessed that without them the Bishops can scarcely accomplish any good whatsoever. Place, if you will, a St. Charles Borromeo in a diocese where the Parish Priests are bad, and what good will be effected by your St. Charles? He might convoke synods, publish pastoral letters, go through his diocese in person, send out visitors, and so forth; yet, if the Parish Priests, who come into immediate contact with the people, be bad, all would remain a dead letter—it would be labour thrown away. Take, on the other hand, the case of a diocese possessing good Parish Priests. Even though the Bishop should not be a St. Charles, still they will do good of themselves. The Parish Priest, in fact, preaches, hears confessions, instructs the children, assists the sick, visits annually all the houses in his parish, comes into contact with all the families, consoles them in their afflictions, and succours them in their necessities. If he discharges properly all his duties, an immense amount of good is accomplished by his unaided efforts, which cannot be hindered by others. From this it is evident, that those who encourage good ecclesiastics to aspire to a parochial benefice, render good service to the Church, and confer a singular benefit on souls; while those rigid ascetics are deserving of grave censure, who would dissuade them from doing so, for the false motives set down above. Even should there happen to be found amongst them some respectable author, we can only say of him "*Quandoque bonus dormitat Homerus*".

CHAPTER II.

ON TAKING POSSESSION OF THE PARISH.

§ 1. The First Sermon.

Of itself, it is not a matter of any importance whether a new Parish Priest takes possession of his benefice solemnly, or privately. Nevertheless, the circumstances or the usages of localities might attach some importance to the solemn function, so that it would not be well to omit it. In this case, the Parish Priest ought to inaugurate his ministry with a thoroughly pastoral discourse, in which he would clearly lay before the people the good intentions with which he is animated, and would warmly exhort them to correspond to the same, so that the measures which he will take for their spiritual good may prove effectual.

A pretentious and ornate discourse, especially on this his first appearance, would mark out the new Parish Priest as a silly man, and one without any heart for his children, to whom he comes to break for the first time the bread of the Divine Word. It would mark him out as a silly man; because he goes begging for compliments, which can be paid him only by impudent pedants who do not know, or do not reflect what the word of God really is: and a man without heart; because he shows that he does not care to make his thoughts and feelings understood by the greater part of his audience, who are really interested in them, and are desirous of receiving spiritual nourishment. Of this, however, I shall have to speak later on, when I come to treat more expressly of preaching.

§ 2. The Inaugural Dinner.

On taking solemn possession, the Parish Priest ought to give the customary dinner, inviting to it the priests of the Parish (or, should they be too numerous, at least the most distinguished among them), the churchwardens, and also the most influential persons in the place, in order to give them proof of his esteem and consideration.

He must take care, however, that this dinner be in keeping with the position, not of a great lord or squire, but of a poor pastor of souls. I say *poor:* because, for the most part, Parish Priests are really poor; and, even where they are not so, they ought to regard themselves as poor, since it is not fitting that they should squander upon their table, that money which they might expend so much more profitably for the benefit of the Church, and of their poor parishioners. On these occasions, some new Parish Priests, whose means are well known to be very limited, expend large sums; and this desire to play the fine gentleman secures to them, at the very outset, the pity of all men of sense, and the sneers of the parish wits. Since the inaugural dinner is a mark of esteem shown to the more respectable parishioners who are invited, it ought to be *respectable*; but it can be all this, without becoming a splendid and sumptuous banquet. It not unfrequently happens that the frivolity of the first sermon, and the sumptuous style of the inaugural dinner, form a bad recommendation which the new Parish Priest gives of himself to his parishioners.

§ 3. THE FURNISHING OF THE PAROCHIAL HOUSE.

One of the first thoughts which occupy certain new Parish Priests is to furnish the new parochial house, and especially an apartment for the reception of visitors. Yet, whilst no one can blame a Parish Priest for having a room set apart and nicely furnished for this purpose, there is no doubt, nevertheless, that the furniture of the entire parochial house, including this reception room, ought to be grave and simple, so as not to exhibit a trace of luxury or effeminacy. A Parish Priest, whose duty it is to preach against worldly vanities, must not let it appear that, whilst he disapproves of them in the houses of others, he considers them suitable in his own.

Some parochial drawing-rooms are so sumptuous or showy, that they might be considered suitable for a nobleman, or for a newly-wedded pair. Still worse is it when they are decorated with profane pictures and prints—and God grant that these same be not, also, somewhat indelicate. In this last case, we should be compelled to form a bad opinion of the Parish Priest, as shall be said later on, when we return to this subject more expressly. The new Parish Priest must take care that the furniture and ornaments of his house exhibit that modesty and grave simplicity which a minister of Jesus Christ, and much more a pastor of souls, ought to teach by word and example.

The new Parish Priest ought to reflect that his drawing-room—that, namely, which he ought specially to regard as such—is the Church, wherein he receives and lodges, night and day, the most august person of the Lord Jesus Christ; and where, to His honour and glory, he performs the most holy and tremendous functions of a supernatural ministry. This is the apartment which he ought to keep beautiful and well adorned, so that it may inspire the people with feelings of respect and devotion, and be a less unworthy resting place for the Holy of Holies. The Parish Priest who shall be very solicitous to keep this apartment beautiful and well-adorned, will not sin before God, and will be excused in the eyes of men, if he shall seem to be careless about his own private dwelling. I shall make a few additional remarks on this subject when speaking, later on, of the care which a Parish Priest should bestow upon his Church.

§ 4. On the Relations to be maintained with the Priests of the Place, and with the Neighbouring Parish Priests.

Before taking possession of his benefice, the Parish Priest should seek for information regarding the character of the priests of the place. He ought more particularly to make these inquiries of the Bishop, and of others, also, who may know them, since the Bishop cannot be informed of everything. Whilst receiving this information (I do not speak now of what he may learn from the Bishop), he must listen to everything that may be told him, being on his guard, however, against placing full trust in all that he may hear either for or against them. For, persons are not always sufficiently prudent and cautious in the judgments to which they give expression: they entertain sometimes secret sympathies and antipathies; and, for this reason, do not always speak with due sincerity. Wherefore, the Parish Priest ought to listen to all; but, afterwards, comparing the different accounts which he has received, he must make it his study to discover which of them he ought to believe.

Having found out who are the best, the less good, and even the indifferent priests in the place, he must make it appear, on going to take possession, that, with the exception of a case to be mentioned afterwards, he holds them all in esteem. Nevertheless, he shall not open his heart except to those whom he thoroughly knows to be good priests, zealous for the glory of God and for the salvation of souls. He will be able to place confidence in these when he wishes to get information, specially regarding the more influential persons in the parish, in order that he may know what he has to hope or to fear from them. Meanwhile, he must be careful to keep secret this special confidence which he reposes in these more trustworthy ecclesiastics, in order not to afford an opportunity for jealousies, which might prove very injurious.

To the less worthy, yet not absolutely bad, ecclesiastics, he ought to exhibit every mark of civility and respect, in order that they may not be tempted to oppose him, or to speak injuriously of his undertakings or intentions. A good Parish Priest, having no reason to expect much assistance from these, ought to adopt every precaution not to provoke their opposition. This prudential measure is particularly necessary on his first entry into the parish; because the people, not having had as yet an opportunity of forming an independent estimate of him, are easily impressed by the opinions of others, and especially of priests, whom they consider the most competent judges in a question of this kind.

Should he find in his parish any priest of indifferent character, but not known as such outside the locality, he must not at first let it appear that he knows anything of his failings; so that this priest may not be able to say that the Pastor's mind had been prejudiced against him by his enemies, and, moreover, that he may be on his guard not to forfeit the esteem, in which he may flatter himself that he is held by the new Parish Priest. But if he should persevere, nevertheless, in his disedifying life, as soon as he must naturally have concluded that the report of his conduct has already reached the ears of the Parish Priest, the latter should correct him in the manner to be indicated later on.

Finally, should this indifferent priest be known as

such even outside the locality, the new Pastor ought not to conceal from him, even from the very beginning, his sorrow at finding such a scandal in his parish; and, both for the edification of his flock, and to diminish the force of the bad example, he ought, without doubt, to abstain from manifesting towards him any mark whatsoever of esteem.

The new Pastor ought, moreover, to put himself in friendly relations with the neighbouring Parish Priest—a matter of great importance, because of the mutual assistance which they can render to one another in many ways. He ought, however, to bear in mind that, if any of the neighbouring Parish Priests were of a strange disposition and not likely to fall in with his views, it would not be advisable to seek to become intimate with him. It is folly to seek for one's friends those who do not share a community of feelings; because, for this very reason, they can never become real friends. To attempt to do so, involves the risk that to an unreal friendship there may succeed open enmity. One acts more wisely in respecting such men, than in seeking to become intimate with them. Contact may produce a violent shock instead of cohesion.

§ 5. On the Pastor's relations with the Authorities, and with the more Distinguished Persons in his Parish.

The new Parish Priest, on entering into possession of his benefice, ought to bestow some thought upon the relations which he may be able to maintain with the civil authorities of the place. If the spirit of the times be friendly to religion and to her ministers, the civil authorities, either from principle and their own individual convictions, or at least from a feeling of respect and deference towards one placed over them, will show themselves well disposed towards the Parish Priest, and favourably inclined to co-operate with him in the exercise of his ministry. In such circumstances, he ought to manifest towards them proofs not only of his esteem, but, also, of his confidence; because in this manner he will secure their valuable support in the discharge of his pastoral duties, nor need he fear that they will require of him in return anything which might do violence to his conscience.

If, on the contrary, the spirit of the times be evil, and those who control public affairs be hostile to religion, the civil authorities of the place will, as a rule, share this feeling, and, in consequence, the Parish Priest can scarcely escape open, or disguised persecution. In these circumstances, the Parish Priest ought to show respect to the authorities, according to the advice of St. Paul "*etiam discolis*"; but let him not aspire to their confidence, because in order to obtain and preserve it, he would sometimes be led to fail in his duty, by culpably conniving at their misdeeds.

The new Parish Priest ought, also, to manifest special marks of esteem towards the leading and more influential persons in the locality; and, even though there should be some amongst them not very pious or edifying, he ought at first to make it appear that he entertains a favourable opinion of all, so that it may not be said that he came into the parish prejudiced against any one, and jealousies and enmities may be thus avoided. On his first entry into the parish, he ought to act as does a father, who believes all his children to be good, until he shall have received proof of their wickedness.

Prudence demands this course of action, in order that the Pastor may be loved and respected by all, and, likewise, that the bad may keep themselves under restraint, and be more circumspect. And, assuredly, if they see that the Parish Priest holds them in esteem, being anxious not to forfeit his good opinion, as happens especially in small places, even though they may not entirely abandon their evil courses, they will, at least, shew themselves more guarded and cautious, which, in itself, is a matter of some importance.

The Parish Priest shall, likewise, take care not to appear the friend or confidant of one family more than of another, especially if feuds or factions should exist amongst them. He ought to make it a point to show equal honour to them all, that he himself may be equally esteemed and respected by all, and thus be in a position to do good to all, as his pastoral office requires. Moreover, this impartiality is far more necessary to preserve harmony, if already existing, among the more distinguished families in the parish, and to create it if absent—a blessing fraught with many happy results for the entire population.

Here the question might arise, whether a Parish Priest would not be guilty of the fault of acceptance of persons, in showing particular marks of deference and honour to his more respectable parishioners. For, acting on that spirit of faith which ought to animate an ecclesiastic, all Christians—be they rich or poor, learned or unlearned, gentle or simple—have in his eyes an equal dignity—that of children of God. However, it is easy to perceive that this doctrine would lead us on to ignore the providential order established by God in human society, in consideration of which St. Paul wrote: "Render therefore to all men their dues . . . honour to whom honour". The advocates of the opposite doctrine would have the Parish Priest pay equal respect to the prince and to the shepherd.

The Parish Priest would indeed fail through acceptance of persons, were he to pay greater attention to the wants of his more respectable parishioners than to those of persons of inferior condition; if, for example, he were to show himself prompt to hear the confessions of the rich, and reluctant to hear those of the poor; if he were to leave poor women seated at his confessional, whilst he went elsewhere to attend to some rich lady, who might be too impatient to wait long in the Church: if he were to visit frequently, and constantly to attend upon rich persons, when sick or dying, whilst he forgot, and almost abandoned the sick and dying of the poorer classes. In these and similar cases, there would be very reprehensible and scandalous acceptance of persons; because spiritual necessities are equal in the poor and in the rich, and both the one and the other have identical rights, to which the Parish Priest ought to attend impartially.

Should he act otherwise, he would not only be guilty of injustice, but would give occasion for remarks and murmurings which are not edifying, and which redound but little to the honour of the sacred ministry.

It is quite another matter, when the distinction made between the rich and the poor has reference merely to worldly compliments and social usages; and it is worthy of remark that even the poor themselves readily submit to be treated in a free-and-easy style, without those marks of respect and distinction, which they themselves know are not due to persons of their condition.

Wherefore, a Parish Priest is not to be censured for showing special marks of esteem to his more distinguished parishioners. In doing so, he simply shows himself acquainted with the truth that whosoever is placed by God in a more elevated position in the social scale, merits particular honour and respect: he simply follows a practice entirely conformable to reason, and to the teaching of St. Paul.

§ 6. OF THE RESPECT WHICH THE PARISH PRIEST OUGHT TO SHOW TOWARDS HIS PREDECESSOR.

The new Parish Priest ought always to hold his predecessor in esteem, and to speak respectfully of him; unless, indeed, he should have been a bad man, in which case, not being able to say anything in his favour, he ought to keep silent altogether. The estimate which some new Parish Priests form of their predecessors, and the manner in which they speak of them, afford evidence of little charity and great thoughtlessness, and give rise to much surprise if not to scandal. To listen to them, you would suppose that everything had been ill-done and mismanaged in the parish through the fault of their predecessor; and they will give you to understand that they are themselves almost done to death, through striving to put matters in good trim, and to remedy all the evils brought about by the ignorance, the negligence, and the incapacity of those who preceded them.

When such men, in their turn, come to have a successor, it is a pretty thing to hear the same old story told by whoever succeeds to their place. Such complaints, even though they be well-founded, are evidence of little charity, whilst they are powerless to remedy an evil already accomplished; and they serve no purpose, unless, indeed, it be to lessen the reputation of another. They argue a great want of judgment; since they evidently spring from a vain desire to appear better than the former Parish Priests, and from not reflecting that sensible people generally allow a large margin for exaggeration in the case of such complaints. Finally, they furnish matter for surprise, and even for scandal; since they serve only to make known to the people the real, or even the apparent or exaggerated, weaknesses and failings of the ministers of the Lord.

Wherefore, a new Parish Priest, if prudent, will always speak respectfully of his predecessor, whether he be living or dead; and should it be impossible to speak well of him consistently with truth, he will be altogether silent on the subject. Moreover, should he find it necessary to apply a remedy to the consequences of his predecessor's ignorance, negligence, or incapacity, he will take care to do so quietly, and without remark. By acting thus, he will shew that he is charitable, sensible, and edifying, as becomes a Pastor of souls.

§ 7. Of the information which a Parish Priest ought to seek concerning the Necessities of his Flock.

The new Parish Priest ought to procure accurate information on these two points, viz., the evil to be prevented, and the good works to be promoted in his parish. Wherefore, he ought to make inquiries from some good priest in the locality, or from a neighbouring Parish Priest, or even from some trustworthy and prudent layman, regarding the disorders of most frequent occurrence in the parish, the reprehensible customs that may have been introduced there, and the bad maxims that may be in vogue. This information is necessary to the Parish Priest, for his guidance in the confessional and in the pulpit, and when studying the opportune remedies, which we shall mention later on, whereby he may prevent sin and scandals.

He should, likewise, inform himself of the good works to be promoted, and especially, of any good institutions that may have been established in the parish, in order that he may maintain them in a flourishing condition, or revive them should they have fallen into decay. Furthermore, he should inquire whether any such institutions be still needed in the parish, with a view to deciding whether it would be advisable to attempt to establish them.

It is thus a gardener acts, when he comes to cultivate a flower-plot. He immediately observes what weeds ought to be plucked up, what plants require watering, what ones must be strengthened, and what specimens he must add to his stock. And as the good gardener sets about his work promptly, in his anxiety that the garden entrusted to his care may quickly become fair and rich in everything beautiful and fragrant, so the good Parish Priest will make no delay in commencing his labours, being eagerly desirous that the parish confided to him may resemble a well-kept and fertile garden.

Let the Pastor take care, however, to place little trust in the reports which may be made to him on his first entry into the parish. For, it frequently occurs that there exist jealousies and factions between families, and often between the inhabitants of different portions of the parish, regarding oratories, almshouses, or the like; and on the occasion of the arrival of the new Parish Priest, each one is anxious, through interested motives, to give him information. It is evident that, if the Parish Priest reposes blind confidence in the information supplied by these persons, he runs the risk of committing grievous mistakes, and of adopting measures which may afterwards compromise him. Therefore, let him listen, by all means, to whatever reports may be made to him, but let him know at the same time how to be distrustful of them all, and let him defer taking any action, until he shall have seen clearly how matters really stand. If a Parish Priest should happen to show himself imprudent or hasty in the very beginning of his career, and should give offence, without good reason, to some influential person or family, to the churchwardens, to a confraternity, or the like, the people would become so prejudiced against him from the start, that it would afterwards prove a matter of very great difficulty to remove the bad impression.

Wherefore, should he discover in the parish any abuse or disorder, provided it be not a crying evil, let him take time to apply a remedy, and to introduce changes. Let him first take counsel, and then act with mature prudence.

CHAPTER III.

ON ADMINISTERING CORRECTION.

§ 1. On the Correction of Priests.

THE sins of priests, because of their special malice, are more offensive to God, and, through the greater force of the bad example which accompanies them, are the most destructive to the Christian flock; wherefore, a good Parish Priest will not neglect to take particular care to correct the erring. It must, however, be confessed that these are cases of correction in which success is most difficult of attainment, and which must be approached with the greatest circumspection and prudence.

It is most difficult to succeed in corrections of this kind; because there is no medium degree of badness in a priest. A priest is either good, or he is very bad. It is impossible that a priest be otherwise than good, who lives up to the obligations of his state, daily nourished and strengthened in the Holy Mass by the *corn of the elect and wine springing forth virgins*. But, on the other hand, it is impossible that a priest be other than an impious wretch, in the most rigorous acceptance of the term, who, ignoring the obligations of his holy vocation, daily ascends the altar in a state of mortal sin, there, like Judas, to betray Christ, and eat and drink the most tremendous judgment of eternal condemnation. Should he persevere in a state so deplorable, he cannot be regarded otherwise than as one obstinately blind, who merits the foremost place amongst those perverse beings of whom the Holy Ghost says that they "*are hard to be corrected*". (Ecclesiastes i. 15.)

Nevertheless, the Parish Priest ought never to despair of such, but, on the contrary, ought to make the utmost exertions for their conversion, awaiting help from on high: and, therefore, he ought to have recourse to prayer, before proceeding to correction. He must himself pray, and he must procure the prayers, especially, of pious persons, in order to effect that difficult conversion.

He will then proceed to correct the erring priest, in the most considerate manner, so as to wound his self-esteem as little as possible; selecting moreover, the time most suitable for this purpose; and employing that method of correction which he has reason to suppose will prove most acceptable and least painful.

Should the Parish Priest find that his efforts prove fruitless, let him acquaint the Bishop of the scandal, and exert himself to have the bad priest removed from his parish. Perhaps it may be objected that this unworthy ecclesiastic will thus go to spread scandal in another parish, as not unfrequently happens. Nevertheless, the Parish Priest cannot dispense himself from removing the stumbling block from the midst of his own people, and he can console himself with the reflection that, should the scandalous priest go elsewhere, the Pastor of that locality will know how to discharge his duty towards him. It is singularly important, for two reasons, that the unworthy priest should not be permitted to remain undisturbed in his sin. It contributes to the edification of the faithful, who are greatly scandalised when they see a crime go unpunished in a Minister of God; and it serves as a warning to other priests, so that if they be not inclined to virtue, they may, at least, be more cautious, and may not create scandals by open disorders.

Should the Parish Priest be unsuccessful in removing the wolf from his flock, he must endeavour as much as possible to keep them from coming into contact with him, and especially by procuring the withdrawal of his faculties for hearing confessions.

Priests who have not the fear of God cannot possess a proper spirit to guide souls in the path of salvation. Being obliged to condemn in others what they approve by their own acts, being bound to stir up in others that love of God which is wanting in themselves, and to exhibit zeal for those virtues which they trample under foot, their language, of necessity, must be feigned and hypocritical. It is a language altogether artificial, and at variance with the sentiments of their heart; and therefore, very naturally, it is impossible that their words can produce a real, and salutary impression upon the hearts of others. It is a well-established fact, that a heart can never be effectually moved, except by sentiments which come from the heart. Artificial sentiments, when well studied, may interest the mind, but they can never touch the heart. Therefore a priest without the fear of God, although he may not wish to do any harm in the direction of souls, must inevitably fail to do any good.

A Parish Priest, even though but little experienced, will have already discovered that spiritual directors who do not possess the holy fear of God, in addition to doing no good, generally inflict a very grave injury upon souls, by permitting them to repose tranquilly in those vices by which they are themselves enslaved. With what facility, with what benignity, do they absolve, *toties quoties*, from certain sins! At their confessional there is always a perpetual jubilee, much more ample in its provisions than the Pope could ever grant. There the penitent need never fear being reproached, or that absolution will be deferred.

Wherefore, there is not the slightest doubt that a Parish Priest ought to exert himself with all his zeal to the end that no bad priest may hear the confessions of his parishioners.

Nor does it avail to say, that all concern about this matter ought to be left entirely to the Bishop, who is responsible before the tribunal of God for the capacity and goodness of the confessors approved by him. We must never lose sight of this solemn truth —that in this world things are not always as they might be, or as they ought to be, but exist as we find them in their stern reality. Now, it is a fact that bad priests easily find unsuspecting or hypocritical persons, sometimes enemies of the good Parish Priest, who not being sufficiently known to the Bishop, bring influence to bear upon him directly and indirectly, in order that he may not give credence to the unfavourable reports sent in by the Parish Priest regarding the morality of certain priests. The Bishop, even though vigilant and well-intentioned, cannot in a moment sift the truth of things. Therefore, fearing lest anyone may suffer injustice, or even be defamed by withdrawing from him faculties for hearing confessions, he wisely delays and temporises, until he sees the guilt of the accused priest made perfectly clear. Meanwhile, this procrastination, whilst it is a prudent measure on the part of the Bishop, does not prevent the spiritual injury inflicted on souls entrusted to the direction of bad guides; and, therefore, the Parish Priest who is perfectly convinced of the utter unfitness of a confessor, even though the Bishop should not proceed against him, ought not to cease employing every means to bring about the cessation of the evil.

And what means are left to the Parish Priest under such circumstances? He ought to continue to make fresh representations to the Bishop, whenever fresh cases occur tending to criminate the unworthy priest. He ought to secure the co-operation of persons who possess influence with the Bishop, that they may support his request. Finally, he ought, cautiously and prudently, to avail himself of every opportunity to withdraw penitents from the direction of the priest in question.

A Parish Priest ought to have for the souls entrusted to him the feelings of a father, or, better still, of a mother, since these latter are more tender. Now a father, and still more a mother, when there is question of rescuing their children from some grave temporal danger, never for a moment calculate what precisely they may be bound to do as a matter of right, and of strict legal obligation. Fathers, and still more mothers, consider themselves justified in removing danger from their little ones, by adopting any means ready to hand, provided it be lawful; and were any one to say to them, "why do you take so much more trouble than the law requires?" they would reply: you have not a father's love, nor do you know anything of a mother's tenderness, otherwise your heart could never conceive such cold and senseless words. For the rest, there is no doubt that the means here suggested to the Parish Priest, in order that he may succeed in effecting his purpose, ought to be regarded as legitimate, nor ought he to be less solicitous to rescue his spiritual children from the risk of an eternal evil.

To return to the relations of a Parish Priest with Ecclesiastics in the matter of correction, whenever there is question of lesser defects and failings, he must be always careful to act with the greatest reserve and affability. Therefore, he ought not to correct priests for slight failings, but only for more considerable ones; the lesser faults he must pretend not to see. Should a priest happen to be somewhat addicted to gossiping (not however with women, or on unbecoming subjects); should he misspend some time, by occupying himself beyond what is necessary in innocent recreations; should he appear somewhat obstinate in maintaining his own opinions, a little irritable or quarrelsome, nay a little covetous, or should he have other like defects—and it is difficult to find a man wholly exempt from them—the Parish Priest would act imprudently who in such cases should constitute himself an Aristarchus.

On the other hand, when there is question of other defects more serious than those just mentioned—such as to celebrate the Holy Mass with indecent haste or without regard for the Rubrics, to dress in a manner unbecoming his state, to utter improper words habitually, to be guilty of excess in drink, to cherish an aversion and ill-will against those who are unfriendly to him, to indulge in miserly and mean habits, and other such notable defects which cause scandal to the people—the Parish Priest must not omit opportune correction. He must always administer it, however, with the utmost good grace, and must make it appear that the advice which he gives is not a correction, or is as little like it as possible. This might be effected by speaking to the priest in general terms, and as it were theoretically, of the defect which he ought to correct, by pointing out its impropriety, the surprise which it causes to the people, the bad example which consequently accompanies it, and such like considerations. In this manner, the advice might be administered without imparting to it the appearance of a personal reprimand.

There is need of special caution in the case of decrepit old priests, when they are subject to any failing which, by long habit, has become with them a second nature. The weakness of their mental faculties does not permit them to be conscious of its existence, or, at least, deprives them of the energy necessary to correct it. In this case every attempt to administer correction is useless, nay injurious; because it serves only to irritate them, since they fancy that persons are wanting in respect to them, precisely because they are old and unable to enforce respect. On the other hand, the Parish Priest, whilst omitting correction in such cases, may set his conscience at rest by the reflection that the failings of these old men are no longer scandalous, since their weakness of mind is known to, and pitied by all.

Nevertheless, if a decrepit priest should grievously violate the ceremonies of the Holy Mass, and, still worse, if there should be reason for suspecting that, because of his mental weakness, he might consecrate invalidly, or because of a tremor in his hand might spill the Sacred Blood, or reject it from his mouth through coughing, or do something else equally serious,—in such cases the Parish Priest ought to inform the Bishop of his condition, and absolutely to prevent that priest from celebrating Mass. And even though the priest in question should be poor, and have strict need of the "honorarium," the Parish

Priest ought at any cost to hinder him from profaning the Holy Sacrifice, and to procure for him some other means of sustentation. He ought to have recourse to the charity of the Bishop, and of other charitable people: he ought even to sacrifice some portion of his own revenue, rather than permit on any account such a profanation.

§ 2. On Administering Correction to the more Distinguished Persons in the Parish.

Next to the sins of priests, those of persons of position in the Parish cause the greatest scandal; because they attract most notice, they are spoken of by everybody, and they seem to justify the sins of persons of inferior condition. Therefore, a Parish Priest ought to take special care to correct the failings of persons of this class. But, before doing so, he ought to take into account whether these transgressors are persons who give evidence that they have faith, and are respectful towards the ministers of God; or whether they parade their unbelief and their contempt for the priesthood.

In the first case, the Parish Priest ought to administer correction; because there is reason to hope that it will bear fruit; and, on the other hand, there is no reasonable fear that it may be productive of evil consequences. He must, however, be careful to administer the correction in a very respectful manner; because the rich, and those honoured by the world, are the least disposed to receive correction from anyone whatsoever; and even though they may entertain religious sentiments and respect for the priesthood, they feel the corrections of the Parish Priest very humiliating. Nevertheless, if the Parish Priest admonish them very respectfully, they may the more readily take it in good part. From the respectful manner of the correction, they become sensible of the fact that their pastor holds them in esteem, and that he admonishes them much against his inclination, and solely in discharge of his bounden duty. Wherefore, their self-love is the less wounded: nay, they are constrained to show themselves sensible of an admonition, which is not only just but courteous. If, on the other hand, the correction were administered with that freedom of manner which one might adopt towards persons of inferior condition, their self-esteem would constrain them to disregard it, precisely for this very reason. Later on we shall allude to the more gentle methods by which correction may be administered.

If there be question, however, of persons of position who make profession of unbelief, and take pride in showing their contempt for the priesthood, a prudent Parish Priest will content himself, generally speaking, with praying for them, and procuring the prayers of others for the same intention; for, it is certain that correction would prove not only fruitless, but even injurious; and, in this case, as Theologians teach, there never is an obligation of administering correction, even though there be question of public crime. However, we shall see afterwards how the

Parish Priest, when preaching the Divine Word, may supply for this private correction which he has omitted.

And here I must remark that there are some who, when there is question of Parish Priests, insist that, at all hazards, without any distinction or exception whatsoever, they ought to correct all their parishioners, in all their failings; and they quote many passages from the Scriptures and the Fathers, with a view to proving that pastors never can be dispensed from this duty. Those who advance such doctrine are persons who know nothing of practical work, and who live, so to speak, in an abstract and theoretical world. If these persons were to discharge, even for a brief period, the duties of Parish Priests, they would be undeceived, and would learn to give a more benign interpretation to the Scriptures and to the Fathers.

In our times, we find amongst the persons most distinguished by riches, knowledge, and rank, a large number of unbelievers, who are singularly haughty, and intolerant of any kind of censure; and who are, moreover, possessed by a malignant spirit of hatred and contempt for religion, and for its ministers. Add to this, that since the establishment of the new dogma of individual liberty, pressed to the extreme limit of asserting that everyone has the right not only to think, but to speak and act as he pleases, without being held accountable to anyone, the exercise of evangelical correction is regarded by such persons as a thing tending to degrade man from his natural dignity, and as the most flagrant violation of one of the chief rights belonging to him.

Now, let us suppose that a person of this class, as happens amongst us now-a-days, should disseminate evil maxims, should fail to comply with the paschal precept, should eat meat on Fridays, should have formed a sinful connection, and so forth, will the Parish Priest be bound, or at least will it be prudent on his part, to present himself before such a one for the purpose of administering that correction which he deserves? What, I ask, can he tell him to correct him? Is it that the Council of Trent and the Papal Bulls have condemned these maxims, and that there is Excommunication for those who propagate them? Is it that, in failing to comply with the precept of paschal communion, he disentitles himself to Ecclesiastical burial? Is it that, by eating meat on days of abstinence, he commits a mortal sin? Is it that he will go to Hell, unless he breaks off that criminal intercourse? Do you not believe that if the Parish Priest were to whisper these things to him, even in the most humble manner, a gentleman of this class would consider himself extremely moderate if he merely treated him as a simpleton, and sent him off quizzing him on the score of his council, his excommunication, and all the rest, even including hell?

But, then, you may ask, will the Parish Priest have no responsibility for these souls? will he allow them to perish precisely through omitting to whisper one word to them? and must he, also, tolerate public scandals, without making an effort to apply a remedy?

I reply that no one wishes to exempt the Parish Priest from these so stringent duties; but I maintain at the same time, that where the inutility, nay the hurtfulness of correction is evident, so that one foresees that unquestionable evil must follow from it without any counterbalancing good effect, the most elementary prudence dictates that correction ought to be omitted; just as it would dictate that a certain medicine ought not to be administered, when one foresees that it must prove not only useless, but injurious to the patient.

However if we consider the matter calmly, we shall see that the Parish Priest, while omitting private and personal correction, has at his disposal other means of preventing the scandal and of admonishing the delinquent. Let us suppose that there is in the Parish a gentleman who notoriously eats meat on Fridays; who keeps a concubine in his house, or the like. Is it absolutely necessary, in order to prevent scandal, that the Parish Priest should personally visit him for the purpose of correcting these sins, and thus expose himself to the disrespectful reception which is certain to await him at the hands of this vile profligate? will he not effect his purpose more successfully, by preaching from the altar and the pulpit against those who violate the laws of the Church regarding abstinence, against those who live in concubinage, and so forth? The voice of the Parish Priest denouncing such disorders will surely be sufficient to caution the people against imitating this gentleman's bad example. Nay, since the sins are public, the people will immediately understand that the Parish Priest, though not naming him, is pointedly directing his discourse against this particular person; and thus the scandal is prevented, better than it could have been by private correction.

Meanwhile, the deliquent himself is likewise admonished. For he either goes to church, and hears the invective which is directed against him; or he does not go, and in that case he will be sure to hear of it very soon from others; and in this manner he receives a true and real correction, of which he may profit, if he only have the desire to do so. Wherefore, it is not true that a Parish Priest must fail in his duty of correction, when, for just reasons, he refrains from administering it personally to the delinquent.

However, one must not conclude from what has been said that the Parish Priest is never bound to have recourse to private correction, in as much as its place may be supplied by public admonition. For, what has been said applies solely to the case in which it is foreseen that private correction would prove fruitless and injurious; in other cases it ought not to be omitted, as being that which exercises the greatest influence on the mind of the sinner. As a matter of fact, in administering private correction, the Parish Priest hears the difficulties, the objections, the reasons or pretexts which the sinner puts forward in his own favour, and he can reply to them and refute them one by one; afterwards, by employing suitable arguments, he can convince and persuade him to change his life—objects which cannot be attained when the correction is publicly administered. Wherefore, private correction, as being the most efficacious, ought not, when opportune, to be omitted. Let us once more return to the parallel case of medicine: the physician has at hand a remedy which he knows to be absolutely the most efficacious; nevertheless, being convinced that, by reason of special symptoms which he sees in his patient, it might prove dangerous in his case, he adopts another remedy, less efficacious, it is true, but yet certain not to do any injury.

Finally, I will remark that the case may sometimes occur when the Parish Priest may prudently have recourse to private correction, even with the irreligious and free-thinking members of his flock. Should they happen to require some service at the hands of the Parish Priest (for example, to secure his influence, or some favour for themselves, or for their families), they usually approach him in a rather obsequious and humble manner. Now and again they have to receive him in their houses, on the occasion of the sickness or death of their relatives; and under such circumstances human pride is much subdued, and faith is somewhat revived. The Parish Priest, seizing upon such opportunities as these, may venture on administering private correction; but he should always do so in the kindest and most respectful manner.

Should it seem to any one that these suggestions savour too much of extreme condescension and diplomacy, I would venture to affirm that he has no experience of the class of whom I speak, and that he does not know their pride and the feeling of contempt with which they regard their Parish Priest.

§ 3. On Administering Correction to Persons of the Lower Order.

One of the most glorious truths of the gospel, which we see confirmed in a hundred ways, is that contained in the sentence: *Beati Pauperes*. The poor, if we only regard them with the light of faith, are always in a better condition than the rich, and can more easily derive profit from all the means of salvation, amongst which we must reckon correction. They, as a rule, entertain no haughty feelings which could induce them to resent correction on the part of their Pastor; and he in turn is never tempted to omit it, since he knows the good disposition with which it will be received.

It must be borne in mind, however, that in administering correction to the poor, a Pastor ought never to look upon himself as dispensed from adopting a gentle and charitable manner towards them. Certain Parish Priests, who scarcely dare to breathe freely in the presence of the rich and powerful, storm and rage when they come to deal with the poor and the lowly. They are incapable of admonishing them without breaking out into shouts, invective, and insulting language. Now, correction ought to be the daughter of charity, and ought always to preserve her amiable characteristics. And if, now and again, the obstinacy and stubbornness of the person to be corrected demand stern and vigorous language on the part of the Parish Priest, he must never give way to bursts of violent passion, which can produce no other effect than irritation and contempt. Even persons of the lower order have their feelings, which must be respected; and when they see that the Parish Priest oversteps the limits of decency and propriety, they consider themselves justified in paying no heed to his words, and even in retorting with abusive language.

We are not, however, of opinion that all the poor ought to be classed in the number of the "Blessed," and of those who are best disposed to avail themselves of the means of salvation left by Christ, and amongst others of correction. In our days, unbelief is by no means restricted to the rich and to those who move in the higher grades of society, but has permeated down to the poor and lower orders, and produces amongst them the self-same results as amongst their betters, namely, pride and a spirit of contempt for the ministers of religion. Whenever the Parish Priest may have to administer correction to poor persons of this class, he must, for the reasons already stated, proceed with extreme caution and reserve: acting otherwise, he would expose himself, without the slightest advantage, to insults and jeers.

Let us, for example, suppose the case of a porter, who, through the influence of bad books or newspapers, irreligious theatrical representations, and the pernicious maxims which he daily hears around him, has lost all respect for our holy Religion, believes its ministers to be impostors and hypocrites, eats meat on Fridays, has given up hearing Mass, and leads the life of a Pagan; let us suppose a Parish Priest visiting such a one, to correct him for the blasphemies and obscenities which he habitually utters, for keeping company with females of abandoned character, for neglecting to comply with the Paschal Precept and so forth,—what advantage, I ask, will the Parish Priest derive from his visit of correction? He must regard himself as singularly fortunate, if a scoundrel of this class will content himself with merely replying with a contemptuous smile: "*Ah, Sir, that style won't do now-a-days: the times are changed*".

Again, take the case of a woman who is leading an immoral life, and who, also, is well acquainted with the current cant of the age on religious and moral topics—is the Parish Priest to go to her house to admonish her on the subject of her immoral life? Most certainly not: to do so would be an act of extreme imprudence. Is he, instead, to summon her to his house? If she be not yet quite hardened in guilt, she will content herself with laughing at the invitation, and replying that she does not attend to any orders except those which come from the police. But if she be one of the brazen class, she will not fail to wait upon the Parish Priest, in order to turn him into ridicule, and be in a position to amuse her companions afterwards with a comic description of the interview.

But, you will ask, are such persons, then, to be

entirely abandoned by the Parish Priest? I can only repeat what I have already said, namely, that the Parish Priest must omit private correction when he clearly foresees that it would effect no good, nay would even be productive of evil. But should there occur a suitable opportunity of speaking with persons of this class under favourable circumstances, and especially should they happen to need any service at his hands, the Parish Priest ought eagerly to take advantage of these circumstances, and discharge his duty with all possible charity and mildness.

§ 4. On the various Methods of Correction.

The first method of correction is to warn the sinner directly of the evil which he is committing. Should he be a person of position, it is necessary, as has been said, to do this with the greatest delicacy, in order that he may take the admonition in good part. The Parish Priest might open the conversation, by giving him to understand that the high estimate which he has formed of his good qualities inspires him with a courage which he should not otherwise feel; that in the few remarks which he is about to make, he intends to give him proof of the esteem in which he holds him; and that, for the rest, he feels himself impelled to adopt the present course of action not so much from a sense of duty, as from an anxious desire for his welfare. He must allude to the fault to be corrected in very simple terms, without, in the least exaggerating it, or depicting it in too glaring colours, a course which would border too closely on the language of reproach.

The Pastor must be persuaded that the force of self-esteem is exceeding great, especially in those who are accustomed to the language of flattery, and never hear a word of reproof. Now if they take up the idea that one is, even ever so little, wanting in respect towards them, they resent it fiercely, at least in their hearts ; and, consequently, they are altogether indisposed to profit by any admonition which may be given to them.

On the other hand, the Parish Priest need have no scruple in adopting a method of correction which borders on flattery; because it is not his intention to flatter, and, in reality, the substance of his conversation is far indeed from flattering. Moreover, the person to be corrected will be sharp enough to perceive that these complimentary expressions are no more than a polite jargon, brought into requisition in order to lessen the bitterness of the pill which his Pastor would have him swallow. Jacob when he met his brother Esau, in order to propitiate him, had no scruple in telling him: "I have seen thy face, as if I should have seen the countenance of God"; and St. John Chrysostom praises him for having acted so. (See *A Lapide* on this passage.)

Should the Parish Priest have reason to believe that the sinner would consider himself insulted by a *direct* correction, such as that just described, the admonition ought to be conveyed to him through his mother, his sister, his wife, or some other relative or friend. This is a much milder method of administering correction, since the sinner is spared the confusion of hearing himself reproached to his face, and the Parish Priest will at the same time have discharged his duty, by committing the charge of correction to any of the persons named above, that they may administer it in his name.

It is very true that this milder method of correction is less vigorous, and, *per se*, less efficacious than the direct method; inasmuch as the Parish Priest has no opportunity of refuting the objections, setting aside the excuses, and cutting short the delays which the sinner might put forward in his own behalf. Nevertheless, since one must not attend so much to the strength of a medicine, as to its suitability in a given case, the Parish Priest ought to adopt correction of a milder type, should he foresee that a more vigorous correction would not be unattended by danger.

But, since even this mild type of correction might seem to some too bitter, especially when there is question of correcting a sinful habit (and undoubtedly some persons would be very much incensed, on finding that the Parish Priest conveyed certain reproofs to them through a mother, a sister, and still worse a wife), there remains yet another, and a still milder, form of correction, of which the sinner could not possibly complain, unless he were prepared to reject altogether, correction of whatsoever kind. This is to write him a respectful letter, couched in most conciliatory and even flattering terms, such as those which we have outlined above. A great deal might be said in a letter: and it would be possible, also, by this means to smooth away the difficulties which the person to be corrected might probably put forward, while at the same time sparing him the mortification of seeing himself corrected to his face, or through his relatives or friends. This, therefore, would be an excellent method of correction.

Should the Parish Priest be of opinion that it would not be prudent to employ any of the methods already mentioned, he has still remaining another method, effective and eloquent in many cases, and especially with persons of position—this is negative correction.

It must be remembered that the sinner, when he is conscious that his fault is known, is always apprehensive lest he may be reproached with it, especially by one such as the Parish Priest, whose duty it is to do so. Wherefore, he is quick to perceive any change of manner towards himself, to remark how he is addressed and saluted, whether he is visited as usual by the Parish Priest, and so forth; and should he really notice any change in these respects, he immediately interprets it correctly as a direct reproof. Hence, a Parish Priest can correct a sinner by speaking to him or saluting him with more reserve and coldness than usual; by ommitting to pay him a customary visit; or, should it be inconvenient to omit the visit, by treating him with more formality and less confidence than he had been in the habit of doing.

In this manner the Parish Priest will sufficiently manifest his displeasure towards the sinner; he will silently point out to him his misconduct; and without speaking a word, will, all the while, exhort him to penance. Let me once more repeat that correction is a medicine, which may be administered in various ways without changing its nature, but still retaining all its efficacy.

We have already remarked that a Pastor may administer correction to particular individuals, even by means of a public discourse.

§ 5. OF THE PERSONS IN PARTICULAR TO WHOM CORRECTION MUST BE ADMINISTERED.

The spirit of charity ought to prompt a Parish Priest to correct, as far as christian prudence will allow, *all* sinners entrusted to his pastoral charge; nevertheless, there are some who have a *special* claim upon his zeal.

First of all, he ought to correct those who sin through ignorance, since they stand in greater need of correction, and are the most likely to derive profit from it.

They have greater need of correction: because ignorance prevents them from knowing their duty. They are the most likely to derive profit from it; because their sins will cease when the cause of them has been removed. However, should the ignorance be accompanied by malice, so that even after the removal of the former, the latter should still remain, a pastor could not hope for a thorough reformation. Nevertheless, on the removal of one of the two causes which occasioned the falls, the sins will be at least diminished, and a partial amendment will have been effected, which in itself is, after all, a result of considerable importance!

Next come those who sin through weakness. Such weakness is never entirely free from malice, and therefore persons of this class cannot be excused from sin, though, at the same time, they are deserving of special compassion. There are certain persons, not viciously disposed, nay some of whom are positively well disposed, who would wish to live virtuously, and who do so live, as long as special occasions of sin do not present themselves; but whenever these occasions do occur, they easily yield to temptation, then repent as quickly, but only to relapse again with the same facility as before. To such as these the Parish Priest must devote himself with unremitting attention, in the hope that he may succeed in confirming them in their good resolutions, so as, at length, to effect a permanent amendment.

A pastor ought to exert himself with special zeal to correct the failings of children, since in their case, ignorance and weakness are generally found combined. They deserve special compassion in many cases because of the bad education which they have received from their parents, and in every instance because of their inexperience, their levity, and the fickleness of their minds. It is worthy of remark that we find greater tractability and less pride and stubbornness in children than in adults, and that, in consequence, correction in their case more readily produces its effects.

Since the Parish Priest need never fear to receive from children the insults and affronts which he might have to endure at the hands of adults, he can very rarely be excused from correcting them; unless, indeed, their parents should happen to be influential persons animated by feelings hostile to Religion and its ministers, in which case the children would be beyond the pastor's control. At the very worst, correction administered to children may prove fruitless, and, therefore, even though their pastor may fail in effecting any good, he can at least do no harm.

If the parents be good, it will be advisable that the Parish Priest should correct the children in their presence. If those who need correction be girls, and still more if they be rather grown-up girls, they ought invariably to be corrected in the presence of their mother, or of some other female relative. It would not be edifying that the Parish Priest should summon young girls before him without a witness, even for the purpose of correcting their faults; and if he should at any time judge it expedient to admonish a young girl without the presence of a third person, he ought to summon her to the confessional for the purpose. These precautions may seem to some too precise; nevertheless, let young Parish Priests be assured that, even when they shall be advanced in years, they will not regret observing them with scrupulous fidelity. It is surprising what a good impression is created in the minds of the parishioners, when they see their pastor scrupulously exact in matters of this kind.

§ 6. Two Counsels regarding Mildness in Administering Correction.

Correction, being the child of charity, ought, as has been already said, to retain the amiable characteristics of the parent that gave it birth. Nevertheless, in as much as charity, ever striving to attain its end which is the salvation of souls, cannot always accomplish its purpose by mild means, and in fact sometimes finds sterner methods more effective, it would be folly to pretend that it can invariably appear in the garb of gentleness; and for the self-same reason correction, which is the offspring of charity, must at times be sharp and vigorous. The example of the mild corrections of Heli, which are censured in holy writ, convinces us of this truth.

Wherefore, if a person who has been already corrected should continue obstinate, the Parish Priest may administer a severe rebuke with due moderation and prudence; and may even proceed to employ threats, provided it be in his power to have the transgressor punished, or to deprive him of some favour, such as a certificate of character, alms, and so forth. But should the Pastor feel that his threats are powerless, and can never proceed beyond mere words, he ought not to employ them; because when the offender knows that the Parish Priest cannot really carry out the threat, he will merely laugh at him, and might even continue in his evil ways for the express purpose of giving him annoyance.

Next to the general recommendation that correction ought to be mild, and administered in a winning manner, another counsel is necessary with regard to the correction of women, more especially if they be young. Women, whether young or old, ought to be treated by their Pastor with charity, just as well as men; for, equally with men, they are our neighbour. Nevertheless, a Parish Priest ought to be very much upon his guard against employing, when they are concerned, tender and endearing expressions; and this precaution must be scrupulously observed even though such expressions might seem to him opportune, and likely to render his correction more effective and fruitful. His charity towards women ought to be extremely respectful, but never, even in the slightest degree, affectionate; otherwise, there would be danger both for them and for him. Let him always employ kind and loving words with men, and they will produce an excellent effect; but let him never use them with women, in whose case the effect would be extremely injurious.

I have never been of opinion that in treating with women one ought to adopt the *sermo brevis et durus*, in the full rigour of that phrase. I believe that, in speaking with them, a Parish Priest need never entertain the slightest scruple as to the number of words necessary to instruct and advise them; and I believe, furthermore, that he ought to guard himself against asperity whether of sentiment or of language in their regard. The conversation of our Divine Lord with the Samaritan woman is a complete refutation of the doctrine embodied in the maxim *sermo brevis et durus* taken in its full rigour. Nevertheless, there is no doubt that one ought to adopt an attitude of respectful reserve towards women, and that this is advisable even should they belong to the very lowest orders; because their weakness always claims from men that respect which might not be due to their rank. But tender and endearing expressions are not words of respect, but rather of confidence, which ought never to find a place in the relations between a priest and women. On this subject I shall have something further to say elsewhere.

CHAPTER IV.

OF THE SCANDALS TO BE PREVENTED.

§ 1. OF SCANDALS RUINOUS TO FAITH.

THE Parish Priest ought to exercise the utmost vigilance to preserve the integrity of our holy Faith; and, therefore, should he learn of the presence of any one in his parish who is engaged in disseminating doctrines and maxims contrary to Faith, he must exert himself with the greatest zeal to put an end to this most pernicious scandal.

Should the author of the scandal be a hired emissary, come to the locality expressly for the purpose of propagating erroneous doctrines, the Parish Priest must not attempt to correct him personally, since it is certain that he would gain nothing by this course except ridicule and insult. These hired agents are persons utterly devoid of every religious and moral feeling; they look upon the Parish Priest as their natural antagonist; and they entertain towards him no feeling except hatred and contempt, especially when they are aware that they can count upon influential support and protection. If the Parish Priest could venture to hope that his remonstrances would be heeded, it would be his duty to appeal to the civil authorities to put an end to the scandal; but, at all events, he must not neglect to inform the Bishop of the entire matter.

In many places there are no hired agents of this class; but almost everywhere, it may be said, there may be found freethinkers, who spread abroad evil maxims, and circulate books injurious to Catholic Faith. In our times such persons inflict upon the Christian flock even a greater amount of injury than results from the action of paid agents, because they are more numerous, and they are more readily admitted into family circles.*

As regards the advisability of administering correction to such as these, we must refer the reader to the counsel already given with respect to unbelievers and those who entertain feelings of contempt for the priesthood.

* It may not be out of place to quote here the words of the Irish Bishops assembled in the National Synod at Maynooth, regarding so-called "liberal" Catholics:—"Catholicorum veri nominis est fidem integre et confidenter tenere et cum opus est profiteri, adeoque eorum exemplum evitare qui ut acatholicis et incredulis placeant, liberales catholicos se vocant. Hi nimirum magisterium Ecclesiæ parvi pendunt, et inter arctissimos limites circumscribunt, Summi Pontificis et Episcoporum hortamenta et consilia fere spernunt, de religione parum caute loquantur, atque sectas quaslibet in omnibus Ecclesiæ Christi æquiparant, quæ eorum agendi ratio fidem infirmat, et recta via ad hæresim aut indifferentismum ducit. Catholici veri nominis diversam prorsus viam tenere debent, ante omnia quærere regnum Dei et justitiam ejus, Ecclesiam diligere, et in ejus prosperitate gaudere, res spirituales rebus temporalibus anteponere et debitum obsequium et obedientiam Ecclesiæ ministris et præcipue Romano Pontifici ejusque decretis præstare."—(Decretum VII., *De Fide Catholica*, n. 10.)

Meanwhile, the Parish Priest must find out what truths are most combatted, and these he must explain more fully to the people, so that they may find in his sermons a powerful antidote against the poisonous errors that are being spread abroad amongst them.

It will, also, prove a most effective check to the dangers which now-a-days threaten the faith, to inculcate frequently upon the faithful the warning of St. Paul: "a man that is a heretic avoid". (Titus iii. 10); and that of St. John: "Receive him not into the house, nor say to him God speed you". (2 John 10.)

Such texts of sacred writ grate harshly on the ears of the enemies of our faith, and they would wish to cancel them, as being too much opposed to that spirit of indifferentism and absolute toleration which characterises our age; but, precisely for this reason, it is all the more necessary to proclaim them to the people, and to inculcate their paramount importance, so that all may fly from the society and companionship of the seducers, and no one may be caught in their treacherous and wicked snares.

The Parish Priest must earnestly exhort his people not to hold friendly relations with those whose faith is tainted, and never to admit them to their confidence; but, above all things, he must especially impress upon the heads of families the duty of excluding every such person from their homes, as they would wish to keep at a distance those infected with the plague.

By pursuing this course, not only will a barrier be erected against the perversion of the good; but, moreover, the free-thinkers, being excluded from the assemblies, entertainments, and society of good and respectable families, can never acquire much credit or influence in the locality. Thus the injuries which they might, otherwise, inflict upon the faith, will be, at least in a great measure, prevented.

The Parish Priest ought above all things, to exert himself in preventing the agents of sects or other unbelievers from opening public schools, even though they should profess to teach nothing beyond reading, writing, and arithmetic; for they avail themselves of this means to instil their baneful doctrines into the minds of the children. But if, despite his opposition, such schools should be opened, the Parish Priest must not neglect to warn and implore the heads of families to keep their children away from them. And in order that the parents may not put forward the excuse that they must get their children educated, and that there are no other schools in the neighbourhood, the Parish Priest, as shall be said later on, must labour zealously to establish in the parish good schools, conducted by religious and God-fearing teachers.

And since unbelievers are in the habit of scattering broadcast irreligious and immoral books, the Parish Priest must likewise be extremely vigilant with regard to this method of making perverts. To this end, he must not only preach frequently against the danger of bad reading, but he must earnestly exhort all those who may have bad books in their possession either to give them up to himself, or to consign them to the flames. He might induce them to surrender such books more easily by giving them good ones in exchange, and in this manner he would place in their hands wholesome food instead of poison.

Let the Pastor bear in mind that his most pressing duty is to preserve amongst his people the integrity of the faith, which is the corner-stone of Religion and of every christian virtue. The man who has faith, even though he be a sinner, may at any moment be converted, by availing himself of the means of justification which are placed at his disposal in the Catholic Church; but against whosoever has renounced the faith, the gospel thunders forth this terrible sentence: "*he that doth not believe is already judged*". (John iii. 18.)

§ 2. OF SCANDALS RUINOUS TO MORALS.

Scandals which tend to destroy faith are the most ruinous if we regard the intensity of the evil resulting from them; but those which aim at destroying purity of morals are the most disastrous if we take into account the extent of the evil which follows in their train; and the reason of this is supplied by the fact that men have a stronger propensity to dissolute habits than to unbelief. Therefore, a Parish Priest must not only be zealous for the integrity of the faith, but he must also most earnestly devote himself to prevent those scandals which imperil the morals of his people.

In this class we may include those scandals which

are caused (1) by theatrical representations, licentious entertainments, and public evening parties open to both sexes; (2) by immoral books; (3) by the exhibition of immodest pictures and statues; (4) by free baths, especially if there be no separation of the sexes; (5) by indecent language and improper songs; (6) by the cynicism of certain incarnate demons who allow themselves to be seen in the commission of the most shameful excesses, in order to scandalise young persons of both sexes; (7) by women of illfame; (8) by the opening of public houses, or the holding of games during the time of divine worship; (9) by the public performance of servile works on festivals of obligation; (10) by the public violation of the law of abstinence; (11) by blasphemies, imprecations, and coarse scandalous expressions.

Should the scandals amount to an outrage upon public decency, the arm of the law ought to be invoked against them. Every Parish Priest, considered merely as a citizen and an individual subject of the state, has a right to demand that the law be put in force, and this right is fully recognised even by freethinkers.

Nor ought a Parish Priest to dispense himself from pressing this right, on the grounds that his action will probably prove ineffective, that nothing came of it on former occasions, and so forth; because when there is question of dealing with vice, the very worst course which could possibly be adopted is to give it peace. If it cannot be entirely crushed, it is well at all events, to keep it in constant trouble, and thus it will be at least prevented from becoming too defiant. Moreover, when the authorities, who previously had been inactive, see the application repeatedly renewed, they may be either unwilling or unable to persevere in resisting demands put forward in accordance with the law.

However, should the Parish Priest, from his knowledge of the character of those with whom the authority rests, foresee that his demand will be unheeded, precisely because it has been made by him, he ought to adopt the expedient of interesting in its favour the most distinguished and influential laymen in the locality; or, better still, induce them to take independent action in the matter, without any reference to himself, and as it were, of their own free accord. Now-a-days, when in so many parts of the world the laity are considered much more respectable than the clergy, a claim based upon law has great force when put forward by laymen; and its force is all the greater if it is believed to be perfectly free from every suspicion of clerical influence.

If, on the other hand, the scandal be one of those tolerated by the law, the Parish Priest ought not on that account to despond, nor ought he cease to combat it by such means as he may have at hand. Active zeal, even unassisted by the law, can accomplish a great deal; and even though there may be no direct means of grappling with the scandal, yet, as we shall see later on, indirect means, no less effective, may be employed.

Let us now touch briefly on the several kinds of

scandal mentioned above, and let us consider how a Parish Priest may be able to apply a remedy to them.

There are to be found in many places certain persons having moderate wealth and no occupation, who promote amateur theatricals and licentious entertainments, in order to train up subjects for the gratification of their own vile passions, and to corrupt the youth of the neighbourhood, especially the young girls. Persons of this class are utterly indisposed to pay attention to the admonitions of the Parish Priest, should he wish to correct them: nay, they take special delight in the pain which their scandals cause him. Therefore, to say the very least, the Parish Priest would be simply losing his time, were he to beg of these persons to discontinue their evil practices; in fact, they would even make it their study to act worse than before, for the express purpose of giving him annoyance. Under such circumstances, a Pastor must rather have recourse to prayer. He must pray himself, and must, likewise, procure the prayers of pious persons (a means always to be understood, even when we do not mention it expressly); and, in God's good time, a remedy will come from on high.

But the Parish Priest must, moreover, exert himself with the more respectable persons in the locality, in order that their influence may be brought to bear against such disorders, so as at least to lessen them, if they cannot be entirely banished. Above all he must leave nothing undone to induce persons of good reputation not only to refrain from taking part in these licentious entertainments, but always to discountenance them. Should he succeed in doing so, these incentives to sin cannot long survive, but will gradually die out of their own accord. A bad custom cannot resist the active and continued hostility of the better class of persons in a locality.

In the next place, a Parish Priest must offer persistent opposition to balls of every kind, whether their immorality be greater or less, whether they be public or private. I say advisedly: "of every kind"; because a certain tincture of immorality is always inseparable from balls at which, in accordance with universal custom, men and women dance together.

A Pastor must set his face against them all, whether their immorality be greater or less, whether they be public or private; because, infallibly, once the custom of giving balls is introduced, even though a beginning be made with less dangerous dances, the more licentious ones as well will quickly be introduced; and because all are the occasion of many sins, especially to the young.

Some people draw a wide distinction between public and private balls, maintaining that the former alone are dangerous, whilst the latter are harmless; and, in confirmation of this opinion, they adduce the fact that private balls are customary even in pious and well-regulated families. I shall not attempt to deny that immorality more easily becomes unblushing at public balls, inasmuch as it is easier for persons of a less refined class to gain admittance to them;

nevertheless, who can deny that young people find most powerful incentives to their passions at private balls likewise, even though they take place in the houses of good and respectable families ? Is it not a matter calculated to shake the solid sanctity of an anchorite, as well as the weaker virtue of a young dandy, that two young persons of different sexes should take each other by the hand, and gaze upon each other while executing most graceful movements, and embrace each other, as is done in some dances, to the strains of the softest music ?[1]

[1] In the Pastoral Letter addressed to their flocks by the Irish Bishops assembled in National Synod at Maynooth, their Lordships, after warning the Faithful against dangerous amusements in theatres and elsewhere, thus speak of improper dances : " To these we must add the improper dances which have been imported into our country from abroad, to the incalculable detriment of morality and decency. Such dances have always been condemned by the Pastors of the Church. This condemnation we here renew ; and we call upon all to whom God has intrusted the care of immortal souls, to use every exertion to banish from our midst what is clearly of itself an occasion of sin. St. Francis of Sales, that most indulgent of spiritual guides, addressing the people of the world, has left it written ('Devout Life,' chap. 23) that innumerable souls are suffering eternal punishment for sins they had committed in dancing, or which were occasioned by dancing. We cannot but admire those heads of families, who, in obedience to the teaching of their Pastors, resisting the torrent of evil custom, have closed their doors against these forbidden amusements, lest they should stain their conscience by exposing themselves or others to the danger of spiritual ruin. God is a faithful rewarder ; and such parents may rest assured that, as in the government of their household they have imitated the holy Tobias, who taught his child, *from his infancy to fear God and abstain from every sin*), Tobias i. 10), so, like him, they shall one day find joy and comfort in the domestic happiness of the children they have brought up so well, and through them be filled, even in this

However indisputable may be the goodness of the families in whose houses such entertainments may be given, yet, by reason of their very nature, they must always be attended with considerable danger. Wherefore, there cannot be the slightest doubt that a Parish Priest will act wisely in offering opposition to all balls of whatsoever description.

Should he, however, find the custom of attending balls general in the parish, he must proceed with great caution and moderation, and must not attempt to effect a revolution in this matter all at once. He can make use of the confessional to combat this practice, according as the different necessities of his penitents may require. Again, when preaching, and especially in catechetical discourses, he can denounce in vigorous language the more licentious dances, and his doing so cannot give offence to anybody. He must speak with greater moderation of balls in general, frequently pointing out their danger, without, however, indulging in over-strong or intemperate language; and he must not omit to praise in the highest terms all, and more especially young girls,

---

life with all good." (Acts of the Synod of Maynooth, pp. 165, 166.)

In the Decrees of the same Synod, the Bishops employ the following very strong language on the subject of *fast-dances*: "Omnibus sacerdotibus tam secularibus quam regularibus qui in ministerio animarum versantur, injungimus ut omni quo pollent zelo saltationes quasdam (fast-dances) recenter in hanc regionem inductas, et modestiæ christianæ plane repugnantes pro viribus impediant. Et sciant confessarii se suo muneri non satisfacere si ullo modo aut sub ullo prœtextu eas permittant aut excusent" (Decretum xxi. n. 216)—*Translator.*

who abstain from attending such entertainments. In this manner the bad custom will gradually become less frequent, and there may be a reasonable hope of ultimately eradicating it altogether.[1]

A Pastor must also combat this custom indirectly by bestowing the greatest care on the cultivation of piety among women and young girls. It is a fact that females who are truly pious do not frequent dances; and, consequently, in those parishes where piety prevails, dances cannot come into fashion to any considerable extent. When those girls who enjoy the highest reputation begin to withdraw from such entertainments, others who might wish to take part in them are likewise induced to absent themselves; and should this feeling of piety become general, dances are sure to prove a failure in the locality. Experience has shown that when an attempt has been made to get up a subscription ball in parishes of this kind, it has been found necessary to bring women and girls from other districts, sometimes even paying

---

[1] Very much might be accomplished in this direction by nuns who are engaged in the education of young girls. In the town where the translator resides, there is a boarding school of the very highest repute, conducted by nuns of the Institute of the B. V. Mary, where the young ladies are not allowed to learn or dance fast, or, as they are sometimes called, "round" dances. This system might well be adopted in all convent schools; and the Irish Bishops seem to have intended that it should be observed in all schools under their jurisdiction; for, in the thirty-second Decree of the Synod of Maynooth we find the following article (n. 300): "Curent Superiorissæ, ne quocumque sub prætextu, choreæ, cantus, vel aliquid hujusmodi in earum scholis introducatur si christianis moribus non conveniat."—*Translator.*

for their attendance; and for this very reason the entertainment fell into disrepute, and failed to recoupe the manager.

Those *conversazioni*, or free social gatherings of persons of both sexes, which are held in many places during the winter evenings, are an evil almost as great as dances. At these parties young men become forward and maidens less retiring; innocence is lost prematurely; and consequences which entail dishonour follow later on. In order to remove these occasions of sin, the Parish Priest must preach against them from the pulpit, must warn his penitents against them in the confessional, and must exert his influence with the heads of families towards the same end. And let him not grow weary or despondent even though, for a time, he should see all his efforts fruitless. By steady perseverance in working out his purpose, he will, sooner or later, enjoy the consolation of witnessing some good results.

A Pastor must, also, carefully guard against the circulation of romances, novels, and lascivious poems amongst his parishioners, and especially amongst the young. And since now-a-days everyone delights in reading, he must take care to provide some good books to be distributed as presents, or at least to be given out on loan. We shall return to this subject in the twelfth chapter.

Let the Parish Priest take care, likewise, that indecent statues or pictures be not exposed in public, or even in private houses. These inflict upon souls

OF SCANDALS TO BE PREVENTED. 73

even greater injury than is caused by immoral books; because they are the occasion of bad thoughts even to those who do not know how to read, and, moreover, the imagination is excited more vividly by the sight of objects, than it is by reading. Wherefore, the Parish Priest ought to exhort those who possess such objects to remove them from positions where they may be seen, whether in public or in private. If his zeal prove successful in inducing the owners of such objects to destroy them altogether, instead of concealing them, he will have performed a work of incalculable service; for, if they be at all preserved, it is impossible to find a hiding place from which the devil will not, some time or another, drag them forth, to restore them once more to the public gaze.

Should the owner wish to palliate the scandal, and to deny the existence of any danger, on the ground that these objects had occupied their present position for several years and that no one any longer heeded them, the Parish Priest must reply that prescription, even of a hundred years, will not hold good in favour of these objects once they are admitted to be indecent; and that from the fact of their having been exposed to view for several years, to the certain detriment of public and private morality, no other conclusion can be drawn except that it is a misfortune that they had not been removed many years ago. He must, moreover, reply that it is untrue to state that nobody any longer heeds such sinful objects; for if they be in a public gallery they attract the attention of every visitor, and if they be in private houses, they come under the observation of all who are in the habit of calling there. He must add that, though they do not let it appear by any outward sign, unfortunately too much notice is taken of these objects by all the members of the family and the domestics who may be viciously inclined, and who find in them subjects calculated to gratify the wantonness of their eyes. Finally, let him remark that such objects excite in a special manner the curiosity of children, who tutored by a disposition prone to evil, and eager from their tenderest years to investigate secrets, have sufficient discretion to pretend not to look at these objects, but afterwards, watching their opportunity when there is nobody by, they will fix their eyes upon them and study them attentively.

Bathing-places are an occasion of frequent scandal in parishes which are situated at the sea-side, or near lakes, or on rivers. There is the scandal which might arise from boys and girls bathing together; the scandal which might be occasioned by shameless men and youths bathing, in a state of entire nudity, close by roads and houses, where immodest women and girls may stand looking at them; the scandal of certain women exposing themselves in places where they can be seen in the act of dressing and undressing; and, again, there is the scandal which might be caused by these women taking with them to the bathing-place their sons, especially if somewhat grown.

In circumstances such as these, the Parish Priest

OF SCANDALS TO BE PREVENTED. 75

ought to raise his voice and give utterance to vigorous denunciations, in order to inspire his people with horror of those outrages upon public decency. He ought, in particular, to administer a severe reproof to those who are guilty of them, and ought not to give them any peace until the abuse has been corrected. And here it may be well to remark, that if the abuse were notorious and general, it would be one of those cases in which the Parish Priest would be bound to have recourse to the civil authorities, in order that, as has been elsewhere said, the provisions of the law in such cases might be put in force. The heads of families especially ought to support their pastor in taking this step, calling for the protection of morality in the interests of their daughters.

Another fruitful source of corruption is the immodest language so frequently spoken, and the licentious songs which are sung. The Parish Priest must labour to correct these sinful abuses, both by preaching and by private admonitions; but in the case of immodest songs, he must, in addition, apply a more positive remedy which cannot fail to prove effective. This is to introduce and spread amongst the people the custom of singing hymns; and since this is a matter of greater importance than may seem at first sight, it may be advisable to enter a little more fully into particulars.

It is a fact that women and young girls in particular, who are engaged in sedentary occupations for long hours and days, like to seek relief in the recreation of singing; and in this they do well ; for, if the theme of their song be good, it will prove a healthy entertainment likewise for the mind.

However, it will be found that, as a rule, most of them are satisfied with the mere act of singing, without caring much about the words of their song. It is to them a matter of indifference whether they sing a love-song or a hymn. Wherefore, if they know good songs by rote, they will willingly refrain from singing bad ones,—the more readily, if exhorted to do so by one such as the Parish Priest, who has authority over them.

A Parish Priest ought, therefore, exert himself to spread through the parish a number of little hymn-books, and to induce the more devout women and girls to teach the others how to sing the hymns. He will easily succeed in doing so, by promulgating the indulgences mentioned in the note at the foot of this page [1]; and in carrying out this project he will

---

[1] The Rev. John Bosco, being most anxious to promote the singing of hymns and spiritual canticles in honour of God, of the Blessed Virgin Mary, and of the saints, petitioned Pope Pius IX. to grant the following Indulgences, which the Holy Father was graciously pleased to do, signing the Rescript with his own hand :—

1. An Indulgence of one year to whosoever teaches gratuitously the singing of sacred hymns, practising them at least sometimes in public or in private; and another indulgence of 100 days each time they are practised in a public or a private oratory.

2. A Plenary Indulgence to be gained at the close of the Month of May, by those who in the course of the month shall have devoted themselves in a special manner to singing in the Church, and who shall have assisted at the devotions of the Month of May.

3. A Plenary Indulgence once a month in favour of those who on, at least, four festivals, or even week-days, shall have taken part in singing, or in teaching others to sing sacred songs; and this

obtain the greatest assistance from good schoolmistresses, if he have such in the parish.

The Parish Priest may attain this object still more effectually by getting a hymn sung by the children, both boys and girls, before he commences to teach the catechism. This affords much gratification even to the adult population, and it attracts a larger number of children to instruction. If pious hymns be sung in the public church on all festivals, the entire congregation will learn them, and on the recommendation of the Parish Priest, these will soon come to be substituted for the indecent and corrupting songs which were sung previously.

Should there be found in a parish any of those incarnate demons who, while in the act of committing the most shameful sins, expose themselves, from wicked motives, especially to little girls, whether on the lonely roads, or in the halls, or on the stairs or from the windows of houses, the Parish Priest must seek out such monsters and reprove them as they deserve; warning them at the same time that, should they be again detected in such infamous conduct, they will be denounced to the legal authorities. Should

---

Indulgence is to be gained on that day on which they shall have approached the sacraments of Penance and the Blessed Eucharist. To gain the above-mentioned Indulgences the hymns must have the approval of the Ecclesiastical authorities.

4. These Indulgences are applicable likewise to the souls in Purgatory.

Romæ apud S. Petrum die 7 Aprilis 1858.

BENIGNE ANNUIMUS JUXTA PETITA.—PIUS P.P. IX.

—*Author's note.*

the Parish Priest not deem it expedient to encounter such characters personally, he ought to see that legal action is taken by the parents of the children who have been scandalised, supported by the other heads of families in the neighbourhood. And since he may easily find them timid or slow to appeal to the civil authorities, he must warmly and zealously animate and encourage them not to defer applying an effectual remedy to such gross scandal. However, should he be unsuccessful in inducing them to bring the offender before the courts, the Pastor ought himself to discharge that duty.

Women of bad character are the source of innumerable scandals in a parish. Some of these are avowed prostitutes, others lead sinful lives privately, and with greater circumspection. It is extremely difficult to bring women of the first-mentioned class to repentance; nevertheless, as we have already said, should a favourable opportunity present itself, the Parish Priest ought to speak to them a word of admonition to which perhaps the Divine Mercy may be annexed. These unfortunate creatures sometimes feel remorse and discontent with their lot, and in such great moments especially, a salutary admonition may produce a good impression upon their hearts. The fact is that, from time to time, some of these receive from God the grace of conversion and the strength to withdraw from the world. Those amongst them who never are converted are the old procuresses, to whom wickedness has become a second nature, like the devils, of whom they are the most fitting representatives. However, even these, when occasion offers, ought to be corrected, since they, too, are capable of receiving the grace of conversion.

The Parish Priest will experience far less difficulty in dealing with women of the second class—those, namely, who sin in private. These have not as yet cast off the modesty natural to their sex, and they still fear to gain the repute of women who have lost their honour. Therefore, they listen with greater humility to the words of the Parish Priest, and it is less difficult to bring them to repentance, especially if the Parish Priest call in the good services of their parents and virtuous female friends to second his pastoral zeal. Persons of this class are weak rather than wicked; and when they are enlightened by grace, exhorted, encouraged, and, above all, recommended to a good confessor, they turn from their evil ways. Let us never forget the story of the adulteress mentioned in the gospel, whom our Redeemer received, and who seems to have belonged precisely to this class.

When women of bad character prove incorrigible, the Parish Priest should use his endeavours at least to have them removed from the parish. Should there be any hope of success, he ought to make application to this effect to the authorities of the place; but if such an application would be fruitless, he ought to address himself to the landlord of the house where such people live, if he be a good christian man. Nor should they be suffered to remain on account of the illusory argument put forward by those who are slow to take action—namely, that *if the scandal be removed from one locality, it will pass on to another.* The fact that the world cannot be entirely freed from robbers, does not hinder any one from taking measures to prevent them from entering into his own house. Moreover, as has been repeatedly said, no system can possibly be more unwise, than to suffer vice and the scandals which spring from it to remain undisturbed.

Great mischief is likewise caused in a parish by the opening of public houses and the holding of games or other entertainments during the hours of divine worship; for by these means, men especially, are induced to stay away from Church, habitually to neglect hearing the word of God, and to devote to feasting, to uncharitable language, to blasphemy, or, at the very least, to idleness, the time that ought to be consecrated in a special manner to the service of God. Wherever it is in his power to do so, a Parish Priest ought to employ all his influence and authority to extirpate this abuse.

There is another abuse almost as bad as that just mentioned, namely that men should stand lounging and talking in the enclosure around the Church, whilst the Pastor is delivering his catechetical discourse. A certain Parish Priest having unsuccessfully tried several means to remedy this abuse, at length adopted the plan of asking the people assembled for instructions to recite three *paters* and *aves* for those who remained outside talking. The result was, that many of those who previously had been in the habit of remaining outside, not wishing to hear members of the congregation saying to them: "We have prayed for you," used, thenceforward, to be amongst the very first into Church. I know a Church in a country town, where the Parish Priest was so successful in eradicating this abuse, that you could never find even two men lounging about the enclosure during the time of divine service.

Let the Parish Priest likewise guard against the introduction into his parish of the abuse of working and of keeping shops open on festival days. If one begins this practice, and the Parish Priest remains silent, many others, influenced by the desire of gain, will follow his example. Should a Parish Priest find this bad custom already established in his parish, he must endeavour to abolish it by preaching and by private admonition.

Still more earnestly ought a Pastor labour, to prevent the introduction into his parish of the abuse of eating meat on days of abstinence. This sin, committed in cold blood, without the incentive of any passion, is a proximate disposition to unbelief or Apostasy. When a man commits a grievous sin, impelled thereto by anger, by the desire of gain, or by lust—all of them violent passions—there is some motive for the sin, and it is possible to understand how it could be committed by one who still retains the Faith. But when one deliberately commits a mortal sin, in order to eat some meat rather than some fish—a matter of such indifference to the passion of gluttony—we can find no intelligible explanation of his conduct, except in the supposition that he has either already lost the Faith, or is on the point of losing it.

Finally, let the Parish Priest exert himself to combat the scandal arising from blasphemies, from cursing, and from licentious conversation. Let him preach vigorously against such sins; let him correct, especially, foul-mouthed parents, who are the chief cause of the evil, and likewise young lads when they begin to make use of improper language. If he be vigilant and exert himself with true zeal, especially in rural parishes and in country towns, where his words produce a greater impression, his efforts will be attended with a large amount of success.

In conclusion, we may remark on the subject of scandals, that it will be found serviceable towards lessening their force and influence, to bear in mind that vice never loses anything of the infamy which naturally attaches to it, so that it never comes to be regarded as a matter of indifference. The common sentiment of mankind, even unenlightened by Faith, regards vice as something abominable, and the vicious as disreputable. Even among heretics, Turks, and idolators, a woman considers herself insulted by being called a prostitute. This common feeling on the subject has never varied, not even in those remote days when the unfortunate women of this vile class held the office of priestesses to the goddess Venus. It is also worthy of remark, that it is not only the notoriously vicious who are looked upon by the world as dishonoured, but that a certain stain of disrepute attaches even to those who follow a profession not indeed necessarily vicious, but which is rarely free from vice. I remember reading the complaints of one of those modern regenerators of the world, regarding "the melancholy fact" that members of the theatrical profession have never yet been able to secure for themselves a position of honour and esteem in society. The wiseacre could not fathom the mystery of this "melancholy fact"!

Nevertheless, vice is making constant efforts to lessen, and, if possible, to remove from itself, the mark of infamy and dishonour with which it is stamped; and that form of modern impiety which calls itself *tolerance* is labouring, now-a-days more than ever, to procure for it an *entrée* into society. And, in truth, if a scandalous person of loose morals could secure everywhere that respect and deference which are due to persons of virtuous and edifying character, the progress of impiety would, indeed, have reached its culminating point.

Wherefore a Parish Priest must study to preserve and strengthen that healthy tone of feeling dictated by universal sentiment—that *vice brings dishonour and infamy in its train*. He must enforce this truth from the pulpit, in the confessional, and in the course of familiar conversation. Nor ought he to refrain from doing so through a charitable feeling towards the vicious; for he may pity them in his heart, whilst utterly detesting the wickedness which has made them what they are. Will anyone be bold enough to pretend that we ought to respect sin through charity for the sinner?

Apropos of this portion of the subject, it may be

well to relate two little incidents which may give some light to a new Parish Priest.

There was in a certain parish a very wanton woman, who was in the habit of frequenting her neighbours' houses in a free and off-hand manner, and of entering into conversation with respectable matrons. Several of these, through good nature and human respect, were unwilling to give her the reception which she deserved, and tolerated her conversation. The Parish Priest summoned two of them to him, and cautioned them that their character would be compromised if they continued to converse with this woman, whom they themselves, as well as all their neighbours, held in bad repute. Whereupon, fearful of dishonour, they mentioned in confidence to their female friends the caution that had been given to them, and all, in consequence, immediately began to shun that woman's society. She quickly perceived that all were beginning to regard her with suspicion, and avoided her company. She was highly incensed at the slight that had been put upon her, and immediately went to take up her residence at a great distance from that parish.

Of what importance it is to put vice to shame may be gathered from another fact which happened in the same place. A woman of ill-fame, who by deceit and false pretences managed to pass herself off as a most respectable person, rented an apartment from a man of christian character. After a few days, he became aware of the fraud which this woman had practised upon him when renting his apartment, and knowing that, if he proceeded in due legal form, he would have to go through a tedious and expensive process before he could eject her, he took into his counsels a good-humoured cobbler, who kept his stall at the porch of the house. The cobbler, thereupon, suspended over the entrance of the porch a lamp which he lighted towards nightfall. The neighbours, on seeing this unusual glare, came running up, as they asked him : " Domenick, what's the matter to-night ?" " Oh," he replied, "this is the anniversary of my wedding, and I wish to illuminate in honour of the occasion." Meanwhile, from the corners of the neighbouring streets, there used to peep out, every now and again, some gallant of the lady's, and not wishing to be seen by those who were standing around the illuminated door-way, he would quickly draw back again. After a while he would re-appear, but only to find the illumination still continuing, while Domenick kept laughing and joking with his friends. The woman was not slow to understand the purpose of this proceeding, and, on the following morning, she relieved the house of her presence.

CHAPTER V.

ON THE CARE OF THE POOR.

THE office of Parish Priest is one which regards the soul, and therefore his primary duty is to provide for the spiritual wants of the faithful. But since spiritual necessities are oftentimes closely connected with corporal wants, to such a degree that the former are frequently the result of the latter, the care of the poor has always been regarded as one of the principal duties of a pastor of souls. Moreover, the exercise of the corporal works of mercy is a most noble virtue, and is commanded by divine precept, from which no Christian and much less a Parish Priest can dispense himself.

§ 1. ON THE CAUTION NECESSARY IN ORDER TO DISCOVER THE REALLY POOR.

In country places the Parish Priest can easily know those who are really poor; but this is not the case in cities, where many flock from the neighbouring country districts to share in the alms which is there distributed, and on account of their habit of constantly changing their lodging from one parish to another, cannot be sufficiently well known.

When poor persons from the country, who have come to live in a city, apply to the Parish Priest for alms, he ought not hesitate to relieve them if their want be urgent; since it is better to run the risk of giving alms to an impostor, than to deny assistance to one who really needs it. But if the necessity be not urgent, the Parish Priest should not place implicit trust in the story told him by the applicant, but ought first to seek for information in the locality whence he has come; for it happens not unfrequently that covetous country people of both sexes, who have plots of ground and houses in their own districts, come from time to time into the city, to play the part of impostors and live upon alms. Such persons are not poor, so much as dishonest; and it is real charity to refuse them that alms which they would be bound to restore, since they obtained it unjustly under false pretences.

A Parish Priest ought likewise to be on his guard against throwing away alms upon big, sturdy beggars, since many of them are idle and vicious, and could earn their bread if they were only willing to do so. In giving alms to such persons, a Parish Priest would be simply abetting immorality. Nay, even though these professional beggars should happen to be really poor, and incapable of supporting themselves by their own labour, a Parish Priest need not give himself much concern about them; for since they spend the entire day going about in quest of alms, they are never in want of necessaries, nor is it a rare occurrence to find that they have something over and above to spend and squander in the public-houses.

We must next consider the case of other poor persons of a more respectable class, who likewise live upon alms, which, however, they solicit secretly from persons in easy circumstances, from charitable societies, and especially from the Parish Priest, from whom, moreover, they receive papers attesting the *bona-fide* character of their poverty.

Amongst these there are individuals and families who are really needy and deserving of assistance, and the Parish Priest ought to be most careful to draw a distinction between them and others of whom we shall speak presently, providing for them relief in proportion to their wants.

But even amongst poor persons of this class, as amongst professional beggars, you may find the idle and the vicious—persons practised in every art of deceit, who know how to excite the pity of the Parish Priest, of the Presidents of charitable societies, and of rich, benevolent individuals, so as not merely to procure a sufficiency for the necessaries of life, but even a superabundance, which is squandered in the gratification of their passions.

Wherefore, when poor persons of this class come to the Parish Priest, unless they happen to be thoroughly known to him, he ought not immediately to put faith either in their own account of their misfortunes, or in the tears which may accompany the recital of them; but he ought, instead, to seek for accurate information, not only regarding their real necessities, but also regarding their morals, requiring from them certificates of character from the Pastor of the locality in which they last resided, and applying for information likewise to other discreet and prudent persons.

Meanwhile let him interrogate them carefully and cautiously as to how many they may be in family, and what may be their means of livelihood. By asking them a good many questions, he will easily discover whether they are deserving of credit, or are imposing upon him.

He must be particularly on his guard against placing trust in those who would wish to persuade him that they have only the very slightest means of subsistence, or none at all, so that it would seem as though they wished him to believe that they lived upon air, as the saying goes. Persons who make representations of this kind are undoubtedly impostors.

Almost the same conclusion may be drawn regarding those women who, when they ask for alms, invariably have tears in their eyes, and make their appeal with such moving pathos, that one would suppose them on the very point of expiring through hunger. If the Parish Priest will only change the discourse and begin to talk of something else, it will be seen that the tears will immediately cease to flow, and they will speak with the greatest composure. This shows that the previous tears and excitement were not natural, but assumed for the occasion; for, were it otherwise, the signs of profound interior sorrow and excitement ought to have continued, even when the subject of conversation happened to be changed.

§ 2. How a Parish Priest ought to act towards the Pretended Poor.

When impostors present themselves to solicit alms, the Parish Priest should he know them to be such, ought to excuse himself with the best possible grace, in order not to provoke their passionate tempers, saying that, just then, he has nothing to give them; that on some future occasion he would see what he could do for them; and so forth. Should they repeat their visits, he must always have some excuse ready in order to send them away graciously; and, in this manner, they will soon come to understand that the Parish Priest has discovered their real character, and they will, accordingly, cease to solicit alms from him.

Some one may, perhaps, suggest, that the Parish Priest would do better by correcting them, and advising them to seek some more honest means of livelihood. But it must be borne in mind that people of this class do not want to listen to any advice about their affairs; and that if the Parish Priest were to correct them, even in the most moderate language, he could expect no result except passion and scorn, perhaps even insults and vile language. Wherefore, in their case, correction would be useless, nay injurious. Nevertheless, the Parish Priest, speaking with them in general, might remark that it was a great shame that persons who could find other means of subsistence should adopt the profession of mendicants; that such as these were usurping the alms left for the really poor; that in doing so they were guilty of real injustice, which is sure not to go unpunished, perhaps even in this world, and so forth: but he should say all this in general terms, without making it appear that such observations are intended to apply to themselves.

But how ought a Parish Priest to act, if mendicants of this class should ask him to interest himself in their behalf with some charitable society, or with some benevolent rich persons; or should ask him for a certificate of poverty; or should claim to be admitted to a share in any general charity which might happen to be in course of distribution?

In the first of the cases stated, the Parish Priest may lay the claim of these mendicants, even though they be undeserving, before those who have control of the administration or distribution of alms; but he ought at the same time to tell them, for their guidance, what he himself thinks of the necessities and moral character of the applicants.

In the second case, he may give a certificate of poverty; for even though the poverty of such people is the result of their own laziness, nevertheless they are really poor. However, the certificate ought to be drawn up in a very cold and dry style, so that any person possessed of judgment, may be able, on reading it, to suspect how the matter really stands. Those who administer the funds of charitable societies, and benevolent rich persons to whom such certificates are presented, easily distinguish those which the Parish Priest writes with a real desire that they should be successful, from those others which he gives, so to speak, *pro forma*, and merely to rid himself of the importunity of the applicant.

In the third case, the Parish Priest need have no scruple in admitting the class of mendicants of whom we speak to a share in general distributions of alms; not only because he would expose himself to lasting annoyance by excluding them, but also, because to admit them is, or ought to be, the intention of those who order such public distributions. I say that to admit them is, or ought to be, the intention of the donor of the alms: because he must forsee that when it becomes publicly known that, for example, five shillings are to be distributed to each of the poor people in the parish, a claim to this dole will be put forward not only by the really poor, but also by all those who, though not poor in reality, are not ashamed to represent themselves as such, and will, therefore, have the presumption to claim their share in the distribution. This, to be sure, is an abuse, but it is an abuse intended, at least indirectly, by the almsgiver, and the Parish Priest is powerless to remedy it. We only, who know by experience what and how great is the insolence of those, whether really indigent or otherwise, who lay claim to a share in public distributions of charity, can realise the trying position in which a Parish Priest would place himself, were he to attempt on such occasions to draw a distinction between the real and the pretended poor.

For the rest, there is no doubt that public distributions of alms (except, perhaps, in the case of cooked provisions) are rather vainglorious displays than real works of charity. Meanwhile we must be resigned to see all who please become sharers in them.

§ 3. On giving Alms to Persons who lead Bad Lives.

A Parish Priest must be on his guard against giving alms to notorious and obstinate sinners. Even though they should be really poor, the Parish Priest, nevertheless, ought to suffer them to endure all the pangs of poverty, in the hope that they may thereby be induced to abandon their evil habits; whereas were he, on the other hand, to show himself touched by their privations whilst they still persevered in their evil courses, he would be simply conniving at their sin, and at the consequent scandal.

But if, on the contrary, persons of this class should happen to be sincerely desirous of changing their lives, they ought to be received with the greatest charity, both because of their real poverty, and also to encourage them to repentance. I have said "*sincerely desirous*": because it frequently happens that when certain unfortunate women are already in great measure cast off by the world, though still unwilling to abandon sin, they pretend to be animated by the very best intentions, in order to move the Parish Priest to assist them; and if he be not well upon his guard, they will continue to support themselves, at one and the same time, by the wages of sin and by charity.

Meanwhile the Parish Priest must test the sincerity of their good intentions, not so much by observing whether they go to confession or to mass— things which certain women do through deliberate hypocrisy ; but by discovering whether they are prepared to place themselves for the future beyond the possibility of continuing in their sinful career. Wherefore, should any of these unfortunates present herself before the Parish Priest, he must propose to her to retire to some Magdalen asylum, or other charitable institution, where she would no longer be within reach of the occasions of sin ; and this he ought to do, even though he should not at the moment have any place of retreat ready to receive her. If the woman be sincerely penitent, she will eagerly embrace his proposal; otherwise she will raise difficulties, and put forward excuses for the purpose of retaining her liberty ; and, should she do so, the Parish Priest ought to distrust the sincerity of her intentions. He ought to distrust it even though her condition were such as would be calculated to excite the disgust of the world; because, being a woman of abandoned character, habituated to idleness, without any honest means of livelihood, and, perhaps, ruined in health, there would be grounds for fearing that she does not wish to abandon her sinful career altogether, but to continue in it, at least as the proprietress of a house of ill-fame.

He must distrust her sincerity still more, should she happen to be yet young, and to retain a portion of her good looks; because if a woman of this kind, who has already lost her character, and who is unable to do any work, as is the case with most persons of her class, were to remain in the midst of the world, she would find it too difficult a task to procure the necessaries of life by honest means. Moreover, notwithstanding all her good intentions, no matter how sincere we may suppose them to be, she would not be able to persevere for any length of time against the violent assaults of her fierce and unbridled passions, and the solicitations of those evil companions with whom she had so recently associated.

Let us, however, put the case that a woman of this class protests that she is really anxious to change her life, but cannot be induced to shut herself up in an asylum for penitents—ought the Parish Priest, under such circumstances, to abandon her? And, again, how is he to act in the hypothesis that she is willing to enter an asylum, but no vacancy exists to admit of her reception?

If the woman in question can point out any means by which she hopes to earn an honest livelihood, the Parish Priest ought not to abandon her, but rather to help her for the purpose of testing her resolution; taking care, meanwhile, to keep a strict watch over her conduct. But if, on the other hand, the woman were merely to *assert* that she would find honest means of support, without, however, *indicating* what these means were, the Parish Priest ought not to trust her; and, under such circumstances, to give her alms blindly would not be to perform an act of charity, but an act of imprudence.

On the other hand, if the unfortunate woman were to declare herself willing to enter an asylum for penitents, but there should not happen to be any institution of the kind ready to receive her, it is evident that in this case the Parish Priest ought to assist her, taking care, however, to bind her down to certain conditions, in order that her conversion might be permanent. These conditions ought to be: that if she should happen to live in the same apartment, or even in the same house, with other women of bad character, she should change her lodgings without a moment's delay; that should an opportunity present itself of living with some virtuous female relative, or other well-conducted woman, she should not refuse to do so; that she should abstain altogether from visiting public-houses, or other dangerous places; that she should not receive into her house any person of the male sex, except her more immediate relatives; finally, that she should frequently hear the word of God, and approach the Sacrament of Penance, leaving it to the judgment of her confessor to decide how often she ought to approach the holy communion. It is certain that if she cannot find shelter in an asylum, the grace necessary to avoid sin, and to persevere in repentance, will not be wanting to her, provided she employs the means which I have just mentioned; for it is always true that "*facienti quod est in se, Deus non denegat gratiam*".

When we said above that a Parish Priest must not admit those who lead bad lives to a share in the distribution of alms, we must be understood as speaking solely of persons *who make a livelihood by sin*, not of those who otherwise fail in their duty as Christians; such, for instance, as those who do not educate their children religiously, who do not observe festivals of obligation, who do not comply with the precept of paschal communion, or who cherish hatred and ill-will even against the Parish Priest himself. To such as these the Parish Priest ought not to refuse alms, if they be really needy; and this, not so much because of their poverty as for two other reasons.

The first is that, when giving alms to such persons, the Parish Priest has always a most favourable opportunity to admonish them and to exhort them to repentance. The spiritual charity of correction, when united to the corporal charity of alms-giving, possesses singular efficacy; and it will very rarely occur that a person who frequently has recourse to the Parish Priest for alms, and receives it, will not, sooner or later, yield to his paternal exhortations. Should he be really hardened in evil, he will prefer to keep away from the Parish Priest altogether, and will turn elsewhere to seek assistance.

The second reason is that, if the Parish Priest refuses to assist such persons in their real necessities, they become annoyed, and more and more hardened in their evil ways. Therefore, to deny them alms would only be to hurry them on to perdition.

In the case of a poor person entertaining hatred towards the Parish Priest, this hatred will infallibly vanish, and will be replaced by kindly feelings, if the poor man experiences generous treatment at the hands of his pastor in the hour of necessity.

To conclude, then, a Parish Priest ought, as a general rule, to give alms to those who are really poor, even though they be sinners, provided, however, they do not make a livelihood by sin. I say "*as a general rule*"; because a Parish Priest may at times threaten to withdraw his assistance from them, and may, occasionally, even carry this threat into execution, should he judge that such a course would be calculated to make them change their lives, as we have already remarked when treating of correction.

§ 4. How a Parish Priest ought to act towards the Really Poor.

A Parish Priest ought to feel towards the really poor a mother's tenderness, and ought, therefore, to manifest the greatest solicitude in providing for their wants. The Parish Priest must show that he has a heart to feel for them in their necessities: when he gives them alms he must do so in a kindly and considerate manner, especially if they be poor persons of a rather respectable class, who find the mere fact of receiving alms very humiliating in itself; and he must take care not to appear annoyed by them, and

ON THE CARE OF THE POOR. 99

not to allow his charitable deeds to be accompanied by complaints and grumblings. Let him remember that "God loves a cheerful giver".

He ought to regard the poor, whom Christ so loved, as his children, recommended in a special manner to his care, since he prides himself on being "Pater pauperum"; and therefore he ought to labour to relieve the necessities of the poor, with the same earnestness which a father displays in providing the necessaries of life for his little ones.

He must relieve the poor out of his own purse, as far as his means will allow; and when his own resources prove insufficient, he must procure further assistance for them from charitable societies and from benevolent individuals. I have said that *he must relieve the poor out of his own purse,* since this is the rule followed in practice by good Parish Priests. It is very true that, if we consult Canonists and Moral Theologians, we might find that a Parish Priest is allowed, now for one reason and again for another, to lay aside a little money to purchase a small farm, to make small investments in the public funds, to acquire a little property for the purpose of leaving it to his nephews, or better still, to endow a chaplaincy out of it, and so forth. Nevertheless, it very rarely happens that good Parish Priests are able to make such savings, more or less justifiable before God, and more or less praiseworthy in the eyes of men. Good Parish Priests, even when they have a large income, spend the entire of it, and would spend still more if they had it, in decorating their

Church, in promoting piety, and in relieving the wants of the poor.

Setting aside, then, all questions whether of Canon Law or of Moral Theology, and adopting an indisputable standard of goodness, such as is the practice of the best Parish Priests, let a Pastor, whilst not neglecting the adornment of his Church and the advancement of piety, give to the poor out of his own pocket as much as he can. By acting thus, he will never have to be deciding cases between his right and his duty; he will be free from troubles of conscience during life, and from fears at the hour of death.

But what are we to say of the case when the Parish Priest should happen to possess some private property, and consequently revenues derived neither from his benefice nor from the exercise of his sacerdotal functions? Ought he to share such monies also with the poor? It is a fact that some Parish Priests regard whatever property they may happen to have from their families as a something sacred, not to be touched on any account, but to be handed down to their nephews, not only in all its integrity, but even increased by the addition of all the profits which may have accumulated from it during their entire life; because, they say, a Parish Priest ought to live upon the income of his benefice, and not defraud his nephews or other relatives of the unbounded expectations which they entertain, that whatever he possesses will one day belong to them.

I do not mean to quote either Canon Law or

Moral Theology in opposition to this doctrine, although a good deal might be said on the subject from a moral point of view. I will merely remark that good Parish Priests have always been accustomed to employ in doing good whatever property really belonged to them; and there cannot be the slightest doubt that the revenue derived from their patrimony really belongs to them. I will add, furthermore, that sometimes, when they judged it expedient, they have employed in good works not only the revenue derived from their patrimony, but even the patrimony itself, disposing of it either entirely or in part.

And who could have the hardihood to censure them for so doing? A secular takes his share of the patrimony, and does with it what he pleases: he may even squander it in the most reckless manner, and the world does not gainsay his right to do so. But when, on the other hand, an ecclesiastic takes his portion, is he supposed to take it, not as its real owner but as a mere administrator, who is obliged to preserve it intact, nay to hand it down to his family improved and augmented? One might fairly say to certain Parish Priests: "miserable stewards, acting for your families, of what use is your property to you? what do you derive from it, except the annoyance of managing it, without even receiving a salary for your trouble? If you were unwilling to employ your money either for the glory of God, or for the good of your neighbour, it would have been better for you to renounce your right to it altogether, and thus get rid of the trouble of thinking about it." On the other hand, it is impossible to believe that when God will one day demand from us an account of the use which we have made of the goods received from Him, He will exclude from the reckoning the revenues derived from our patrimony, or will be satisfied if we answer Him that we have saved them all up for our relatives.

However, since very rich parishes are rare, and few Parish Priests are possessed of family property, a Pastor, as a general rule, will not be able to provide out of his own purse for all the poor of his parish; and, therefore, to supply the deficiency, he must appeal to charitable societies, and to benevolent individuals, especially on occasions of extraordinary necessity, such as, for instance, in time of famine, of pestilence, of war, or of any similar calamity, whereby the number of the poor is augmented, and the wretchedness of their condition becomes aggravated. The Parish Priest must likewise remember that he is bound to see that on such occasions the civil authorities are not wanting in their duty of providing succour for the poor and suffering. I have often noticed, during outbreaks of cholera, how necessary it is that the Parish Priest should be vigilant in this respect.

But though a Parish Priest ought to employ his influence with rich and charitable persons in order to procure relief for the poor members of his flock, nevertheless he must be careful not to make too frequent demands on their purses, without real necessity. Certain Parish Priests who are always begging, either for their Church or for the poor, become exceedingly troublesome, and are regarded as a nuisance. If the Lord sends a Parish Priest enough to keep his Church decent, and to provide sufficiently for the wants of his poor, in a manner suitable to their lowly condition, he ought to be satisfied, and look for nothing more.

Instead of annoying all the rich people of his acquaintance, by continually importuning them for money—a matter which is, in itself, always disagreeable—let him urge them to employ their wealth in co-operating to promote the glory of God and the salvation of souls, by such means as are most called for by the circumstances of the times; such as, for example, by supporting the Catholic Press, by establishing or assisting good Catholic schools, and so forth.

Let Parish Priests bear in mind that, where there is a want of discretion in asking for money, there is reason to fear that the zeal for spending a good deal on the Church, or in giving alms, has its origin and motive in a vain-glorious desire to attract attention by one's good works. I say this, however, with the express reservation: *"where there is a want of discretion in asking for money"*.

§ 5. OF THE CLASSES OF POOR PERSONS TO WHOM A PARISH PRIEST MUST GIVE A PREFERENCE.

Since, in relieving the wants of the poor, a Parish Priest ought to be animated solely by charity, and since charity acts according to rule, he must always prefer the virtuous poor to the vicious, and even amongst the virtuous he must prefer the very best. For the same reason, he must help those whose wants are greatest, before those who stand less in need of his assistance.

Respecting this matter, however, two cautions are necessary. The first is that this preference must be kept a profound secret from the rest of the poor; for, otherwise, wretched jealousies would be sure to spring up, from which the favoured poor would have to suffer just as well as the Parish Priest himself.

The second caution is, that the Parish Priest be on his guard lest the poor feign piety and devotion, in order to receive alms from him more abundantly. For poor men, and more especially poor women, are constantly to be met with, who, taking it for granted that a Pastor ought to be more liberal towards pious persons than towards others, go to confession to the Parish Priest himself, and do so frequently; ask permission to communicate on days of devotion, are always in Church on festivals, and often on weekdays, and yet, all the while, are no better than designing knaves and hypocrites. If the Parish Priest will be on his guard, and instead of trusting blindly to appearances, will take the trouble to examine matters more closely, he cannot be deceived by manœuvres of this kind for any considerable length of time.

Wherefore, let him distinctly tell those penitents who come to make known to him in confession their temporal necessities, that he will not pay the slightest heed to such stories once he has left the confessional, no more than he will pay heed to the sins which he has been hearing there. Sometimes he might even say to them with advantage: "I would have you know that were I to discover from your confession that you were likely this very day to die of hunger, I would not come to your assistance, unless I should happen to acquire a knowledge of the fact otherwise than through the medium of the confessional". If treated in this manner, certain persons, for the most part women, will abandon the system of coming to confession more for the purpose of asking alms than to seek absolution from their sins. However, should the Parish Priest, in the course of confession, become acquainted with certain wants which closely affect the conscience of the penitent—such as, for instance, the want of a bed to provide separate sleeping accommodation for brothers and sisters—he must direct the penitent to inform him of the state of affairs outside the confessional, in order that he may be able to verify the existence of the want, and the subsequent result of the precautions taken.

Should he discover any case of imposture, he must administer a paternal correction to the hypocrite; and should this person again return to his confessional, he must direct him to confess in future to some other priest. Meanwhile, should the person be really poor, he must not be refused the ordinary alms.

Here it may not be out of place to put new Parish Priests and confessors on their guard against certain impostors, who keep travelling about through town and country, and who show a decided preference for young confessors, in order to extract alms from them, occasionally even in considerable sums. These persons sometimes pretend that the officers of justice are on their track, and that liberty or life is at stake, unless they receive immediate assistance to make good their escape; and so practised are they in the art of deception, that, when at the feet of the confessor, they are able occasionally to weep like children, and to tremble like aspen leaves. Now, whoever gives alms to persons of this class ought to have serious scruples for encouraging them in their sacriligious trade; because when they have succeeded in deceiving one confessor, they proceed with the same story to another, and so on to several in succession. Even though a confessor should believe that he has evidence of the sincerity and real poverty of a penitent who asks him for alms, nevertheless, he ought not to trust anyone under such circumstances. Even though he should be in a position to relieve his necessities on the spot, yet he must insist on his stating his case outside the confessional; then let him examine into the truth of the statement; and when he shall have, as it were, thus thoroughly probed that sincerity and destitution, the existence of which he had already suspected, let him, by all means, relieve the wants of his penitent. By acting in this manner, his charity will be judicious and meritorious.

Just as the virtuous poor are to be preferred to those who are less good, so those who are in greatest need are to be relieved in preference to the less needy. Now there is no doubt that, generally speaking, we must reckon amongst those who are most needy, orphan children, widows—and more especially young widows with little children—the old and the infirm.

The Parish Priest must endeavour, if possible, to place orphans with their relatives, provided these happen to be good and pious people, so that there may be grounds for hoping that the children will receive a Christian education. Otherwise, he must take measures to have them received into some religious institution, or placed under the guardianship of some charitable people. Above all, he must have a special care of orphan girls who may be somewhat grown, inasmuch as they are exposed to great risk of being seduced or corrupted.

Poor widows with children merit special consideration, and therefore ought to receive more abundant alms. A pastor ought to be still more particular to relieve their wants should they happen to be still young, and, consequently, in greater danger of being tempted and seduced.

However, he must be very careful not to exert himself to get them married, as a means of rendering them assistance. If a young widow wishes to get married, she will be quite competent to conduct the negotiations herself; her relatives and female friends will assist her; and there will not be the least necessity for the intervention of the Parish Priest's zeal—zeal which the world would pronounce imprudent and suspicious, and which might leave a stain upon his character. We shall return to this subject when treating of matrimony.

Finally, the Parish Priest must show special charity to poor aged persons, and to the infirm who are dangerously ill, and are unable to provide themselves with the sustenance necessary for them.

And here I must remark that we occasionally meet with aged and infirm persons, who cannot procure in their own houses that food and attendance which their condition requires, but who might, if they chose, find shelter in some charitable institution or hospital; yet, so absurd and wrong-headed are they, that they prefer to remain in their own homes, and to endure there every species of privation. Amongst this class are frequently found persons who are most careless in all that concerns their eternal salvation; who never approach the sacraments, or hear the word of God; and who do not even assist at Mass on festivals of obligation, either because they are unwilling to do so, or are unable to attend conveniently.

Now there is no doubt that the Parish Priest will perform an act of great charity, if he succeeds in inducing such persons to leave those dens of wretchedness and filth which they call their houses (where it is to be feared they are in many cases detained by the devil), and procures admission for them into some charitable institution, where provision will be made for their wants both corporal and spiritual.

However, should they obstinately refuse to yield to the exhortations of the Parish Priest, he must, nevertheless, assist them, as best he can, not only in their spiritual, but also in their corporal necessities; for many of these poor people are so blinded by prejudice, that they really are not open to conviction. And even in the hypothesis that their obstinacy were positively culpable, they should be assisted, nevertheless, for the love of God, which obliges us not to allow our neighbour to perish, even when he wishes to perish through his own fault.

CHAPTER VI.

ON THE CARE WHICH A PASTOR OUGHT TO HAVE OF HIS CHURCH.

§ 1. OF THE CHURCH COMMITTEE.[1]

THE Church Committee is not a matter of ecclesiastical institution; nay, it is tolerated rather than desired by the Church, at least in the form in which it exists amongst us. Nevertheless, since the Parish Priest must resign himself to its existence, he must regard it as what it ought to be—namely, an organisation composed of his most influential and respectable parishioners, for the purpose of assisting him

---

[1] I have translated the Italian *Fabbriceria* by the expression "Church Committee," for want of a better word. As a matter of fact, such an institution as the *Fabrica* does not exist, in its canonical sense, in English-speaking countries. Its origin and functions are thus described by Craisson: "Ad providendum variis Ecclesiarum necessitatibus institutæ fuêre Fabricæ, seu corpora administratorum quibus cura demandabatur administrandi res ecclesiæ, sumptus suggerendo necessarios ædificationi ac reparationi sacrarum ædium, et aliis ad cultum divinum requisitis; ideo sic vocantur, quia institutæ fuêre præcipue ad reficiendas et *fabricandas* sacras ædes" (*Manuale totius Juris Canonici*, n. 5308).

The *Fabrica* in its canonical sense is found at present only in those Catholic countries where the Church is established by law; and even in some of these, as in France, and of recent years in

in providing the material requirements of divine worship, and in regulating other matters to which he cannot himself conveniently attend, owing to the arduous labours imposed upon him by the administration of the sacraments, the visitation of the sick, the care of the poor, and the other spiritual duties of his sacred office.

Considered in this light, a Church Committee could not be displeasing to a Parish Priest, and he ought not to exhibit any hostility towards it; for to do so would be an act of great imprudence, and might entail upon him serious trouble and annoyance.

If it be urged that the Committee is oftentimes composed of persons in whom the Parish Priest cannot repose confidence, it by no means follows that he could therefore prudently assume an attitude of hostility towards it; nay, it is precisely under such circumstances that he ought to treat the members of the Committee with more than usual consideration,

---

Italy, its functions have been in a great measure usurped by the State, in opposition to the spirit and the letter of the Canon Law (see Craisson, n. 5311, et seq.). But though the *Fabrica*, strictly so-called, does not exist in English-speaking countries, yet Priests charged with the care of souls in these countries continually find it advisable, and often indispensable, to associate with themselves committees of their lay parishioners, to assist them in matters connected with the building and repairing of churches, and other temporal affairs of the parish. The rules, therefore, laid down in the text for the guidance of a Parish Priest in his relations with the members of the *Fabrica*, will, *mutatis mutandis*, be found applicable to the relations which ought to subsist between Priests in English-speaking countries and the lay members of their Church Committee. — *Translator*.

as they might otherwise involve him in trouble, and, indeed, in greater trouble than he may be able to foresee. The Church Committee is a legally constituted body, on which the Parish Priest is dependent in many things. Therefore, if the members of the Committee be at variance with him, they may give him a good deal of annoyance, more especially if they be not pious men. If, on the other hand, the Parish Priest treats them with respect, and shows deference to their views and arrangements, they will, in turn, entertain friendly feelings towards him, or, at least, will not adopt an attitude of hostility; and where mutual friendly confidence between a Parish Priest and his Church Committee is impossible, it is a great blessing that there should be, at least, no open rupture between them.

No matter how the Committee may be composed, it ought to be the constant aim of the Parish Priest to keep on friendly terms with all its members; and he will undoubtedly succeed in doing so, if he allows them to act as they please in whatever belongs more particularly to their province, such as repairing the Church and keeping it in good order, looking after the Church furniture, the choir, and other like matters. The Parish Priest not only may, but ought, give expression to his own views, whenever there is danger that the funds of the Church may be squandered in extravagant expenditure. Nevertheless, since he has but a single vote on the Committee, and is therefore powerless by himself, should he see the Committee resolved on executing some repairs, or purchasing some furniture, he must be careful not to cling obstinately to his own views, but rather to vote with them, unless, indeed, there should be question of committing some act of injustice involving the guilt of sin—a case which will not occur, perhaps, once in a hundred years. In this manner, by letting the members of the Committee see that he is ready to accommodate himself to their wishes, and to vote with them, he will be certain to gain their goodwill; and they, in turn, will be disposed to entertain favourably any proposals which he may, from time to time, put forward.

Some Parish Priests, perhaps, may be of opinion that it is cowardly and weak to yield in this manner, even when there may be valid reasons for opposing some measure advocated by the committee. However, when one gives way for the sake of peace, in a matter where there is no question of sin, it is rather an act of humility and charity, and, in the present case, of christian prudence likewise, as we shall see presently.

Now it is evident that, as a general rule, a Parish Priest can yield to the views of his committee without any risk of incurring the guilt of sin. For though it is true that they often wish to incur expense, and to contract debts that are extravagant considering the poverty of the Parish—a matter which of itself would be unjust—nevertheless the injustice ceases, when we consider that the views of the committee, to whom it belongs to collect the funds, are shared by those who contribute them, since these latter are aware of the expenditure of the committee, and yet do not protest against it. Therefore, if the Parish Priest, for the praiseworthy motive of maintaining peace with his leading parishioners, becomes a consenting party to this extravagant outlay, he cannot be charged with doing wrong. There would, indeed, be grounds for the charge of injustice, if debts were contracted so enormous that there could be no likelihood of their ever being paid. But this is to put a highly improbable case; for though the committee may venture to contract debts which cannot be paid until after the lapse of several years, they will never contract liabilities which they do not expect to discharge at some time or other. Moreover, the creditors of the committee foresee and calculate all the risks which may occur in their dealings with them.

Let us, for instance, put the case that the committee should wish to order a very expensive peal of bells, though their Church is poor, and would require more necessary, and less expensive furniture. There is no doubt that, in such a case as this, it would be the duty of the Parish Priest to point out to the committee the incongruity of such expenditure, and to exhort them to postpone it for a while, or at least to curtail it. Nevertheless, should they, who, perhaps, have already come to an understanding on the subject with the more wealthy parishioners, show themselves determined to incur this expense, can the Parish Priest be charged with doing wrong if he consents to it, for the purpose of maintaining peace and harmony with his committee? I, most certainly, would not endorse such rigorous doctrine; and I would be of the same opinion were there question of providing a choir, or of undertaking any other work which would entail an inconvenient outlay.

That the Parish Priest should yield in this manner, and accommodate himself to the wishes of his Church Committee, is nothing more than an act of christian prudence; for when he yields to them in temporal matters, they are bound to second his views in whatever concerns the spiritual welfare of his flock. If he sanctions their arrangements regarding the bells, the choir, and such like matters, they will approve of his selection of a preacher for Lent, or for a mission, and so of other spiritual affairs. When they see that he allows them to act as they please with regard to the material requirements of the Church, they, in turn, will permit him to do as he pleases in all that concerns matters of devotion; and thus the Parish Priest will be in a position to attend much more freely to the sanctification of his people, which is his first and most important concern.

Many Parish Priests are constantly engaged in disputes with the members of their Committee—disputes most prejudicial to the spiritual interests of their people, and concerning purely material affairs, in respect of which the Parish Priest, no doubt, has privileges and rights, but privileges and rights which must always be sacrificed to the supreme good of harmony between himself and his most influential parishioners. The Parish Priest who succeeds in preserving this harmony, even at some sacrifice, is truly wise, and at the same time must be regarded as singularly fortunate, because he thereby gains an ascendancy over their hearts, and moulds them as he wills. Moreover, it comes to pass by degrees, that not only is he not opposed, but his wishes are consulted and gratified, even in what concerns the material interests of the Parish. Sometimes he succeeds in controlling the very election of the committee, so that it comes to be composed of his own adherents; and once this is gained, disputes become impossible, and the entire management of the Church rests practically in the hands of the Parish Priest.

And in this matter we must not allow ourselves to be deceived by that pretext which is commonly put forward by some Parish Priests: "If I yield, I not only injure myself but my successor, who will be unable to regain his right, after I shall have renounced it". For there is no question whatever of renouncing rights, but merely of yielding in cases where it is necessary to do so for God's greater glory, which must always be our first consideration. By such a course of action, your successor loses no right; nay, he himself, should circumstances require it, will have sufficient humility and charity to give way sometimes for the preservation of peace. And here, perhaps, it may not be out of place to ask, whether we really are so very zealous for the rights of our successor as we pretend to be? Charity towards our successor ought to stimulate us, above all, to hand down the parish to him in a condition of peace and harmony, and well prepared to derive benefit from his pastoral solicitude.

And since it is a matter of such importance that a

good understanding should exist between a Pastor and his Church Committee, he must strive by every means in his power to create this good feeling where it is absent, and to foster it where it already exists. Wherefore, it would be advisable that, occasionally during the course of the year, he should invite the members of his Church Committee to dinner, and show them all those marks of consideration and affection which he may judge opportune.

Let the Parish Priest be careful to consult the committee, whenever there may be question of taking legal proceedings to defend the interests of the church and of the parish. There are some Parish Priests who wish that the Committee should resign entirely into their own hands whatever appertains to legal matters, since they believe that they know best how to manage such affairs. This may be very true, especially in the case of country committees, whose members have little or no knowledge of legal proceedings; however, it will never be necessary that the Pastor should carry on the suit personally, appearing before the courts, and acting as though he were the sole mover in the case. The Parish Priest may, and sometimes must, consult lawyers; so far from blindly handing over to the Committee the entire management of the suit, he must exercise supervision over their proceedings; but he must do all this unostentatiously, letting it appear as though they managed the entire affair themselves, and that he took little part in it. In this manner, he will save much time, which may be more usefully employed in looking after spiritual concerns, and he will avoid the risk of incurring odium, which might prove very injurious, should the lawsuit happen to be carried on against any influential parishioner. It is always much better that in matters of this kind seculars should deal with seculars, and it is less injurious that any one should entertain a bad feeling against the committee than against the Parish Priest.

Let him likewise take care that the committee keep a regular account of their receipts and expenditure, so that the financial condition of the Parish may be always known at a glance, and those mistakes avoided which occur through negligence or fraud. Should he discover any serious irregularities, he must endeavour to apply a remedy, but always with prudence, and in a gracious manner, so as not to give offence to anybody. Should he find that matters are managed substantially well, he must be on his guard against appearing suspicious and exacting, since this would destroy the harmony existing between himself and the committee, the maintenance of which is of far greater importance, than that everything should proceed with all that exactness and precision which one might desire. Let him always bear in mind that he holds the office of Parish Priest, first of all, for the spiritual good of souls, and, in the next place, for the material good of the church and of the parish. Wherefore, though the material interests are not only useful, but even necessary, for promoting the spiritual interests, yet he must never prefer the well-being of the former to the well-being of the latter; and there is no doubt that it is far more conducive to the spiritual good of his flock, that he should maintain friendly relations with the members of the church committee, than that he should insist on a very rigorous audit of their accounts.

§ 2. OF THE ASSISTANTS EMPLOYED ABOUT THE CHURCH.

The Parish Priest must take care that those who are employed about the Church are moral and pious persons, and especially that they observe that reverence which is due to the holy place. This latter point is to be insisted on the more strongly, because such persons generally fail in this respect, not from any bad disposition or want of faith, but simply through thoughtlessness, and that habit of taking liberties with holy things, which insensibly grows upon those who are constantly brought into contact with them.

For this reason it often happens that the most irreverent persons in a Church—those who walk about there, and chat, and laugh, and joke as if they were in the street, and omit to genuflect, even when the Blessed Sacrament is exposed—are those very attendants who are employed in the service of the Church. The Parish Priest must, therefore, be vigilant on this point, and must not omit to reprove those whom he finds culpable in this respect.

In many places women and girls, selected for the purpose by the Parish Priest, have charge of keeping the Church clean. This custom is on the whole commendable; because women are better suited for such work than men, and wherever they are in charge the Churches are kept remarkably neat—a matter which is a source of great edification. Nevertheless, the Parish Priest must be careful not to employ in this service women who are rather young and good-looking; to select only those who are elderly and steady; to see that they are never alone with the male assistants when the Church is closed; and, above all, that they do not, as might easily happen, make themselves too much at home in his own house—a circumstance which would be fraught with danger for himself, and might give rise to disedifying reports.

§ 3. OF THE CLEANLINESS OF THE CHURCH.

It is not necessary that all parochial Churches should be rich and sumptuously adorned, but it is expected that they should all be kept extremely neat and clean. This result will be obtained, if the Parish Priest exercises strict supervision over those who have charge of the Church.

The Baptistry, the Altars, and the sacred vessels should be kept scrupulously clean and neat, as shall be said later on when we come to speak of the Sacraments. The same remark applies to the fonts for holding the holy water, which should never be wanting in parochial Churches. And let the Parish Priest take care that the holy water be not unworthy of its name—*aqua lustralis*—for it sometimes happens that respectable persons are almost forced to withdraw their hands from the fonts, owing to the filthy condition both of the font and of the water. Let him be careful, therefore, to have the fonts often washed, and the water renewed, so that no one may feel any repugnance to sign himself with it when entering the Church, and that this Sacramental, which has been held in such respect from the earliest ages of Christianity, may suffer no profanation.

§ 4. Of the Sacristy.

I shall say barely one word about the Sacristy, and it is that the Parish Priest must not allow it to become a meeting place for idlers, and must not permit persons to indulge there in useless conversation, or to speak in a loud tone of voice. These abuses are of every-day occurrence in Sacristies. Persons who have nothing to do pass entire hours there, chatting about all the topics of the day; and conversations are carried on in a loud tone, so as to disturb not only the priests who wish to make their preparation for, or thanksgiving after, Mass, but sometimes even those persons who are engaged in their devotions in the Church.

CHAPTER VII.

OF THE CURATE.[1]

§ 1. OF THE QUALITIES WHICH A CURATE OUGHT TO POSSESS.

A PARISH Priest usually has a Curate, and it is advisable that he should never be without one, as we shall show later on. Now, since the Curate ought to be the *alter ego* of the Parish Priest, he should possess all those good qualities which are required in a Pastor;

---

[1] I have been somewhat perplexed in determining what English equivalent I should select for the Italian word *Vice Parrocho*; and my perplexity arose from the fact that, as on the Continent, so, too, in English-speaking countries various names are given, in the vernacular, to those clergymen who assist the Parish Priests in the discharge of their parochial duties, and who are called in Canon Law *Vicarii* or *Coadjutores*. I have finally decided on using the word *Curates* throughout this chapter (and elsewhere), as it is the name universally employed in Ireland to designate the priests in question.

However, in order to understand some allusions in the text, it is necessary to remember that the author speaks of *Vicarii* such as they are in Italy, where, as a general rule, they are nominated not by the Bishop, but by the Parish Priest with the approbation of the Bishop. This system, though in accordance with the Common Law of the Church, (Vide Bouix *De Parocho*, p. 450; Ferraris *Vicarius Parochialis*, No. 43), is not followed in any English-speaking country, in which the Bishops alone have the power of appointing and removing the "Vicarii".— *Translator*.

and if there is a single one with which we might, perhaps, dispense as not being absolutely necessary, it is the capacity for preaching, since the Parish Priest might supply for this want by means of others. As a matter of fact, it is the duty of a Curate to hear the confessions both of those who are in health, and of those who are sick, to attend the dying, to visit the houses of the parishioners for these and other purposes, and oftentimes to assist the Parish Priest in eradicating disorders and preventing scandals. Therefore, he must hold intercourse with all classes of persons, pretty much like the Parish Priest himself; and, consequently, he ought without doubt to be a well-instructed, exemplary, prudent, pious and zealous ecclesiastic, so that the Parish Priest might be able to repose entire confidence in him on all occasions, and under all circumstances. But, above all, he must be a man of irreproachable morals, a qualification which is the most essential in every ecclesiastic, and especially if his duty obliges him, as is the case with curates, to treat at all times with women and young girls, among whom there is always to be found a considerable number possessed of but little steadiness and little prudence.

Wherefore, it is greatly to be regretted that Parish Priests sometimes, when looking for a curate, require in him one solitary qualification—namely, that he be a man of sound and robust constitution, so as to be capable of enduring all the physical labour that may be placed upon his shoulders, just as one would select a porter (excuse the comparison) for his capacity to carry heavy loads. Provided the curate be able to attend sick calls in the wildest and most distant parts of the parish, to sit up whole nights with the dying, and knows how to keep the parochial books, certain Parish Priests are perfectly satisfied, and look for no further qualification. That he may be very ignorant, that he may be unable to speak two words of comfort to the poor sick people whom he attends, that he may be boorish in his manners, and even not sufficiently cautious and edifying in his conduct, does not give them the slightest concern.

The Parish Priest ought to reflect that, when he entrusts his duties to another priest, the latter ought to be a person capable of discharging them in a proper manner, not merely materially, but formally as well; moreover, that he ought to look upon his curate as a companion, and not as his servant or almost his slave; and that, consequently, he ought to treat him with charity and respect, and take a share with him even in the hardest and most disagreeable duties, instead of throwing them over on him altogether. I have been led to make these remarks, because certain Parish Priests fail very signally in this respect.

§ 2. OF THE ADVANTAGES OF HAVING A CURATE.

It is easy to understand how important it is that a Parish Priest should not be unaided in the government of his parish, but should have a curate who may be able to supply his place. The Parish Priest may occasionally be ailing, and even though he were always in the enjoyment of perfect health, it is advisable that he should have an assistant, especially in winter, when the sick are more numerous, and attendance on them becomes more laborious. Moreover, it sometimes happens that all the parishioners have not entire confidence in the Parish Priest; and it is, therefore, very convenient that there should be another priest in the parish, to whom they may be more willing to apply in their spiritual necessities. Finally, there is no doubt that if there are two priests in a parish to take charge of the souls of the faithful, the good fruit produced will be double what it would be if there were only one. Therefore, both for his own sake and for the sake of his parishioners, it is most important that every Parish Priest should have a curate.

The foregoing considerations merit the attention of certain Parish Priests who are always, or frequently, without a curate, either because they wish to save the stipend which they should have to pay him, or because they pay him a stipend so paltry that it would not satisfy any respectable priest. The advantages of having a curate are so great, that to secure them a pastor ought to make even a notable sacrifice. Wherefore, if a Parish Priest can spare from his own income enough to pay a curate, he ought not hesitate to do so; and should he not be in a position to provide the entire sum required, he ought to supply a portion of it at least, and find some other means of procuring the remainder.

It cannot be denied that there are parishes so small, and so poor, that they scarcely afford maintenance to the Parish Priest, and, unfortunately, such parishes are pretty numerous. Nevertheless, it cannot be denied, also, that we, Parish Priests, sometimes regard our income as a something sacred, which cannot be touched, and from which not a farthing is to be deducted for the benefit of any other priest who may wish to share our labours, for the simple reason that we have a right to the entire of it ourselves. But, since this reason would not be considered valid by any one, and would be accounted mean even by ourselves, we more usually put forward the other excuse of the impossibility of supporting a curate, owing to the poverty of the parish, the number of the poor, the pressing wants of our relatives, and so forth—a plea which is more plausible.

§ 3. How Advantageous it is that the Parish Priest and Curate should Live together.

As has been already said, a Parish Priest ought to look for a curate endowed with every good quality, so that he may possess his entire confidence; and when he has found such a one, it will be of the greatest advantage to lodge him in his own house. This is, in fact, a matter of such signal importance, that to effect it a Parish Priest ought even to make a sacrifice. When the curate lives in the Parish Priest's house, the Parish Priest comes to know and understand him better; when any duty turns up, either in connection with sick calls, or some service in the church, he is always on the spot to discharge it; and both the pastor and his assistant quickly, and almost of necessity, become one heart and one soul, for the furtherance of every good work.

But, should neither the Parish Priest nor the curate happen to have any relative living with them, another very great advantage follows from the system which we advocate, and it is that it removes one of the most serious, yet least regarded, dangers to which an Ecclesiastic can be exposed—that of living alone with his servant. Let us make the hypothesis that she is irreproachable, pious, and of mature years, yet she is always a woman. Let us suppose, again, that the Ecclesiastic who lives alone with her possesses in a high degree prudence and piety, yet he is all the while a man. Meanwhile, if he has nobody in the house with whom to exchange a word during the time of meals, or in the long winter evenings, except that servant, who, without being conscious of it, repays confidence by confidence, and for every mark of kindness shows a corresponding sense of affection, (always however within the limits of propriety), there is reason to fear lest, one day or another, the limits of propriety may be overstepped. This fear, which is suggested by reason, has been more than once justified by experience; and, therefore, by having his curate to live with him, the Parish Priest will, by this one act, remove danger from four souls.

However, it must be confessed that, in practice, it cannot always be arranged that the Parish Priest and curate live together; and, when this is so, God will not fail to assist those who invoke His aid, if, as shall be said elsewhere, they on their part observe all due caution.

CHAPTER VIII.

OF RELIGIOUS FUNCTIONS AND PIOUS PRACTICES.

THE fitting celebration of the services of the Church contribute very largely to preserve and revive faith among the people; and it is for this reason that they are decried so much by Protestants, by freethinkers, and by all the modern disciples of indifferentism. But this also is the very reason why the Parish Priest ought to strive earnestly to carry them out with the greatest decorum, and with all possible pomp, so that they may produce a more lively impression upon the minds of the faithful.

It is a signal favour of the divine mercy that, in this age of unbelief, solemn religious functions are of much more frequent occurrence among us than was the case formerly; for they are most efficacious to preserve the spirit of piety among the faithful, who are beset by so many snares and temptations.

Wherefore, a Parish Priest must keep up those religious functions which he finds already established in his church, and must be careful that they lose nothing of their accustomed pomp and decorum. He must celebrate with special pomp the principal solemn festivals of the year, which afford an excellent means of recalling to mind the principal mysteries of our religion, and of reviving the faith of the people in connection with them.

Let him endeavour, also, to celebrate in his church some of those feasts which are best adapted to re-awaken the sentiments of piety in his flock; such as, for example, the feasts of the Sacred Heart of Jesus, and of the Dolours of the Blessed Virgin Mary.

Let him strive, moreover, to cultivate those pious practices which entail in a special manner the frequentation of the Sacraments, such as the devotion of the Fridays of March, and of the Sundays in honour of St. Aloysius. These are especially recommended to the young.

It will be very useful to have the Church provided with statues of the Sacred Heart, of our Lady of Dolours, of our Blessed Lord, and of St. Aloysius. Should there be none of these already in the Church, yet, by providing one each year, the expense would be only a mere trifle even to a poor Church. But in any case, even though there should be no statues, the Feasts and pious practices of which we have spoken ought not to be omitted.

Above all, the Parish Priest must promote the devotion of the month of Mary, now so general throughout the entire Church, and so productive of good results. This devotion has been so visibly blessed by God, that it cannot be doubted that He wishes His Virgin Mother to be honoured in this manner. Wherefore, it is very advisable that on each day of this month the Pastor should address to his people a short, stirring discourse suitable to the occasion, or at least read a lecture for them from some of the many books published for the month of May.

It would be well, also, that the Parish Priest should determine some Festivals, occurring at regular intervals throughout the year, to be celebrated with a general Communion. The first general Communion after Easter ought to take place during the month of May; another might take place in August, or in September; and another in December, or in January, when the Spiritual Exercises might also be given. In this manner, a fresh incentive to approach the Sacraments will be supplied, from time to time, to lukewarm christians, including those who may not have complied with the precept of Paschal Communion.

In small places, the Parish Priest must not omit on such occasions to invite some extraordinary confessors, not only for the convenience of the penitents who frequent the Church in large numbers, but likewise for the benefit of certain persons who may be ashamed to confess to Priests to whom they are known.

Let the Parish Priest be careful to celebrate all religious functions at the hours most convenient to the people, so that they may be more numerously attended, and may be productive of greater good to the faithful. He must be particularly careful to fix the most convenient hours for the catechism and for religious instruction.

It is very desirable that on week-days Mass should

be celebrated at an early hour, so that pious persons, who are obliged to go to business or to work early in the morning, may have an opportunity of assisting at the Holy Sacrifice.

It is an excellent practice to assemble the parishioners in the evening to recite the Rosary, and in this manner a visit to the Blessed Sacrament is also secured. It would contribute largely to the promotion of piety amongst the Faithful, if, after the Rosary, a short meditation were read for them by the Parish Priest, or by some one commissioned by him, as is done in some places.

CHAPTER IX.

OF THE BLESSING OF THE HOUSES.[1]

THE blessing of the houses must not be regarded simply as a means of compiling the statistics of the parish, or as a source of gain and parochial revenue; but we must look upon it as a most effective help towards the good government of the parish. I shall briefly point out the advantages which a good Parish Priest may derive from this practice.

---

[1] Of the blessing of houses, De Herdt writes: "Quatuor in rituali Romano assignautur benedictiones domorum ; 1a, in Sabbato Sancto cum aqua e fonte baptismali ante infusionem sacrorum oleorum desumpta; 2a, alio quocumque tempore facienda, ad libitum postulantis ; 3a, pro nova domo ; 4a, pro loco vel domo, ut ex oratione patet." (Sacræ Liturgiæ praxis, tom 3, n. 296.)

The first of the blessings here mentioned takes place annually in Rome and in other parts of Italy, where the Parish Priests, on the afternoon of Holy Saturday, visit and bless all the houses of the Parish, according to the form prescribed in the Ritual. It is evident, however, that this rite could not possibly be carried out except in very small and compact parishes, and that its observance would be utterly impossible in the extensive parishes which exist in English-speaking countries.

The second blessing mentioned in the Ritual, to be given by the Parish Priest whenever he may judge fit, is that to which our Author refers in the text; and though it would be possible, in the course of the year, to give this blessing even in extensive parishes, yet it is not customary to do so in English-speaking countries. It

The first is that he thereby comes to know his parishioners, as the good shepherd knows his sheep. In cities, especially, it is impossible to acquire this knowledge without the blessing of the houses.

In the next place, he discovers whether such disorders as separations between married persons, concubinage, and the like, exist in any families of his flock. It may, perhaps, be said that those families in which grave scandals do exist will not admit the Parish Priest, when he comes to bless the house. But this is not universally true; because some of them, and especially the poor, who wish to have their names on the parochial register, with a view to receiving alms, will admit the Parish Priest, and the more readily if they hope that he will merely ask

---

is evident, however, from the text that our Author regards this blessing of the houses, principally, as a *means to an end;* and the end is that the Parish Priest should, in the course of his visits to the different houses, acquire a thorough knowledge of his parishioners, and of their spiritual and temporal wants. The acquisition of this knowledge is the point on which our Author insists in the present chapter—knowledge which every Parish Priest is bound to acquire, in virtue of a Divine precept, as is evident from the words of the Council of Trent: "*Cum præcepto divino mandatum sit omnibus quibus animarum cura commissa est, oves suas agnoscere,*" &c. (Sess. 23, Cap. 1, De reform.) The Fathers of the first Provincial Council of Westminster give the following instructions on this point to Incumbents of churches: "In case this has not been already done, let him traverse the whole extent of the district under his pastoral care, and write an exact report of it, and make out a *Liber status animarum,* in the manner prescribed in the Roman Ritual, as far as circumstances will permit." (Decree xxv., n. 2.) See also the statutes of the National Synod of Maynooth, Decretum xxi., art. 211.—*Translator.*

their names, and will abstain from putting any further questions. But should they refuse him admittance, he will then have good reason for presuming that there are in the house, at the very least, suspicious characters—a discovery which will prove useful to him in many cases.

Thirdly, he finds out whether there are any grown-up children who have not yet made their First Communion; and it is particularly necessary to get information on this point in city parishes, where unknown families are daily arriving. The Parish Priest has likewise an opportunity of ascertaining whether the children above seven years of age are sent for instruction in the Christian Doctrine, and are taken to confession.

Fourthly, he will be enabled to find out whether there are sufficient beds in the house, so that brothers may not be compelled to sleep with sisters, or children with their parents,—an abuse for which the Parish Priest ought to provide a remedy without delay.

Fifthly, he is afforded an opportunity of seeing whether there are in the house scandalous pictures, prints, or other objects of an indecent tendency.

Sixthly, he becomes acquainted with the poverty of certain families, who, having fallen from a position of respectability, are ashamed to beg, although they are in dire distress, without bedding, clothing, or even a sufficiency of food.

These are the advantages derived from the practice of blessing the houses—advantages which render this practice as important for the Parish, as the Episcopal visitation is for the Diocese.

However, the objection may be raised that the blessing of the houses involves a great deal of trouble, especially in extensive parishes, and still more so where the Parish Priest happens to be somewhat advanced in years. This is very true; but it is likewise true that the visitation of the Diocese is very troublesome to Bishops, who, as a general rule, are older than Parish Priests. Now, if Bishops, for the good of the Diocese, are bound to undergo the toil of a visitation, surely Parish Priests are bound, for the good of their parishes, to submit to the toil of blessing the houses. But if the Parish Priest were very old, and could not bless the entire parish every year, he could bless at least a portion of it, so that every two or three years the entire parish might be blessed and visited by him.

Nor does it avail to reply that the curate could perform the blessing of the houses, could make his observations on everything in course of his visits, and afterwards hand in a suitable report to the Parish Priest. For a Bishop, in like manner, could do the self-same, namely, send visitors through the Diocese, while he himself remained at his ease in his palace, awaiting their reports—a proceeding which (not to mention the administration of confirmation, which belongs exclusively to a Bishop) would not meet with the approval of anyone, who understands what a wide difference there is between acquiring a knowledge of things through the report of others, and seeing them with one's own eyes. Moreover, a Pastor of souls, whether he be Bishop or Parish Priest, receives a special gift from God to find out and provide for the wants of his flock.

Wherefore, there is no doubt that, if we except the case of real impossibility, the conduct of those Parish Priests is reprehensible, who delegate to the Curate the duty of blessing the entire Parish, reserving to themselves merely some few houses of rich gentlemen, which they bless on Holy Saturday.

I will remark, in conclusion, that it will be very useful if the Parish Priest, when announcing the blessing of the houses, will explain every year to the Faithful the importance of this sacred rite, the spiritual blessings to souls which flow therefrom, and its utility, from a temporal point of view, to the health and interests of those families who receive it in a spirit of faith; pointing out, at the same time that to refuse it, as some do, might be attended by evil consequences.

CHAPTER X.

OF THE EPISCOPAL VISITATION OF THE PARISH.

IN speaking of the Episcopal visitation, we must draw a distinction between the parishes of the city in which the Bishop resides, and those other districts where he is rarely or never seen, except on the occasion of his visitation. In the Parishes of the place where he lives, his pastoral visitation produces but a slight impression; because, as he resides there all the year round, his presence even on the occasion of a visitation does not awaken any particular interest in the people, who are accustomed to see him every day; and, on the other hand, since everything in these parishes is constantly under the supervision of the Bishop, he can give suitable directions concerning all matters, at any time, even outside the occasion of his visitation.

The very opposite of this happens in those parts of the diocese where the Bishop does not reside. There the arrival of the Bishop on his visitation tour excites considerable interest, and his presence exercises a wholesome influence on the population. Moreover, on these occasions he comes to know many things of which he was previously ignorant, and he gives such directions as the circumstances may require.

It must be borne in mind, however, that not even in these districts will the visit of the Bishop prove as beneficial as it might, unless the Parish Priest employs his solicitude and zeal in co-operating towards this end.

A Mission, or at least a Retreat, will be a good preparation for the visit of the Bishop, so that a well-attended general communion may be one of the most striking features of the occasion. Even the most lukewarm and negligent will readily take part in this, in order to have the honour of receiving the Holy Communion from the Bishop's hands, and not to appear unwilling to approach the Holy Table on so solemn an occasion.

The Parish Priest must be careful to prepare for Confirmation not only the children, but likewise those adults who may not yet have received this Sacrament. And since these latter sometimes evince a disinclination to be confirmed, owing to a foolish feeling of shame, the Parish Priest ought to instruct them on the great importance of this sacrament, and to impress upon them that, if they allow the present opportunity to pass by, they may very probably die unconfirmed.

In small parishes, the Parish Priest ought to provide a sufficient number of confessors for the day of confirmation, and the day preceeding it. The confessions of several hundred children of both sexes will have to be heard, of whom many have not been to confession for a considerable period, and who present themselves in the tribunal of penance, rather to be disposed by the Confessor than actually disposed to receive absolution. In such circumstances, if there be not a sufficient number of confessors, the Parish Priest will find himself placed in a position of great embarrassment, and tempted to give absolution in a perfunctory manner.

The Parish Priest must strive also to awaken a holy enthusiasm in his flock, so that they may receive their Bishop with all that respect and homage which is due to his exalted office. The more the faith of the people in the Episcopal dignity is awakened, and the more they are filled with a sentiment of veneration for the first Pastor of the Diocese, the more fruitful will be his exhortations. Moreover, the people must be urged to abstain from all servile work and business on the day of the visitation, and to observe it as a holiday, in order that all may be able to assist at the sacred functions in the Church, and to listen to the discourse of the Bishop.

Meanwhile, should there be any good work to be promoted in the parish, or any abuse requiring correction, the Parish Priest must request the Bishop to speak of it to the people. The words of the Bishop will produce a great impression upon the faithful; and if the Parish Priest will not suffer their good dispositions to grow cool, but will at once begin to carry out his project, he will see his desires crowned with success. This success will be doubly assured, if the Parish Priest requests the Bishop to speak in a special manner to the leading parishioners, that they may assist their pastor in the good work which he proposes to himself.

In this manner, the pastor will succeed in establishing in his parish any good institutions which may be required there; he will be enabled to revive, or to infuse fresh vigour into those which may have perished or remained inoperative; and to extirpate bad customs, even though they may have been tolerated during many years.

Moreover, the Parish Priest must avail himself of the occasion of the visitation to bring under the notice of the Bishop the priests of the place, in order that the good may be encouraged by him, and urged to renewed exertions for the glory of God, and the salvation of souls, and that those who may not be living up to the requirements of their state may be admonished and corrected.

He ought also avail himself of the Bishop's visit to offer to the members of the church committee, and to the superiors of oratories and confraternities, whatever suggestions he may deem conducive to the decorum of divine worship, and the good of souls; but he must be at the same time careful to act in this matter with great prudence, so as not to let it appear that he had been making complaints to the Bishop, and had brought down his reprimand upon them. This, however, must be understood to apply merely to the case of trivial abuses; for if the abuses happened to be serious, the parties themselves would understand that the Parish Priest could not keep silent under the circumstances. Meanwhile, of whatever kind the abuses may be, the Bishop will know how to act with the proper discretion in giving such exhortations, admonitions, and directions as he may judge suitable.

CHAPTER XL

OF CONFRATERNITIES AND SODALITIES.

IN our times, when almost all the evil that is committed is effected through the combination of wicked men, good associations are to be encouraged more than ever, in order to prevent and diminish the evil effects of societies of an opposite character.

§ 1. OF ADULT CONFRATERNITIES.[1]

There does not perhaps exist a parish in which

---

[1] For the better understanding of this section, it is necessary to remember that our author supposes the confraternity (*a*) to be erected in strict canonical form, in accordance with the Constitution of Clement VIII. *Quæcumque* 7 Decemb. 1604 (see Ferraris *Confraternitates*, art. 1); (*b*) to possess a private or public oratory of its own, and to have a chaplain of its own; (*c*) to enjoy certain exemptions from the jurisdiction of the Parish Priest, within the limits of the Decree of the Congregation of Rites, 10th December, 1703. (This decree may be read in Craisson *manuale totius juris canonici*, n. 618.)

These conditions are very rarely verified in the case of any confraternity existing in English-speaking countries, if we except, perhaps, some of those attached to the Churches of Regulars. Hence, many things laid down by our author in the text, though applicable to the status of Confraternities in Italy and elsewhere, do not apply equally to the position of confraternities in English-

there is not to be found some confraternity of adults, in which persons of either sex are enrolled. The principal object of these confraternities is to accompany the funerals of the faithful, and to aid by their suffrages the souls of departed members.[1] This, perhaps, may constitute the sole object of the confraternity, and beyond this the members may effect scarcely any other good; yet, even so, it ought not to be accounted a slight good, both because the Church has always highly approved of the honour paid to the bodies of those who die in the Lord, sanctified by the Sacraments, and destined after the resurrection to shine in heaven with ineffable glory; and because the suffrages which are procured for the souls of the faithful departed must be reckoned among the most precious acts of Christian charity. Wherefore, the Parish Priest should never say that the confraternity does little good, even though it were to do nothing else than attend the funerals of the faithful, and get prayers and masses offered for their souls.

speaking countries. However, even so, the rules of practical prudence laid down by the author will be found, *mutatis mutandis*, of much advantage in regulating the action of a pastor towards confraternities, as they exist amongst ourselves.—*Translator.*

[1] It is the almost invariable custom in Italy, that the heirs of deceased catholics should invite the members of the parish confraternity to assist at the funeral, wearing their peculiar uniform. There are, moreover, certain confraternities which have for their special object the burial of the dead—more particularly of the destitute poor. Such, for example, is the *Archconfraternita della morte*, in the Via Giulia at Rome.—*Translator.*

However, it not unfrequently happens that there are found in the confraternity wrong-headed, and even fanatical, persons, who wish everything done in accordance with their own ideas, and who, provided they can carry out a whim, never reflect on the consequences which may follow from their action. Wherefore, the confraternity is sometimes the occasion of disputes and disagreements, which cause no slight trouble to the Parish Priest; and on such occasions he is tempted to assume an attitude of hostility towards it, to humble it, and to suppress it altogether if possible.

It must be observed, however, that these evils might be prevented, entirely or in part, by prudence and charity on the part of the Parish Priest. And, in fact, if the Parish Priest were persuaded that it is his duty to bear with patience the failings of his parishioners, especially such as spring from zeal, however misguided; if, from the very beginning, he were to show particular kindness to the more zealous members, and then were not to insist so rigorously on certain trivial matters affecting his rights and dignity: if he were never to complain, except of patent and notable abuses, and, even then, in a quiet way, without exhibiting any bad feeling or anger, he might remedy all, or at least many of the evils for which the confraternity is blamed. He would see those very persons who were wrong-headed and fanatical become more moderate in their pretensions, and he would win the sympathy of the general body of the members. And even should a Parish Priest, through following a different course, have erred in the commencement, and so happen to be at variance with the confraternity, yet, by at once correcting his mistake, and acting with greater prudence, toleration, and charity, he would gradually succeed in restoring that peace and harmony which is so much to be desired.

When the Parish Priest is in friendly relations with the confraternity, he must exert himself to promote through it two other good works. The first is the frequentation of the sacraments, by persuading the members of the confraternity, both male and female, to approach the Sacraments once a month, or at least on the principal Festivals, and on the Feasts of the Blessed Virgin. The second is the exercise of charity towards the sick, by inducing the confraternity to give them some temporal relief should they be poor, and to elect out of their own body a few competent men and women, whose special care it would be to assist them.

Speaking in general of confraternities, I would observe that, in our times, it is particularly necessary to promote and revive all institutions which nourish the Faith, and call it into action; such as are those confraternities which sprang into existence in those ages when the faith was stronger and more pronounced than at present, and which, in fact, have no motive for their existence outside the faith. Perhaps it may seem to the Parish Priest that, in the case of such bodies, the exercise of faith is altogether material, and mixed up with many defects; that the interests of the confraternity are opposed to the interests of the parochial Church, since the faithful take their offerings to the oratory of the confraternity rather than to the Church of the Parish ; and he may believe, moreover, that, because of the confraternity, the spiritual interests of his flock will suffer, since many, through hearing mass in the oratory, absent themselves from the parochial mass, at which the Gospel is explained to the faithful.

Let us grant all this, for the sake of argument ; yet, nevertheless, I am of opinion that the Parish Priest ought to look favourably on the confraternity, and ought to promote its interests ; because that exercise of material faith contributes largely to the preservation of the faith and to its formal growth. As a matter of fact, the minds of the members are constantly occupied by concerns which in themselves are religious and pious ; these are shared in by all the principal families in the place, and so, ultimately, by the entire population. Then, as regards the defects : a Parish Priest ought not to scrutinise them too closely ; for there is no institution in the world under the management of men which has not its defects, and if good works were to be censured on this score, there would not be found a single one which could pass unscathed.

However, should the defects be very serious—such as to carry on public functions in the oratory of the confraternity during the parochial mass, to profane the sacred functions with unbecoming festivities, and the like—the Parish Priest ought to lay the matter before the Bishop, if he cannot succeed in remedying the evil by the exercise of his own charity and prudence.

And here I must allude briefly to certain functions and processions which take place in the oratories of confraternities, and which are not always conducted with that spirit of devotion and piety, which ought to accompany all the practices of our holy religion. With the exception of such of them as have been condemned by synods, or in the pastoral letters of Bishops, I am of opinion that a Parish Priest ought not to attack these practices, and this for several reasons. First, because if he offer opposition to these functions and processions, he will be sure to provoke disturbances in the parish. Secondly, because in our times, above all others, we ought to promote all external religious demonstrations which help to revive the faith, and to stir up the religious enthusiasm of the people. Thirdly, because whatever faults, in the matter of piety and devotion, happen to be mixed up with these functions may, as a rule, be easily corrected. I would, therefore, say that, instead of condemning them and endeavouring to prevent them altogether, the Parish Priest ought rather direct his efforts to correcting the abuses which are found in connection with them; and this he will infallibly succeed in accomplishing, by the employment of much prudence and a gracious manner. For, the members of the confraternity, if permitted to carry out their practices substantially, will readily submit to a modification of their programme in matters of minor importance; and they will do this the more readily, if the inconvenience arising from them is pointed out in a gracious manner.

Then, again, it is not a fact that the success of the oratory will prove detrimental to the interests of the Parish Church; for, even if the oratory never were in existence, the parishioners would not expend for the benefit of the Church all that they expend upon the oratory. In fact, they have a real passion for the oratory, when it is under their own management; and they take a peculiar interest in it, which they do not, and can not feel for the parochial Church. Moreover, there are grounds for believing that the more active the faith is maintained amongst the people, the better will it be for the prosperity both of the oratary and of the parochial Church.

If the Parish Priest enjoys the goodwill and esteem of his parishioners who are members of the Confraternity, they will not omit on Festivals to assist at the parochial mass and at his sermon; and if their affection for the oratory induces them to go there afterwards to hear a second mass, it will be all the better. Besides, it may happen that when there is mass at the oratory some might assist at it, who, perhaps, might otherwise omit hearing mass altogether.

In conclusion: good Parish Priests are in the habit of promoting every good work, including the Confraternity, which is also a good work, although it is liable to many defects, which the Pastor, however, may correct, or at least diminish, by the exercise of charity and prudence.

§ 2. Of Congregations of Young Persons.

It is of the utmost importance that in every parish there should be two sodalities, established for the purpose of cultivating the spirit of piety amongst young persons of both sexes.[1]

The young people belonging to these congregations ought to have a Rule of Life, specially drawn up with a view to making them frequent the sacraments and the preaching of the Word of God, and to preserving undefiled the purity of their morals. This Rule ought to be very simple, and adapted to the circumstances of all. It is well, therefore, that it should be limited to the following points:—(1) Morning and night prayers, with three Hail Marys in honour of the purity of the Blessed Virgin, and the ejaculatory prayer—" *Dear Mother, preserve me from mortal sin*"; (2) attendance at the preaching of God's Word, and especially at the Catechetical

---

[1] In parishes where convents are established, it might be found convenient to place the female sodality under the charge of the Nuns. The Irish Bishops seem to have contemplated the adoption of this system in Ireland, for in the Maynooth Decrees (XXXII., art. 298) we find the following : " Sodalitates religiosæ, ab ordinario approbatæ, pro puellis quæ scholas frequentaut, in unoquoque conventu instituantur". The Decree speaks only of girls who are still frequenting the schools ; but it might be easily arranged that, even after they have ceased to attend school, the girls and young women should continue to assist at the Sodality meetings held in the convent on Sundays and holidays. As a matter of fact, this is done in several parishes.—*Translator*.

discourse; (3) monthly confession; (4) the total separation of the sexes in all games and pastimes; (5) the avoidance of bad company'; (6) the prohibition of profane songs, and of dangerous books and entertainments, such as theatres, balls, and so forth. If one aims at anything beyond this, the chances are that he will attain far less. If anything additional be required, it had better be left to the discretion of the Confessor, who can vary the details of the Rule, to suit the requirements of his several penitents.

The Parish Priest must be cautious not to admit into these congregations any boys except such as are steady and pious, or who are at least well-disposed, so that they may afford grounds for hoping that they will turn out well; for if bad boys be admitted, they will do no good themselves, and will be sure to bring ruin on the sodality.

Nor ought we listen to the specious pretext which is sometimes put forward—that if wayward and badly-disposed young persons of either sex are excluded from the sodality, they will be deprived of this means of improvement, and will daily become worse. For, experience teaches that when the bad associate with the good, so far from imitating their good example, they corrupt them; just as rotten apples placed beside sound ones, instead of themselves becoming sound by the contact, communicate to them their rottenness. Therefore, while reserving the sodalities for those who are good, at least in disposition, the Parish Priest must adopt other expedients to reform the bad, such as advice, correction, and the like.

From time to time, the Parish Priest must call together separately the members of each sodality, in order to give them some appropriate instruction and exhortation, calculated to promote in them the growth of piety and of the holy fear of God.

These sodalities are a great blessing to a parish; for from them go forth those young men who are most regular in frequenting the sacraments, who are distinguished by their good conduct and piety, who devote themselves to the advancement not only of their own welfare but likewise of that of others, and who in many ways assist the Parish Priest by promoting pious practices, and by contributing to the beauty of God's house.

From these sodalities, likewise, go out the most pious and edifying maidens; and among them some, who being animated by a special zeal for the instruction of little girls neglected by their own parents, bring them to the Catechism, and when necessary teach it to them themselves. They make them frequent the Sacraments, and keep a watch over them, so that they be not corrupted by evil example, and the temptations of the world.

§ 3. OF CHARITABLE SOCIETIES.

Should there be already established in the parish any charitable society for the assistance of the poor and the sick, the Parish Priest must be careful to maintain it in a state of efficiency; and should none such exist there, he must introduce them. These societies are the means of drying many a tear, of lightening many a burden, of relieving many a wretched being; and they keep alive among the people the spirit of charity, which is the spirit of a true christian.

Worthy of special commendation in our days is the Society of St. Vincent de Paul, which is effecting so much good throughout all Europe, and which, while relieving the wants of the body, provides likewise for spiritual necessities, and exercises a great influence upon the morals and religious conduct of those whom it assists.

There are also other charitable associations which in several places are not regarded with favour by Catholics, because they are often made the instruments of religious or of political perversion, by forming among the people bodies of freethinkers or of conspirators, through the introduction of a spirit of hostility to all religious practices, and a spirit of emancipation from the control of all authority. These are the *Benefit*, or friendly societies.

Nevertheless, such associations would be, *per se*, good, and in several cases they might prove exceedingly useful; inasmuch as they aim at relieving the wants of the poor, by establishing, through small weekly payments, on the part of all the associates, a considerable fund, capable of affording relief to each one of them, in proportion to the necessity in which he may happen to be placed at any time.

Wherefore, such associations are not to be absolutely condemned; nay, they are rather to be praised and encouraged, provided they be in good hands, and under the direction of religious and pious persons, as might easily be contrived by the Parish Priest. In fact, if he employ his influence to have these associations started by good men, if he watch over the drafting of their rules, and if he be careful that irreligious and bad men do not control their management, these associations will prove not only harmless, but even extremely useful, as is shewn by the experience of several localities.

It must be borne in mind that it is not wise to disapprove of everything which the wicked turn to bad account; for even the very best things may sometimes be abused. On the contrary, it is true wisdom to wrest good institutions from the hands of the wicked, or, better still, to prevent them from ever passing under their control, so that they may not be able to make a bad use of them. This may be accomplished by placing good men at the head of them, who will make them prosper to the advantage alike of Religion and of Society.

§ 4. Of other Pious Sodalities.

There is a very large number of other pious sodalities approved of by the Church, and enriched with many indulgences, which aim at promoting spiritual interests, and which nourish the spirit of piety among the faithful in a manner at once attractive and substantial. Of these the principal are the sodalities of the Most Holy Sacrament, of the Sacred Heart of Jesus, of the Holy Rosary, of Our Lady of Mount Carmel, of Our Lady of Dolours, and of the Most Holy and Immaculate Heart of Mary for the Conversion of Sinners. Let the Parish Priest strive to introduce and foster among his people, if not all, at least some of these; since it is certain that they will contribute largely to preserve and increase the faith among them.

Above all, he must exert himself to establish in his parish the first of the above-named sodalities, and to maintain it in a flourishing condition, so that there may be always a large concourse of people at the public exposition of the Blessed Sacrament, and a respectable number to accompany the Viaticum when borne to the sick.[1]

Let him also labour in a special manner to extend the last-mentioned sodality, which has been so warmly recommended by the Sovereign Pontiff and by the entire episcopate, and which, having spread, in a wonderful manner and within a few years, over

---

[1] The Fathers of the First Provincial Council of Westminster speak as follows of this sodality: "It is expedient also, in order to promote devotion to the Divine Sacrament, that, where it is practicable, the sodality of the Most Holy Sacrament be established; the members of which shall provide for the service of the altar, for processions and other functions. This sodality and the Confraternity of Christian Doctrine should, according to the First Provincial Council of Milan, be established in every congregation, prior to all others." (Decree xviii., n. 11) — *Translator.*

the entire world, has been most fruitful in bringing about very remarkable conversions.

I cannot omit to recommend a pious practice which likewise takes the form of a sodality, namely the Perpetual Adoration of the Most Holy Sacrament.[1] This pious practice is admirably adapted to multiply the great blessing of prayer among the people; because, as we shall see when we lay the Rule before our readers, it constitutes so much prayer more than we would otherwise say, and it awakens in the faithful great devotion towards the most wonderful pledge of the Saviour's infinite goodness. Later on we shall mention other pious sodalities, in regard of which a Pastor may profitably exercise his zeal, when we come to treat more expressly of this virtue. (See Part III., Cap. ix., § 3.)

[1] The rule will be found in an Appendix, at the end of this work.

CHAPTER XII.

OF THE SCHOOLS.[1]

ALTHOUGH, now-a-days, the schools are independent of the Parish Priest, and he has no direct control over them, nevertheless they have a claim upon his zeal and attention, because of the powerful influence which they exercise on the training of youth.

This is not the place to speak of the efforts which have been made, and which are still made every day, to hand over the education of the young to persons who are hostile to Christian faith and morality—

[1] In this chapter, the author contemplates a condition of affairs which, though it is the rule in Italy and France, and in other continental countries, has not yet, thank God, been fully realised among ourselves. In Ireland, especially, there is a very considerable amount of freedom in the matter of education, though the full rights of Catholics in this respect have up to the present been persistently refused. However, it would be folly to deny that the tendency of our age, and of the most powerful State parties both at home and in the colonies, is strongly in favour of a purely secular system of education; and that all English-speaking Catholics will have henceforth to struggle, as they never struggled before, to secure freedom of education for their children. How they may succeed, it would be extremely difficult to forecast; but should the education of the people ever come to be conducted on the same principles which are at present in vogue in most continental countries, it is clear that the clergy must have recourse to some such expedients as those suggested in the text, to provide for the moral and religious training of the young.— *Translator.*

efforts which have proved only too successful in accomplishing their wicked purpose. I shall, instead, confine my observations to pointing out how the Parish Priest may counteract, at least partially and indirectly, the evil consequences of this deplorable fact.

Since "the children of this world are wiser in their generation than the children of light" (Luke xvi. 8), the Parish Priest ought to reflect with what zeal, perseverance, cunning, and dexterity the wicked have striven heretofore to obtain the appointment of even one irreligious and immoral teacher, in schools where the other masters are pious and moral men; and therefore the Parish Priest must employ, in a corresponding degree, zeal, perseverance, vigilance, and address, to procure the appointment of even one good master, where there are, unfortunately, so many who are undeserving of that name. And there is no doubt that, by combining prudence with energy, he will often be able so to manage matters with the authorities of the place, that on the occasion of electing a master, a good man, nay the best among the candidates will get the preference.

The Parish Priest must also bear in mind that as in times past the corruptors of youth sought to effect through clubs and places of recreation frequented by the young what they were unable to effect in the schools, so now that the Parish Priest is banished from the schools, he must effect by means of sodalities, young men's societies, and juvenile social entertainments, what he is not permitted to do in the schoolroom. In the sodalities he would have a splendid field open to him for explaining at length to the young those truths that are most attacked or misrepresented: in social gatherings he might inculcate them still better, and thus oppose an antidote to the poison of the enemy.

Societies for the young, which are everywhere useful, become strictly necessary in places where there are bad schools; and in such places it would likewise be especially necessary to provide innocent recreations for the young on festival days. The young men who take part in these entertainments are kept aloof from bad companions, they are withdrawn from the danger of evil conversation and bad example, their minds are continually nourished with good maxims, and innumerable other advantages follow, which need not be more particularly specified.

It must be observed that, when giving such entertainments to girls, the Parish Priest ought never take part in them himself, but should entrust the management of them to pious and sensible young women or widows, who will take the place of the pastor in rendering the entertainment useful towards the promotion of piety and good morals.

These entertainments are of singular importance wherever good schools do not exist; but they are likewise useful in every other place as well. In addition to the fact that their usefulness has been tested by experience, we have the example of those saints who devoted themselves in a special manner to the care of the young, and who always regarded such entertainments as a most effectual means to promote the spirit of piety among them.

It is scarcely necessary to say that, when the schoolmasters are moral and pious men, the Parish Priest ought to consider himself singularly fortunate. He ought therefore to treat them with the greatest kindness, and to shew them every possible proof of esteem and goodwill, so as to animate and encourage them the more to co-operate with him in promoting the welfare of the young.

Should the masters, on the other hand, be men whose moral conduct and religious views are open to suspicion, he ought still to show them signs of friendship and esteem, so long as they keep up good appearances. By this means they will be anxious to preserve at least the semblance of goodness, and will consequently refrain from insinuating erroneous maxims and principles. Moreover, by adopting this course, another most desirable result will be secured: namely, that if cordial and perfect harmony, with all its attendant blessings, be impossible between the Parish Priest and the schoolmaster, at all events there will not exist between them open hostility with all the evils which spring from it.

Finally, should the masters be notoriously immoral or irreligious, then would the case arise when the Parish Priest ought to say: *quæ conventio Christi ad Belial?* Therefore, for the edification of his flock, he ought to make it manifest that he holds no relations with them, and that their presence in the parish is to him a source of extreme pain. He ought to warn good parents to keep a watch over the instruction given to their children, and he ought himself to inculcate from the pulpit those truths and sound maxims, which he knows to be impugned or misrepresented by the bad schoolmasters. He must, however, be careful not to mention their names publicly, and also not to speak badly of them in private with unreliable persons, lest he might rouse their resentment, provoke their vengeance, and come into collision with the authorities, who, when they tolerate bad masters, are not to be supposed over friendly to the Parish Priest.

CHAPTER XIII.

ON PROVIDING WHOLESOME LITERATURE FOR THE PEOPLE.

It is most important that the Parish Priest should promote the circulation of good books among his flock, not only because of the actual benefits to be derived from them, but also to prevent the very serious evils which are caused by bad reading.

We cannot shut our eyes upon the fact that, now-a-days, every one is given to reading, and that the thirst for knowledge is more general and widespread than it ever was in times past. Now, I certainly am not of the number of those who deplore this thirst for knowledge, as though it were the bane of religion and society. For who will deny that ignorance is a curse, and knowledge a blessing? and that it is praiseworthy in any one to seek to improve his mind by reading? But the real evil lies in the diffusion of a poisonous literature, which is brought within easy reach of the masses, by so many vile books and newspapers, which may be found in the hands of everybody, and which are the plague of modern society.

Instead then of bewailing uselessly, and in a great measure unjustly, the modern thirst for reading and knowledge, our efforts ought rather to be directed to the diffusion of a wholesome literature, from which the people might derive real and solid instruction, and which would, at least partially, supplant that poisonous literature of which I have spoken; for whosoever acquires a taste for reading good books, gives up the perusal of bad ones.

Wherefore, should the Parish Priest observe that his people are much given to reading, he must make it his study to bring good works within their reach; so that those who have a passion for books may be enabled to gratify it to the full, and, if possible, even to satiety. If he points out a clear spring to those who are ready to quench their thirst at the muddy stream, they will unquestionably run to it in preference.

If this course had been adopted at the time when bad books and newspapers first began to flood the world, we would not now have to shed so many useless tears over evils that are almost irremediable. Wicked men, banded together in the hellish project of effacing from the human mind the principles of faith and morality by means of a corrupting press, were not deterred from their purpose by the prospect of having to make most serious sacrifices. They freely contributed their money, and taxed their intellectual powers, to insure the accomplishment of their design, and they now exult over a success greater, perhaps, than they had ever ventured to anticipate.

Meanwhile good men, terrified by the flood of poisonous literature which had been let loose over the world, without taking any practical steps to encounter the evil, contented themselves with fruitless lamentations and complaints. They considered that they had discharged their duty, by merely shedding cheap tears over the great misfortune which had overtaken religion and society, and they added the consoling reflection—which in the mouth of one who can and will not work, is a proof of cowardice, not of faith—that *God would provide a remedy in His own good time.* Yes; God, no doubt, will provide a remedy; but, meanwhile, He has permitted this deplorable inactivity, in punishment of past transgressions on the part of the people.

What has not been done to crush this evil in its very commencement, ought now to be done to lessen its growth; and, therefore, it is especially incumbent on Pastors to leave nothing untried towards providing wholesome reading for their flocks, in order that poisonous literature may not be still more widely circulated, and that, as we may hope, some who have been led astray through its influence may again open their eyes to see the error of their ways.[1]

---

[1] The English Bishops, assembled in the First Provincial Council of Westminster, speak as follows on this most important subject (Decree viii., n. 4). "Since the vilest tracts, attacking the Catholic Religion, or assailing it with calumnies, lies, and abuse, are in a marvellous way scattered abroad everywhere, and are even brought to the houses of Catholics, or put into their hands, let the faithful be admonished to refrain from reading them; nay more to cast them away altogether, being reminded by their Pastors of the penalties declared by the Church against those who read such kinds of books. But the more effectually to check this pestilence, let the priest furnish himself with a supply of pious and edifying books, or provide a library suited to the capacity of his people, whence even the poor

To this end the Parish Priest must endeavour to have a supply of good books, of a class suitable for the people, for the purpose of lending and circulating them among them. This object will be more securely and permanently attained by the formation of a parochial library, where he and other pious persons may place good books, to be lent out to such as ask for them. A library of this kind is very easily established. One might begin with even a few books, to which additions could be made by degrees. Care and regularity are required, however, in the managment of these libraries, in order that the books may not be lost or kept out too long by any one person, so that all may have an opportunity of reading them in turn. For this purpose, the Parish Priest must appoint a librarian and an assistant, to keep an accurate record of the books lent out, and to call them in, if not already returned, at the appointed time.

Should the Parish Priest wish occasionally to give

and ignorant may imbibe useful knowledge by having books lent out to them, for a time, to read. Let him also do his best to spread amongst his flock the pious works of Catholics, which are daily issuing from the press."

The Irish Bishops, assembled in the National Synod of Maynooth, also urge strongly the formation of Parochial Libraries. We subjoin their words taken from the 9th Decree, art. 20:—"Optandum quoque est ut libelli pii et qui fidem Catholicam defendunt, quam plurimum disseminentur. Rejiciendi autem omnino sunt libri damnati, et qui ad errores disseminandos conscripti sunt. Hic vero pastores eorumque vicarios monendos esse arbitramur, quantum emolumentum ex Bibliothecis parochialibus rite ordinatis, fidelis populus consequatur ; quapropter easdem in singulis parœciis instituendas volumus ; et ubi jam institutæ habentur eas omni diligentia fovendas et promovendas hortamur."—*Translator.*

premiums to the children, he ought to select good books for this purpose, in preference to other objects of devotion ; because they are quite as useful as any other kind of premium to stimulate the little ones, while in addition, they serve to instruct them, and are read, moreover, by the members of their families. In many places there is a very laudable custom of distributing pious pictures and medals on the occasion of a general communion, especially at the close of the month of May. But would it not be better on such occasions to distribute copies of some devout and moral little book, which would unquestionably be more useful to the recipient, and would moreover do good in his family, where it would be read likewise by others who had taken no part in the sacred function ? And let it not be said that a little book of this kind would be more expensive than a picture or a medal. For if a number of Parish Priests combined their efforts in this direction, they might get a little book printed which would not cost more than a penny, or even a half-penny per copy, and which would be productive of far more good than could be expected from the distribution of pious pictures or medals.[1]

---

[1] The facilities for obtaining good books at a merely nominal cost are far greater now than when our author wrote. I have recently seen a Catalogue issued by the Messrs. Chamney, 4 Lower Ormond Quay, Dublin, which contained a list of 146 different little works, for sale at *one penny each!* The list included several of St. Liguori's smaller treatises. In the Catalogues of the well-known Catholic houses of Duffy & Son, Dublin, and Burns & Oates, of London, will also be found lists of a great number of little books, suitable for children, which are marvels of cheapness, ranging in

The Parish Priest must not neglect to become a subscriber to some sound Catholic magazine and newspaper, and to encourage such of his parishioners as can afford it to become subscribers likewise. This is indispensable in localities where bad newspapers circulate; for otherwise their sophisms, misrepresentations, and calumnies would pass unchallenged. He ought also use his exertions that magazines and newspapers of this kind should not be confined to the hands of the subscribers, but should circulate among several.

In order to induce those of his parishioners who can afford it to subscribe to good periodicals and newspapers, he ought to impress upon them that one of the most suitable and necessary acts of charity which one could perform in our time, one of the works most pleasing to God and most useful to our neighbour, is to expend some of their money in placing wholesome reading within the reach of the masses, which is, in fact, the sole means left to combat effectively the evils caused by a wicked press.

price from one penny upwards. I have no doubt that, notwithstanding the extremely low figure at which these little books have been brought out, a still further reduction in price would be made to priests who should purchase them in considerable quantities.— *Translator*.

CHAPTER XIV.

OF PREACHING.[1]

IT was stated in the first chapter of this work, that capacity for preaching is a necessary qualification in a Parish Priest. We explained, however, that this does not imply the possession of any rare oratorical gifts, but simply the ordinary ability to expound

[1] Throughout this chapter, our author supposes a Parish Priest to preach regularly TWICE on every Sunday and Festival of obligation. The first sermon is supposed to be delivered at the parochial mass, in the morning, and is to consist in the explanation of the Gospel, or of some other portion of the liturgy of the day. The second sermon is supposed to be delivered in the afternoon, and is to take the form of a *catechetical instruction* to the adults of the congregation; and it must be carefully borne in mind that this catechetical instruction is something *quite distinct* from the instruction in catechism given to *the children*, which is supposed to take place sometime between the morning and evening sermons.

As a matter of fact, the Council of Trent imposes on Parish Priest these *three distinct obligations* with reference to the instruction of their flocks. Scavini refers to the subject in the following words: "Proprie loquendo *triplex* est parochorum obligatio circa verbum dei: una prædicandi, nempe divinam legem populis enunciandi; altera pueros instruendi; tertia fideles in christiana doctrina erudiendi. De prima loquitur Tridentinum, Sess. 22, cap. 8; de secunda sess. 24, cap. 4; di reform; de tertia, sess. 5, cap. 2, de reform" (Scavini, Theol. Moral. Tract, 3 disp. 1, cap. II., Q. 5, in nota.).

The evening instruction is scarcely practicable in country parishes, as it would be almost, if not wholly, impossible to

plainly and clearly the truths of faith and of christian morality, and to exhort his parishioners, in warm and zealous words, to practise virtue and to avoid sin.

assemble a congregation ; it might be given, however, in cities and towns, and even in villages. The Fathers of the First Provincial Council of Westminster are very explicit with regard to this catechetical instruction. The following are their words : (Decree VIII., n. 3), "Besides teaching catechism every day in school, let there also, on every Sunday, be a public catechetical instruction in the church, in which the mysteries of faith, and the commandments of God and the church, and the doctrine of the Sacraments, should be explained in a plain and clear manner. Moreover, whilst the priest accommodates his language to the understanding of little ones, let him speak in a way not to be tedious to the well-instructed ; on the contrary, by his weighty words, and by aptly illustrating his discourse with numerous appropriate texts of Holy Scripture and by the Examples of the Saints, let him attract even adults to listen and to learn."

The various difficulties which might be put forward, to claim exemption from this duty of the catechetical instruction, are summed up and answered by Scavini in the following passage : "Neque instructionis locum tenet concio matutina ; sunt enim diversa munera, ac *duo potissima onera a Tridentina Synodo Curatoribus animarum imposita festis diebus,* uti ait laudatus Benedictus XIV. Adde concionem jam supponere fidelem primis fidei rudimentis informatum ; cum hæc nonnisi leviter atque cursim in concione attingantur. Neque ab hoc gravissimo munere parochus liberatur ob exiguum numerum audientium, qui plerumque ex Rectorum negligentia dimanat ; etsi unus tantum ex suis audiat, Parochus imitetur Christum, qui pro una Samaritana sermonem habuit (Joan IV.) Neque excusatur ideo, quia alii supplent ; nam ipse ordinarie tenetur qui est parochus. *Neque valet proferri immemorabilis consuetudo contraria ;* quæ enim sunt de necessitate salutis, non præscribuntur : hinc Pontifices hanc non quidem consuetudinem, sed corruptelam et abusum dixerunt eliminandum omnino. Iterum Benedictus XIV. Notificatione IX et X." (Scavini, Theol. Moral. Tract III., disp. I., cap. II.), cf. Benedictus XIV. Const. *Etsi nemine,* 7 Feb., 1742.—*Translator.*

Supposing, then, that a Parish Priest is capable of doing this much, we will now proceed to examine how he ought to discharge the duty of preaching.

§ 1. Of Preparation for Preaching.

Preachers, and especially Parish Priests, are subject to a temptation of vanity, which often induces them to assert untruly that they preach without writing their sermons, and sometimes even without thinking beforehand of what they are going to say. In making this statement they have a two-fold purpose. If the sermon be a success, they wish you to infer that they are men of such ready genius, and such fluency of speech that they have no need of preparation; if, on the other hand, the sermon prove a failure, they would have you attribute the fact, not to any lack of ability on their part, but solely to the entire absence of preparation. But these are mere pretences. As a general rule, those who do not wish to become objects of ridicule or pity, and who have some little respect, if not for God's word, at least for their own reputation, invariably make some preparation before preaching.

In truth, those who succeed in preaching a solid and interesting sermon without preparation are extremely few; and if they seem to be more numerous than they really are, it is because braggarts, who form a pretty numerous class, place themselves in this category. Wherefore, it is undeniable that all, as a general rule, have need of preparing their sermons, and this must be understood of every kind of sermon, if we except, perhaps, a short exhortation occupying not more than a few minutes, which many persons are capable of delivering without any, or at least, with very slight preparation.

I have said that preparation is necessary for every kind of sermon, intending to include in this statement the exposition of the gospel, and the catechetical instruction delivered in the most homely language. Some, perhaps, may be inclined to question my views on this point, and to maintain that Parish Priests, who for many years have been explaining the gospels appointed for the different Sundays, have already at their command such a store of reflections on the several gospel subjects, that they never can be at a loss for something to say; and likewise that, having explained over and over again the various portions of the Christian doctrine, they will have abundant matter for a catechetical instruction, without any previous preparation.

I reply that, at the very utmost, this would prove nothing more than that a Parish Priest who has had long practice in preaching will never want words; but it by no means proves that if he preaches *extempore* he will announce the word of God with effect.

As a matter of fact, these *extempore* preachers are often remarkably inexact in matters of doctrine. They do not make those reflections which are best suited to the circumstances of their audience, but content themselves with the most trite and commonplace thoughts, which they never vary, and which they develop in a very poor and pitiable style. The few good sentiments to which they may happen to give expression are lost in a very ocean of meaningless words. Their preaching is insipid and wearisome, and they must be held accountable for the fact that the parishioners absent themselves from the sermon, and thereby remain ignorant even of those points of dogma and Christian morality which are the most necessary to be known.

And, assuredly, it must be confessed that the parishioners have often need of great virtue, and above all of great faith, to keep listening morning and evening to their Parish Priest, while he declaims, with little elegance and considerable confusion of ideas, in one eternal, unvaried strain, and lets it be seen that he does so simply to be able to say that he has preached, thus discharging his duty with all the negligence of the daily labourer, who has no other concern except to get through the material task marked out for him.

This occurs more usually in country parishes, where the Parish Priest knows that he has not a very cultured audience. And it is sometimes a piece of singular good luck for the parishioners, if some of the more educated people of the place, or some stranger who may be on a visit in the locality comes to the sermon; for then the Parish Priest, fearing the criticism or ridicule of such persons, makes preparation before he undertakes to explain the Gospel or to deliver his catechetical instruction. And yet, there is Another who is always listening to him, and who deserves far more respect than those cultured critics.

If the Parish Priest really wish to fulfil his duty, he must read over in the course of the week the Gospel appointed for the following Sunday; he must draw from it those reflections which he may judge most useful, considering the wants of his congregation and of the times; and he ought to write out at least a rough draft of his discourse, so that he may be able to read it over a few times, and commit it to memory. By adopting this course, everything will present itself to his mind in a clear and orderly manner, when he afterwards appears on the altar or in the pulpit; and thus he will be enabled to impart real instruction, to persuade, and at the same time please his audience. He must adopt the self-same method in the preparation of his catechetical discourses, so that he may be exact in his exposition of dogma, moderate in all that relates to moral doctrine, and attractive by reason of the orderly and fluent style of his discourse.[1]

---

[1] Some persons, when sitting down to prepare a sermon, begin with reading a number of sermons by different authors on the subject which they have chosen for their discourse. This is a most injudicious and bewildering plan; and is criticised by Blair in the following passage, in which he also points out the true method to be pursued in the preparation of a discourse—"When a preacher sits down to write on any subject, never let him begin with seeking to consult all who have written on the same text or subject. This, if he consult many, will throw perplexity and confusion into his ideas; and if he consults only one, will often warp him insensibly into his method, whether it be right or not. But let him begin with pondering the subject in his own thoughts; let him endeavour to fetch materials from within; to correct and arrange his ideas; and

Here we may ask whether those Parish Priests make due preparation for preaching, who, having preserved old sermon books, written perhaps years ago, in which they had jotted down some points on the Gospel or the Catechism, content themselves with merely taking these up once more, and reading them over a few times. If these notes had been originally compiled with proper care, this custom could not be censured; for the sermons of such priests would be the Word of God announced with respect, and it could not be without fruit. Nevertheless, this system does not merit unqualified approbation, and this for two reasons. First, because those members of the congregation who have good memories, hearing always the self-same thoughts put before them invariably in the self-same style, become so tired and weary of the performance, that they go to sleep even while they seem to be awake. Secondly, because these notes, written several years previously, cannot be suited to the actual wants of the audience. In the course of

form some sort of plan to himself; which it is always proper to put down in writing. Then, and not till then, he may inquire how others have treated the same subject. By this means, the method, and the leading thoughts in the Sermon, are likely to be his own. These thoughts he may improve by comparing them with the track of sentiments which others have pursued: some of their sense he may, without blame, incorporate into his composition, retaining always his own words and style." (Lectures on Rhetoric. Lect. XXIX – Eloquence of the Pulpit.) Of course, there are some persons who are incapable of following the system here laid down. Their best plan, since they cannot dispense with books to supply them with thoughts, is to select some *one* good book of sermons, and to confine themselves to it.—*Translator.*

a number of years, notable changes always take place in the habits of the people, and the Parish Priest ought to accommodate his preaching to these changes. Wherefore it is necessary that, at least as far as regards his moral discourses, the Parish Priest who may wish to make use of notes compiled several years back should introduce some alterations, in order to meet the wants of the times; and, in doing this, he will at the same time remove the other inconvenience to which we alluded above, of forcing the people to listen to him perpetually singing the same old song to the same old tune.

We would, moreover, recommend that a Parish Priest should not always follow a uniform style in his sermons, especially if it be somewhat antiquated. This remark applies more particularly to city parishes, where the people have frequent opportunities of hearing distinguished preachers, whose sermons are in harmony with the taste of the times. This taste is entitled to consideration, provided it be not so vicious as to be opposed to the fruit to be derived from the Word of God; and for this reason, also, it is difficult for one who has spent a long time in the ministry to make much use of the sermons which he composed in his earlier years.

§ 2. OF CLEARNESS AND INTELLIGIBILITY IN PREACHING.

The first quality required in a sermon, and especially in a pastoral discourse, is, that it be plain and very clear, so as to be suited to the capacity of all, even of the most ignorant, whose spiritual wants give them a strict right to expect that the preacher will make himself intelligible, when he announces to them the Word of God.

There is a style of preaching which may be called "the showy," and which serves to impart splendour to the sacred functions, just like fine music and the other accessories of divine worship—a style of preaching which resembles a poem, and, in reality, often is poetry in the garb of prose. Of this kind are the panegyrics of Italian preachers, which are delivered not that they may be understood by uneducated persons, but that they may be admired and applauded by the learned. *Unusquisque in sensu suo abundet.* To my mind this style of preaching seems an abuse of the Word of God, and it seems so, because the Word of God ought always to be directed to the sanctification of God's people, of whom the greater number, and in some places all, belong to the uneducated classes.

But if any one should wish to reply that at great functions there must be elegant and polished discourses, in keeping with the splendour of the occasion, I would not wish absolutely to dissent from the proposition; but yet I would be inclined to ask whether the preacher might not judiciously employ his skill, so as to compose a most beautiful and elegant discourse, in language which would be, at the same time, intelligible to every one? I am of opinion that a true scholar ought to be capable of pronouncing a most finished and elegant panegyric of the Saints, or of the Mother of God, which would still lie within the mental range of everybody, and which would charm the learned while it instructed the ignorant. However, this is not the place for discussing this subject further.

The Parish Priest's sermon ought invariably to be plain and intelligible to everyone, both as regards the thoughts and the language; and therefore he ought never employ abstruse thoughts or subtile arguments, even though he should have borrowed them from St. Augustine or St. Ambrose, for the simple reason that they would not be understood by the greater portion of his audience. Many things which we read in the Fathers would come suitably from a Professor's chair, but would be entirely out of place in a pulpit. The language employed in the sermon ought likewise to be simple, and such as is in common use. Otherwise, should the Parish Priest seek out unusual or high-sounding words or phrases in which to clothe his thoughts, they will prove, in the case of his less educated hearers, so many obstacles to the understanding of the Word of God. "Jesus Christ (St. Alphonsus Liguori used to say) knew rhetoric better than we do; and yet, in order to make himself understood by the crowds, he never adopted any other style than that of the commonest parables and similitudes. We, also, are engaged in preaching to the crowds, and if the people do not understand us, we produce no impression upon them, and all our labour is lost." (Tannoia, "Life of St. Liguori," Bk. 2, ch. 35.)

And, in truth, it is difficult to understand how there can be found men of learning and taste, who are willing to sacrifice sense to mere words and phrases. When I can employ a phrase understood by everyone, why should I, instead, make use of a phrase which may not be understood by one half of my audience? Instead of addressing my flock in plain, homely words, which they will all understand, why should I select words which will have no meaning for them, and will be intelligible only to scholars?[1] A misdirected admiration for classic writers, an extravagant love of elegance and purity of language, sometimes blinds even the most sensible men, and they wish to employ in the church, where most of the audience are ignorant or but poorly educated, language which would be suited to the halls of a University.

§ 3. OF THE AFFABILITY WHICH SHOULD ACCOMPANY PREACHING.

When in ordinary conversation we wish to con-

[1] Preachers who affect the style which the Author here so justly condemns, do so in the hope of gaining a reputation for eloquence; and yet they only prove thereby that they are utterly ignorant of what constitutes true eloquence. "No man," says Blair, "can be called eloquent who speaks to an assembly on subjects, or in a strain, which none or few of them comprehend. The unmeaning applause which the ignorant give to what is above their capacity, common sense and common probity must teach every man to despise. Usefulness and true eloquence always go together; and no man can long be reputed a good preacher who is not acknowledged to be a useful one." Lectures on Rhetoric, Lect. xxix.— *Translator.*

vince a person of any truth, or to induce him to perform some good action, we are accustomed to do so in the most gracious manner possible, in order to conciliate him, and win over his sympathies. Now the self-same method must be adopted when addressing the public, and especially by a Parish Priest, who must speak to them as a father, and consequently with the affection which a father entertains towards his children.

Wherefore we must entirely disapprove of the rough, offensive, ironical manner adopted by some preachers—a manner which alienates the minds of the people, and renders them indisposed to profit by the word of God; and, for this reason, those who have a naturally hot temper must be on their guard lest their zeal should degenerate into passion. Zeal ought to be sweet, like the charity from which it springs: a "bitter zeal" is disapproved of by St. James (James III., v. 14), and invariably fails to attain its object. For what is the object of zeal? To withdraw souls from sin, and to make them practise virtue. Now, to attain this end, one must first captivate men's hearts, in order afterwards to soften and bend them, and to bring them to love what they formerly abhorred, and to abhor what they once loved; and to accomplish all this, one must of necessity employ a gracious, gentle, and attractive manner.

Some one may say that it is necessary to thunder loudly against vice, and that if this be not done, sinners will repose tranquilly in their sins, and become hardened in iniquity. This is very true; but it means no more than that the preacher ought to put clearly before the people the injury that sin does to God, and the temporal, and, above all, the eternal loss which it entails on man. This he must do in a lively and forcible manner, so that sinners may rouse themselves from their lethargy and do penance; but, at the same time, he must let sinners see that he entertains for them feelings, not of contempt, but of love, not of aversion, but of sympathy, and that the object of his sermon is not to disgust and offend them, but solely to make them better, and to save their souls.

It must never be forgotten that, since all human hearts are made to love, they understand no language so well as that of love. The very hearts that are most brutalised by vice retain this disposition; so that we might fairly interpret in this sense the words of the Apostle: "Overcome evil by good" (Romans xii. 21). Let the preacher, then, be loud in his denunciations of sin, but yet in such a manner that no one may suspect him of denouncing the sinners, for whose souls he must entertain no other feeling than the most tender charity, as has been enjoined upon us by the Redeemer.

Above all, the Parish Priest must be on his guard against using any language which may savour of personal invective, and especially if he should happen to denounce faults which may be in any way directed against himself.[1] Those who are, or who suppose

[1] It may not be out of place to quote here the words of the

themselves to be, the object of such invective, become thereby greatly incensed against him, and grow obstinate in their evil courses, even for the express purpose of giving him annoyance. Moreover, the employment of invective under such circumstances is displeasing to all sensible members of the congregation, who regard it simply as an outburst of unbridled passion, and consequently a profanation of the Word of God.

Some persons pride themselves on their power of invective, and are never done telling of their exploits in this direction, taking malicious pleasure in the public shame which they have brought upon their opponents. They think, moreover, that by pursuing this course, they make the people respect and fear them. This is a very grave mistake. In addition to shewing that they are ignorant of the Spirit of Christ, they render it impossible for themselves to effect any good in the Parish, which becomes for them a bed of thorns, so that sometimes they are even forced to resign, as being the lesser of two evils.

Let the Parish Priest, then, when addressing his people, adopt the most gracious manner possible, in order to win to himself the love and confidence of his audience. They will thus come to regard the voice of their Pastor as the voice of a loving Father,

---

National Synod of Maynooth on this subject: "Vetamus etiam ne quis sacerdos, inconsulto episcopo, quacumque de causa, nomine, aut designatione propria quæ in idem incidat, in aliquem ex altari invehatur aut publice aliquem denunciet." (Decretum xxi., art. 203).—*Translator.*

who always speaks to his children for their good, and who, even when he may have occasion to speak harshly to them, lets them understand that the harshness proceeds not from hatred but from love. In particular, should there be question of injuries or affronts offered to himself, he must preserve an attitude of unalterable mildness, which requires of us not to shew resentment for wrongs suffered, but generously to pardon them. And to mildness he must unite that loving charity which alone possesses the greatest efficacy to soften hardened hearts, to win over the obstinate, and to cement the bonds of union between a Pastor and his flock.

§ 4. Of the Earnestness which ought to accompany Preaching.

There are some preachers who are very learned, polished and elegant, who are universally reputed eloquent, and who are listened to with pleasure by crowded audiences, yet who, through the absence of earnestness, produce no fruit, so that their sermons neither convert sinners nor improve the good. There are others, again, who are very poor indeed in the above-mentioned qualities—men whom nobody ever thinks of calling eloquent—and yet, because their sermons are full of zeal, they produce abundant fruit, they excite sinners to repentance, and kindle in the hearts of the just the desire of attaining to still higher perfection.

One of the qualities most indispensable to a

preacher is unction, and if a Parish Priest wishes his sermons to produce fruit they must possess this quality. Wherefore it is necessary that a Parish Priest be a man endowed with a lively faith, ardent charity, and burning zeal, so that his words, as if of fire, may touch men's hearts, inflame their wills, captivate them, and compel them to give themselves up cheerfully to the practice of virtue.

It must be observed, however, that this fervour of spirit is not a thing to be got up for the occasion, if one does not really feel it. Some persons affect this fervour, by emphatic declamation and studied gesture; but all such artificial expedients are vain. They may astonish many, but they never succeed in touching the heart of even one. It is possible to counterfeit feelings successfully on the stage, where people do not look for, or expect, anything but acting; but in the pulpit, where men expect to find sincerity, feigned sentiments are worthless, or may even produce an effect the very opposite of what was intended. Let the Parish Priest, then, cultivate in his own heart a real spirit of holy zeal, and this will impart force and efficacy to his sermons.[1]

[1] I may be excused for quoting from Blair, though a Protestant Divine, the following most appropriate and solid remarks on this subject: "In a preceding Lecture, I endeavoured to show, that on no subject can any man be truly eloquent, who does not utter the *veræ voces ab imo pectore*, who does not speak the language of his own conviction, and his own feelings. If this holds, as, in my opinion, it does, in other kinds of public speaking, it certainly holds in the highest degree in preaching. There, it is of the utmost consequence that the speaker firmly believe both the truth and the importance of those principles which he inculcates upon others;

It is worthy of special remark that we, Parish Priests, easily become cold in our sermons, because we accustom ourselves to preach from habit—simply to discharge a duty which we regard as monotonous, and to rid ourselves of a burden which seems to be ever pressing on us. Every Sunday and Festival of obligation, we deliver the invariable explanation of the Gospel and the invariable catechetical instruction. This routine continues all the year round, and for many years—nay even for our entire lives. We have always before us the same audience, and never enjoy any of those special consolations, which are experienced when one preaches before a vast mixed congregation, where one can see the effect produced by his words, and from which great sinners go out, touched by an extraordinary grace of repentance, to throw themselves at the preacher's feet, and bear witness to the effectiveness of his discourse. For these reasons we often become cold in our sermons, and, almost without being conscious of the fact, we preach because we are in the habit of preaching, and because our duty requires of us to do so.

and, not only that he believe them speculatively, but have a lively and serious feeling of them. This will always give an earnestness and strength, a fervour of piety to his exhortations, superior in its effects to all the arts of studied eloquence: and without it the assistance of art will seldom be able to conceal the mere declaimer. A spirit of true piety would prove the most effectual guard against those errors which preachers are apt to commit. It would make their discourses solid, cogent, and useful; and it would prevent those frivolous and ostentatious harangues, which have no other aim than merely to make a parade of speech, or amuse an audience." Lectures on Rhetoric. Lect. xxix.—*Translator.*

It is only a well-sustained effort to revive our faith which can save us from that coldness which, little by little, steals upon our hearts, and makes the word of God, as it were, dead, when it issues from our lips. Let us, then, revive our faith in the importance of our preaching, as a means towards accomplishing the eternal designs of God, in regard of the manifestation of his own glory and the salvation of the souls redeemed by Christ. Let us revive our faith in the immense good which it is in our power to effect in the church, by announcing to the faithful the word of God; and the result will be that as at present, perhaps, we preach coldly, almost without being conscious of the fact, so then, almost without adverting to it, we will preach with such fervour that *os, lingua, mens, sensus, vigor confessionem personent, flammescat igne charitas, accendat ardor proximos.*

Let us for a moment suppose that the propagandists of impiety were afforded an opportunity of addressing the people as they pleased, once a week or oftener, in order to indoctrinate them with their errors, and to hurry them on still further in the career of perversion to the fullest extent of their wishes—they would assuredly believe that no more desirable means than this could be afforded them for the accomplishment of their purpose. Nay, they would be prepared to forfeit every other means, in order to secure this one. For the sake of it, they would even resign the aid of the press, powerful though it be; because every one knows that the living word is more effective than the dead letter.

Now this most efficacious means is placed in our hands, and if we only strive to make our sermons attractive, so that even the most tepid will be eager to hear them, and if we preach with that zeal and fervour which one ought to feel when treating of the eternal interests of the glory of God and the salvation of souls, we will achieve miracles, so to speak, and nothing further will be required for the sanctification of the people.

Alas! we scarcely ever reflect on the importance of our preaching! On listening to the coldness with which we expound the eternal truths, the promises and the threats of the Omnipotent God, one would be inclined to say that we did not believe our own words. And yet we do believe. The evil is to be attributed to that absence of reflection with which we often reproach our flocks, but which we fail to recognise in ourselves, although we too must plead guilty to it, and it is far less excusable in our case, since we are the ministers of the Lord. The only means by which we can remedy this evil, is by studying to become men of prayer, which alone can revive our languishing faith. But of this we shall speak again, elsewhere.

§ 5. Of Assiduity in Preaching.

As prescribed by the laws of the Church, a Parish Priest is bound to preach the word of God to his people on all Festivals of obligation. He will discharge this duty by expounding to them the Gospel, by explaining the Christian doctrine to the children, and by delivering a catechetical instruction to the adults.

I cannot explain how there has crept into certain places the custom, or rather the abuse, of giving vacation from preaching, just as schoolboys get vacation from their studies. In some churches they require two months' exemption from explaining the Gospel, from the catechetical discourse, and even from teaching the Catechism to the children. Why is this? Is it because the Parish Priest stands in need of a two months' holiday at the seaside, or elsewhere? Should such be the case, he ought to provide a substitute during his absence. But, as a matter of fact, the Parish Priest does not require this holiday. He remains all the time in his own house, or if he does go away at all it is merely for a few days. Why, then, does he not preach? He may, perhaps, reply that his parishioners are away on their holiday. But no one could venture to give this answer in sober earnestness; for every Parish Priest well knows that not ten per cent of his parishioners have it in their power to enjoy a holiday during the summer months. Why, then, I ask again, does he not preach? He may say that he stands in need of a little rest. But can any one seriously pretend that to preach on one day out of seven involves such arduous labour, that, because of it, the Parish Priest requires rest for two months every year; and rest so absolute, that he must not even attempt to teach the Catechism to the little children?

I can understand how a Lenten Preacher, who has been in the pulpit every day during the forty days of Lent, has need of rest for a week or two afterwards; but it is impossible to understand how a Parish Priest requires two months' absolute repose, because he has preached on the Sundays and Festivals throughout the year.

Meanwhile, two evils result from this system. The first is self-evident; namely, that during all that interval the parishioners do not hear the Word of God. The second is less noticed, but most real, nevertheless, and it is that some of the parishioners, having become accustomed during that period to sanctify the Sunday by merely hearing Mass, continue to sanctify it in the same manner even after the Parish Priest has resumed his sermons.

A Parish Priest, then, if he be observant of the laws of the Church, which have never sanctioned the abuse of taking vacation from preaching, will sanctify all the Sundays and all the Festivals of obligation by preaching the word of God; and he will give his parishioners an opportunity of being able to sanctify them likewise by coming to hear it. In a circular addressed to his Parish Priests, St. Liguori once wrote: "Doctors teach that Parish Priests cannot be excused from mortal sin who omit to preach for a month consecutively, or at intervals which, taken together, would amount to three months." (Tannoia Life of St. Lig., Bk. 3, Chap. 22.)

Again, in certain other places there prevails the abuse that the Parish Priest should omit preaching, or at least give up the catechetical discourse in the afternoon, in order to attend some festival in a neighbouring parish. Because of these festivals in a single Church, the people of several neighbouring parishes are very frequently deprived of instruction, either entirely or in part; and thus these functions prove very detrimental to the glory of God and the good of souls.

In other places, under circumstances of this kind, the Parish Priest, in order not to omit the afternoon instruction, tacks it on to the sermon in the forenoon. Thus, after explaining the gospel of the day, he gives an instruction in Christian doctrine to the children, and a catechetical discourse to the adults—a medley that would require a miracle to prove of any advantage. Just fancy a man hearing confessions, saying Mass, explaining the gospel, explaining some portion of the Christian doctrine to the children, and delivering a catechetical discourse to the adults, one after the other! Whoever should attempt such a task, would do so merely to be able to say that he had attempted it. Meanwhile, how will the people spend the remainder of the Sunday? In idleness, in gambling, and in such like practices. Wherever such abuses as we have described may have been introduced, the new Parish Priest should take counsel with the Bishop, and be guided by his advice.

§ 6. Counsels regarding the Instruction of the Children.

In order that the teaching may be uniform, the

Parish Priest, when instructing the children, ought to adopt the little catechism of his own diocese. He must next endeavour, as far as possible, to make all learn thoroughly the material words of the catechism. This material knowledge of the words is more easily remembered, and it is, likewise, the best means to fix in the minds of the children a knowledge of the substance or meaning of what they learn.

In addition to this, the Parish Priest must explain the catechism clearly to the children, in a manner adapted to their capacity, in order that they may understand it the better, and that the truths contained in it may produce a more lively impression upon their minds. I have said "*in a manner adapted to their capacity*"; because, as a rule, they are incapable of understanding profound and subtle explanations and arguments. They ought to be taught merely the principal points, and always, so to speak, in rather a general way, without descending to too minute particulars.

The Parish Priest will act wisely in preparing the children against the objections which are commonly put forward against the truths of Faith, and which they will be likely to hear from unbelievers, who are now-a-days becoming so numerous. These objections he must refute by the most obvious and palpable arguments, which are the only ones that children are capable of understanding; and he must be careful not to touch at all upon those difficulties which cannot be met by arguments of this kind.

The Parish Priest must strive to impress upon the

children the most exalted idea possible of God, and this he may do by imparting to them some knowledge of the greatness of His divine attributes—of His wisdom—of His omnipotence—of his immensity, and so of the rest. He must dwell in a special manner on the greatness of God's goodness—that attribute which, according to our manner of thinking, best includes all that is calculated to awaken sentiments of love. Therefore he must make them understand that God is not only good, but that He is Goodness itself, without limits, without bounds; that no human mind can imagine and understand how good He is, so that no one—not even the angels and saints in heaven, or the Blessed Virgin herself—can love God as much as He deserves; and that, consequently, though great be the goodness of the saints and angels, and of Mary their queen, yet it is all nothing in comparison with the goodness of God.

The Parish Priest must also strive that the instruction of the children in the Christian doctrine be not a mere cold, dry teaching of the truths of Faith —such as :—*There is a God; there is a Hell; there is a Heaven; there are Seven Sacraments;* and so-forth—but that it be, instead, a teaching full of unction, which will, at one and the same time, enlighten the mind and train the heart. This may be attained by combining practical and moral truths, good maxims, and the like, with the purely speculative and doctrinal instruction. The following truths will furnish examples to illustrate what I mean :—

I. That *God has placed us in this world to know*

Him, to love Him, and to serve Him, and afterwards to enjoy Him for ever in Heaven. That, consequently, God has not placed us in this world to eat, and drink, and amuse ourselves; but *to know* Him, by learning well the Christian Doctrine, which is the only science capable of imparting to us a knowledge of God. That we have been placed here *to love* God, —to love Him above everything else, and even more than ourselves. That we have been placed here *to serve* God, by showing ourselves obedient in everything enjoined upon us by the Ten Commandments, and also by the Precepts of the Church, which command us in His name, and by authority received from Him. Finally, that having done all this, we may, one day, go to enjoy Him in Heaven, contemplating for ever the splendour and brightness of His infinite beauty, and tasting in beatific love how dear and sweet is His infinite goodness.

It is of the greatest importance to make the children realise that whosoever is not in the world to know, to serve, and to love God, does not fulfil the end for which he was placed in the world, and deserves to be removed from it; just as the vine that brings forth no grapes, or the fig-tree that produces no figs, deserves to be rooted out of the soil which it encumbers.

II. That *of all the acts of the Christian virtues, we ought especially to practise acts of the love of God.* Theologians agree in teaching that as soon as children arrive at the use of reason, they are obliged to make acts of the love of God. Nevertheless, as a general rule, we omit to teach and to urge them to fulfil this duty, to which they pay little or no heed themselves, through want of reflection.

Wherefore, after having impressed the children with an exalted idea of the Divine goodness, as has been said above, and having touched, also, on what the Lord has done for our salvation, the Parish Priest must endeavour to excite them to make acts of the love of God, which, as St. Teresa says, are as it were the fuel which keeps alive, and increases in our hearts the holy fire of charity. It is most important that he should, likewise, suggest to the children the practice of making such acts frequently in the course of the day, by means of ejaculations, saying, for example : *My God, I love Thee above everything—Lord, I love Thee with all my heart—I love Thee more than myself*, &c. If Parish Priests will inflame the virgin hearts of children with a love so pure and beautiful, they will afterwards have the consolation of seeing them reject every filthy profane love.

III. That *the grace of God is the greatest treasure in the world.* Wherefore he will teach the children (a matter of which even adults are sometimes unfortunately ignorant), that *sanctifying* or *habitual* grace is a gift of God, by which a christian becomes the friend of God, a child of God, an heir to paradise, and the brother of Christ—the greatest gift which God can bestow upon His creatures—a gift which confers sanctity on men here below, and upon the blessed in Heaven, including even Mary, their Queen. He will make them understand that all souls, free from the guilt of mortal sin possess this grace; that it is mortal sin alone which can rob us of this gift; that whosoever dies enriched with this treasure will infallibly be saved, and whoever dies without it will most certainly be damned; that, consequently, this treasure ought to be prized above everything else, and that to preserve the grace of God in our hearts, we ought to forfeit even an entire world, were it ours, and were the preservation of grace dependent on our doing so.

IV. That *the greatest of all evils is sin*, which, if it be mortal, deprives us of sanctifying grace, and makes us the slaves, the brothers, the children of the demons, and deserving of Hell fire. That, therefore, it would be an infinitely less evil to keep a deadly serpent in our bosom, than a mortal sin upon our soul; and that, as it would be impossible for a man who kept a venomous snake in his bosom to eat, sleep, or enjoy himself, through the ever-present fear that he might at any moment be stung to death, so it ought to be impossible for a christian to eat, sleep, or enjoy himself, as long as he has sin upon his soul, since it may, at any moment, hurl him into Hell. That, consequently, should there happen to anyone that greatest of all misfortunes—to fall into mortal sin—he ought immediately to make lively acts of contrition, and go to confession as soon as he possibly can.

V. That *whosoever keeps bad company needs no devil or other enemy to tempt him on in the path to hell*. He must make the children understand that sometimes a bad companion inflicts greater injury upon the soul than would be inflicted by a devil; and that the promiscuous companionship of boys and girls, if not actually bad, is at least always dangerous, and is displeasing to their angels guardian.

VI. That *it is better never to go to confession, than to make bad confessions, by concealing sins through shame.* This maxim must be impressed especially upon little girls, who more easily allow themselves to be overcome by shame. For this reason it will be well to relate some melancholy examples of bad confessions which have been punished by God.

VII. That *a true client of the Blessed Virgin has never been lost.* And when speaking on this subject, the Parish Priest must endeavour to instil into the hearts of the little ones this tender and warm devotion, impressing upon them to regard Mary as a loving mother, and to have recourse to her in all their necessities. Among other practices that might be suggested to the children, the following would be easy, and productive of the greatest good—namely, to recite each morning and evening three *Hail Marys*, with the ejaculatory prayer: *Dear mother, guard me from mortal sin.*

By mixing up these and other like good maxims with the doctrinal instruction given to the children, they will increase in the holy fear and love of God, and will become fervent christians.

Finally, the Parish Priest must employ with children sweetness and patience, in order to attract them to his instruction. One who is unable to make allowance for the defects inseparable from their tender age would fill them with aversion towards him, so that his instructions would be in a great measure shunned, and would generally prove fruitless. The good Parish Priest will ever bear in mind how Christ acted in the midst of children.[1]

Should there be anyone who has not yet reflected well on the example which Christ has left us, and who should think it beneath him to devote himself personally to teaching the catechism to children, let him listen to the following words of John Gerson: "*Sinite parvulos venire ad me. O bone Jesu, quis ultra verecundabitur esse humilis ad parvulos, quando tu usque ad castissimos puerorum amplexus te inclinas? Absit ergo ut indignum sit parvulorum animas plantare et rigare. Venite, ergo, parvuli, ad me; ego doctrinam vobis, vos orationem impendetis; sic angelos nostros lætificabimus*" (De trahendis ad christum pueris).

§ 7. REGARDING THE INSTRUCTION OF ADULTS.

In many parishes it is the custom to teach the little Catechism aloud to the children in the middle of the Church, when the adults are already assembled for the catechetical discourse. This is a good custom:

---

[1] A very judicious paper, entitled "Qualities of a Successful Catechist," will be found in the *Irish Ecclesiastical Record* for July, 1869 (New Series, Vol I., p. 472), and will repay the perusal of all priests engaged in imparting catechetical instruction to children.—*Translator*.

because there may easily be found amongst the adults some who do not know, or do not sufficiently understand, the principal truths of the christian doctrine, and to whom they must consequently be taught and explained ; and if the Parish Priest teaches and explains them aloud to the children, the adults, likewise, will receive that instruction of which they stand in need. ˙ Wherefore in places where it is the custom to teach the childrens' Catechism in some building adjoining the Church, the Parish Priest ought, for the purpose just mentioned, to cause some children to remain in the Church itself, to whom he will explain aloud the principal, and more elementary truths.

Nor can it be urged, in opposition to this system, that these same truths can be explained in the regular catechetical instruction delivered to the adults. Because, since the catechetical instruction for the adults proceeds according to a regular methodical plan, embracing the entire Catechism, it must happen that a long interval will elapse before the Parish Priest will return to speak of these primary truths; and when he does come round again to treat of them, those who require to learn this or that particular truth, not being invariably present at the instruction, may miss the explanation on that occasion, and must consequently wait for another long interval, before this subject again comes under discussion. If, on the other hand, these truths be frequently explained, a little at a time, while teaching the Catechism to the children, even if missed on one occasion, they are sure to be heard on another; and, through being frequently repeated, they become clearly and distinctly imprinted on the memory, as they ought to be.

There is another point to be borne in mind by the Parish Priest with regard to the catechetical instruction for adults, and this is not to treat the subjects too diffusely, in order that he may be able to come back again upon them as frequently as possible. I know a Church where the explanation of the Creed lasted through four years. If a corresponding number of years were allowed for the explanation of the Decalogue, of the Sacraments, of the Lord's Prayer, of the Seven Deadly Sins, and so forth, the result would be that a youth would almost have become an old man, before he would have heard an explanation of the entire christian doctrine.

It will very much conduce to brevity if the Parish Priest will omit all points of doctrine which are superfluous for the people. Having once, when a young man, casually entered a certain Church, I found the Parish Priest explaining the fifth commandment, and he was deliberately, and at great length, laying down, for a few poor women who were listening to him, the conditions which are required to render a war just! He did not reflect that these poor creatures would never have to declare war, except against the rats and mice which, perhaps, infested their houses.

In order to consult for brevity, one must, also, avoid that system of hair-splitting in moral questions, which induces some persons, under the impression that they are thereby making a display, to lay down all the distinctions made, and all the possible cases contemplated, by moral Theologians. This is simply labour thrown away. The people are not capable of understanding all these subtile distinctions invented by Theologians, and the cases put forward by them are more often hypothetical than real, or, at least, are of extremely rare occurrence. It is even worse than labour thrown away; for it is, moreover, labour which does harm, because it confuses the minds of the audience, and creates scruples and anxieties in those who have delicate consciences. To say the very least, it is highly ridiculous to pretend to teach Theology to the simple Faithful; and it is still more ridiculous to pretend to teach it to them in the catechetical discourse on Sunday. Students, whose minds are developed, spend several years in this study, devoting to it many hours each day; and is it to be expected that the people will learn it during an hour's instruction on a Sunday? The dogmas of Faith and the moral truths must be taught to the people in a broad, general way, suitable to their capacity, which is always limited, if for no other reason, because of the absence of preliminary studies. Those who, because of their particular avocations and professions, stand in need of further instruction, can obtain it more suitably from their confessors.

It is also unwise that in his instruction a Parish Priest should touch upon disputed questions, regarding which he must in the end inform the people that some Theologians hold one opinion, while others think differently. This scandalises the people, who are thereby made to believe that not even the Theologians know what one ought to teach and to do, and that the Christian Doctrine is full of uncertainties.

A few remarks are also necessary regarding those witticisms, with which some Parish Priests are in the habit of adorning, so to speak, their catechetical instruction. In the first place, to be at all tolerated, such expressions should be really witty, and not merely exhibitions of silliness and buffoonery. Secondly, they must be employed sparingly. Witty expressions ought to be, as it were, the salt of a discourse. Now every one knows that too much salt renders even the best viands unpalatable. If the witticisms be really pointed and amusing remarks, sparingly introduced into the catechetical discourse, they will serve to keep up the attention of the audience. Otherwise, they will simply disgust persons of sense, and will prove to all an occasion of distraction and of unseemly laughter, so that both the Catechist and his audience will be wanting in the respect due to the word of God.[1]

---

[1] St. Alphonsus makes the following remarks on this subject in his Institut. Catechetica: "Facetias illas, quæ naturaliter a materia oriuntur non reprobo ; sed quædam facta vel fabulas ridiculas ut populus rideat, dedita opera, enarrare, idem est facere, ut instructio concidat in fabulam, quod inconveniens est: homines delectantur, sed quid inde percipiunt? Sunt alii modi ut populus se præbeat attentum, et fructus percipiat." (Apud Scavini. Theol. Moral, Tract viii., Disp. 1., Cap. iii., in fine.)—*Translator.*

§ 8. On Preaching in Chapels-of-Ease.

Many town parishes, and some city parishes, also, have chapels-of-ease attached, where Mass is celebrated on Festivals of obligation, for the convenience of the Faithful who live at too great a distance from the parochial church. These Chapels, therefore, supply one serious want, namely, that of hearing Mass on Festivals; but it is well to remember that the Faithful have another want no less serious, and it is that of hearing the word of God, for which, consequently, provision should likewise be made. I have said: "*a want no less serious*"; because, although the obligation of hearing the word of God does not bind on every Sunday and holiday, as does the obligation of hearing Mass, neverthelesss, it is an obligation from which, as a general rule, the Faithful cannot be dispensed, since they usually have no other means of receiving instruction in the truths of Faith and of Christian Morality; and such instruction is as indispensable to the people as it is to hear Mass, and, in some cases, it is even more indispensable, as, for instance, in case anyone should be ignorant of the primary truths of Religion.

Wherefore a Parish Priest cannot rest content with merely having Mass celebrated in the chapel-of-ease, but he ought also take measures, if possible, to have some instruction given to the people by the officiating priest; so that those who assist at Mass there, may not be continually deprived of the spiritual nourishment of God's Word. I say: "*if possible*";

because sometimes the priests who officiate in chapels-of-ease are altogether incapable of preaching a sermon of any kind. Should this case occur, however, the Parish Priest ought to make some other provision, either by sending some one, or by going himself from time to time, to give instruction to the people of that locality. And though, now-a-days, it would seem a most unusual course to adopt, yet, it would be no less useful if the Parish Priest arranged that, in case the Priest attached to the chapel-of-ease were unable or unwilling to preach, he should at least read distinctly for the people some short instruction, as was directed to be done in his diocese by Cardinal Durazzo, archbishop of Genoa, in the middle of the 17th Century— a period when the education of the clergy was not so well attended to as in our times. I have seen a circular issued by His Eminence, in which he ordered those Parish Priests who did not preach to read an instruction for their people on all Festivals of obligation.[1]

It must be observed that a Chapel-of-ease in which

---

[1] Where the Priest is *unable* to preach, it would, no doubt, be advisable that he should at least read an instruction for the people; but surely it is going too far to say (as the author seems to do), that a Parish Priest who is simply *unwilling* to preach can discharge his obligation by merely reading an instruction for his flock. I find the following passage in Gury on this subject: "Parochus autem, qui pios libros auditoribus legit, non obit munus suum prædicandi: quia lectio non est prædicatio ; nisi quis adeo sit labilis memoriæ, ut aliter facere non possit: tum vero identidem debet curare, ut per alium populo sermones habeantur, vel episcopum de impedimento commonefacere." (De Statibus Particularibus, n. 112.)— *Translator.*

a sermon is never preached becomes the occasion why many persons never hear the Word of God, who would hear it if the Chapel-of-ease were not in existence. For these persons, not wishing to lose mass on Festivals, would go, even at great inconvenience, to the parish Church, where, together with the mass, they would hear a sermon. But when they are enabled to comply with the obligation of hearing mass without leaving their own locality, never reflecting on the obligation of hearing the Word of God, they remain deprived of it altogether.

Wherefore, I cannot understand how those Parish Priests are excusable, who not only neglect to provide for the preaching of God's Word in Chapels-of-ease, but even positively forbid preaching there, under the pretext that, otherwise, persons would be kept away from the parish Church, and would no longer go to hear the words of their Pastor. These Parish Priests do not reflect that there are several who, if they have an opportunity of hearing mass near home, will not put themselves to the inconvenience of travelling some distance to hear an instruction; and even though some might submit to this inconvenience, the majority would not do so, and would thus remain unprovided with the spiritual food of God's Word. Could a Parish Priest ever be excused who, for the sake of having an additional dozen or so of persons to listen to his own sermon, would permit, and almost wish, that some hundreds of his parishioners should be deprived of the opportunity of hearing the Word of God?

Theologians are agreed in teaching that a Parish Priest is obliged to instruct the ignorant even individually and in private, if they should otherwise remain ignorant of the knowledge necessary to attain eternal salvation. Can we ever suppose, then, that they would permit a Parish Priest to hinder, nay positively to forbid, these poor people to enjoy a convenient means of instruction, such as would be afforded by a sermon preached in the Chapel-of-ease of the district? Parish Priests will say in reply that the law supports their view of the question. But they ought to observe that the law favours them, only in the hypothesis that the parishioners can conveniently hear the Word of God in the Parochial Church; and if this hypothesis be not verified, every *human, ecclesiastical* law, which might otherwise be in their favour, must give way before the *natural, divine* obligation, by which they are bound to provide the means of instruction for all the Faithful committed to their care.

§ 9. ON THE MODERATION TO BE OBSERVED BY THE PARISH PRIEST, WHEN TREATING OF MORAL QUESTIONS.

In the last century, great injury was done to souls by the prevalence of certain rigid opinions; and these opinions continued to exercise their baneful influence, until the works of Saint Alphonsus Liguori became for the clergy the standard authority on Moral Theology, and supplanted in the hands of the Faithful all works of devotion which inculcated views differing from those which he put forward.

For a long period the Church has suffered from the two-fold scourge of laxity on the part of the irreligious, and rigour on the part of the pharisaical. The former spurred on to impiety those whose inclinations already tended in that direction; the latter frightened pious souls. Wherefore, while some were smoothing and widening the path which leads to irreligion, others would make a devout life almost impracticable. This second scourge was not less baneful than the first, and it aroused greater indignation. For, it is but natural that the patrons of impiety should favour its development; but it is too outrageous that those who profess to promote holiness, should direct their efforts towards its destruction. This second scourge has now almost entirely disappeared, and God made use of the pen of St. Alphonsus as the instrument to bring about this happy result— a fact recognised by everyone, especially in Italy and in France.

Nevertheless, it must be borne in mind that the books printed at that period are still in existence, and there are still extant catechisms, or instructions in Christian doctrine, which, though written in good faith, are tinged with that undue severity of which I have spoken. It usually happens, in fact, that every prevailing error is surrounded, as it were, by an atmosphere of poisonous ideas, which are censurable in a greater or a less degree, in proportion as they approach or recede from the error itself; but which, at the same time, can never be pronounced perfectly harmless, as long as they remain in any degree within the circle of error.

It happens, likewise, that certain good men, in the delusive hope of being able to lessen the divergence between sound and false doctrine, when the latter already enjoys a certain degree of popularity, in their effort to be conciliatory, unconsciously enter a little within the circle of error; and if they do not actually entertain views which are identical with the error of the day, they hold some which are at least closely allied to it. This is why we may so easily meet with courses of Catechetical Instructions, written by good authors, who err on the side of excessive severity—a severity which does no good to the wicked, and serves only to discourage the good.

Now that God has been pleased to bless the world with the moral and ascetic works of St. Alphonsus, which leave nothing to be desired, whether in point of erudition, or of clearness, or of solidity, the Parish Priest, in preparing his Catechetical instruction, must not trust blindly to any author, no matter how respectable. He may, if he please, consult the works of such authors for the division of his subject, for illustrations, examples, and so forth; but where moral doctrine is concerned, he should not repeat to the people everything which he may find in any of these books. Let him carefully note whether the opinions of this book agree with the teaching of St. Alphonsus; and should he find that they do not, let him abandon this author's views, and follow the doctrine of St.

Liguori. Wherefore it is desirable that every Parish Priest should have by him Saint Liguori's *Moral Theology* and *Homo Apostolicus*, as well as the *Love of our Lord Jesus Christ reduced to practice*, the *Spiritual Treatises*, the *Glories of Mary*, the *Catechism for the People*, and as many other works of the Saint as possible; for though they are numerous, yet he could never have too many of them. In addition to St. Liguori's Moral Theology, he might have also those of *Gousset* and of *Gury*, especially the Roman edition with the notes of Ballerini, which seem to have aspired to no other distinction than that of copying the spirit and doctrine of the Saint.

Let the Parish Priest, then, in explaining the Catechism, adopt the mild opinions of Saint Alphonsus, and let him not be afraid of incurring thereby the imputation of laxity. There was, indeed, a time, which is still remembered by old priests, when the saint was freely accused of laxity, and when his opinions were combatted with the same ardour with which one ought to combat doctrines subversive of sound morality. But that time is now past, and St. Alphonsus excites a more profound feeling of veneration, inspires a greater sense of security, and enjoys a more wide-spread reputation, than any other Theologian since the days of St. Thomas. Throughout the entire world it is his Moral Theology which may be said to be in the hands of everybody, and to regulate the consciences of all. And should there still be found some gloomy individual, who prides himself in combating the doctrines, and denying the authority of the saint, we can only allow him to enjoy his own growling, like dogs which "bay the moon," and pity him through a feeling of charity.

Here, however, I must reply to an objection which might make an impression on some minds, and lead them into error; it is that, in preaching, one ought always to put forward strict and severe views, which may afterwards be relaxed and made milder in practice; whereas if, on the other hand, mild doctrines were preached from the pulpit, and were made milder still in practice, we would at once find ourselves going headlong on the broad road of real laxity.

At first sight, this objection seems to have considerable weight; yet it is based upon a principle of false prudence, which is expressly calculated to deceive, rather than to instruct, the faithful.

Both from the stand-point of Reason and of Faith, the most sacred thing in the world is Truth. It is so sacred, indeed, that it can never be lawful for any motive to alter, to counterfeit, or to disguise it. Would it, in fact, ever be lawful to preach that a man who has stolen a hundred is bound to restore a hundred and one, even though by this assertion one might obtain some great good, or avert some serious evil? Most certainly, never. The simple truth must be told, and especially when one speaks from the chair of truth. Therefore, a Parish Priest who alters, counterfeits, or disguises the truth, even for a good purpose, commits a grave fault which nothing can excuse.

Now, having established this principle, it follows

that whenever we know the more severe opinion to be true, we must preach it; but if, on the contrary, the milder opinion is known to be true, we must preach the milder opinion. And should it be feared that the abuse of laxity will follow therefrom in practice, the Parish Priest must find some other means to prevent this evil result, but he must never do so by distorting the truth. Let us take an example: It is sufficiently certain that in order to sanctify the Sundays and Festivals, as far as regards merely the precept of the Church, nothing further is required than to hear mass, and to abstain from servile works. Nevertheless it is certain that if the Parish Priest were to teach in his catechetical discourse, without a word of comment: "in order to comply with the precept of sanctifying the Sunday, it is enough to abstain from servile works and to hear mass," many would abuse this doctrine, and would utterly neglect all religious instruction. Now, in order to apply a remedy to this very probable abuse, must the Parish Priest alter his doctrine? No, certainly not. On the contrary, he must expound the true doctrine which teaches that, in virtue of the Church's precept, a Christian is bound to abstain from servile works, from buying and selling, and so forth, and is moreover bound to assist at Mass; but he must add that, in addition to the obligation imposed by the Church's precept, one is bound to assist at the instructions given upon Festivals, in order that he may not be ignorant of those truths of faith and morals, which he is bound to know; and that, for this very reason,

Parish Priests are obliged by a most rigorous precept of the church to impart such instructions to the people. And in this manner he prevents the danger of anyone abusing the doctrine laid down above, while at the same time he offers no violence to truth.

Again, it is a very safe doctrine, and, as Saint Alphonsus teaches, intrinsically more probable, that if a penitent, after having received absolution, should remember some sin which, through forgetfulness, he did not confess, he may communicate without further confession, postponing the declaration of this sin until the next occasion on which he shall approach the sacrament of Penance. Now if a Parish Priest, fearing lest some one, unable to distinguish one case from another, should go to communion after deliberately concealing a sin, were to teach the people that whosoever should reduce to practice the doctrine laid down above, would be guilty of sacrilege, just like the person who should communicate after having concealed a sin in confession—could we approve of such a course? Most certainly we could not. The Parish Priest ought instead to explain clearly, and to impress well upon his audience, that he is speaking of a sin omitted in confession through *forgetfulness*, and therefore already pardoned with the others; and that he is *not* speaking of a sin *purposely concealed*, which would render the confession sacrilegious. Would not every danger of applying the doctrine erroneously be thus removed, without in the least altering the truth?

Let it be observed, moreover, that it is not the

province of the Parish Priest to decide, but simply to expound, the various theological opinions. Wherefore, he cannot command his parishioners to believe what is believed by himself, or by some moral theologian who is a particular favourite of his. His parishioners have a right to know from him whether a certain thing is lawful, and if it probably is so, he could not deny them the right to avail themselves of this opinion in practice.

For example: A respectable parishioner of mine finds a crown under the dust, in a street which is trodden every day by thousands of persons. No one can tell how long it has lain there: it is impossible to discover the owner. Now, according to the most rigid opinion, my parishioner is bound to give that crown to the poor: according to the more benign opinion, he may keep it himself. Will it be lawful, then, for me to tell him decisively that he is bound to give that crown to the poor, and that, failing to do so, he would be guilty of mortal sin, by retaining what belongs to others? Would he not have a right to be informed by me, his Parish Priest, that, according to a solidly probable opinion, he may, if he like, retain the money himself without the slightest scruple? And is it just that, with my rigid views, I should impose upon him the necessity either of giving away the crown or of committing a mortal sin? Whence did I acquire this high authority of being able thus to force my opinion upon my parishioner?[1] Let us never forget that the Church alone has the power to decide

---

[1] Let those confessors who are quick to bind persons to restitu-

theological controversies, and that she alone, in deciding them, has authority to say: "If you follow this or that other theological opinion, you will commit a mortal sin".

Nor does it avail to reply that theologians frequently decide certain questions, placing a *peccat mortaliter* against whosoever does not follow this or that doctrine, although it may happen to be disputed in the schools. For theologians write for theologians and confessors, who know well what weight is to be attached to that *peccat mortaliter*—that is to say, they know well that a *peccat mortaliter*, which has no other support beyond the private opinion of some theologian, is a mere assertion which decides nothing, which does not trouble anybody, and which some laugh at without the slightest scruple. On the other hand, if the simple Faithful, who are ignorant alike of the value and of the existence of certain scholastic opinions, hear the Parish Priest laying down: " whoever does this action, commits a mortal sin," they fancy that this is the doctrine of the Church, which must never again be questioned. Therefore, the decisions laid down by theologians in their books produce no evil

---

tion in doubtful cases, take notice of the following question in Gury :—

"An Confessarius ad restitutionem teneatur si proprias opiniones imponat cum damno pœnitentis ?

Resp. Affirmative cum Bouvier : si enim confessarius urgeat. v. 9. obligationem restitutionis in casu, in quo duplex datur opinio probabilis inter theologos, urget injuste cum damno pœnitentis ; sed ille qui est causa injusti damni, ad restitutionem tenetur : Ergo etc." (Casus conscientiæ, Casus de Conse. ix., ad q. 3.)—*Author's note*.

consequences; but those, on the other hand, laid down by Parish Priests from the Altar or the Pulpit might entail very serious and most injurious consequences, because they would serve to deceive rather than to enlighten the people, and they would force consciences to do things to which no one could bind them.

And let not the Parish Priest imagine that the more rigid he is in his sermons, the more moral and pious will his flock be. The very opposite might easily happen. He who is too rigid in his sermons will be judged *extreme* by the good sense of the people; and, consequently, they will always discount liberally whatever he says, and will not attach full credit to his words, even when he speaks with exactness and caution. Moreover, they never care to hear him; and, precisely for this reason, many of the parishioners absent themselves from his instructions. Preachers of the rigid school succeed only in keeping sinners away from hearing the Word of God, and in discouraging pious souls. Sometimes even Confessors are compelled to tell their penitents that they must not place blind faith in certain assertions of the Parish Priest, and must not regulate their conduct by them; and, should the penitents be very scrupulous, they are obliged to counsel them to attend the sermons of some other preacher, if there be one in the place, or to give up attending sermons altogether, if there be no one to preach except the Parish Priest.

Experience proves that the greatest licentiousness prevails where the most rigid doctrines are preached. Cardinal Gousset has confessed that such was the case in France, at a period when rigid doctrines were most in vogue there. The most rigid opinions of Tertullian were preached from the French pulpits; doctrines were taught which were better suited to Anchorites than to Christians living in society; it was pretended that one should be almost an Angel to approach the Holy Communion; and yet, meanwhile, evening parties, banquets and theatres were distinguished by a dissoluteness of morals little better than pagan, and the prevailing licentiousness did not seek to hide itself, but rather paraded its infamies everywhere, commencing on the steps of the throne and descending to the mire of the streets. Yet, since it was also the fashion at that time to comply with the Paschal Precept, this manner of life did not prevent anyone from approaching the Holy Communion at Easter time.

In addition to employing great moderation and suitable mildness in his exposition of the Christian Doctrine, the Parish Priest must also be careful not to touch upon those subtle questions, which, instead of enlightening the people, would serve only to create scruples and doubts in consciences. This is a point on which the most learned catechists, who are thoroughly versed in all the distinctions of theologians, sometimes exhibit a want of judgment and prudence. I have seen a catechist apply himself to teaching the people the several ways by which a venial sin might become mortal, and he told them that this might happen: 1, through *an erroneous conscience* —if one believed that his sin was mortal; 2, by *excessive attachment* to it—that is, by being so disposed that one would not hesitate to commit the sin, even though it were mortal; 3, by *contempt of the law or of the superior*—that is, intending to commit that sin as a formal act of disobedience towards the one or the other; 4, through *an intention grievously sinful*— that is, by intending to produce a grievously bad effect by means of a sin in itself venial; 5, through *a bad effect foreseen*—that is, when one foresees that a venial sin may produce a notable bad effect. Now these theological distinctions are all very just and reasonable; nevertheless anyone possessed of the least discernment can see that the majority of the audience will not understand them all, at least without altering their form considerably, while persons of delicate consciences, on examining whether any of these five conditions may be found in their own venial sins, will be sure to fancy that they can discover the presence of even several of them. Nay, the very fact of remembering that a venial sin may become mortal in so many different ways, will become to them a source of perpetual anxiety; so that they will suffer from constant apprehensions lest they may be committing mortal sin by every act of impatience, or by every officious lie of which they may be guilty.

It is certain that the people ought to be taught the elementary doctrines, and the more obvious consequences deducible from them, after the manner employed by Saint Alphonsus in his catechism for the people. Everything else ought to be left to the natural good sense of the audience, who, when they find themselves involved in any particular doubt, will declare it to their confessor, by whom it will be solved as far as may be necessary, and suitably to the resspective capacity of each one. Those who affect great subtilty in their instructions, do not enlighten, but confuse the people; they do not remove doubts but multiply them; and, we repeat once more, the attempt to teach the people theology, whether dogmatic or moral, is an undertaking at once fruitless and ridiculous.

There is another most important point to which the Parish Priest ought to attend when explaining the catechism, and it is not to set down anything as a mortal sin, unless it can certainly be classed as such, as, for example, the theft of something valuable, fornication and bad desires, the omission of Mass on Festivals of obligation without an excusing cause, non-compliance with the precept of paschal communion, and so forth. As regards those bad actions which are not manifestly mortal sins, the catechist ought to confine himself to simply stating that they are sinful. Nor does it avail to say that such or such another bad action is declared a mortal sin by this or that theologian. As we have already said above, this or that theologian is perfectly at liberty to give his opinion; but his opinion does not change the substance of things, and cannot make a mortal sin of that which perhaps is not one, or justify me in calling it a mortal sin. A catechist ought never pronounce a sin mortal, unless it has been declared such by the Church, or by the consensus of all theologians. Whenever the point is disputed, we ought to refrain from pronouncing a decision in the case.

Let us illustrate this by an example. Some theologians say that it is a mortal sin to steal a *franc*, while others maintain that a larger sum is required to constitute a grievous sin. A prudent Parish Priest will never say that the theft of a *franc* is a mortal sin, but will simply say that it is a sin, and nothing more. Those rigorous catechists who lightly assert that such and such sinful actions are mortal, really cause mortal sins to be committed, through the erroneous consciences which they form in their audience.

It must, furthermore, be remarked that even when theologians with common consent hold a certain action to be a mortal sin, prudence sometimes dictates that we should not declare it to be such in our sermons, when we have reason to believe that we would fail to persuade our audience of the truth of the assertion, or that, in any case, they would still continue the practice, even after the warning of the Parish Priest. Let us take superstitious practices to illustrate my meaning. These, if invested with all the malice which is supposed to belong to them, are really, *per se*, mortal sins. Meanwhile, if we pass from theory to practice, you will not perhaps find one in a hundred superstitious women who believes, or is prepared to believe, that her vain observations are a grievous offence to God. And if some of them could be induced, on the authority of the Parish Priest, to believe that such is the case, yet they would not cease to practise them; so great is the force of prejudice, of fears arising from ignorance, and of habit! Wherefore the Parish Priest will act prudently in pointing out the absurdity of superstitious practices; in declaring that they are real offences against God, and in denouncing those (for the most part women), who practise them; but let him not say that they are mortal sins, which moreover, generally speaking, would not be true. As a matter of fact, we do not generally find in these superstitious acts, when reduced to practice, that malice which theologians suppose in them in the abstract. Theologians teach that they are mortal sins, because they suppose in them a deliberate compact, expressed or implied, with the Devil—a condition which, as a general rule, is not verified in practice. Superstitious women never for a moment dream of having anything to do with the Devil, when they seek to find out the numbers that will be drawn at the lottery, or when they cure sicknesses by vain observations, and other naturally inadequate means which they employ, or when they conjecture the future from cards. It is simply an almost beastly ignorance that makes them superstitious. This, however, must be understood to apply to cases of this kind merely as a general rule; because occasionally you may find women filled with hellish malice, who, to work out their ends, would not hesitate to accept any service from the Devil; but these are very few, and they are, moreover, thoroughly aware that they commit mortal sins by these superstitions, without waiting to learn the fact from the Parish Priest.

The Parish Priest must also be careful not to

preach that other rigid doctrine, which would have us believe that invincible ignorance is impossible with respect to matters forbidden by the Sixth Commandment; and that, consequently, if any one had sinned against modesty in his youth without knowing the malice of his act, when he does come to discover it later on, he is obliged immediately to confess the act, under pain of otherwise committing sacrilege. Such a doctrine as this must appear exceedingly strange to any one who reflects that children are kept as much as possible in the dark regarding the malice of this sin, and that people would wish them to be ignorant even of its very existence. In fact if we would insist at all hazards that children must know the malice of impurity, so as to sin absolutely and grievously every time they commit indecent actions, charity and justice would demand that they should be carefully instructed on this matter, that all seasonable warnings should be given to them, and that, in every possible way, they should be put upon their guard against committing such sins.

Some one may say that children are made sufficiently aware of the malice of these actions by the very shame which they cause them, since they would shrink from committing them where they could be seen by anybody. To solve such a frivolous objection as this, it is quite sufficient to reply that there are other perfectly innocent actions—such as to comply with the wants of nature—which are likewise accompanied with shame. Besides, if shame were a certain proof of guilt, it would follow that even married people could not be excused from sin, since they also experience a feeling of shame when discharging their conjugal duties. Moreover, it is a fact that good children of both sexes, who through ignorance commit immodest actions, when they are better informed through some instruction heard, or some caution given them, immediately amend their conduct on discovering that such actions are sinful, and even make that extraordinary effort which is required to resist the very strong force of the habit already formed. Now can we believe that these children, who are so well disposed as to amend on the first warning, would be damned if they had died before the warning had been given to them? And yet they must infallibly be damned, unless we are prepared to admit in their case invincible ignorance? I do not well know how to designate opinions of this kind, and I cannot understand how they ever came to receive the support of even a single theologian.

But if, nevertheless, some Parish Priest of rigorous views should still have some scruple on this point, he will quickly lay it aside if he but reflect that St. Alphonsus Liguori did not hesitate to teach the opposite doctrine even to nuns. Here are his words: "As regards acts of levity or immodest jokes which took place in childhood, without a knowledge of their malice, there is no obligation to confess them. Nor is it a certain proof of malice to reflect that they were done in secret, because certain natural actions are likewise done by children in secret, and yet they are not sins. Wherefore we are not bound to make

OF PREACHING. 221

special mention of such matters in confession, unless when we remember to have committed them with a consciousness of mortal sin, or at least with serious doubts whether they were mortal sins." (The Nun Sanctified, cap. 18, n. 14, of Confession.) Wherefore, according to the doctrine of the Saint, even though the little boy or little girl may have known that these actions were culpable, yet if they regarded them merely as acts of levity or jokes which did not exceed the guilt of venial sin, not even in this case would they be bound to confess them afterwards, when, having attained more mature years, they should have come to know their heinousness.

This prudent system employed by St. Alphonsus to rescue from the danger of committing sacrilege some over-modest nun, who, without knowing its malice, might have been guilty of some failing in her childhood, ought likewise to be adopted by the Parish Priest towards these timid souls who are to be found among the faithful, and who suffer an almost insuperable shame in confessing the immodest actions of their childhood, committed through levity, without a knowledge of their wickedness, or at least without advertence to their grievous sinfulness.

§ 10. COUNSELS REGARDING SERMONS ON THE SIXTH COMMANDMENT.

Since this subject is more delicate, more dangerous, and, taken all in all, more important than every other, it seems to me to call for some special counsels. The first of these, however, is that the Parish Priest should preach frequently and warmly against this vice, which alone, according to the saying of St. Remigius, hurls into hell a greater number of Christian souls than all other vices taken together. And we must convince ourselves that, as far as this vice is concerned, there is not any notable difference between city and country parishes, between gentle and simple, between one nation and another, since it is everywhere a predominant vice.

Wherefore the Parish Priest must preach against this vice frequently and zealously; and those Parish Priests are deserving of censure who, as though all their parishioners were angels, never touch upon this subject in their instructions, perhaps under the pretext of not creating a knowlege of sin where none already existed. In the first place, it must be observed that a knowledge of this sin is far more wide-spread than is commonly supposed, and that those souls who are really ignorant of it are very few in number; and it is not just, for the sake of these few, to omit to warn, to frighten, and to forearm the innumerable others who are perfectly well acquainted with it. These few souls, and the sanctity of God's House, and the reciprocal weakness of him who speaks and of those who listen are all deserving of respect, and for this very reason a preacher ought to treat this subject with extreme caution and reserve; but it is no reason why he should observe absolute and perpetual silence on the subject.

Without doubt, the first care of the Parish Priest

ought to be to speak of this vice in such a manner, that whosoever knows nothing of it already can understand nothing, and that those who are already acquainted with it may have nothing indecent or immodest presented to their minds. The Parish Priest ought to picture to himself how an Angel would speak on such a subject, and endeavour himself to speak in a similar fashion.

Wherefore he ought always to speak of it with repugnance, and with a show of disgust, as one does who is forced through necessity to speak of nasty subjects in the presence of respectable persons. Moreover, he ought to guard carefully against speaking in a jesting manner, or employing pleasantries which might be permissable in treating of other subjects. Still worse would it be were he to make use of some witty expression which might be capable of an equivocal meaning, and would be calculated to excite mirth amongst the audience. This would be a profanation which would do grievous injury to the character of the Parish Priest. For there is no doubt that, from the manner in which one speaks of this vice, it is easy to know whether he is chaste or the opposite. Could a pure soul ever speak of such defilement with a smile upon his lips?

He must also guard against the fear of not being sufficiently understood, whereby he might be led to use too plain and really scandalous language—scendalous for those who may be unacquainted with this vice, because they must of necessity acquire a knowledge of it, and scandalous for all the others as well, in as much as it would bring before their minds dangerous and seductive images. It must be remembered that even though one's language on this subject be extremely discreet and carefully veiled, yet those who have need of understanding it will be sure to understand it thoroughly. Even the most dull and stupid persons exhibit in this respect acute and ready intelligence.

By speaking of this vice with due caution and reserve, by employing extremely modest and grave language, and by letting it be seen that he entertains towards it a feeling of horror and disgust, there is not the slightest fear that the Parish Priest will injure any soul by his sermon; nay, he will do good to all without exception, and he will even inspire the innocent, if not with hatred of a sin that is unknown to them, at least with hatred of sin in general.

In the next place, the Parish Priest must recommend above all things the avoidance of whatever is an occasion of, or incentive to, this vice; and he must inculcate upon the faithful to be cautious in small things as in great, and vigilant in the lesser dangers as well as in those which are more considerable; since no one escapes its defilement except he who entirely distrusts himself, and guards against little beginnings, which are, as it were, sparks, capable, each one of them, of producing a terrible conflagration.

He must likewise continually exhort his parishioners to strengthen themselves against this vice by prayer, by frequenting the Sacraments, by devotion to the Blessed Virgin, by avoiding idleness, and by all the other means calculated to preserve the holy fear of God in their souls.

Let the Parish Priest be persuaded that as many souls as he shall make chaste, so many he shall save. It must be a case of extremely rare occurrence that a Christian soul is lost without sins of impurity. Whoever, with the aid of Divine grace, has strength to overcome the most seductive, and at the same time the most violent of all the passions, will have strength to overcome all the others, which are less seductive, and have less power over the human heart. Let a Pastor, then, make his people chaste, and he will make them saints. Let him be persuaded that in preventing sins against purity, he prevents innumerable other evils—evils of every kind, both spiritual and temporal, which I must not even attempt to allude to here, as the enumeration of them would occupy too much space.

What has been already said might be considered sufficient upon this subject; nevertheless when we reflect that it depends in a great measure upon the education given by parents to their children, whether these will be free from, or slaves to, this most destructive of all the passions, I must further lay down a few cautions to be given by the Parish Priest to parents.

The first is, that they be themselves extremely careful not to give scandal to their children; for they must not imagine that these little ones are either shortsighted, or deaf, or dull of comprehension. It seems impossible, yet it is a fact, that this vice, while still in its very germ and undeveloped, can make tender children so watchful, so curious, so inquisitive as they are, and yet without their giving evidence of it. What is most to be deplored is, that they treasure up with a most retentive memory whatever they see and hear; so that even if they should happen not to understand, at the moment, something wicked, they will understand it afterwards when they are a few years older.

Moreover, let him in his sermons caution parents to be on their guard lest brothers and sisters should give scandal to one another, or receive it in their intercourse with their companions or neighbours; to observe what places their children frequent, and with whom they associate; and not to take them to theatres or balls, or permit them to retain in their possession books which treat of profane love, or other incentives to vice.

Finally, let him impress upon parents not to allow their sons to contract too intimate familiarity, and above all in private interviews, with the young girls whom they intend to marry. I have used the words "too intimate familiarity," and "above all, in private interviews"; because it would be, to say the least, useless to preach that betrothed lovers should never meet one another. Visits of this kind are partly necessary, in order that young people may come to know one another, before entering into the indissoluble bonds of matrimony. Moreover, they would at all hazards visit one another through an impulse of mutual affection, and this, when it has marriage in view, is a matter which, *per se*, cannot be condemned.

Moreover, it must be remarked that these visits are not of themselves so dangerous that they ought to be generally forbidden; for good young couples do visit one another without committing sin, being assisted by divine grace, which cannot be wanting to them in a matter both legitimate and suitable, such as is that of wishing to know one another before entering into matrimony. It is true that those who are bad, sin on the occasion of such visits; but such persons sin on all occasions. They sin when conversing with females on matters of business, or on the ordinary concerns of life; they sin in walking through the streets; they sin in the Churches; they sin even in solitude.

However, the Parish Priest must earnestly recommend parents to be very vigilant on the occasions of such visits, and to insist that they take place under due prudential restraints. Let them exercise great vigilance, so that the conduct of the young people may be in accordance with the strictest propriety; and to this end, they must have them always within range of their own observation. Let them, moreover, insist that the visits be regulated by a due regard to prudence, so that they be not extended over a period of several years or months, or be of daily occurrence, or too protracted; for in such cases it could not be presumed that divine grace would assist the young people, inasmuch as they were pursuing a course of conduct neither necessary nor suitable, and which, from this very fact, would become extremely dangerous.

Wherefore, as we have already remarked elsewhere (p. 72), those free evening parties should not be tolerated which are customary especially in towns and villages, where young men are in the habit of making love to young women, even for years and years, under the pretext, or even with a vague hope of marriage. Such *reunions* are a source of innumerable sins, an occasion of grave disorders, a real plague in a parish, and a cause of damnation to those imprudent parents who permit them. The only visits to be tolerated are those which are prudent with regard to frequency, which are moderate in their duration, which take place under the supervision of prudent and cautious parents, and which are necessary, in order that the young people may come to know each other before entering into the indissoluble bonds of matrimony.

§ 11. OF THE FITNESS OF INSTRUCTING THE PEOPLE ON THE EXCELLENCE AND MERIT OF VIRGINITY AND PERFECT CONTINENCE.

The Parish Priest must not content himself with merely preaching frequently and earnestly against the most baneful of all the vices; he must also remember the most beautiful of the virtues, and tell its praises to his people, so that many may become enamoured of it, may be induced to practise it, and may glory in the practice. This is the virtue of virginity and perfect continence, the excellence of which, owing to a most lamentable prejudice, is too rarely brought under the notice of the people. This prejudice consists in regarding perfect continence as a virtue so difficult to practise, that no one ought to aspire to it without a special vocation from God; and in looking upon it, in consequence, as a something peculiar to priests, to monks, and to nuns. Certain preachers and catechists, under the influence of this prejudice, never speak of the excellence and value of this virtue. It seems to them something so sublime, that it surpasses and exceeds the capacity and strength of ordinary persons, and of all who live in the midst of the world. Just as it would seem out of place to explain from the pulpit the theories of mystic theology, and to bewilder the people with its hidden divine communications, so it seems to them altogether unsuitable to describe the excellence of perfect chastity, and to inspire the people with a love of it. And so profound, in fact, is the silence which they observe with respect to this virtue, that one would imagine they wished to apply to it the *nec nominetur in nobis* which Saint Paul inculcated with regard to vice. (Ephes. v. 3.)

This prejudice is in direct opposition to the teaching of Holy Writ, and especially of Saint Paul, who, in a general way, counsels perfect continence to all christians: *volo enim omnes vos esse sicut me ipsum* (1 Cor. vii. 7). It is contrary to the sentiment of the holy Fathers, who, when explaining the text of the Gospel—*non omnes capiunt, verbum istud*—

unanimously explain it to mean that *non omnes capiunt, quia nolunt capere* (see Corn. a Lapide on this passage). It is contrary to the experience of all ages, which shows us that there have ever been in the church virgins and celibates in great numbers, who, as secular in the midst of the world, led spotless lives.

To remove this prejudice, it will be enough to observe that celibacy or perfect continence is a virtue which, though not commanded, at least one half of the human race must profess to observe through necessity. This is a proposition which astonishes at first sight, and seems paradoxical, but it is nevertheless a palpable truth. As a matter of fact, putting out of our reckoning children not yet arrived at puberty, whom we are willing to regard as free from temptation, let us see how many there are who are bound to perfect continence. All girls are bound to it, as a general rule, up to their eighteenth or twentieth year, or even for a longer period; and young men are bound to it up to their twenty-fifth, or thirtieth year, or even longer still; because, as a rule, neither women nor men have the opportunity or the possibility of getting married before the ages mentioned. Then again, men of even more mature years are forced to observe continence, either because they are serving in the army, or because their income is not sufficient to maintain a family, or because for several other reasons they are unable to marry. Many young women are similarly situated, either because of absolute poverty, or from corporal defects, or from the operation of various other causes. It is evident, then, that very many persons of both sexes are necessarily compelled to grow old in the state of celibacy. In addition to those named, there are, moreover, many in a state of widowhood, who cannot get married a second or a third time. All these whom I have mentioned are bound to observe perfect continence, and they constitute a class so numerous, that it is evident they comprise more than one-half of those who have attained to puberty.

However, should anyone be still inclined to dispute the fact, he may be enlightened by the census of the Province of Genoa, taken on the 31st December, 1857. The total population amounted to 313,402 individuals. Of these there were 102,962 married, while the celibates and those in the state of widowhood amounted to 210,610—that is to say, more than two-thirds were actually obliged to observe perfect continence. From these figures we ought to subtract those who had not reached the age of puberty, the number of whom is not given in the Census Tables; but it is easy to understand that the boys under fourteen years and the girls under twelve cannot amount to a third of the population. Therefore there is not the slightest doubt that those obliged to observe perfect continence constitute more than half of the adult population; and, consequently, as a matter of fact, more than half the population is obliged to practise this virtue of perfect continence, and to practise it, as we know, under pain of mortal sin and of eternal damnation.

Well then, can it be said that a virtue, from which, as a matter of fact, so large a percentage of the population cannot be dispensed, nay, which seculars, living in the midst of the world and all its seductions, find themselves bound to practise under a penalty so terrible, is so difficult that it cannot be preserved without a special vocation from God? Can it be called a virtue peculiar to priests, to monks, and to nuns? If this were true, what should we say of the goodness and the Providence of God? Could He, under pain of mortal sin and eternal damnation, exact from more than half the human race the observance of a virtue, which could scarcely be practised by a few specially chosen souls? This reflection will suffice to remove the prejudice of which we have spoken, and to persuade every one that perfect continence is a virtue which whosoever pleases may observe, provided he seeks the assistance of God's grace, which is given to all who ask it, and employs those means which are necessary for the preservation of continence, and which are familiar to every Parish Priest.

Having removed this very injurious prejudice, I would next point out that preachers, and especially Parish Priests, ought, for two reasons, to instruct the people regarding the excellence of virginity and perfect continence. The first is, that all those who, from personal or family motives, are prevented from entering the marriage state, may make a virtue of necessity, and preserve continence undefiled of their own free will, and in such manner that it may prove meritorious. The second reason is, that the number of those who would voluntarily select this state may be increased—a matter to be most earnestly desired, since it is from the soil of virginity and perfect continence that those plants spring forth which are most valuable, and which produce the best fruit for the church and for society.

It is from among young men who embrace this happy state that, of necessity, recruits are drawn for the ranks of the secular and regular priesthood, who attend to the sanctification of the faithful, and furnish those missionaries who carry the true faith to the Gentiles. There is no doubt that it is most desirable to swell the ranks of the priesthood, considering the necessity that exists at the present day for zealous ministers of God, to oppose a barrier to the impiety which everywhere inundates the world; and it is likewise most desirable that apostolic men be multiplied, to spread the light of the Gospel through those many nations which still sit in darkness and the shadow of death, especially in the present age when, owing to increased facilities of communication, this object can be effected much more easily than in times past.

Those of the laity also who more usually consecrate their lives and property to the service of the Church and of society are always to be found in the ranks of the celibates, who, not being obliged to trouble themselves with family cares, concentrate their thoughts instead on the spiritual and temporal interests of Humanity.

It is of almost equal importance that the love of holy virginity should be fostered amongst young maidens likewise, since in our times they are called by Providence to a kind of priestly office, and to a real apostolate unknown to all the ages past. It is true that in the past there flourished very many congregations of holy virgins, the fragrance of whose virtues made heaven rejoice, and sanctified the earth; yet these, however, attended solely to the attainment of their own salvation. But in our times, when rampant infidelity and unbridled moral corruption have almost legalised wickedness, God, Who to the greater confusion of His enemies and the exaltation of His own Omnipotence opposes them by means which, naturally, are most inadequate, has raised up an army of pious virgins, who, flying from the mad and wicked world, and fired with the courage of heroes, wage a holy war; combating vice and promoting virtue in schools, academies, and hospitals without number, in prisons and convict establishments, on the battlefield, in the foreign missions among the heathen in every quarter of the globe; in one place planting, in another reviving, in another strengthening, the faith of Christ, among people who are filled with admiration on beholding such intrepidity in a sex so weak. Nor can I be accused of exaggeration when I call them *an army*, seeing that in France alone these new heroines number nearly three hundred thousand. The congregations and institutes of these sisters, who are as it were priestesses and real apostles, are multiplying wonderfully from day to day; and so great is the harvest which they have to reap that they always have need of additional workers, and therefore welcome indifferently the rich and the poor, praying that many may be inspired to join them, even with no other dowry than a good disposition.

And still more consoling is it to perceive that this apostolic spirit is spreading also amongst young women who remain in the world in the midst of their families, and who organise here and there pious unions of truly wise virgins, who, not content with keeping their own lamps replenished and lighted, wake up their sisters who are slumbering, lest their lamps may be extinguished, or may be found untrimmed when the heavenly spouse shall call them. Such young women possess a spirit of burning zeal which produces immense good in their own families, and in their entire neighbourhood, where they make true piety flourish in various ways.

Nothing of all this good could be effected without an esteem and a love for holy Virginity, coupled with a resolution to preserve it. Wherefore the ministers of the Lord, and especially Parish Priests, ought to speak to the people with great zeal and earnestness of the angelic excellence of this virtue, so that very many young people of both sexes may become enamoured of it, and, renouncing the vanities of the world, choose it for their portion; thus fitting themselves to fill the places of those who from time to time fall asleep in the Lord, and to swell the ranks of those who survive, as the daily increasing need for such services requires.

To this end it will be well that, in addition to preaching, the Parish Priest should circulate among the members of his flock good books, setting forth the excellence of this virtue, and calculated to inspire young people of both sexes with a love of it. It was thus that the ancient Fathers acted, in imitation of the example of St. Paul who wrote "*volo enim omnes vos esse sicut me ipsum.*" (1 Cor. vii. 7.) All of them warmly exhorted Christians to embrace a state of perfect continence, and the most illustrious among them wrote books for the express purpose that where their voice could not reach, their writings might proclaim the praises of this beautiful virtue. This was done by St. Cyprian, by St. Gregory Nazianzen, by St. Jerome, by St. Augustine, by St. Ambrose, and others. When we reflect on all this, we see still more clearly how deplorable and culpable is the practice of remaining silent on the subject of this virtue.

However, the most effectual means to excite in young people the love of holy virginity is not to be found in sermons, or in books, but in the frequent reception of the most Holy Eucharist. This "corn of the elect," this "wine springing forth virgins" (Zach. ix. 17) renders everything that is sensual so insipid and nauseous to the soul, that young persons who communicate frequently, experience such a sweet attraction towards holy virginity, without knowing how or why, that they cannot be lured away from it.

I have a very long and constant experience of this fact. Young people who persevere in frequently receiving the Holy Communion will not listen to the subject of matrimony. The blind world thinks them deluded and bewitched, but it is all the while only the effect of the Blessed Eucharist, which frees them from every illusion and snare of the flesh. Let us multiply the communions of the young, and we shall multiply virgins.

And since this is a matter of paramount importance, I must not omit to solve a difficulty which might easily present itself. This is that St. Philip Neri wished young boys to confess frequently, but to communicate rarely. The authority of the Saint, were we to understand him as laying down a general rule without exception, might deter some one, not only from promoting, but even from permitting frequent communion among young boys. It must be observed, then, that the Saint spoke of young boys in general, most of whom, unfortunately, through thoughtlessness, through levity of disposition, and also through bad and vicious habits, are not disposed to receive the Holy Communion very frequently. But I am speaking, on the other hand, of those good pious youths, regarding whom we may conclude that they approach the Lord's Table with due respect and suitable dispositions, even though they may not be exempt from certain defects belonging to their time of life, and which one ought to condone precisely because they are natural to their age.

Among young people of both sexes we find some

endowed with good dispositions, some simple souls, some pliable hearts, especially those who have been brought up in the holy fear of God, and who from their earliest years have conceived a great love for piety and a great horror for sin ; and if these be properly directed they turn out extremely well. Young persons of this class may approach the Holy Communion very frequently, without risk of profaning or abusing it. These young people, constantly nourished with the Bread of Angels, will become angels upon earth, and will swell the great train of the Lamb, whom virgins follow whithersoever He goes —" *Quocumque tendit virgines sequuntur* ". I have been taught the truth of this, I repeat, by very long experience. I would wish that a trial of it were made by new Parish Priests, and likewise by all confessors, who can effect almost as much as Parish Priests in increasing the number of those who cultivate holy virginity.

§ 12. OF LENTEN COURSES, MISSIONS AND RETREATS.

Preaching is a personal obligation imposed upon the Parish Priest, so that, except when lawfully prevented, he must not discharge it by deputy. This, however, must be understood of the ordinary preaching on Sundays and Festivals; for it is very advisable that, from time to time, he should give his people an opportunity of hearing a strange preacher. This is of advantage in order to bring within the influence of

God's word some rather negligent persons, who do not go to hear their own Parish Priest, either because he fails to please them, or because they love novelty even in the matter of preachers; and it is furthermore of advantage, because a stranger produces a greater impression, inasmuch as he fixes the attention of the audience better.

If the Parish can meet the expense of a course of Lenten Sermons, at least on the Sundays, it would be of great importance that the Parish Priest should procure this advantage for his flock. The Lenten preacher, in addition to the good effected by his sermons, will confer another benefit upon the Parish at Easter time, by hearing confessions. In small places, where there are only a few priests, who know, and are known to everybody, it may easily happen that some persons will be found who are ashamed to confess to them, and who, consequently, allow themselves to be tempted by the Devil to conceal sins in confession; but if the strange priest who preached the Lenten Course be in the parish, even for a few days, at Easter time, they will readily make a full and entire confession to him, since he knows nobody.

The Parish Priest ought be careful, however, to secure a preacher endowed with sufficient learning, who will announce the word of God with fervour, and who will be moreover, a man of piety. Otherwise but little fruit could be expected from his sermons, and his assistance in the confessional, likewise, would not be a matter to be desired.

Of far greater importance, still, are Missions and

Retreats, since on these occasions many souls are roused from the sleep of sin, who, otherwise, would have continued in it, notwithstanding the sermons of the Parish Priest and of the Lenten preacher. It is a fact that a Mission never takes place which does not effect the conversion of many, or a Retreat which does not result in the conversion of some at least; and for this reason zealous Parish Priests are accustomed to have a Retreat in their parish every year, and a Mission from time to time—say every twelve or fifteen years.

The good effected by Missions, if no other proof of it existed, would be abundantly demonstrated by the fact, that, whenever a Mission is proposed, the project meets with opposition from the worst characters in the parish. Wherefore it seems incredible that there are some Parish Priests, who not only show themselves indifferent and cold with regard to a work so excellent, but even sometimes, when good people are anxious to forward it, offer opposition to such an extent, that the Bishop has to interpose his authority to make them accept a Mission. These Pastors are accustomed to allege, in defence of their wrongheadedness, that Missions disturb and unsettle the consciences of the people. Now it is possible that there may be some so simple as to put forward this excuse or pretext in all sincerity; but, on the other hand, there are occasionally grounds for suspecting that some Parish Priests may have another more cogent motive, which would redound but little to their credit. In fact, we need not be afraid of incurring the guilt of judging rashly, if we say, that a Parish Priest who is opposed to Missions, is either very stupid or very bad.

As regards Retreats, it is well that they should be given once a year; and if in poor country parishes it should not be possible to procure a competent preacher, zealous Parish Priests, rather than omit the Retreat, might assist one another by giving from time to time a course of spiritual exercises, each in the other's parish. In this manner, in addition to the advantages arising from the sermons, there would be secured the further advantage of having a strange confessor, for the benefit of those who may be ashamed to confess certain sins to the Parish Priest, or to any other priest of the parish.

And here I must caution new Parish Priests against a prejudice, which has great weight with some—namely, that if a Retreat be given every year, it makes but a slight impression upon the parishioners, and does not produce much fruit. In truth, if the principal fruit to be derived from a Retreat were to consist in producing great religious excitement in the parish, there is no doubt that the more rarely one takes place, the greater will be the excitement. In fact we see that where a Retreat has not been given for a very great number of years, it produces far more excitement than in parishes where it is an annual occurrence. But since the real benefit of a Retreat does not by any means consist in this religious excitement, but in the conversion of sinners, and since no year passes in which there will not be souls who stand in need of conversion, the satisfaction of seeing a great religious revival amongst the people every ten or twenty years, must be sacrificed to the consolation of witnessing a certain number of sinners converted every year, through the instrumentality of the spiritual exercises.

CHAPTER XV.

OF VARIOUS DUTIES REGARDING THE TEMPORALITIES OF THE PARISH.

SINCE in this world everything spiritual requires, to some extent, material support (as a matter of fact, the very dogmas of faith require paper, on which they may be written and transmitted without change to posterity, and even the sacraments require some of them water, some bread, some oil, and so forth), though the office of Parish Priest is of itself purely spiritual and entirely directed to the eternal salvation of souls, nevertheless it has need of several things which are in themselves material, but on which his spiritual functions in many ways lean for support; and, consequently, the Parish Priest has various duties to discharge with regard to these material interests.

§ 1. OF THE PAROCHIAL REVENUES.

Some of the revenues of a parish are fixed and others variable. Of the fixed revenues, some are derived from lands and tenements, others from rents, annuities, and so forth. The Parish Priest must be careful to preserve them all in their integrity, so that his successors may not be injured by any action of his.

Wherefore, though a Parish Priest might personally be willing to renounce some portion of his income, it would never be lawful for him to do so to the prejudice of his successors, through leaving the property of the benefice so circumstanced, that they would be unable to exact some portion of their income, or could not exact it in its entirety without considerable difficulty. It sometimes happens that Parish Priests, rather than undergo the annoyance of legal proceedings, are prepared to renounce some source of parochial income. Now, so far as they are personally concerned, it would be quite within their power to make such renunciation, but it is by no means within their power to do so in so far as it may affect their successors; and, therefore, they are bound to adopt every means, no matter how troublesome, which may be necessary to maintain the integrity of the revenues, appertaining to their Benefice.

As regards lands and tenements, it is of the utmost importance that they should be maintained in good condition by the Parish Priest, so that they may not pass to his successor almost destroyed, or greatly deteriorated. Some Parish Priests draw from such property the revenue which it annually produces, whilst they entirely neglect to keep it in good condition, by omitting to make the improvements and repairs which might be necessary from time to time. It happens as a natural result, that, when the parish becomes vacant by death or resignation, the parochial property is found in a deplorable state of dilapidation, so that it can yield but little revenue, and requires a considerable outlay to put it in good condition. There is no doubt then, that a Parish Priest ought to take care of the freehold property of his parish, and maintain it in good condition, precisely as he would care and preserve it had it been his own private estate.

The variable revenue of the parish consists in the so-called "stole fees" for marriages, funerals, &c. These also are to be maintained in their integrity, so that a Parish Priest ought to require the payment of these fees even though he should not need them, or should be ready to renounce them as far as he is personally concerned. This however must be done with due discretion, as we shall point out when speaking of disinterestedness (Part III. chap. 7). Were he to remit these fees too easily, the parishioners would no longer regard the payment of them as a duty, and his successor would find it very difficult to exact them.

§ 2. OF THE PAROCHIAL ARCHIVES.

Since Parish Priests are charged with the safe custody of those records which are of the greatest importance to religious and civil society, such as are the registers of Births, Marriages and Deaths, and are furthermore the custodians of all papers containing the instructions which emanate from the Bishop from time to time, of the dispensations and privileges granted by the Holy See, of the title-deeds of the parochial property, of the books recording the foundation of masses, and of the historical records of the parish, it is quite clear that they ought to have archives, wherein all these documents may be carefully preserved, quite apart from all other books and papers which may belong to them.

Since the preservation of these documents is of such great importance, the place in which they are deposited ought invariably to be kept locked, and the Parish Priest should not allow any one to have access to it, unless it be some one who possesses his entire confidence.

It occasionally happens that persons who are either perfect strangers, or who are not sufficiently trustworthy, ask for some of the parochial books in order to institute a search for some matter in which they are personally interested; and, should this search happen to be somewhat protracted, the Parish Priest, not having patience to superintend it, gives the books over altogether into the hands of these persons. It is evident that, under such circumstances, they would have a most favourable opportunity of making erasures or alterations of the most serious consequence. Wherefore, in cases of this kind, the Parish Priest ought either to examine the books himself, or, should he permit the persons interested to do so, he ought to superintend the examination until the books are again handed back to him. The books and papers belonging to the parochial archives are a sacred deposit, not to be handed over to persons who are either unknown, or not sufficiently trustworthy.

The archives ought to be in a dry place, so that the damp may not affect the papers; they ought to be well closed, so that mice may not be able to injure them; and they ought to be placed at a safe distance from the fireplace, so that they may run no risk of being burned. It is not enough, then, that the Parish Priest guard them from fraudulent treatment at the hands of men, but he must also adopt every precaution to preserve them from accident.

Moreover, the case in which these documents are kept, ought to be reserved exclusively for the custody of the parochial books and papers; and it would be well that it should have painted upon it the words: *Parochial Archives,* so that it may always be easily distinguished from the personal property of the Parish Priest. Otherwise it might happen that, on the occasion of his death, his heirs might look upon it as an article of furniture, forming a portion of the inheritance, and, taking possession of it on this title, might fling the papers into a heap in some corner of the parochial house. The inscription mentioned above will prevent any usurpation of this kind.

The Parish Priest should also be very careful never to leave any parochial books or papers lying loose outside the archives; because, in the event of his death, and especially should he die unexpectedly, his heirs, more particularly if ignorant people, might possess themselves of these books and papers, in common with other books and papers which were the private property of the Parish Priest, and destroy them or sell them as waste paper, as has sometimes occurred. Moreover it must be borne in mind that when the parochial books or papers are left outside the archives, there is always danger that they may be lost or stolen. Wherefore, whenever the Parish Priest has occasion to take them out of the archives, he ought to be careful to put them back again when he has done with them.

§ 3. OF THE MANNER OF KEEPING THE PAROCHIAL BOOKS AND OF AN INVENTORY.

In addition to the register of births, marriages, and deaths, the Parish Priest ought to keep also a register of the persons confirmed, another of legacies left for masses, and finally a *liber status animarum*.

The registers of births, marriages and deaths in particular ought to be made of very strong paper, because they are supposed to be preserved for centuries. These books, moreover, ought to be written in very distinct characters, and with such precision that no particular ought to be omitted which they are expected to contain. Furthermore, the entries ought to be made in them out of hand; and it is a very grave irregularity to note the entries in the first instance on stray sheets of paper, with the intention of afterwards transferring them to the proper Register. These stray leaves may easily get lost, and so the entries that had been made on them are never registered.

In the book recording the legacies left for Masses, the Parish Priest ought, each year, to record the discharge of the obligation regarding them. In the *liber status animarum* he ought to note down such observations as may prove useful to him in the government of the parish, unless he should happen to have a special book for this purpose.

The Parish Priest ought also to keep in the archives an exact statement of all the freehold properties belonging to his benefice, of its boundaries, and of the revenues derived from it, distinguishing the revenues allotted for the support of the pastor from those destined for the maintenance of the fabric. In the same manner he should have an accurate statement of the revenue derivable from rents, tithes, &c.

He should likewise have an inventory of all articles of value belonging to his church, so that in the event of a vacancy in the parish, they may not be abstracted, or, should this happen, that his successor may be in a position to demand an account of them from the person who had them in charge during the vacancy.[1]

---

[1] Regarding the inventory of church property in each parish, the Irish Bishops, assembled in Synod at Maynooth, passed the following decree: "Præcipimus omnibus parochis, aut parœciarum administris, necnon locorum piorum quæ ab episcopis pendent curatoribus, ut statim post publicationem hujus concilii constitutionum, bonorum, tam mobilium, quam immobilium, quæ ad ecclesias suas vel parœcias, vel ad loca pia prædicta spectent, inventarium conficiant. In hoc inventario diligenter vasa sacra, sacramque omnem suppellectilem, quæ in suis ecclesiis existat, describent; si quæ sint prædia ecclesiæ, si domus aut scholæ parochiales, si redditus denique permanentes, eos omnes recensebunt. Onera autem non omittant quibus ecclesia vel loca pia subjiciuntur. Confecto inventario singularum ecclesiarum et locorum piorum, unum exemplar, a parocho vel ab alio ad quem spectat subscriptum, episcopo Diœcesis mittetur ab eo in archivo episcopali custodiendum; alterum penes ipsam ecclesiam de qua agitur in loco tuto asservabitur." (Decret xxix. art. 271, 272.)—*Translator.*

PART II.

OF THE SACRAMENTS.[1]

CHAPTER I.

OF THE SACRAMENTS OF BAPTISM AND CONFIRMATION.

§ 1. OF THE BAPTISTERY.

IT is scarcely necessary to observe that the Parish Priest ought to see that the baptistery is of the proper form, as prescribed by the sacred rites, and also by

---

[1] I would here take the liberty of remarking that no English-speaking priest who wishes for a safe practical guide in all that concerns the administration of the sacraments, should be unprovided with the admirable work entitled *Notes on the Rubrics of the Roman Ritual regarding the Sacraments in general, Baptism, the Eucharist, and Extreme Unction,* by the late Rev. James O'Kane, Senior Dean, St. Patrick's College, Maynooth. Here will be found discussed all those difficulties which in English-speaking countries often perplex priests, and stand in the way of the strict observance of the rubrics. The extrinsic authority of Fr. O'Kane's book is very great; for having been examined by the *Congregation of Rites,* it was pronounced *Vere commendabile et accuratissimum opus* in a decree dated Feb. 14, 1868.—*Translator.*

synodical decrees, and by the Bishop of the Diocese.¹ He must see that it be kept clean, decent, and suitably decorated, as befits the most sacred thing in the church, after the altar. If the Church Committee have made no provision for this, the Parish Priest himself ought by all means to do so, asking help for this purpose from his parishioners, and, if necessary, contributing a portion of his own revenue to defray the expense. A shabby baptistery is one of these things which are least tolerable in a church, and it affords one of the clearest proofs we could have that the Parish Priest is an indolent man possessed of little faith.

He ought also to bestow care on the preservation and purity of the Baptismal water, of the holy

[1] On this subject DE HERDT writes as follows: "Locus in quo fons baptismalis ponitur, esse debet decens, mundus, et convenienter ornatus cum imagine S. Joannis christum baptizantis, vel columba spiritum sanctum repræsentantis, vel etiam cum altari S. Joanni dedicato, ubi commode fieri potest. Baptisterium seu fons baptismalis debet esse in decenti forma; ex materia solida, ut marmore aliove lapide polito, quæ aquam bene contineat; decenter ornatus et cancellis circumseptus; decoro operculo tectus, sera et clave munitus, nisi ipse locus semper et bene clausus sit; atque ita observatus, ut pulvis, insecta vel aliæ sordes non penetrent. Si fons sit æneus, stanno fusili ab interiori parte sit illitus, ne aqua ærugine inficiatur. Oportet ut binæ sint claves, a parocho vel ejus vicario servandæ. Ipse fons in duas partes dividi potest, quarum una aquam baptismalem continet, et altera vacua, in quam aqua e capite defluit, et in cujus fundo parvus est canalis, per quem aqua in sacrarium decurrit; vel juxta fontem, a parte qua infans sub baptismo tenetur, in eadem circiter altitudine, parva statui potest piscina ad modum pelvis, in quam aqua e capite defluens excipitur, et in qua similiter parvus est canalis, per quem aqua in sacrarium defluit (Sac. Liturg. Praxis, tom 3, n. 154).—*Translator.*

SACRAMENTS OF BAPTISM AND CONFIRMATION. 253

oil and chrism, and of the vessels set apart for containing them; and he should likewise see that the *vestis candida* be kept really clean, because, owing to grave negligence, it is sometimes found in a condition which contradicts its name.

§ 2. OF THE BAPTISM OF CHILDREN IN DANGER OF DEATH.

The Parish Priest must not forget to teach his people how to administer Baptism in case of necessity; and he must teach them this frequently, not only when explaining to them the doctrine regarding this sacrament, which ordinarily cannot occur except at long intervals, but also when teaching the Catechism aloud to the children, in the manner mentioned in a preceding chapter (see p. 197). He must return repeatedly to this point, and ask the children how they would proceed to act, should it become necessary for any one of them to baptise a dying infant. This instruction is of paramount importance, in order that the parishioners may frequently hear how this Sacrament is to be administered in case of necessity. It is generally taken for granted that everybody knows how to administer Baptism in case of necessity, and yet ignorant persons are liable to commit most serious mistakes in this matter. Thus, they might pour the water on the head of the infant saying merely: *In the name of the Father, and of the Son, and of the Holy Ghost,* omitting altogether the words: *I baptise thee;* or sometimes, instead of pouring the water, they might content themselves with dipping into it the tips of their fingers, and then making the sign of the cross with them upon the child.[1]

When Baptism has been administered privately in case of necessity, and the child is afterwards taken to the church that the ceremonies may be supplied, the Parish Priest ought to interrogate *directly* the person who has administered it, in order to discover whether it ought to be repeated conditionally, or at all. He cannot place full reliance in information supplied to him on this subject at second hand, especially if the informants were not present at the ceremony; and even if they had been present, he cannot put absolute trust in their evidence, unless they should happen to be very intelligent persons. Experience has taught me that this is a matter of great importance, and that if I had acted blindly upon the information supplied to me at second hand,

---

[1] Almost everything of importance regarding this matter is briefly and fully summed up in the 16th Decree (n. 9) of the first Synod of Westminster, in the following words:—" Since Catholic mothers are frequently attended by surgeons or midwives, who are not Catholics, and who care nothing about the baptism of infants in danger of death, the faithful of both sexes must be carefully instructed, as to the manner of baptising in case of necessity, as it is called; that no child depart this life without the saving bath of regeneration. Should the child recover, it must be brought to the church, that the ceremonies may be supplied. Let the priest, however, inquire diligently how the baptism was administered, and in coming to a decision on the case, let him incline to the safer side; and if he think proper, let him not hesitate to baptise conditionally."—*Translator.*

I should sometimes have committed grave mistakes. Wherefore let the Parish Priest adopt the custom, and introduce it where it may not already exist, of asking the person who has baptised the infant to give an account of the manner in which the ceremony was performed. When it is the custom to ask this information from everybody without distinction, no one in particular can take offence at it; the more so if the Parish Priest states in public the reason for requiring this information, and explains to the people how wrong it would be, on the one hand, unnecessarily to repeat the ceremony of baptism even conditionally, and, on the other hand, how great the risk of not repeating it, should cause for doing so exist.

The Parish Priest ought furthermore to take care that when an infant survives after having received private baptism, because of the danger of death, it shall be afterwards taken to the church for the purpose of having the ceremonies supplied in accordance with ecclesiastical law; and it must be borne in mind that, should any unnecessary delay occur in complying with this law, the child may again relapse into its former dangerous condition, and may actually die before the ceremonies have been supplied.

The Parish Priest ought also to make known to his people in his public instructions, that if the danger of death be not immediate, lay persons ought not themselves to baptise the infant, but should summon the Parish Priest, who, when called for such a purpose, ought to attend without a moment's delay.[1] However, there is no need to be over-scrupulous on this point, for it will be a lesser harm that a lay person should administer baptism, than to run the risk of allowing the infant to die unbaptised through waiting for the priest. Therefore let him preach absolutely that when the life of the child is believed to be in danger, baptism ought to be administered by anyone who may happen to be present; but that should the child be merely sick, and not actually in a dying condition, the Parish Priest ought to be summoned to perform the ceremony. And since an accident is always possible, let him caution the people that, while awaiting the arrival of the Parish Priest, some one should remain constantly with the

[1] "When a priest is called on to baptise in a case of necessity, in a private house or in any other place than the church, it is certain that he is not allowed to perform any of the ceremonies which precede the application of the matter and form, even though there be no danger of the infant's death until all the ceremonies could be completed. He should vest in a white stole, and after pouring on the water, apply the ceremonies which follow, leaving those that precede, and for which the violet stole is worn, to be afterwards supplied in the church. This has been expressly decided by the Sacred Congregation, 23 Sept. 1820." (O'Kane's Notes on the Rubrics, n. 382).

A question might arise whether this rule holds in Ireland where, as we shall see presently, baptism is permitted to be administered solemnly in private houses, under certain circumstances. O'Kane remarks that in certain Dioceses, as for example in those of the province of Dublin, the observance of the Decree of the Congregation of Rites (23rd Sept., 1820) quoted above is strictly enjoined, notwithstanding the Irish custom which had already been sanctioned by the Synod of Thurles, and he concludes thus: " wherever, then, in Ireland, the old custom has been thus ex-child, having water at hand, so as to be ready at any moment to administer baptism, should the infant begin to fail more quickly than was expected.

§ 3. OF THE CARE WITH WHICH A PARISH PRIEST OUGHT TO IMPRESS UPON HIS PEOPLE NOT TO DEFER THE BAPTISM OF THEIR CHILDREN.

The Parish Priest ought to inculcate frequently in his instructions that it is extremely dangerous to defer the administration of this Sacrament, which is of the very first necessity; and, on becoming aware of the birth of an infant in his parish, should he observe that the parents allow several days to pass by without presenting it for baptism, he ought to request them to do so without further delay.

Wherefore, to guard against any unforeseen acci-

pressly abolished (as in the Province of Dublin) the Priest, when required to baptise outside the church, must adhere to the present rubrics, omitting the ceremonies that precede baptism, and using common water when he cannot get water from the font" (n. 397). However the Synod of Maynooth, which was held after the publication of O'Kane's work, would seem to extend this rule *to all Ireland;* for when treating of baptism administered by a priest in private houses in case of necessity, it expressly directs that the ceremonies which *follow* the ablution should be immediately applied, in *compliance with the decree of the Cong. of Rites;* from which we may lawfully infer that those which *precede* the ablution are to be omitted, in accordance with the same decree. The following are the words of the Synod: "Ex decreto vero Sac. Cong. Rituum Sep. 23, 1820, cum sacerdos in casu necessitatis infantem privatim baptizat, ceremoniæ quæ subsequuntur ablutionem, scilicet, chrismatio, traditio vestis candidæ, atque lampadis ardentis statim post ablutionem adhibendæ sunt" (Decret xi., de Baptismo, 33)—*Translator.*

dent, he should be careful not to grant permission to parents to defer the baptism of their children beyond three days, even though the child should be strong and nursed with care. For if it once become known in the parish that the Parish Priest is indulgent in a matter involving such risk, the people will lose that salutary feeling which they have regarding the risk itself, and they will venture to defer the baptism of their children for motives of family convenience, or even through mere caprice. Moreover, if the Parish Priest permits a delay of four, five, or six days, in the case of parents whom he knows to be cautious, he can no longer refuse the same indulgence to those whose care and anxiety he has reason to doubt; for he cannot say to them: I am unable to place the same reliance in you that I place in some others of my parishioners.

It is very true that if the parents be unwilling to bring the infant to the church within three days, the Parish Priest has no means of compelling them to do so. However, he will find it of advantage to be in a position to say: I do not permit any delay beyond three days, because I would be afraid to burden my conscience with the risk of doing so; and thus it will become known that those who defer the baptism of their children beyond this limit will incur his formal disapprobation. By adopting this system, he will prevent the introduction into his parish of a custom which might prove fatal to the eternal Salvation of some child; and he will gradually succeed in abolishing the custom, should he find it already established.

SACRAMENTS OF BAPTISM AND CONFIRMATION. 259

Should the parents, through extreme carelessness or want of faith, defer the baptism beyond eight days, and should they manifest no intention of bringing the child to the church immediately, the Parish Priest ought to inform the Bishop of the fact, that he may interpose his authority to avert the danger. As there are usually some diocesan regulations respecting cases of this kind, the Parish Priest ought to conform to them.

Now-a-days there are some fathers so irreligious that they leave their children unbaptised for an indefinite period, and even for years; and there are some others who, having embraced some heretical sect, get their children baptised by their minister, thus leaving the validity of the Sacrament extremely doubtful. In case the infant has been baptised by a heretical minister, let the Parish Priest, if possible, persuade the mother to take it secretly to the church and have it baptised conditionally. Should he find any other relative, or some person in the service of the family, willing to assist in this holy work, the Parish Priest, to avoid acting with imprudence, ought to consult the Bishop, or at least some prudent and learned ecclesiastic, before taking any steps in the matter. However, should the child be really in danger of death, and no time left for deliberation, the pastor ought to exhort any one who has the opportunity to administer baptism, of course, conditionally, in case the ceremony had already been performed by the Protestant minister.

§ 4. OF THE CIRCUMSTANCES UNDER WHICH THE PARISH PRIEST OUGHT TO SEEK PERMISSION FROM THE BISHOP TO BAPTISE IN PRIVATE HOUSES.

In some dioceses Parish Priests often ask and obtain from the bishop permission to administer Baptism privately, either because of the absence of the child's father, or of one of the sponsors, or for some other like motive of convenience. Nevertheless, if we consult theologians, we shall find that there is *one only* case allowed in which Baptism may be administered privately in the house, and this is the case of *necessity*, when the infant cannot be taken to the church without exposing it to personal danger. Outside this case of necessity, theologians do not admit any other reason or motive from separating the Sacrament from its solemn administration.

All the sacraments have their own proper rites or ceremonies with which they are administered, as prescribed by the church; and so ancient are these rites that their origin is unknown to us, so that we may refer them, at least in their substance, to the Apostolic age. No theologian has ever even hinted that these ceremonies may be omitted in the administration of the sacraments, for reasons of mere convenience; or that it is within the power of the Bishop to sanction the separation of a sacrament from the rites prescribed in its administration. To administer baptism without its solemn ceremonies would be substantially the same as to consecrate and receive the sacred species without saying mass; for, as a matter of fact, the mass is but a ceremonial rite which accompanies the holy sacrifice. I repeat, then, that necessity, and *necessity alone* justifies the omission of the ceremonies. Wherefore it would seem almost a lesser evil to administer baptism in a private house solemnly and with all its ceremonies, even though in violation of the canons, than to administer the sacrament apart from its ceremonies; for the ecclesiastical, apostolic ordinance which prescribes that baptism be administered with its proper rite, is a more ancient and sacred law than the other which forbids it to be administered solemnly in private houses. I have said " would almost seem a lesser evil ": because in reality this could not be done in the face of the prohibition of the canons, and the universal practice of the church, which do not permit baptism to be solemnly administered in private houses, except in the case of the children of sovereigns and princes.[1]

[1] This must be taken with considerable modifications as far as English-speaking countries are concerned. "In missionary countries, and in places where there are no baptismal fonts, special faculties are granted, in virtue of which baptism is usually administered with all the ceremonies in private houses, and the water blessed for the occasion, if there be not a supply of what has been previously blessed. During the operation of the penal laws, and until very recently, such a custom prevailed pretty generally in Ireland and England. But measures were adopted by the Synod of Thurles (De Baptismo 7° 8°) and the first Synod of Westminster (Dec. XVI. De Baptismo, n. 4) to abolish the custom wherever the provisions of the ritual regarding the place of baptism could be conveniently carried out" (O'Kane Notes on the Rubrics, 385, 386.)

The Synod of Thurles allowed the old custom to be continued in

Wherefore a Parish Priest must never ask for permission to baptise in private houses for motives of convenience, or the like. Should it happen, however, that the parents obstinately refuse to bring the infant to the church, and that it must consequently remain without baptism, the danger to which the child's salvation would be thus exposed, would con-

three cases: *(a)* in places where it could not be abolished "sine magno incommodo," of which the Bishop was to be the judge; *(b)* when the Priest baptises an infant in danger of death; *(c)* when the child's parents reside at such a distance from the church that there might be danger in bringing the infant there for baptism. The Synod of Maynooth restricted the custom still further, and does not allow Baptism to be conferred solemnly in private houses *nisi infantes ob magnam distantiam ab ecclesiis vel ob gravem aëris intemperiem ad eas tuto ferri non possint.*

The Synod of Westminster also, while prescribing the observance, generally, of the law of the Ritual, excepts the case in which baptism is administered at a station remote from the church or chapel, and visited by the Priest either at stated times or when he is called on. In such circumstances baptism is still administered with all the ceremonies "*Extra Ecclesiam*".

"The custom prevailing in the United States of America was pretty nearly the same as in England and Ireland. The decree of the first Provincial Synod of Baltimore, referring to the custom, directs that care be taken as far as possible to have the Sacrament of Baptism conferred in the church, but leaves it entirely to the Bishops and missionary priests to determine the circumstances in which such a regulation might be enforced.

"It is worthy of note that the decree, in its first form, ordered that in towns where there is a church, Baptism be administered only in the church, but was altered to its present form by direction of the Sacred Congregation. The words, which will be found with the decree in the appendix, are important as showing clearly that the Sacred Congregation is unwilling to interfere suddenly with an established usage, even when that usage is opposed to the provisions of the Rubric regarding the administration of the sacraments" (O'Kane, loc. cit. 388, 389).—*Translator.*

stitute a case of necessity, not absolute but relative, in which the Parish Priest could and ought procure permission to baptise it in the house. Baptism is a matter of real necessity for the infant: if, through its parents' fault, it cannot receive the sacrament in the church, it has a right to receive it in whatever way it can best be administered.

§ 5. OF THE SPONSORS.

The Parish Priest must observe all that is prescribed in the Ritual regarding the Sponsors; nevertheless he must be careful not to judge anyone a public sinner, so as to forbid him to fill this office, unless he has certain and notorious proof of the fact. I say *certain*, because he ought not to be influenced by stories or reports brought to him by persons who do not merit entire credit; and I say *notorious*, because though it may be known to the Parish Priest that the person selected to act as sponsor is immoral or irreligious, yet, if he be not publicly known as such, he ought to be permitted to act in that capacity.

Wherefore a sponsor ought not to be rejected merely because he has not complied with the precept of Paschal Communion, except in a place where the fact is known to all, or unless he has himself publicly boasted of it, thereby showing his contempt for the laws of the church. The Parish Priest, as a general rule, knows those who do not approach the sacraments even at Easter: but others can only form suspicions on the subject. Regarding this subject, I must refer the reader to what I shall say in the appendix, on refusing ecclesiastical burial.

§ 6. OF CONFIRMATION.

Should his parish be situated in the city where the Bishop resides, there is no necessity for recommending the Parish Priest to be careful that his parishioners have frequent opportunities of receiving the Sacrament of Confirmation; for each year the Bishop administers it to those children who are capable of receiving it, and the Parish Priest need have no other anxiety except to dispose them for its reception. Should the parish, on the other hand, be situated outside the episcopal city, he ought to be careful not to allow many years to pass without requesting the Bishop to administer to his parishioners this sacrament, which is so important in itself, and is particularly necessary in our times, when the faith of Christians is exposed to more violent temptations than in the past. He must remember, moreover, that if several years pass by without having this sacrament administered in the parish, many persons will die without having had an opportunity of receiving it. We must refer the reader to what we have already said on this subject when speaking of the episcopal visitation.

Should the Bishop happen to be engaged in administering confirmation in some neighbouring parish, a Parish Priest might avail himself of this opportunity to take there such of his own parishioners as may require to be confirmed.

If the Bishop be in the habit of going to administer this sacrament to the sick, the Parish Priest should give him timely notice, so that no one may die deprived of it.

CHAPTER II.

OF THE MOST HOLY EUCHARIST.

§ 1. OF THE ALTAR AND THE SACRED VESTMENTS.

THE Altar on which the Sacrifice of the Cross is daily renewed ought to be an object of most profound veneration to every Christian, and especially to the priest —the Pastor of souls—who ought to make it his most particular study to see that nothing is wanting to its suitable adornment.

All altars cannot pretend to be rich and splendid, especially if the churches be poor; nevertheless poverty is by no means irreconcilable with decency and neatness, and a poor altar, if tastefully fitted up and clean, is not unsuited to the sacrifice of Him who was pleased to die on Calvary, stripped of every wordly possession. Nay more, it inspires sentiments of humility, of devotion, and of love. On the other hand, it is intolerable to see certain altars broken and splintered in several places, with soiled altar cloths, with candlesticks battered and blackened, with flowers drooping, covered with dust, and one might almost say with filth. Altars of this kind speak very badly for the Parish Priest, and are a certain proof that he is a man of little faith, or of extreme carelessness.

On these altars one may see crucifixes broken, or with the figure badly fastened to the wood, torn paintings, and statues coated with dust—objects which seem to be kept there for the express purpose of frightening people away from their devotions.

What has been said of the furniture of the Altar may likewise be said of the Sacred Vestments. It is not necessary that they be always rich and magnificent: in many churches this would be impossible; but it is very necessary that they be decent, and not torn or dirty, as frequently happens in some places.

And here I must remark that no weight attaches to two excuses which are commonly put forward on this head. The first excuse is, that this inferior description of Church furniture and vestments is reserved for week-days. Now, we are quite willing to grant that it would not be right to use every day the rich vestments and ornaments which are set apart for the more solemn festivals; but it by no means follows that one may, therefore, use on week-days vestments which, through age or constant wear, are not in keeping with the decorum and the respect due to the sacred mysteries. Poverty would be admissable in the vestments and the ornaments of the altar even on the most solemn feasts; but indecency is intolerable even on week-days, since there never can be a day on which it is lawful to disrespect the most Holy Sacrament, the House of God, and sacred things.

The other excuse is, that it is not the duty of the Parish Priest but of the Church Committee to provide for wants of this kind. This is very true; and there is no doubt that the members of the Church Committee are wanting in the discharge of a most serious duty, when they fail to provide for the decent celebration of Divine Worship. Nevertheless, it is incumbent on the Parish Priest in the first instance, and more so on the Committee, to watch over the decorum of the sacred functions, and especially of whatever appertains to the celebration of the Holy Mass. Therefore should the members of the Church Committee fail in their duty, the Parish Priest is bound at any cost to see that the altar and whatever appertains to it is kept in a becoming manner; and to attain to this end, he should, when necessary, solicit alms from pious persons, and expend likewise some of his own income.

Some new Parish Priests, when they find the church furniture and the vestments in a bad condition and unfit for Divine Worship, are accustomed, if the parish be poor, to give permission to women to work on Festivals (outside the hours of Divine Worship), on condition that whatever they earn will be devoted to the purchase or repair of vestments and altar furniture. In this manner they, in a short time, make abundant provision for the wants of their Church.

However, I would not approve of the practice of those who give such permission, likewise, in cases where there is no real necessity, and cause their female parishioners to be continually working on Festivals, with a view to collecting large sums wherewith to furnish the Church in a sumptuous manner, or to conduct religious functions on a scale of great pomp. These do not seem to be matters of such necessity and importance, that because of them a Parish Priest can assume the authority to sanction labour which is strictly forbidden by the Church on Festivals.

Moreover, some account must be taken of the scandal which may indirectly arise from this practice. If the people see that the Parish Priest permits servile labour on Festivals without any urgent necessity, they will easily accustom themselves to it, they will lose that holy repugnance towards it which is felt by all good Christians, and, having once acquired the habit of working for the Church, they will afterwards begin to work for their families.

For the rest, it is worthy of remark that the precept enjoining abstinence from servile work on Festivals is also useful, nay as a general rule necessary, for the preservation of corporal health. Physicians agree in saying that, after six days of continuous labour, the body has even physical need of some repose. Wherefore Parish Priests who would permit much and sustained labour habitually on Festivals, would be wanting moreover in charity towards their parishioners.

In conclusion, I will remark that though those negligent Parish Priests deserve very great censure, who tolerate in their Churches unbecoming ornaments and furniture, and allow the sacred functions to be conducted there in a mean and beggarly fashion, yet we must not on this account bestow unqualified praise on those parish priests who, on being appointed to poor Churches, set their hearts on adorning and enriching them, and aim at carrying out functions that would be suitable in Cathedrals and Basilicas, sometimes even adopting improper means to accomplish this end, which is frequently suggested by vanity and ambition—our secret and constant foes.

§ 2. Of the Tabernacle, the Lamp, and the Sacred Vessels.

As the throne of Christ in Heaven (excuse the comparison) ought to be the most beautiful among the ornaments of Paradise, so the Tabernacle, where the same Christ dwells night and day, ought to be the most beautiful object among the ornaments of our Churches. Unless a Church be extremely poor, a little richness is desirable in the Tabernacle. Indeed it is so small that it will require but little to decorate it; and it is very consoling to see in many Churches the Tabernacle, in which the Most Holy Sacrament reposes, splendid and elegant, with its little silver door, and the interior all lined with cloth of gold, richly embroidered.

Nevertheless, not even in the tabernacle is richness an essential requisite: even in the tabernacle our Lord is satisfied with simple neatness and propriety. A small door of gilt wood and a little white silk will be enough to make it decent. And it must be borne in mind that it is not merely the tabernacle wherein the Blessed Sacrament is regularly kept that ought to be decent, but the same applies to the tabernacles of the other altars, in which the Blessed Sacrament is placed from time to time during the year, on the occasions of feasts that may be celebrated at them. And yet how many of these do we find with the door blackened, broken, and half unhinged, while on the inside they are begrimed with dust and stains!

It is furthermore the duty of the Parish Priest to take care that the lamp is always kept burning before the most Holy Sacrament.[1] Wherefore, he must see that the oil be sufficiently pure, so that the lamp may not become extinguished, especially in the long winter nights.[2] Nor could he justify his negligence in this respect by the excuse that the Church Committee had supplied oil of inferior quality; for it would be his duty to substitute good oil in its place, rather than suffer the lamp suspended before the Blessed Sacrament to remain extinguished.

---

[1] The Synod of Thurles required a lamp to be kept lighting before the Blessed Sacrament always during the day-time, but at night only in those churches where this could be done with safety. The Synod of Maynooth, however, struck out the clause, "*ubi tuto fieri potest*," and enacted as follows: "in Ecclesiis in quibus SS. Eucharistia asservatur diu et noctu una saltem lampas semper accensa colluceat". — *Translator.*

[2] Regarding the oil to be used in the lamp, O'Kane writes (n. 615): "The oil used should be Oil of Olives; but in places where it cannot easily be procured, other oil may be used. A recent decree of the Congregation of Rites (9th July, 1864) has decided the point, but requires that what is substituted be, if possible, a vegetable oil." This decree is quoted in the *Irish Ecclesiastical Record*, No. II., November, 1864. — *Translator.*

He ought also guard against the unworthy penuriousness of placing in the lamp a wick so small that it will give only the very feeblest light, and may easily go out during the night-time. I know a church where it was a rule that the wick should consist of not more than three threads of cotton. Such economy as this, is simply an insult to God, and a scandal in the eyes of men.

The Parish Priest must also take care that the chalices, patens, ciborium, and the lunette of the Remonstrance are suitably gilded. Let him be careful, likewise, that the sacred vessels are not in any way broken, insecure in the joinings, or even simply discoloured.

§ 3. OF THE HOSTS AND THE WINE FOR THE MOST HOLY EUCHARIST.

The Parish Priest must be careful that the hosts and particles to be consecrated are always fresh, since it is most unbecoming to use stale ones. Wherefore he ought never lay in a larger quantity than he knows will be sufficient for the requirements of a few days.[1]

---

[1] Though the Rubrics direct that the particles to be consecrated shall have been *recently* made, they do not determine how recently. Modern Theologians teach that the altar-bread for consecration ought not to be older than about *fifteen* days (see Scavini, Tract IX., Disp. IV., Cap. II., *De materia et forma Eucharistiæ*). Again, though the Rubrics prescribe that the consecrated species should be *frequently* renewed, they do not specify the intervals of time at which this should be done. There

He must be careful, likewise, not to consecrate such a number of particles as may be likely to last longer than a week, and, according to the direction of the Roman Pontifical, he ought to renew the Host for benediction every eight days. Negligence in these matters is one of the most convincing proofs of carelessness, or of little faith, on the part of the Parish Priest. When there is question of the matter and the species of the Most Holy Sacrament, there is question of something very far different from the candlesticks, the vestments, the tabernacle, the pyxis, and the chalice; and it is easy to understand how the very least negligence becomes intolerable when it affects the Most Holy Sacrament directly.

Here I feel called upon to offer a remark regarding those places where it is the custom to have the particles made in the house of the Parish Priest. In such places it occasionally happens that particles are consecrated which are broken, split through the centre, soiled, brown, and covered with small fragments, just as they left the hands of the Parish Priest's servant. This is most unbecoming. It also happens that in some places the particles are made so very small that they resemble wafers for sealing letters. Economy of this description, while it saves

---

is a very general custom of doing so every *eight days*, and in Ireland, at least, the renewal of the consecrated species every eight days is *obligatory*, having been commanded by the Synod of Thurles (*De Eucharistia*, n. 17), and again by the Synod of Maynooth (Decret xiii. n. 47). See O'Kane, Notes, &c., chap. xi. s. viii. — *Translator.*

but the merest trifle, is extremely sordid in a matter of such grave importance.[1]

It must also be remarked that, when purifying the pyxis, all the small detached particles ought first to be carefully removed before pouring in the wine; for, otherwise, having become moist, they will adhere to the sides of the pyxis, nor can they be removed, no matter how much one may pass the wine round the interior. The result is that, when the pyxis is dried, these particles adhere to the purifier, where, consequently, the Blessed Sacrament evidently remains. The pyxis must be carefully purified in the very same manner as the paten, and when this is done, it is not necessary to wash it with wine, which I think is nowhere prescribed.[2]

As regards the wine for the Holy Sacrifice, the Parish Priest ought to be even still more careful. He must not only see that the wine to be consecrated has no bad taste, or acidity, or sediment in it—defects which ought never to be tolerated in the wine which is to be changed into the blood of our Lord Jesus

---

[1] The Synod of Maynooth decreed as follows, regarding the matter of the Holy Sacrifice : "Maximam diligentiam adhibeant sacerdotes ut panis consecrandus sit recens, purus et albus. Hostiæ pro communione populi sint rotundæ, et non nimis parvæ. Curant episcopi ut ratio aliqua adhibeatur qua vinum sincerum pro Missæ celebratione obtineatur, utque sacerdotes nullum aliud adhibeant. Ob frequentem corruptionem tum farinæ triticeæ tum vini quæ hodie obtinet, hoc statutum rigore urgendum est" (Decret. xiii. n. 62).—*Translator.*

[2] O'Kane treats exhaustively the various methods which have been suggested for purifying the ciborium or pyxis (*Notes on the Rubrics,* n. 622).—*Translator.*

Christ; but he must be particularly careful to see that it is really the juice of the grape—a matter which must not invariably be taken for granted. There are wines made from cherries, from peaches, from apples and other fruits: there are wines manufactured by blending water with spirituous liquors and various drugs; and sometimes it is not easy to distinguish these from wine made from the grape. It is evident that if these spurious and artificial wines were used in the celebration of the Mass, the consecration would be invalid, and there would be no sacrifice. Wherefore, the Parish Priest is most strictly bound to know whence the wine is procured which is destined for altar purposes; and he ought never use any wine unless he positively knows it to be the unadulterated juice of the grape. Nor could he excuse himself by saying that he trusts the wine merchants, or that he must use the wine supplied to him by the Church-wardens. Wine merchants have not invariably very delicate consciences, especially if they suppose that the wine which they are selling is intended not for altar purposes, but for the table of the Parish Priest. The Church-wardens, on the other hand, are often unreflecting, stupid persons, who do not inquire very closely into such matters. The Parish Priest might trust the wine merchants only when he thoroughly knew them to be honest and pious men, incapable of deceiving him; and he could place reliance in the Church-wardens only when he felt quite certain that, in providing the altar wine, they were accustomed to use every possible precaution and care. For the rest, no Parish Priest will for a single instant suppose, that any consideration of economy or of human respect could possibly justify the enormous crime of consecrating invalidly, through the absence of proper matter for the Holy Sacrifice.

Therefore, those Parish Priests are guilty of a most serious neglect of duty, who do not hesitate to purchase their altar wine from hotels and taverns. Not only is it highly unbecoming to purchase it in such places, but there is moreover an evident risk of consecrating some of those various compounds of water and liquor, which are manufactured and sold under the name of wine, simply because they have the appearance of wine.

Consequently, the Parish Priest ought to take care that neither the Church-wardens nor the brothers of the Oratory give a contract for altar wine to the clerk of the church, or to an agent. This is done in some places, where a certain sum is annually furnished to these persons, with the obligation of providing altar wine for the church; and it is easy to understand that the chief concern of these ignorant and not over-scrupulous men will be to seek for the cheapest wine they can procure, in order to make a little profit on the transaction.

§ 4. OF THE DEVOTION WHICH A PARISH PRIEST OUGHT TO SHOW TOWARDS THE BLESSED SACRAMENT.

The Parish Priest is not only bound to cultivate in

his own heart a most intense devotion towards the most Holy Sacrament, but he ought likewise to manifest this devotion by outward act, for the edification of his people.

First of all he ought to manifest this devotion when celebrating Mass, which is the most holy and divine action of the priestly office. When seculars are engaged in hearing Mass, they have a very quick power of discernment, which enables them to distinguish a priest who is pious from one who is not so. If they perceive that a Priest celebrates without devotion, they immediately form an unfavourable opinion of him, nor do they consider themselves guilty thereby of a rash judgment; so much so, that this very exhibition of a want of devotion is quite enough to determine them not to select such a priest as their spiritual director.

Let the Parish Priest reflect what judgment the people will be likely to form of him, should they see him celebrate Mass in a hurried manner, utterly regardless of the rubrics, and without any appearance of gravity and recollection. I once heard a rough sailor saying to his companions: "When Father N. is at the altar he is like a mountaineer aboard ship"; meaning thereby that the priest in question had just as nice appreciation of priestly gravity and demeanour, as a mountaineer would have of a seaman's duties on board a vessel.

But the Parish Priest ought to show profound veneration towards the most Holy Sacrament, not only when he is at the altar, but also both before and after Mass. The Parish Priest is in the habit of inculcating upon seculars the obligation of duly preparing themselves for Communion: it happens, nevertheless, that some Parish Priests frequently, and perhaps habitually, before going to the altar to celebrate Mass, will remain chatting about some indifferent or useless subject, and will continue so to chat while putting on the sacred vestments, and even up to the very moment that he is leaving the Sacristy. And should no opportunity present itself of conversing with anybody, you may see him pacing up and down the Sacristy, like a man who wants to kill time until the hour arrives for going to the altar. What must seculars think of such thoughtlessness, who have been taught by this same Parish Priest that they must prepare themselves devoutly for communion? And their astonishment must be considerably increased, if they observe that the Parish Priest, on returning from the altar, has no sooner laid aside the chalice, than he resumes the useless, or at least, for the time, inopportune conversation which he had interrupted; thus acting in a manner which might lead one to suppose that he does not know where he is coming from, what duty he has just performed, and who it is that he has at that moment lodged within his breast. And greater still must be their astonishment, since they know that when he speaks to the people of the Holy Communion, he inculcates with great warmth, as he is bound to do, the necessity of thanksgiving. They must surely say to themselves: We seculars are obliged to remain for some time after Communion in devout recollection, in prayer and thanksgiving; is it possible that the Parish Priest is dispensed from this duty? These are failings which cause the faith to grow weak and cold in the hearts of the parishioners.

Here some one may ask whether we ought to censure the custom of going direct from the confessional to the altar to celebrate, and of returning again at once, after having taken off the vestments, to resume the work of hearing confessions—a practice which is common enough even with good priests.

It must be admitted that this custom does not scandalise seculars, since they suppose that the work of the confessional may supply for the preparation and thanksgiving before and after mass. But, even so, the practice cannot be approved, and cannot be positively edifying. When there happens to be a great concourse of penitents, and when the Parish Priest knows that certain persons cannot wait long, he may undoubtedly omit his preparation and thanksgiving for Mass. Whoever should hold that a Parish Priest ought on no account omit the usual preparation, and a long thanksgiving, even of half-an-hour, would require too much, and would show that he had never discharged the duties of a Pastor. When the Parish Priest has at his confessional persons, and especially poor persons, who cannot remain long in the church, whether it be a week-day or a festival, he ought not to spend much time in his preparation for, and thanksgiving after, Mass. He ought, on the contrary, to shorten both the one and the other, and dismiss his penitents expeditiously: for, should he act otherwise, after having waited some time in the church and being unable or unwilling to delay any longer, they will go away without confession, it may be in a state of sin, and will not, perhaps, return again for a considerable period.

Nor should the Parish Priest imagine that, because of shortening his preparation or thanksgiving, he will himself suffer some spiritual loss; for, in consideration of the holy and meritorious work of hearing confessions, the Lord will supply for this in some other way, and will enable him to draw for himself fervour of spirit, not only from those holy souls who have a superabundance of it, but even from the hard hearts of sinners, when He will give him grace to move them to tears of repentance. It frequently happens that we leave the confessional with a heart more inflamed with fervour, than when we rise up from prayer. Since the confessor is the channel through which Divine grace, with all its precious gifts, is conveyed to the souls of his penitents, it can never happen, if he only exercise his ministry with pure and holy intentions, that this flood of grace will flow through him without enriching himself likewise.

However, as has been already said, it would not be commendable to omit absolutely all preparation for, and thanksgiving after Mass. A brief preparation and a brief thanksgiving will not subtract any notable time from the duties of the confessional; and, consequently, to omit even this much would be a proof of carelessness which could not be justified. Wherefore, should any Parish Priests or confessors be habitually guilty of this omission, they ought to correct themselves in this respect.

The Parish Priest is also in the habit of recommending the faithful to pay frequent visits to our Lord, reposing in the tabernacle under the Eucharistic species; and it would be, therefore, becoming that he should himself be the very first to set them an example in this respect. And yet it happens in many places that the parishioners never see their Parish Priest paying a visit to the Blessed Sacrament, except on those occasions when it is publicly exposed. It is very true that the Parish Priest might be there at other times when the church is closed; but the parishioners are not disposed to believe this; and I have observed that the poor people are accustomed to bring forward as a proof of exceptional goodness in a Parish Priest, the fact that he pays visits to the Blessed Sacrament, and is sometimes seen assisting at Mass in the church.

It sometimes happens, also, that the Parish Priest displays in church such a want of reverence and recollection—talking, walking about, laughing and jesting—that he acts, in fact, as though he regarded it as his private house, where he is at liberty to do as he pleases. This is a matter which does not edify the parishioners, who reflect that the church is rather the House of God, and that it deserves greater respect on account of His Divine presence.

§ 5. OF THE HOLY COMMUNION.

It is well known that it is not the right of the Parish Priest, nor even of the Bishop, to lay down any law regarding frequent, or even daily communion; and that it is the exclusive privilege of their confessors to direct or permit the faithful to communicate with more or less frequency, according as they may judge it expedient for their spiritual advancement.

Nevertheless it is a fact that, as a rule, the Church approves not only of frequent, but even of daily communion. Here are the words of the Council of Trent: " Optaret quidem Sacrosancta Synodus, ut in singulis missis fideles adstantes non solum spirituali affectu, sed sacramentali etiam Eucharistiæ perceptione communicarent" (Sess. 22, cap. 6). On these words Barbosa remarks : " Expresse concilium in præsenti supponit esse conveniens, laudabile, et consulendum, ut quotidie Eucharistiam sumant fideles, dum optat ut in singulis Missis adstantes communicent ; quod sic intellixit Sacra Congregatio Cardinalium, &c." (Coll. Doct. in Conc. Trid. hoc loco.) Still more clear are the words of the Roman Catechism, which must be taken, in the strictest sense, to be a faithful exponent of the doctrine of the Church : " Est S. Augustini norma certissima, *Sic vive, ut quotidie possis sumere.* Quare Parochi partes erunt fideles crebro adhortari, ut, quemadmodum corpori in singulos dies alimentum subministrare necessarium putant, ita etiam quotidie hoc sacramento alendæ et nutriendæ animæ curam non abjiciant. Neque enim minus spirituali cibo anima, quam naturali corpus indigere, perspicuum est. Vehementer autem proderit hoc loco repetere maxima illa et divina beneficia, quæ ex Eucharistiæ sacramentali communione consequimur; illa etiam figura erit addenda cum singulis diebus corporis vires manna reficere oportebat; itemque sanctorum Patrum auctoritates, quæ frequentem hujus sacramenti perceptionem magnopere commendant. Neque enim unius Sancti Patris Augustini ea fuit sententia: *quotidie peccas, quotidie sume;* sed si quis diligenter attenderit, eumdem omnium Patrum, qui hac de re scripserunt, sensum fuisse, facile comperiet" (Catechis. Rom. de Euch., n. 60). From this passage we may clearly conclude that it is the duty of a Parish Priest often (crebro) to exhort his flock not only to frequent, but even to daily Communion; and that in this matter he ought to avail himself of the authority, not of certain modern masters of the Spiritual life, but of the Ancient Fathers, who all teach with St. Augustine, that, notwithstanding daily defects and lighter failings, it is advisable that the faithful should communicate every day. This, of course, must be understood with the permission of their confessors, as was laid down by Innocent XI. in his decree cited by St. Alphonsus (op. Mor. lib. vi., n. 256).[1]

---

[1] The little work entitled *The Holy Communion* by Mgr. De Segur, which is now so well known, received very high commenda-

Now, this much being established, how is it that, here and there, we find certain Parish Priests who not only do not promote frequent communion among their own penitents, but cannot even endure to see it promoted by other confessors among those who are under their direction? How is it that they are bold enough to disapprove of it, and condemn it, and sneer at it in their ordinary conversation, and sometimes even to give more or less publicity to these views of theirs in their instructions on the Christian doctrine? How does it happen that we are sometimes forced to listen to the Parish Priest inveighing against *devotees*, in a manner which leaves not the slightest doubt upon any person's mind that by this term he intends to point out those who frequently and daily approach the Holy Table? How comes it that sometimes certain Parish Priests refuse to communicate such persons, or at least keep them waiting for a long time, in order that they may grow weary, and may give up the practice of approaching the Holy Communion so frequently? These are things which we might well suppose impossible, and yet they are facts which

---

tions from his late Holiness, Pope Pius IX., who said that it contained the true doctrine of the Council of Trent. His Holiness added, furthermore, that he would wish to see a copy of it presented to all children on the day of their first communion, and that he would desire likewise to see it in the hands of every Parish Priest. (See 2nd Florentine Edition.) This little work might enlighten many Parish Priests and spiritual directors regarding frequent and daily communion. As Pope Pius remarked, the book has already effected a great amount of good, and daily continues to do so in France, in Italy, and wherever else it is read.—*Author's note.*

justify us in forming a low estimate of certain Parish Priests.

Good Parish Priests are accustomed earnestly to exhort the faithful to approach the Holy Communion as frequently as possible, in accordance with the teaching of the Roman Catechism; and to this end they are careful to have an early mass in their Churches, even on week days, so that those persons who would be unable to assist at a later hour, may have an opportunity of communicating sooner and more conveniently. Good Parish Priests pride themselves on the fact that several communions are daily made in their Churches, and that they have amongst their parishioners a considerable number of pious souls, who nourish themselves even daily with the bread of Angels; being fully persuaded that, with the exception of some rare case of hypocrisy, these are the souls who live most free from sin, who are richest in virtues, who are most zealous for the glory of God, and are the "good leaven" and "good odour" of Christ in their parishes.

The Parish Priest ought to take care that the vase which is placed upon the Altar for purifying the priest's fingers be kept clean, and that the water in it be often changed. In some Churches this vase is frequently found filled with discoloured water, because whole months are allowed to elapse without having it renewed. He must also see that the communion cloths, which are suspended from the altar rails, are always clean and respectable. In some Churches these cloths are so filthy, that respectable people experience a feeling of disgust in using them when receiving the Holy Communion.

§ 6. OF THE FIRST COMMUNION OF THE CHILDREN.

Good Parish Priests ought to have three principal anxieties regarding the first Communion of the children. The first is, to admit them to it as soon as they are capable of receiving it, in compliance with the precept of the Church. It does not rest with Parish Priests to give first Communion whenever it may please them. The precept of Paschal Communion binds every Christian as soon as he is capable of receiving the Blessed Eucharist, and the Parish Priest cannot defer the fulfilment of this obligation without sufficient reason. He is merely authorised to judge whether children have the dispositions which are required in order to be admitted to Communion; and, therefore, should he find that they do not possess the necessary discernment or knowledge, he may and ought defer their first Communion, but otherwise he ought to admit them to it.

And here it must be carefully borne in mind that the discernment and instruction required in the young ought to be proportionate to their capacity, which is not that of well-instructed adults, but of children, whose minds and judgment are but little developed, and who are capable of acquiring only a limited amount of knowledge. And if we occasionally meet with children whose minds are more fully developed, who are endowed with a sound judgment, and are capable of acquiring a more extended knowledge, this is no reason why all children should be required to come up to the same standard.

Our Lord Jesus Christ not only did not repel children from Him, but took pleasure in associating familiarly with them, without exhibiting any displeasure because of the defects natural to their years; and so, too, notwithstanding these defects, he will willingly receive them at present, and admit them to share His divine banquet. As regards their intelligence, no more is required than that they be able to recognise the presence of Jesus Christ in the Blessed Eucharist: and, as far as instruction is concerned, it will be enough if they know what dispositions are required to receive the Sacrament worthily.

But since intelligence and knowledge would not suffice if moral goodness were wanting in the children, let us see what the Parish Priest ought to require on this head.

If there be question of interior and secret sins, the confessor only, and not the Parish Priest, is in a position to judge of them; and it is evident that if the child's Parish Priest should happen moreover to be his confessor, he could not make use of the knowledge acquired in the confessional, to put off the child's first Communion, when the time for making it had evidently arrived. In this case he could merely, in his capacity of confessor, exhort the child in the tribunal of penance not to seek to approach the Holy

Communion, so long as he continued in the habit of grievous sins.

If there be question of exterior and known failings, we must first consider whether these are ordinary childish faults, which of themselves are not mortal; such as lies, obstinacy, want of devotion at prayers and so forth. It is clear that the Parish Priest could not put off the child's first Communion on account of such failings, just as it is clear that a confessor could not defer the fulfilment of the Paschal Precept because his penitent might be in the habit of very frequently committing venial sins. Moreover, to postpone the first Communion of children in the hope that this will make them become better, is an entirely useless experiment, as experience invariably proves. However, should there be question of serious sins, such as, for example, grave violations of the fourth commandment, refusing to hear Mass on days of obligation, eating meat on forbidden days, grave acts of theft, sins of impurity, and such like—in these cases, undoubtedly, the child's first Communion ought to be deferred. Nevertheless, even in cases of this kind, as a general rule, the matter might be left to the judgment of the confessor, unless the child's conduct were notoriously scandalous, so that he might be regarded as a little public sinner.; for in that case, so long as he continued obstinate in sin, he ought not be permitted to approach the Lord's Table, both in order to prevent its profanation, and to serve as an example to others.

When children possess the proper dispositions, they

ought, ordinarily, to be admitted to first communion at the age of ten years, as St. Charles Borromeo and St. Liguori teach. St. Alphonsus in one of his instructions to Parish Priests, writes: " Children ought to be made comply with the paschal precept, as a general rule, between the ages of nine and ten, or at most, at the age of twelve years" (Tanoia, Book 3, ch. 22). Wherefore a Parish Priest ought to bring his influence to bear upon parents, to induce them to send their children, when ten years old, to the instructions for first communion. Should he then find that they have the required capacity, he will admit them to communion, otherwise he will put them back until the following year.

Another anxiety felt by good Parish Priests with regard to the children preparing for first communion is that they are well and thoroughly instructed, by having imparted to them all the religious knowledge which they are capable of receiving. This is a matter of the very utmost importance, not only for the actual worthy reception of the Sacrament, but also for two other reasons. The first is that if the children be well and solidly instructed at that age, the truths of faith make a profound impression on their minds, and will sink deeply into their hearts; so that it is difficult that they be ever afterwards forgotten, and they will continue to exercise in the future a powerful influence over the entire conduct of their lives. The second reason is that if children be not well instructed when they are admitted to first communion, there is great danger to fear that they will never be well instructed. It is a disagreeable but undeniable fact, that many, after having received their first Communion, never afterwards attend catechetical instruction, either because of the negligence of their parents, or of their own sloth; and, consequently, these, who constitute so numerous a class, will never afterwards be able to supply the want of that early instruction which precedes first Communion.

The Parish Priest will do well not to hand over to any priest or cleric the instruction of the children who are preparing for first Communion, but to reserve it to himself, as a most important part of his pastoral office.[1] But should it be necessary to entrust it to

---

[1] In populous parishes, such as are almost all parishes in English-speaking countries, it would be impossible to follow out the system here laid down by the Author; and while the Parish Priest personally superintends the preparation of the children for first Communion, he must of necessity avail himself of even lay assistance to a considerable extent. The following observations from Fr. O'Kane's work will be found useful for priests in English-speaking countries: "There ought to be in every parish a confraternity of the christian doctrine, the members of which are charged with the duty of catechising children. This confraternity is earnestly recommended to the Bishops of the church by Pope Innocent XI., in an encyclical letter, 16 Junii, 1686. It is enriched with many indulgences; and special facilities are granted for its establishment in every parochial church (Vide Bouvier, *Traité des Indulgences*, IIme Partie, Cap. I., art. II., § 1, Except 2°). Such a confraternity, properly organised and directed, would lighten very much the labour of the priest, and enable him without much difficulty to ascertain those who might be admitted to first Communion. It would be easy to form these into a separate class, or into two or more classes according to their degrees of proficiency. *Select members* of the confraternity could be charged with the care of these classes, and a few

others, he should be satisfied that the person ap-. pointed to act in his place is thoroughly competent to do so. And indeed in this case there is not question of merely making the children learn the material words of the catechism, for this they could do of themselves, since every child now-a-days is able to read; but there is question of explaining and developing for them the Christian doctrine regarding the principal mysteries of faith, the theological virtues, and the dispositions necessary for the proper reception of the Sacraments, and to do this the teacher must have a sound knowledge of theology, or else he will teach notable and serious errors, as has occasionally happened.

Prudent Parish Priests do not permit seculars to explain and develop the Christian doctrine to the children; because, not being themselves well instructed in theological matters, they unconsciously alter the doctrine of the church whilst explaining and developing it. It is evident that the self-same risk would exist if the catechism were explained by a badly-instructed cleric or priest; since neither the ecclesiastical dress nor the priestly character can supply the defect of want of knowledge. Parish Priests are aware that, unfortunately, some priests may be met with who are very badly instructed, and it would be only natural to suppose the same of

instructions from the priest would then suffice to complete the preparation of the more advanced. It is only by adopting some such plan that the priest, in a populous parish, can at all perform the duty." Notes, &c., n. 644.—*Translator.*

clerics before they have completed their studies. Wherefore, should the Parish Priest be unable to satisfy himself thoroughly that his substitute possessed the necessary capacity, he ought himself to teach the catechism to the children, and prepare them for first Communion even at his own personal inconvenience.

As regards the instruction of young girls, the Parish Priest ought never assign this office to men. Among the girls to be instructed for first Communion, there will be always found some rather grown and good-looking, and these might prove an occasion of dangerous temptation to a young and incautious master; the more so, when we reflect that the instruction preparatory to first Communion is given every day, lasts for a considerable time, and, consequently, may serve as an occasion for the development of that passion to which human nature is most prone.

Finally, the Parish Priest must endeavour to make the first Communion of the children a very special function both in the church and in the family circle. The day of our first Communion is an epoch in our lives; and it is well to imprint it deeply on our memories, by celebrating the auspicious day with solemnity. The function in the church, although religious, ought to wear the appearance of a brilliant and most joyous festival;[1] and the Parish Priest ought

---

[1] The Synod of Maynooth expressly orders that the Mass at which the children receive first Communion be celebrated with all

to make the children a present of some small object of devotion, in order to remind them of that great day. Even after the lapse of many years, the sight of some object which recalls to mind our first Communion is accustomed to produce a good impression upon us. Although, as a general rule, the Parish Priest cannot exercise much influence in regulating family festivities in honour of the day of the children's first Communion, nevertheless he can let it be seen that he approves of them as an edifying custom, and can promote them at least indirectly.

The better to attain this twofold object, he must endeavour to prevent children from receiving first Communion privately and singly. Some may labour under the erroneous impression that the first Communion of children must be more devout, and therefore more fruitful in good results, if divested of every external manifestation of show and pomp. This is a mistake. Sacred functions are more devout in proportion as they are more simple, when there is question of people who do good influenced solely by pure piety—a circumstance of rare occurrence. But all other persons require a certain amount of outward show, to produce an impression on the senses; and children, above all others, stand in need of this, since they have but little power of reflection, and possess a very large share of sensibility and imagination. Wherefore if we wish that the great act of partaking

possible solemnity—" Missa in qua prima vice pueri sacra Synaxi reficiuntur, ea qua fieri potest maxima solemnitate celebretur." (Decret xiii., n. 53.)—*Translator.*

for the first time of the Bread of Angels should make a special impression upon their hearts—as it is most desirable that it should—we must never allow it to be divested of that exterior pomp and solemnity which is so well calculated to awaken in them faith, and, consequently, veneration and love.[1]

I must not omit an observation regarding the right of Parish Priests to admit children to first Communion. The Roman Catechism does not suppose them to have an exclusive right in this matter. In fact we read there the following words: "qua vero ætate pueris sacra mysteria dauda sint, nemo melius constituere poterit quam pater, vel sacerdos, cui illi confitentur peccata" (De Euch., n. 63). And to this St. Charles Borromeo evidently refers, when he imposes on secular confessors the obligation of examining children who confess to them on the points on which they have already received instruction, and of giving them a certificate to be presented to the Parish Priest, in order that he may admit them among the number of

---

[1] In several parts of Germany a custom prevails of making the children approach the Holy Communion in a body, every month or every two months, for a period of two or three years after they have received their First Communion. By this means the children become habituated to approach the Sacraments regularly, and are, moreover, impressed more deeply with the solemnity of this religious duty. The Provincial Council of Cologne held in 1860, alludes to this custom in the following terms:—Consuetudo salutaris in multis locis observata, qua per duos vel tres post primam communiouem annos singulis, si fieri potest, vel alternis mensibus ad sacram synaxim recipiendam omnes congregantur, ubi viget, retinenda, ubi desideratur, introducenda est." (Conc. prov. Col. 1860, p. 133.)—*Translator.*

those who are to comply with the paschal precept. (Instruction for fathers of families. Short instruction, &c.)

However, the custom prevails now-a-days, and in several places it is further confirmed by Synodical decrees, that the Parish Priest should possess the exclusive right of admitting children to first Communion; and therefore those confessors would be deserving of censure, who should direct their young penitents to make their first Communion, without having previously obtained permission to do so from their Parish Priests.

Nevertheless it must be observed that this right belongs to the Parish Priest so long only as there may be reason for doubting the capacity of a child for the reception of this Sacrament, that is to say, up to the age of fourteen years, which St. Charles Borromeo, following Suarez, fixes as the extreme limit to which first Communion may be deferred. Wherefore, should it happen, through the carelessness or caprice of the Parish Priest, that children of fifteen or sixteen years of age might be met with who had not yet received their first Communion, any confessor who should consider them sufficiently disposed ought to command them to approach the Holy Communion. There cannot be the slightest doubt that at such an age children are bound to comply with the Paschal precept, just as they are bound to hear Mass on Festivals; and the Parish Priest has no authority to dispense from this precept at pleasure. And should any one suppose that children are not bound to comply with the Paschal precept until after they shall have been admitted by their Parish Priest to first Communion, I reply that this would be true solely when there might be reason for doubting of their capacity, but it would not hold good when there existed no doubt whatever on this head. This must appear evident if we reflect that, were the principle laid down above to be admitted absolutely and without restriction, we should be forced to admit that a young man of even twenty years of age would not be bound to comply with the Paschal precept, should it have happened that his Parish Priest, through some whim or other, had up to that age refused to admit him to first Communion. And yet not even the Pope could dispense him from it, since there is question of a precept which is Divine as well as Ecclesiastical. However it must be distinctly understood that I do not speak here of those dissolute youths whose first Communion ought to be indefinitely postponed, since they will not show any signs of amendment in their conduct, (though they continue, all the while, bound by the Paschal precept, just as they are bound to amend their lives), nor of simpletons, respecting whom other questions might arise; but I speak of youths who are ordinarily well-conducted, and are possessed of sufficient intelligence.

I must next make a few remarks regarding those children who are by nature so dull and stupid, that not even at the age of fifteen or sixteen years are they capable of learning and retaining the Christian doctrine. The Parish Priest must employ particular diligence in instructing persons of this class; being careful, however, to teach them only very few things, and these the most indispensable, and to teach them in the clearest and most material manner possible. He must then admit them to Communion, even though they should understand and retain but little of the Christian doctrine. There is no doubt that if he wait until they be better instructed, he will never be able to admit them to first Communion, since some minds are so obtuse that they are incapable of development, and continue to old age in irremediable ignorance.

The very few and most indispensable points which ought to be taught to persons of this class are the following:—that there is a God, the Creator and Supreme Master of the entire world; that He rewards the good and punishes the wicked; that in this God there are three Persons, the Father, the Son, and the Holy Ghost; that the Father is God, that the Son is God, that the Holy Ghost is God, and yet that there is one only God; that the Second of these Persons became Man, and suffered and died as man through love of us; that we must confess all our mortal sins in order to obtain pardon of them; that in the Holy Communion we receive the Lord, and that we must approach it with our fast absolutely unbroken, and in the state of grace. This much they must learn as best they can, according to their capacity.

It is not necessary to instruct such as these in the doctrine of the theological virtues, because the Parish Priest and Confessor can excite them to make acts of these virtues from time to time; nor is it necessary to teach them what is required for Confession, since the confessor can make sure that no one of the necessary conditions is wanting, by himself examining their consciences, exciting them to contrition and so forth; nor need other matters regarding Communion be explained to them, for it is sufficent for them to know what it is they receive, and to receive it with respect. The Sacraments have been instituted for all men: all have need of them, and all have a right to them; and the Parish Priest cannot refuse them to any one, except he should happen to be positively unworthy of them, or should wish to abuse them, or it should be foreseen that he will not be able to receive them with due reverence, even without any fault on his own part.

Wherefore Holy Communion ought to be given to simpletons, not only at the point of death, but also once each year, unless there should be reason to fear that they may offer it any disrespect. The Parish Priest ought to suggest to persons of this class the acts of the theological virtues in the following manner: *Do you believe that there is one only God in three distinct persons, &c.? Do you believe that He will reward the good and punish the wicked, &c.?* and to each question he will make them answer: *Yes.* He will likewise ask: *Do you hope for Heaven, &c.? Do you love God above all things, &c.? Are you sorry for your sins, &c.?* He must question them respecting their sins, then give them conditional absolution—*Si es capax*—and afterwards admit them to Communion. This is the practice of all intelligent and zealous Parish Priests, founded on the authority of the common opinion of theologians. Unfortunately, however, there are Parish Priests who regard these unhappy beings as incapable of receiving Sacraments, and keep them away from them during their entire lives. They consider that they are doing a great deal, if they give them a conditional absolution and Extreme Unction at the point of death.

I will add one word about Deaf-Mutes. It is impossible for these unhappy creatures to learn the truths of faith, and to render themselves fit to receive the Sacraments with fruit, unless they be specially instructed in a manner proportionate to their circumstances. Wherefore if a Parish Priest have any deaf-mute in his parish, he must devote himself earnestly to his instruction, taking care that his parents, if in good circumstances, have him taught enough to know the truths of faith, and to be capable of receiving the Sacraments. Should the child's parents be poor, he must strive to induce the municipal authorities or some pious benefactor to take up the case; and should he fail in doing so, he ought to open a subscription list, in which his own name should stand first, and in this manner he would raise a sufficient fund to enable the child to acquire the more necessary instruction. A year, or a little more, would suffice to prepare deaf-mutes for the reception of the sacraments.

§ 2. OF ADMINISTERING COMMUNION TO THE SICK.

Chronic invalids who are unable to go to the

church ought to have the Holy Communion administered to them in their houses at least at Easter; and indeed this custom is universally observed. However the Parish Priest ought not rest content with giving them Communion once a year, but ought to do so more frequently, especially should they express a desire to receive it. Those Parish Priests who show themselves unwilling to administer Communion to sick persons of this class except at Easter, give little edification to their flocks.

Since these Communions can be foreseen and arranged before hand, the Parish Priest will be enabled to make provision for having the Blessed Sacrament accompanied in even a more becoming manner than when it is borne to the sick *per modum Viatici*, which is ordinarily done in a hurry. By announcing to the people on the preceding Sunday, the day and hour when he would proceed to administer Communion to the sick, he would be sure to have a good attendance of the faithful to accompany him.[1]

---

[1] Priests in English-speaking countries, owing to local circumstances, cannot carry out the prescription of the Rubrics regarding the manners in which the B. Sacrament is to be borne to the sick, and are allowed to carry it privately, without lights or any other external manifestation of pomp. "Nevertheless (say the Fathers of the 1st Counc. of Westminster, Decret. xviii., n. 12) no priest should forget that he has his hidden God clinging to his side, and that he is bearing Him along with him for the solace of his people. Reverently therefore, nay devoutly and as if fixed in contemplation let him convey to the house of the sick the most Holy Sacrament, having it suspended from his neck in a bag decently or richly adorned."

Regarding the last words just quoted from the Council of Westminster, it may be remarked that the Roman authorities have

OF THE MOST HOLY EUCHARIST. 301

It is a matter of great importance to have the Blessed Sacrament thus becomingly accompanied when it is borne to the houses of the sick, as it is a public act of lively faith highly expressive of the piety of the people, and serves to strengthen and increase devotion towards the most august pledge of divine love. Wherefore a Parish Priest ought to exert himself to have the Blessed Sacrament respectably

---

repeatedly insisted that when taking the Blessed Sacrament to the sick the pyxis should repose on the priest's breast, and not be placed in a pocket of the vest as is sometimes done. Thus in the instruction of the S. Congregation of Propaganda (25th Feb., 1859) regarding the manner of taking the B. Eucharist to the sick it is expressly stated: "injuncta vero presbyteris *stricta obligatione* semper in hisce casibus Sanctam Hostiam super pectus deferendi" (See Statutes of the Synod of Maynooth, Appendix vii., p. 228). Again, in 1868, when the Rev. James O'Kane (whose excellent work we have so frequently quoted) submitted his "Notes on the Rubrics" to the Congregation of Rites for examination, he was required to correct an assertion made in the first Edition, viz., that priests in Ireland might carry the pyxis containing the B. Sacrament in a special pocket made in the vest for this purpose. The distinguished author thus alludes to the matter in a subsequent Edition: "Whatever it (the bag containing the pyxis) be made of, it should not be permitted to hang loosely from the neck, but be made fast on the breast, as the rubric here directs, so as to prevent the danger of the pyxis falling, or of the Blessed Sacrament being shaken out. This may be done, as the words of the rubric—*alligare, adstringere*—would seem to suggest, by means of strings attached to the case or bag. In our first edition we said that it might be done also by putting the pyxis with its covering into a pocket made in the vest for this purpose, and used for no other. But the Sacred Congregation of Rites referring to this matter, requires that, when the Blessed Eucharist is carried privately, what the Rubric prescribes be observed in every particular—*in hoc casu adamussim servetur quod præscribit Rubrica*"—*Notes on the Rubrics*, &c., p. 807, 3rd edition. —*Translator*.

accompanied each time it is borne to the sick; and this he will succeed in doing by frequently exhorting his flock to take part in this demonstration of faith, as soon as they hear the sound of the bell inviting them to it. But he will attain this object still more securely, if he take care to have in his parish a flourishing sodality of the Blessed Sacrament—a sodality which ought to exist in every parish.[1] This sodality will supply all the material requisites for the procession, and will, moreover, furnish many associates to take part in it.

[1] The chief object of this confraternity is to honour our Lord in the Sacrament of His love, and to repair the many outrages He has there to suffer. It may be established anywhere by the authority of the Ordinary of the diocese, and the members become entitled at once to all the privileges and indulgences that have been granted, or may hereafter be granted to the confraternity at Rome. "O'Kane," Notes, &c., n. 790, cfr. Bouvier *Traité des Indulgences*, IIIme part., chap. II., sec. II., art. I.—*Translator.*

APPENDIX I.

OF ASSISTING THE SICK AND DYING.

§ 1. How Vigilant a Parish Priest ought to be in order that the Sick may be fortified in due time by the Holy Sacraments.

In city parishes, especially if they be extensive, the Parish Priest cannot ordinarily know whether there are any sick persons who stand in need of the Sacraments; and, as a rule, he has no intelligence of the dangerous condition of the sick, until he is summoned to administer to them the last rites of the Church. Under such circumstances there remains nothing for the Parish Priest to do, except to visit the sick person at once when called; so that, if fortunately the call be not too late, as often happens, at least the little time left to the dying person may be turned to the best account.

It is easier for a Parish Priest in a town or country parish to find out whether any members of his flock are dangerously ill; but, whether a parish be situated in a city or out of it, whenever it comes to the knowledge of the Pastor that any one of his parishioners is ailing seriously, he ought to take care that the Sacraments be administered to him in good time. And here I must remark that the Parish Priest ought not to place too implicit trust in the relatives of the sick person, even though they should happen to be pious; for it often occurs that even pious relatives delay too long in warning the patient of his danger, through fear of alarming him; and still less confidence should be reposed in the relatives, should they happen to be persons of but little piety.

It may be asked, then, whether the Parish Priest ought to pay a personal visit to the house of the patient, in order to satisfy himself of his condition, and to prevent delay in the administration of the Sacraments, should he believe the sick person to be in danger? This depends upon circumstances. If the family be poor and humble, the Parish Priest may visit with the certain assurance of being well received. As a general rule, both the members of the family and the patient will consider themselves honoured by the visit of their Pastor; and should he, moreover, think it necessary to administer the Sacraments, they will readily yield to his wishes.

New Parish Priests, above all, ought to be persuaded of this practical truth, that poor persons who are pious, and even those who are not very pious, provided they be not actual unbelievers, receive the Parish Priest into their houses with pleasure on the occasion of sickness; and that sick persons of this class do not become alarmed when it is announced to them that they must receive the last Sacraments, so that, as far as they are concerned, there is no need of those studied discourses which must be employed with the rich, and with persons belonging to the upper classes, in order that they may not be frightened at the bare mention of the last Sacraments. Whether it be that the poor, being less cultured, are less given to reflection, or that, being possessed of little, they are more detached from worldly goods, or perhaps from both reasons combined, the fact remains indisputable that the approach of death does not alarm them. Thousands of times, when I have had practical proof of this truth, I have been forced to exclaim : " Even in this respect the saying *Beati pauperes* is verified". These are they who at the approach of death are most detached from life : they readily dispose themselves to receive the last Sacraments, and consequently they rarely die deprived of them. Wherefore the Parish Priest must take advantage of these good dispositions to visit the families of the poor with perfect confidence ; and should he find among them any sick person who may appear to stand in need of the Sacraments, to exhort him, as far as may be necessary, not to defer receiving them.

Should the family on the other hand belong to the better classes, the Pastor must adopt a different method. In the first place, it will be difficult for him to gain access to the sick person, until the Physician shall have directed that he be summoned to administer the last Sacraments; and even after this order has been given, some time will probably be lost before it is carried out. Hence proceed those deplorable delays, through which so many die without

Sacraments, or receive them when they no longer know what they are doing. The physician delays as long as possible, and the relatives, in addition, delay yet another while. It is a fortunate circumstance for the poor patient should his conscience happen to be in a good condition, and his accounts adjusted with God! Should the Parish Priest become aware of these dangerous delays, he must do all in his power to put an end to them, so that the poor sick man may not be betrayed by the false love of his relatives and friends.

Should it fall to the lot of the Parish Priest to have to announce to the sick man that he has to receive the last Sacraments, he ought invariably to make it his study to do so as delicately as possible. Such an announcement ought to be made in the kindest and least alarming manner, even to the poor, though they are least shocked by it; but this precaution must be specially attended to when one has to deal with the wealthy and better classes, since it is almost impossible to find one among them who will not be more or less alarmed. Charity and Christian prudence demand this; because, otherwise, there is danger that the patient may grow worse, and that his death may be accelerated: there is danger, also, that he may become irritated, and consequently indisposed for the reception of the Sacraments. The thought of death, when it is announced as already close at hand, disturbs even the most pious persons; and we must respect this human weakness which must be supposed to exist in all the children of Adam, including even the most virtuous. Therefore, even though recovery should be altogether impossible, the Parish Priest must not tell the patient not to deceive himself any longer, that his malady is of too long standing, that his case is hopeless, or make use of similar expressions which serve only to persuade him that he is dying. What is of importance to the Parish Priest is to dispose the sick person to die well: it is of no importance to take away from him every hope of life. He must not indeed positively flatter him with the hope of recovery, for this would be to deceive him; but his efforts must be directed, instead, to making him resigned to the will of God, while allowing him at the same time to hope for recovery and life.

Not even when he is on the point of his agony, ought the dying man be given to understand that he is about to expire. Even then he must be told to leave himself tranquilly in the hands of God, to offer to Him his sufferings, and to protest that he desires only the accomplishment of God's will, and that He would dispose of him, His creature, precisely as He may please. Sentiments of conformity to God's will are those which are most perfect and most meritorious; and they preserve that tranquillity of spirit which is always so truly desirable and precious, but is especially so at the point of death.

Some one may, perhaps, say, that by informing the patient that the world has ended for him, and that he must very soon present himself before the tribunal of God, he will think more earnestly of his spiritual necessities, and will make better provision for them.

I reply that this is very doubtful: that, on the contrary, he may, perhaps, become irritated against the person who announces his end to him too plainly, thinking him guilty, at the very least, of an unpardonable want of charity and prudence. In the meantime, while his mind is thus excited, the love of life, which is so very powerful, may easily persuade him that there is no real danger, and thus, perhaps, he will die with less perfect dispositions. These dangers of which I speak are not mere hypotheses, for they have many times been realised in practice. It is possible to persuade the patient of the propriety and obligation of settling his accounts with God, and of arranging everything as he would wish to have done at the moment of death, without obliging him to believe that he has finished his course in this world, and that he is at last arrived at the threshold of Eternity. It must be borne well in mind that since we, Parish Priests, are accustomed to see others die, their death does not produce any great impression upon us; but it makes a very great impression upon those who have actually arrived at that dreadful moment, as it will upon ourselves, when the hour of our death comes round. Let us then use towards the dying every possible delicacy and consideration, as charity and christian prudence require.

Should the sick person be a member of a family which is irreligious, but yet does not belong to any sect, the Parish Priest, on becoming acquainted with his dangerous condition, ought endeavour, as prudently and politely as possible, to gain access to him; and even though the attempt should prove fruitless, it will, all the while, edify the people, since they will come to know that their Pastor has not been wanting in the discharge of his duty. Should the family, however, belong to any sect, it would be imprudent on the part of the Parish Priest to present himself at the house, since he could expect nothing except a discourteous refusal.

It may be well to remind young Parish Priests that those who despise the Sacraments during life are generally deprived of them at the hour of death. They either die suddenly, or the priest is not summoned in time, whether through their own fault or that of their relatives. When I was a young Parish Priest I asked an old man how I should act in case certain persons should happen to be dying, and his reply was: "Be assured that they will give you little trouble". After thirty years' experience, I can no longer doubt the truth of the saying.

§ 2. On the Integrity of Confession on the part of the Sick and Dying.

Whenever we hear confessions we must keep before us that golden principle laid down by De Lugo, and recognised as true by St. Alphonsus and all sound theologians, namely, that the obligation of the examination of conscience and, consequently, of the integrity of Confession, belongs to the penitent, and not to the confessor; so that when the penitent, according to his capacity, has done all that lies in his power, the confessor is not obliged to interrogate him further, even though he should perceive that the examination of conscience and, consequently, the accusation might be more exact from a theological point of view. As regards the integrity of Confession, the confessor is obliged to supply by his questions only what may have been culpably omitted by the penitent (See De Lugo, Disp. 16, de Pænit. 9, 14, n. 589).

If this principle is to be kept in view when we hear the Confessions of persons who are in health, in order not to give way to vain scruples regarding the integrity of Confession, and not to render this Sacrament a burden both to the confessor and to the penitent, much more ought a confessor attend to it when hearing the confessions of the sick and dying, in order not to worry himself, and injure his penitent both in body and in soul. Wherefore when the Parish Priest is called to attend a sick person, he ought to observe the actual condition of the patient's health; and instead of calculating the time that would be necessary to make an exact confession, he must rather consider what time can be devoted to it without doing him injury. As a matter of fact, a sick man may be able to sustain a conversation for five or ten minutes, when he could not do so for half an hour or an hour without increasing his illness. Consequently, if an accurate confession of all his sins would require half an hour or an hour, while at the same time the state of his health will not permit him to make a confession of more than five or ten minutes' duration, the confessor ought to be content with a confession made within five or ten minutes. The sick man under the circumstances, is morally and even physically prevented from making a confession materially entire, but it will be, nevertheless, formally entire, in as much as the penitent will have done all that he is actually capable of doing at the time.

In many cases the Parish Priest or Confessor must simply ask the penitent what time has elapsed since his last confession, must interrogate him in a general way, rather concerning the species than the number of his sins, and having thus obtained, in outline, an idea of his life, after briefly but fervently exhorting him to contrition—which is the most important consideration of all—he must immediately give him absolution. It frequently happens that the sick person is in such a state of mental prostration, that if he were wearied with many questions there would be danger, not only of his becoming very much worse, but of his losing his senses altogether before receiving absolution, and this would be the greatest misfortune of all. In such cases, the confessor ought to be far more on his guard against putting too many, rather than too few, questions. Even though he should ask but little, there will always be the matter necessary for Confession, and, consequently, supposing the penitent contrite, there is no danger of his justification and salvation. But if, on the other hand, his senses fail him, he will be no longer capable either of disposing himself, or of being disposed by the confessor for absolution. Wherefore, whenever we are summoned to hear the confessions of sick persons who are very seriously ill, let us be on our guard against being too scrupulous in the matter of integrity: under such circumstances the penitents are not obliged to it, and should they afterwards recover, they can then make a more accurate confession.

Nor does it avail to say that, should the patient recover, he will, perhaps, no longer reflect on this obligation, and consequently will never discharge it; for should he really never again reflect upon it, he can never be bound to discharge the obligation, that is, to make the confession over again; and the sins that have been already cancelled cannot return again to stain his soul afresh, and imperil his salvation. The evil of not repeating the confession would in this case be purely material, without sin, and free from the consequences of sin, just as if one should fail to pay a debt through forgetfulness. Nevertheless the confessor might caution the sick person that, in case of recovery, he would be bound to complete that confession which he had made with such haste; this, however, should be done only when there is a real hope and a possibility of recovery, and when there would be no reason to fear that such a caution would trouble the sick person.

There is another point to be kept in mind when we are summoned to attend a sick person who is not fully in possession of his senses. In such circumstances it would be a very grave mistake to defer giving absolution, in the hope that the patient may improve later on; for it may easily happen that he may grow worse, and may lose the little reason that yet remains to him. Wherefore we ought to lose no time in hearing his confession as best we can, and giving him absolution. Should he afterwards recover the more perfect use of his senses, we can hear his confession again, and again absolve him; and this we must do as promptly as possible, lest he may once more lose the use of reason which he had recovered.

It must likewise be remarked that should the Parish Priest be summoned to a sick person to whom the last Sacraments have been ordered, or to whom they ought to be ordered considering the grave nature of his ailment, and should the patient beg a little more time to prepare himself better for confession, the Parish Priest ought to insist, in the most gracious manner possible, on his making his confession at once; assuring him that he will himself assist him in doing so, and that in this manner he may be disposed for the Sacrament forthwith. A delay of this kind might be fatal, as frequent experience has proved.

In like manner, should the Parish Priest discover that the patient has committed reserved sins, or has incurred censures, even such as are reserved to the Pope, he ought not to delay absolving him, under the pretext of taking counsel, or of seeking for faculties. Every reservation ceases in danger of death, as well as *in Articulo mortis;* and therefore the confessor, having suggested or imposed upon him whatever he believes at the moment to be most expedient, or of obligation, ought to absolve him without delay, in order to make his eternal salvation secure, in case any sudden change should accelerate his death. Having done this, the Parish Priest might take counsel with learned persons, and, for greater security, seek faculties from his Ecclesiastical Superiors, and then, returning to the patient, he might do whatever still remained to be done either as a matter of duty or of expediency. But, above all, let him be most scrupulous not to defer absolving the sick person on any account. Many a time, through like delays, souls have been lost which otherwise would have been saved. When the harm is done, the Parish Priest excuses himself by saying: *I could not have foreseen that change for the worse;* but if the soul has been lost, meanwhile, this excuse will not save it. For the rest, the Parish Priest knows that when there is question of a reserved censure, even though it be removed in danger of death, the sick person is still bound, should he recover, to present himself to the proper authorities for absolution, under pain *reincidentiæ*, that is, of again falling under the same censure.[1]

§ 3. SOME REMARKS REGARDING THE CONFESSIONS OF WOMEN IN PRIVATE HOUSES.

Some scruple to hear the confessions of sick women in a private house, unless the physician has ordered

---

[1] In the case of a reserved sin *to which no censure is attached*, the penitent is not bound, on recovery, to present himself to the Superior (Cfr Layman, lib. 5, tract. 6, cap. 12, n. 15). — *Translator.*

them to receive the Sacraments, or they should happen to be chronic invalids, so that one foresees that they will never, or at least only after a long interval, be able to go to the church. This is simply a prejudice. Whosoever, without distinction of sex, is prevented from going to the church may be heard anywhere, and there is not, nor can there be any law to the contrary, which would be extremely dangerous, since it would hinder souls from availing themselves of those means which Christ has left them for the purpose of recovering lost grace.

It must be remembered that when a sick woman asks for Confession, even though her sickness may involve no danger of death, it is possible that she asks for it because she finds herself in a state of mortal sin. Unhappily many men and women live in sin, and then fall sick in this state. Now, could the Church require a woman to remain without the grace of the Sacrament in a case of such grave necessity? And yet we cannot draw distinctions between a woman who may be in a state of mortal sin, and a woman who may be free from it; because, we could never for a moment oblige a woman to make known outside the confessional that she was in a state of sin. It must be remarked, furthermore, that certain maladies do not present any dangerous symptoms, for a considerable period, and then become extremely dangerous, so as sometimes even to render it impossible for the sick person to make a confession. This is the strongest reason why there is not and cannot be a law forbidding Confession to sick women whose illness is not dangerous.

Wherefore we must conclude that it was a real oversight on the part of St. Alphonsus, to lay down that confessors ought not to hear the confessions of sick women, *excepto casu gravi infirmitatis* (Homo. Apostol. Tract. ult. punct. x.). Suppose a woman, be she ever so healthy, is unable to go to the church because she is a cripple, is she to be denied every opportunity of Confession? The Parish Priest, then, can never refuse to hear the confession of any sick woman who is unable to go to the church; nay, he ought rather to approve and commend the devotion of those who make such a request.

What has been said up to the present evidently applies to cases where there is no actual or probable danger; but should the illness exhibit symptoms which would indicate possible danger, in that case the Parish Priest ought not to content himself with waiting until the sick woman should send for him, but ought to find some polite way of making it known that he would wish to be summoned in order to administer the Sacraments. In doing so, he would only be acting in conformity with the decrees of the Council of Lateran under Innocent III. and St. Pius V.

Finally, it is unnecessary to recommend the Parish Priest to be most cautious and reserved when hearing the confession of women in private houses. In addition to keeping the door of the room invariably open, he must be careful to remain at a suitable distance from his penitent, and never to keep turned towards her, or to look her in the face, which is not only dangerous, but causes shame to bashful women, and discourages them, should they have to accuse themselves of certain sins. To this point, however, I shall return again, when speaking of chastity.

§ 4. Of the time for Administering the Holy Viaticum.

The same rule cannot be laid down for the Holy Viaticum and for Confession, because the former cannot be administered except in case of necessity, that is of severe, and therefore dangerous, illness. Nevertheless, the Parish Priest must remember that to administer the Holy Viaticum there is no need of the express permission of the physician. When the sickness is of itself evidently serious, and is considered such by the medical attendant, the Viaticum may always be given; and it may be given even though the medical attendant should still entertain strong hopes of the patient's recovery, or should certify that, even should he grow worse, the nature of the illness will still allow time for the administration of the Sacrament later on. Nay, even though the physician should positively forbid the administration of the Viaticum, it might still be administered as soon as the sickness is pronounced serious. In fact, as all theologians are agreed in saying, it is simply required for the administration of the Viaticum that the illness involve the danger of death, and it is clear that every serious illness is necessarily of this description. Wherefore, whenever the illness is severe, the Parish Priest may always administer the Viaticum; and should the sick person ask for it, he not only may, but ought administer it, since the patient has a strict right to receive it.

A Parish Priest would be in error who should say that the Viaticum ought not, or worse still, could not be given without the authorisation of the medical attendant. The permission, nay the obligation to administer the Viaticum, arises more from the gravity and danger of the illness, than from the certificate of the physician. Very frequently the physician knows, and openly admits, that the illness is dangerous, nay very dangerous, and yet will still put off giving directions for the administration of the last Sacraments. Must the Parish Priest, and still more the poor patient, be dependent on the small amount of discretion of such people in a matter of so great importance?

Another very necessary remark has reference to children who have not yet been admitted to their first Communion. Many Parish Priests have no scruple in allowing them to die without the Holy Viaticum, for the sole reason that they have not yet been admitted to Communion, that they possess but little judgment, and are insufficiently instructed. It must, then, be borne well in mind, that every child who has reached the age of seven years is obliged by a divine precept to receive the Holy Communion. The fulfilment of this precept is deferred for several years, in order that the children may be better prepared, and such is the custom of the Church, which can on no account be censured. This delay, however, is not admissible when the child is in danger of death, and it is foreseen that if the precept be not then complied with, it will never be complied with at all. Wherefore, whenever a child is in such danger, the Viaticum ought to be administered, even though the little patient have but a small amount of judgment and but little instruction. It will be enough, as all theologians with St. Thomas teach, if the child knows that in the consecrated particle he is receiving the Lord.[1] It will be enough that he knows, or that he is taught, as well as circumstances will permit, the principal mysteries of faith, a knowledge of which is likewise required for absolution and for Extreme Unction; then the Pastor, after having exhorted him to receive the Lord de-

---

[1] The question of administering the Viaticum to children is discussed at length by Benedict XIV. (de Syn. Dioces. lib. vii., cap xii.), and the following passages exhibit, in brief, his teaching on the subject: "Recte et sine reprehensione poterit Episcopus Synodali constitutione Parochos compellere ad administrandum Sanctissimum Viaticum pueris mox decessuris, si eos compererint tantam assequutos judicii maturitatem ut cibum istum cœlestem et supernum a communi et materiali discernant; haud enim leviter delinquere credimus, qui pueros etiam duodenes et perspicacis ingenii siuunt ex hac vita migrare sine Viatico, hanc unam ob causam, quia scilicet numquam antea, Parochorum certe incuria et oscitantia, Eucharisticum panem degustarunt. . . . . Verum Doctores fere communiter fatentur tantam non desiderari ætatem, ut quis in mortis articulo et possit et debeat Sanctissimo Viatico muniri. Quinimo Suarez expresse docet omnibus qui sunt doli capaces, positis in vitæ discrimine, illud esse ex divino præcepto porrigendum. . . . . illis scilicet, quos Parochi, diligenti præmisso examine, tanta compererint pollere ingenii perspicacia, ut latentem sub speciebus Sacramentalibus Christum et firmiter credant, et reverenter adorent."—*Translator*.

voutly, ought to administer to him the Holy Viaticum. Was not the Blessed Eucharist administered in the Ancient Church even to children immediately after Baptism? The reason for doing so was, because it was believed to be of advantage to them, even though they were as yet devoid of understanding and of instruction. Is it not a well-known fact that the Sacraments produce their effects immediately, when there is no impediment placed by sin, or rather by the affection to sin? Wherefore, there cannot be the slightest doubt that the Parish Priest ought to administer the Holy Viaticum to all children who have reached the age of seven years; but he ought not to administer it before that age, (unless the child should happen to be unusually precocious), because such is the practice of the Church from which we ought never deviate.

§ 5. OF THE TIME FOR ADMINISTERING EXTREME UNCTION.

Regarding the time at which Extreme Unction is to be administered, Parish Priests ought to attend carefully to the doctrine of St. Alphonsus, which is as follows: " Dicunt communiter Doctores, sufficere ut infirmitas sit periculosa mortis, licet *remote:* ita Suarez, Laym. Castrop. Bon. Coninc. Salm. et alii". Wherefore, it would be sufficient that the sickness involved even remotely the danger of death; and the Saint goes on to prove this doctrine by the authority of several councils. He then continues : " Sed clarius hoc confirmatur a Bened. XIV. in præfata Bulla (Eucholog. cit. § 46) ubi dicitur, ne sacramentum Extremæ Unctionis ministretur bene valentibus, *sed iis dumtaxat qui gravi morbo laborant.* Unde recte dicit Castrop. quod quoties potest infirmo non jejuno præberi Viaticum, potest et expedit dari Extrema Unctio" (Homo Apost. de Extr. Unct., n. 7.). This salutary practice of administering Extreme Unction immediately after the Viaticum prevails in several places, including even Paris.

Unfortunately among ourselves, on the other hand, not only seculars, including medical men, but also (the truth must be confessed), a good many Ecclesiastics, and among them many Parish Priests, entertain a rooted prejudice which makes them think that it is not suitable, or even lawful to administer Extreme Unction whenever the Viaticum may be given. Nay they believe that in order to administer it they ought to await a further crisis of the illness; and some even require that the sick person's recovery should be altogether despaired of, and that the danger of death should not only be near, but, in fact, seem imminent.[1] This opinion is unfortunately held by not a few, and among them by several who have

[1] We may appropriately quote here the words of the Roman Catechism on this subject : – Iis etiam qui adeo periculose ægrotare videntur ut ne supremus illis vitæ dies instet metuendum sit hoc sacramentum præberi debet. In quo tamen gravissime peccant, qui illud tempus ægroti ungendi observare solent, cum jam, omni salutis spe amissa, vita et sensibus carere incipiat. Constat enim ad uberiorem Sacramenti gratiam percipiendam plurimum valere, si ægrotus, cum in eo adhuc integra mens et ratio viget, fidemque et

continually in their hands the Moral Theology of St. Alphonsus as their favourite text-book.

It happens not unfrequently that pious persons, after having received the Viaticum, ask the Parish Priest, or the Priest who is acting in his place, to administer to them Extreme Unction, but are immediately told that it cannot be administered yet awhile, that it is not yet necessary to do so, that they must wait for the Doctor's certificate, &c., and from this the sick person and his relatives conclude that a greater danger of death is required for Extreme Unction than for the Viaticum—perhaps even extreme danger. Meanwhile the physicians, seeing that the Parish Priest has a scruple about administering the Sacrament as long as there still remains some hope of the patient's recovery, and that he submissively awaits their certificate, become more and more confirmed in their prejudice.

When there is a question of rich gentlemen, a scene not unfrequently takes place which deserves special notice. In order not to alarm them, the Sacraments are ordered to be administered even to pious persons of this class at a time when their illness is not only dangerous, but already past hope. The physicians direct the last Sacraments to be administered, at that stage of the sickness when they

religiosam animi voluntatem afferre potest, sacro oleo liniatur. Quare Parochis animadvertendum est, ut eo potissimum tempore cælestem medicinam adhibeant, illam quidem semper vi sua admodum salutarem, cum eorum etiam pietate et religione qui curandi sunt magis profuturam intellexerint." (Pars II. cap. vi., n. 9).—*Translator.*

are at length compelled to acknowledge that "*there is nothing more left for them to do;*" and that, "*beyond the remedies already tried, medical science supplies no other means which could afford any hope of success*".[1] It is only then that the Viaticum is administered; and when it has been thus administered, long after the proper time, it is even still considered too soon to administer Extreme Unction. They would wait until the danger had become yet more urgent, and therefore they request the Parish Priest to bring with him the holy oil, not indeed to administer the Sacrament then and there, but in order that he may have it ready at hand when the crisis arrives. The physician warns the relatives not to allow the Parish Priest to go away from the house, because he tells them openly the patient is in such a very low state that he may pass away at any moment; but since he may linger on yet a few hours, and continues to retain the use of his senses, they are unwilling to alarm him for some time longer by the administration of Extreme Unction. Sometimes when he ought to be commencing the Recommendation of a dying soul, when he ought to be reciting the *Proficiscere*, the Parish Priest has not yet received permission to speak to the dying man about Extreme

---

[1] Among the Decrees of the First Council of Westminster we find the following: "Let the Priest admonish the friends of the sick man, and oftentimes also remind the faithful, when in health, that, if they are attended by a doctor who is not a Catholic, they insist and frequently urge him to let them know, as soon as ever there is danger, lest by some sudden attack their soul be deprived of the benefit of this Sacrament" (Decree XX., n. 3).—*Translator.*

Unction! Thus it comes to pass that the patient either dies without receiving the Sacrament, should death come on, as sometimes happens, without any previous agony, or he receives it when life and sense begin to fail him, that is, at the moment when the saying of the Roman Catechism is verified: "*gravissime peccant qui illud tempus ægroti ungendi observare solent, cum jam omni salutis spe amissa, vita et sensibus carere incipiat*".

In order to do away with such prejudices and abuses, the Parish Priest ought frequently to inculcate the true doctrine which we have laid down above, namely, that Extreme Unction ought not to be administered at the last moment of life, but in every case of serious, and therefore dangerous illness; and that it is not only lawful but commendable to administer it after the Holy Viaticum. He ought to teach this doctrine not only in the Church, but when he is visiting the sick: and he should impress it upon the sick persons themselves, upon their relatives, and especially upon the medical attendants. Above all, he must carry it out in practice, which will be the most effectual means of removing the prejudice and the abuse from the parish.

§ 6. OF VARIOUS DIFFICULTIES WHICH THE PARISH PRIEST MAY HAVE TO ENCOUNTER IN ADMINISTERING THE SACRAMENTS TO THE SICK.

There are five principal difficulties which a Parish Priest may have to encounter in administering the

OF ASSISTING THE SICK AND DYING. 325

Sacraments to the sick. The first of these difficulties arises should it happen that the sick person refuses to avail of his ministry. In this case he must have recourse to prayer, which is the most effective remedy. Let him pray fervently himself, and ask the prayers of pious souls likewise.[1] It will be also well in such circumstances to make some promise to the Blessed Virgin, in order to interest her maternal heart in favour of the sick man; and it would be advisable, moreover, to place under his pillow a medal of our Blessed Lady, since wonderful conversions have often been brought about by this means. Then, should he be allowed access to the patient, he ought to speak to him in the gentlest and most insinuating manner, taking no notice of any rude or insulting replies which he may receive. He must also endeavour to soften

[1] Regarding this difficulty the Roman Ritual says: "Quod si æger aliquis hortationibus ac monitis sacerdotum vel amicorum et domesticorum consiliis adduci non potest ut velit peccata sua confiteri, tunc non omnino desperanda res est, sed quamdiu ille vivit, repetendæ sunt frequenter variæ et efficaces sacerdotum et aliorum piorum hominum exhortationes ; proponendaque æternæ salutis damna, et sempiternæ mortis supplicia ; ostendendaque immensa Dei misericordia, eum ad pœnitentiam provocantis, ad ignoscendum paratissimi. Adhibendæ sunt etiam tum privatæ, tum publicæ ad Deum preces, ad divinam gratiam impetrandam pro salute miseri decumbentis" (de visitatione et cura infirmorum). Commenting on this passage, Baruffaldi writes: "Verbis primo utendum est ad convincendos pertinaces, deinde orationibus ; sed præ cæteris posterior modus validior est, a quo abhorrere non debent tum parochus, tum adstantes. Itaque genibus flexis et omni humilitate jacentes tam parochus quam domestici, et si qui alii sint, orent super eum enixis precibus, *ut audiantur et videantur a pertinace infirmo*". The italics are my own.—*Translator.*

his heart, by employing for this purpose the charitable assistance of persons who are on friendly terms with him, and have influence over his mind. In a word, as long as life remains to the sick man, the Parish Priest must not omit to do for him, all that an active, zealous, and earnest charity can suggest.

It is a rare, but not impossible occurrence, that the sick person should demand the Sacraments, and that unbelieving members of his family should refuse to summon the priest, in order that he may thus die deprived of them. On becoming aware of this barbarous tyranny, the Parish Priest ought to proceed to this unfriendly house, and demand access to the sick person, with all possible mildness of manner, and with all the pressing importunity of pastoral charity. Should his efforts prove unavailing, he ought, if time permit, to inform the Bishop of the circumstances, in order to be advised by him, and also that even the Bishop himself, should he think it advisable, might make an effort to see the sick person. Meanwhile he ought to interest in the matter all those who have most influence and authority with the relatives of the patient, in order to win them over from their impious resolution; nay, should this occur in a place where considerations of religion and humanity are respected, he ought even to apply to the civil authorities, in order to be assisted by the arm of the law. In this second difficulty, as in all the others, he ought moreover to have recourse to prayer, as has been said above.

The third difficulty arises when the sick person

may happen to be living in concubinage: and in this case we must make a distinction.

In many cases the concubinage is secret, at least in the locality where the patient resides, and the persons who are cohabiting are commonly regarded as man and wife. In this case, should the Parish Priest become aware of the concubinage through the Sacramental Confession of the sick person, and should both the man and the woman be free to contract marriage, he ought to marry them as soon as possible, having first asked and obtained the necessary permission for this purpose from his penitent, in order not to violate the seal of confession. Should time permit, he ought to seek the authorisation of the Bishop to act in this manner; but otherwise he ought to perform the marriage ceremony on his own authority, since under such circumstance the law regarding the publication of the banns and other such regulations do not bind, as is agreed upon by theologians and canonists. Should the sick person afterwards die, or recover, the Parish Priest ought to inform the Bishop of what he had done, and ask his instructions regarding the registration of the marriage, &c.

This is the general theory on this subject, which is universally received and approved. Nevertheless, the Parish Priest must guard against being too hasty to marry, without the permission of the Bishop, persons living in concubinage; for there might be reason to anticipate serious evils, especially should the sick person recover, which would dispense the Parish Priest from celebrating the marriage. Should the Parish Priest foresee that, in the event of the patient's recovery, the marriage would prove unfortunate, that the relatives would have a right to hinder it, or that it might lead to some difficulties with the civil authorities—in these and such like circumstances the Pastor ought abstain from marrying the parties, and act as if the celebration of the marriage were impossible.

Nor does it avail to reply that the Parish Priest is bound to administer the Sacraments to those who ask for them, even at his own personal risk; for this obligation holds only when there is question of those Sacraments which are necessary for salvation, such as Baptism and Penance, but it does not apply to Matrimony, without which any one, and especially a dying person, can be saved. And still more would the Parish Priest be dispensed from this obligation, should he foresee that the marriage would prove unfortunate for the contracting parties themselves.

In case the concubinage is secret, and the party that is in health refuses to contract marriage, or should any impediment exist between them, the sick person ought to promise, in the event of recovery, to separate at any cost from his or her supposed spouse, unless the other should afterwards consent to marry, or a dispensation should be obtained in the case of an impediment. Moreover, the sick person ought to promise to break off at once all intercourse or familiarity which might partake of the nature of concubinage; or, at the very least, to oppose it as far as possible, and not to consent to it on any condition, no matter what allurements or threats may be employed. Once such promises have been made, the Sacraments might be administered to the sick person.

On the other hand, should the concubinage be publicly known, the Parish Priest ought to insist on a separation as the very first step, unless the necessity for administering the Sacraments to the sick person should be so urgent that his paramour could not leave at once, (for instance, in the night time), or even should refuse to leave on any terms. In this case it would be sufficient that the sick person declare, in the presence of some witnesses, that he is penitent, and is resolved to break off the connexion from that moment as far as possible. I have said *in the presence of some witnesses;* so that afterwards these may be in a position to bear testimony to the repentance of the sick man, and thus remove the public scandal which might otherwise ensue, from the fact of having the Sacraments administered to one who had been living in concubinage. When the Parish Priest administers the Sacraments with this precaution, he ought nevertheless to require the sick person to keep his paramour away from his bedside as far as possible ; and this he ought to do not only for the sake of good example, and in order to give proof of the sincerity of his repentance, but also to avoid the risk of bad thoughts and dangerous familiarity, which long habit and the Devil might suggest.

When this has been carried out, the Parish Priest might administer the Sacraments, even though he should foresee that, in case of recovery, all the good intentions and promises made by the sick person will be cast to the winds, and that both parties will resume their former sinful union, as in fact almost invariably happens in such cases. For it must be remembered that the Sacraments produce their effects according to the *actual* dispositions of the penitent, and not according to the dispositions which he *may possibly have* after a month, a week, or even a day shall have elapsed. Now it is exceedingly probable that a sick man who finds himself at death's door will sincerely detest his sins, at least with attrition, and will have a real purpose of amendment; and in this case it is evident that, with such sorrow and such a resolution, the Sacrament confers grace immediately. And even though the sick person, on recovering, should again fall back into his sinful practices, this new bad disposition could not invalidate the acts of the previous good disposition, in virtue of which he would already have received justification. Even when persons who are in health confess to us, how often do we give them absolution though we foresee that they will fall again? We give, and we are bound to give, absolution, whenever the penitent in the act of confession shows that he is disposed; and it would be a very grave error, nay a real injustice, to deny it under such circumstances, because of a future bad disposition which as yet has no actual existence. God condemns no one to Hell, or even to Purgatory, because of a future bad disposition; nor would it be lawful for us to refuse the Sacraments to anyone because of a possible bad disposition of this kind.

Therefore, when the separation of the parties who have been living in concubinage is physically or morally impossible, the Parish Priest ought to administer the Sacraments to the sick person.

The Parish Priest may have a fourth difficulty to encounter, in cases where the sick person has obligations with which he is unwilling to comply. Here however one must weigh well whether these obligations are really *certain*, so that there cannot be any doubt as to their existence. For example, if the sick person had stolen five pounds, and was unwilling to make restitution, one could not administer the Sacraments to him even at the point of death, since he would be evidently indisposed. The Parish Priest could do nothing for him, except to employ every means in his power to induce him to discharge his obligation.

If, however, the sick man's obligation were not certain according to the unanimous opinion of theologians—if, for example, he had found the five pounds, and, being unable to discover the owner after having made the necessary enquiries, should wish to retain the money as his own and bequeath it to his heirs,— the Parish Priest could on no account oblige him to give that money to the poor, or to expend it in some other pious work : and the case would not be altered in the least by the fact that some, or even many, theologians maintained a different opinion. Not even if he had fifty theologians on his side could a Parish Priest presume to pronounce definitively upon a question which the Church leaves free among moral theologians. Therefore, should the sick man's obligation be a disputed question amongst theologians, even though it may appear quite certain and evident to the Parish Priest and though this view may be supported, moreover, by the authority of many authors, yet if the sick person himself refuses to recognise it, the Parish Priest can not on this score refuse him the Sacraments. But it may be said: how will it fare with the dying man before the tribunal of God, in case the obligation should be true and real in His Divine Sight? I reply that such an objection as this would be unpardonable coming from any theologian. The sick man will have nothing to fear on this account before God's tribunal; because God does not judge our actions by the standard of the moral truths as they are in themselves, but as they are understood by us. If we believe that those moral theologians can be saved, who teach and defend disputed opinions which are not condemned by the Church, we ought also to believe that those persons can be saved who follow out their opinions in practice.

The Parish Priest may have a fifth difficulty to encounter, should the sick person have incurred some censure, and yet refuse to acknowledge it. It is quite possible that the sick man, influenced by reasons which seem to him probable, or by the authority of persons whom he judges competent to decide in such matters, should really believe that he had not incurred the censure—let us say of Excommunication. In this case the Parish Priest ought to reflect whether there might not be a doubt, after all, whether the man had ncurred the censure; for, as theologians teach, no one, in case of doubt, ought to be judged to have fallen under censure. In any case, if the Parish Priest can suppose that the sick man is really in good faith, he can administer the Sacraments to him, not only without danger of failing in the discharge of his own duty, but also without imperiling the salvation of his penitent; who, even though he should be in error, and should have really incurred the censure, would nevertheless be absolved from it by the confessor, from whom no censure is reserved at the point of death.

But should the sin by which the sick person had incurred the censure be public, and should he be commonly reputed as under censure, though he should himself refuse to admit the fact, the Parish Priest ought, necessarily, to consult the Bishop and receive his instructions, if he have time to do so. Should the time at his disposal not admit of his adopting this course, the Parish Priest must again reflect whether the sick man might not really be in good faith; for circumstances might possibly arise in which he would be excusable before God. Let us suppose that persons of authority, or who at least were regarded as such, had assured the sick man that the law imposing the censure did not extend to that particular case, and that when committing the sin he did not believe that he was really offending against the law of the church, in such circumstances, there would be wanting the *contumacia* necessary to incur the censure. In like manner, should he be persuaded that the law had become obsolete, or that it was no longer in force, the Parish Priest, being able in such circumstances to suppose *bona fides* in the sick person, ought to require of him to recognise explicitly the authority of the church, and to profess obedience to her in all cases where there is no doubt; and having done this he might administer the Sacraments to him. Meanwhile, to remove surprise and scandal, the Parish Priest ought to say that the sick man had done his duty, and had died reconciled to the Church and submissive to her authority.

The same course should be pursued when the exacting of a public acknowledgment of the censure would be attended with serious evil consequences, which would be well known to the public. Under such circumstances, the Parish Priest ought to require from the sinner (of course outside Sacramental Confession) a declaration of repentance, and a promise that, in case he should survive, he would submit to whatever the Church might impose upon him. This should be done, if possible, in the presence of some discreet witnesses. Then he might administer the Sacraments, and it would be sufficient to state afterwards, in general terms, that the sick man *had made everything right*. In this manner the people would know that if the Parish Priest had imposed no further conditions on him, it was because he could not do so without risking deplorable consequences. Meanwhile it would be said that both the Parish Priest and the sick man had recognised and respected the Ecclesiastical law, and that the Sacraments were not given and received in defiance of it, which would be sufficient to remove the danger of scandal.

This, however, must not be understood to apply when there is question of some notorious sinner who is under a censure, and from whom it might be supposed that the Church would at any cost require some sign of public retractation. In this case the person under censure ought at least to make a declaration, in the presence of some witnesses, that he recognises the authority of the Church, and that in the event of his recovery he will do all that he may be bound to do.

Finally, should the sick man refuse to believe that he had incurred a censure, because it is his opinion that the Church had not authority to inflict it, this would be inexcusable presumption, nor could such a one be at all considered disposed for the reception of the Sacraments. The theory that each individual among the Faithful is to constitute himself judge of the exercise of the Church's rights, and that her laws do not bind Titus or Sempronius, except when Titus or Sempronius may happen to be persuaded of their equity, is a theory which is something more than schismatical—it is heretical. He who goes to the other world believing that Holy Mother Church abuses her power, and despising her constitutions as arbitrary and tyrannical, cannot receive from the Sacraments any help towards salvation. Under such circumstances there can be no possible reason for administering the Sacraments to the sick man, nor ought any account be taken of the consequences which may follow from refusing them to him. In a case of this kind a Pastor ought to attend solely to the evangelical precept, "*nolite sanctum dare canibus*".

§ 7. OF ASSISTING THE DYING.

Having administered the Sacraments, the Parish Priest ought to assist the sick person to the very last moment; and we must highly disapprove of the custom, or rather the abuse, which prevails in some places, where the Parish Priests are in the habit of administering the last Sacraments to the sick, and, having done so, never afterwards return to visit them.[1] Such a custom could scarcely be tolerated in winter time, in certain localities where one would have to perform a most painful journey on foot, amidst ice and snow, and hurricanes dangerous even to life. Scarcely could a Parish Priest in these

---

[1] When forwarding (June 2, 1873) to his Eminence Cardinal Cullen a letter of instructions regarding some matters to be discussed in the approaching Synod of Maynooth, the Cardinal Prefect of Propaganda enclosed, with other documents, copy of a letter written by him on June 9, 1863, referring to the assistance to be given by priests to the dying. The original of this letter, which is in Italian, may be found in an Appendix to the Statutes of the Synod of Maynooth (Appendix XXV., p. 347). I subjoin a translation. . . . "As regards the first point, I am informed that it is customary in several dioceses that the priest (almost invariably the curate) goes to the sick person when seriously ailing to administer to him, one after the other, the Sacraments of Penance, the Eucharist, and Extreme Unction; but that when this has been done he does not again return to see the patient, unless he is expressly summoned to do so, so that the sick rarely have the consolation of being assisted by the priest at the hour of death.

localities, after having administered the last Sacraments and given the indulgence *in articulo mortis*, recommend the patient to the charity of some pious person who might assist and comfort him, leaving directions, however, that he should be summoned again without delay, should the sick person have any special need of him, as for instance in case his conscience should not be quite tranquil.

Nevertheless it cannot be maintained that a Parish Priest, or whoever supplies his place, after having administered the Sacraments, must not stir from the bed-side of the sick person until he either dies or has made marked progress towards recovery, as is the custom in some other places. If the abuse first mentioned is one of defect, this latter abuse errs on the side of excess, and it is a bad custom. First, because it obliges the Parish Priest, or his substitute, to remain beside the sick person for days and nights,

---

I am free to admit that, in certain places and under certain circumstances, this may happen through necessity, considering the scarcity of priests, and the number of sick persons who are sometimes to be found at the point of death at the same time. But that this system should be habitually followed in certain dioceses, as I am assured is the case, is foreign to the spirit of the Church as well as to the practice inculcated by the Roman Ritual, and confirmed by the Sacred Congregation of the Council when the following doubt was proposed to it by the Bishop of Bagnorea, April 14th, 1821 :—An et quomodo teneatur canonicus curatus ægrotos ruricolas visitare iisque assistentiam præbere dum morti proximi reperiuntur ? The Sacred Congregation replied: "Affirmative ad formam Ritualis Romani, et Episcopus curet providere parœciæ Capellanum Curatum ne ruricolæ vel civitatis incolæ spirituali assistentia careant" . . . .—*Translator.*

without being able to occupy himself with the other duties of his ministry, or to take the repose which is necessary for him. Secondly, because when the Parish Priest knows that the relatives of the sick man expect this constant attendance once Extreme Unction has been administered, he is strongly tempted to defer the administration of this Sacrament as long as possible, in order not to deprive himself too soon of his liberty, and be obliged to nail himself, as it were, to the bed of the dying person.

If the people of any parish should set up any such claim as this, the Parish Priest ought to instruct them on the advisability of administering Extreme Unction at an early stage of the illness, both in order to make sure that the sick person will not be deprived of this Sacrament, and that he may derive therefrom more abundant spiritual advantages. He should, next, impress upon them that, once the Sacrament is administered, constant attendance at the bedside would be useless, when the danger of death is still remote. Meanwhile, the Parish Priest ought to administer Extreme Unction when the sick person is still strong, and there is no immediate danger apparent. The relatives would not then be so unreasonable as to expect that the Parish Priest should remain to assist their sick friend, when there was really no need of his presence. Moreover, by administering this Sacrament to the sick in good time, many of them would recover, and it would become every day more evident that this constant attendance was unreasonable. He might add that the Church does not require it from Parish Priests; explaining to them the words of the Roman Ritual : " ingravescenti morbo, Parochus infirmum frequentius visitabit, et ad salutem diligenter juvare non desinet; monebitque instante periculo se confestim vocari, ut in tempore præsto sit morienti". Wherefore the following is the course which ought to be adopted by a Parish Priest —first, to administer the Sacraments to the sick at a very early stage of their illness; then to visit them frequently (even several times in the day, should the distance and other occupations not prevent him from doing so), and the more frequently in proportion as death approaches, or the patient exhibits a greater need of spiritual consolation; to recommend the relatives to inform him without delay of any sudden change for the worse which may take place; and, finally, not to leave the sick person any more, once he perceives that death is imminent.[1]

And in this connection some few additional remarks may not be out of place. The first is that, in assisting the dying, the Parish Priest should take care to make his presence useful and edifying to their families. This is the seasonable time to administer corrections, and to excite them to do good; because, with the dying man before their eyes, his relatives and

---

[1] In the decrees of the first Council of Westminster (decree xxv. n. 7.) we find the following: " In visiting and assisting the sick and dying let him (*i.e.*, a priest having the care of souls) be solicitous ; and let him not abandon them altogether, after they have received the Sacraments; but let him continue to visit them often, even daily if he have time, and assist them in their agony".—*Translator.*

friends are better disposed to receive the impressions of faith, than they would be under any other circumstances. The most favourable moment of all is when the Parish Priest is about to take his departure from the house, after the sick person has expired, and he has offered up the prayers for a departed soul. Let him avail himself of this moment, which is always serious and solemn, to make a few brief and appropriate reflections, which must necessarily produce on the hearts of those who are present a salutary impression which cannot be effaced.

It is easy to understand how wrong it would be for the priest who is assisting the dying, to indulge in useless conversation, or, still worse, in jokes and pleasantries, under the pretext of alleviating the sorrow and affliction of the relatives. By acting in this manner, the Minister of God would give proof that he was possessed of but little heart, little judgment, and little faith. Little heart, because he would show himself insensible to the most painful scene which this world can present, that, namely, of a human being struggling with death ; little judgment, because he does not understand how ill-suited is such levity on so solemn an occasion; and little faith, because he shows that he does not realise the importance of the passage to eternity, which his fellowman is just then making, and which he himself must likewise make at some future time.

And what could we say were the Minister of God, with the dying man before his eyes, to indulge in frivolous conversation with young women and girls from the neighbourhood, who might be attracted by curiosity to the house of death? If God's Minister ought to preserve an edifying deportment under all circumstances, how much more ought he to do so by the bedside of the dying!

The Parish Priest must also take care not to allow in the room of the patient persons who can be of no possible assistance to him, and who would only disturb him, and distract him from the good thoughts which ought to occupy his mind—the more so, should they happen to indulge in vain or imprudent conversations, or to speak on matters in which he may be deeply interested. Above all, should a young man happen to be dying, he ought to prevent him from being visited by the young woman who is betrothed to him, and *vice versa*, as such visits would be attended with great danger. The Parish Priest could easily find an excuse for excluding such persons from the sick room, observing, for instance, that the presence of many visitors would vitiate the air of the apartment; or, that the conversation and even the mere movements of several persons tend to aggravate the sickness very much, considering the critical condition to which the patient is reduced. In the last-mentioned case, however—that, namely, of lovers—should the relatives be pious persons, the Parish Priest ought to point out the danger clearly to them, remarking, moreover, that such visits would serve only to embitter the last moments of the dying person—an argument which will be appreciated even by relatives who are not pious.

The Parish Priest must also be careful that whilst the dying person appears to be in a lethargic condition, no one should begin to praise him in his presence, saying for example: *he is an angel, he will go straight to heaven*, &c., for sometimes when the sick appear to be entirely unconscious they hear all that is said, and, in such circumstances, words of praise would be a temptation to them. In like manner, no one should say : *he cannot hold out much longer : he will not survive until morning;* as such expressions might cause too much alarm to the dying person. It is also very annoying and discouraging, and is, moreover, in the case of women, and especially of young women, a proof of little caution and prudence, that the assisting priest should be constantly feeling the pulse of the sick person, as some rude and inconsiderate priests are in the habit of doing.

When engaged in assisting the sick, some other matters will also claim the attention of the Parish Priest, which at first sight seem rather foreign to the pastoral ministry, but which in reality are very proper to it, since it is not purely and simply a ministry of religion alone, but of charity as well.

Wherefore he must see that the sick person is provided with whatever may be necessary for him in his illness; and should he observe that his relatives are careless or negligent in this respect, he must remind them of their duty as prudently and as politely as possible, and must caution them in a special manner not to allow the invalid to want medical assistance and medicine. Sometimes when the relatives see that the patient is growing worse they become discouraged: again, if he be old and useless to his family, they feel no great interest in his recovery; and in both cases they become very negligent, to an extent which may prove fatal to the life of the sick person. In these cases the Parish Priest must exercise a charitable vigilance, and must do for the dying man as he would for a relative or friend, and as he would wish others to do for himself in like circumstances.

Frequently, poverty and wretchedness are the principal causes of this deplorable negligence; and when this is the case, the Parish Priest must regard it as his strict duty to come to the assistance of the invalid. For this purpose let him have recourse to charitable societies and to benevolent individuals; let him contribute from his own purse; and, in a word, give efficacious assistance to the poor sick person. Should the Parish Priest perceive that, considering the poverty of the family, the invalid cannot receive at home all the care that he requires, he must endeavour to persuade him to allow himself to be taken to the public hospital, provided his strength will permit it, and the physician certifies that he may be removed without danger. Many persons die in their own homes through want of attention, who would recover if taken to the hospital.

Should the Parish Priest observe that the sick man has no thoughts of giving instructions regarding his temporal affairs, or of discharging obligations by which he may be bound, he ought to caution him, or have him cautioned by some other person, to make all necessary arrangements concerning such matters while there is still time.

Finally, I must not omit a remark which concerns the personal safety of the Parish Priest himself. It is that, when going out at night to assist the sick, he should always have some one to accompany him. And I say *always;* so that it may be known that the Parish Priest never goes out at night unaccompanied, and does not trust any one who may summon him, unless he should happen to be some person well-known to him. The courage which prompts men to face danger without necessity is simply foolish rashness. Parish Priests, even without being aware of it, may have enemies, who, as has sometimes happened, may avail themselves of the pretext of calling them to the sick, in order to wreak their vengeance on them. If it be known that the Parish Priest, despising every danger, is accustomed to go out by night unaccompanied, his enemies are by this very fact encouraged to lie in wait for him; but, on the other hand, they will abandon the idea, if it be known that he never leaves his house in the night-time unattended.

APPENDIX II.

OF REFUSING ECCLESIASTICAL BURIAL.

THE Roman Ritual points out clearly who those deceased persons are who ought to be deprived of Ecclesiastical burial. Nevertheless, since the rigour of discipline has been somewhat modified in practice, it will be well to make some appropriate remarks on this subject, so that the Parish Priest may not be perplexed, or in danger of compromising himself, as occasionally happens, with the relatives of the deceased or with the Civil Authorities.

When there is question of deceased persons not belonging to the Catholic Communion there is ordinarily no difficulty; but difficulties frequently arise when we come to deal with the case of persons who were Catholics, at least in name, who were baptised in the Catholic Church, who belonged to Catholic families, but who, nevertheless, lived without practising their religion, led immoral lives, and despised the laws of the Church and her censures. Such persons, on the ground that they have not expressly abjured the Catholic faith, claim the rites of the Church after death, and would consider themselves covered with infamy were they not interred in consecrated ground. Their relatives carry out this unjust pretension, and are sometimes supported in their action by the Civil Authorities.

Now the first counsel which I would give to a Parish Priest is a very general one, namely, never on his own authority to deny Ecclesiastical burial to any one of those who may appear unworthy of it, but to lay the case before the Bishop, and await his instructions. By acting in this manner, the Parish Priest will relieve himself of all responsibility; for no one could ever reasonably ask him to disobey the orders of his Bishop. By following this counsel, the Parish Priest will avoid a great deal of trouble, and perhaps evil consequences. Wherefore, in cases of this kind, he ought at any cost to have recourse to the Bishop, even though his parish should be at a distance from the Episcopal residence, so that he could not go there without expense or inconvenience. And here I will remark that he ought not to transact business of this kind through the Post-office, lest the Bishop may not receive the letter in time, and may thus be prevented from sending a prompt reply. The Parish Priest ought to go in person to the Bishop, or at least to send some trusty messenger to him, with a letter stating the full particulars regarding the death of the person who is about to be buried, and the same messenger could bring back the Bishop's reply without loss of time.

Should the Parish Priest, through difficulties arising from local circumstances or through want of time, be unable to take counsel with the Bishop, he ought to act upon the principle of never denying Ecclesiastical burial, except when to grant it would be a certain and evident violation of his duty. And let it be remembered that, in the absence of this certainty and evidence, he must not act upon the views of some Theologian or Canonist whose opinion might be for refusing Ecclesiastical burial. The private opinion of any author, even though he should be a man of great repute, can never make an opinion certain and evident. To render it such, there would be required either clear, manifest, convincing reasons, or the common consent of theologians. Whenever, then, a doubt may exist as to the unworthiness of the person who is to be buried, the Parish Priest, if unable to consult the Bishop, ought to grant him Ecclesiastical burial.

Now, having established this principle, if a man should die suddenly who had been living in concubinage, but who, nevertheless, kept the concubine in his house in the capacity of housekeeper, servant, or the like, so that the fact of concubinage, though generally suspected, could not be proved, the Parish Priest, in case he have no opportunity of consulting the Bishop, ought to grant such person Ecclesiastical burial.

The same rule holds good when there is question of a man who may have incurred some censure, provided the censure be not publicly known, or had been incurred a long time previously, so that people had probably forgotten all about it, or that it might be supposed that he had already complied with all that conscience required. The same course should be likewise followed if the deceased had filled some office or situation, which could not *per se* be justified by well-instructed persons, but which was not viewed in the same light by public opinion, or in respect of which we might suppose the man, who was himself incapable of knowing the truth, to have been in good faith, because he was imposed upon by persons whose authority had influence with him. In one word, it would not be enough that he had probably, or even certainly incurred the censure, if this were not generally known, or if he could be plausibly excused before the public.

It may be remarked in this connection that as regards excommunicated persons who are publicly known as such, and who die impenitent, the Sacred Penitentiary, on being consulted as to how a Parish Priest or Bishop ought to act when there is grave and imminent danger of public disturbance, and of the intervention of the Executive, if the funeral be not carried out, replied "*passive se habeant*".

Those who do not comply with the Paschal Precept, and who die without having time to be reconciled with God, or without being able to give signs of repentance, would deserve to be buried outside consecrated ground. Nevertheless, the custom prevails that, if they be guilty of no other crime, they should be buried in consecrated ground, and in this case it is not even necessary to consult the Bishop. Formerly, Parish Priests kept an exact account of those who complied with the Paschal Precept, but this is no

OF REFUSING ECCLESIASTICAL BURIAL.   349

longer done. The names of those who transgressed in this particular were published on the church door, but the custom has ceased to be observed. In those days everyone took the most lively interest in proving that he had complied with the Precept, even though he may have done so after the appointed time had elapsed; but now-a-days this is no longer the case. Nay, it frequently happens that confessors, whether authorised or not, permit those who fulfil the precept outside the appointed time to communicate outside their own parish. From all this it follows that the Parish Priest can no longer know with certainty which of his parishioners have transgressed the Precept; and even though he did know them without the possibility of mistake, yet his knowledge would be private, and such as he could not make public. In fact, it would never be lawful for a Parish Priest, of his private authority to put in practice an Ecclesiastical regulation already abolished, or fallen into disuse, which might be attended with most serious consequences, such as is the rule of publishing the names of those who transgress the Paschal Precept. Therefore, for all these reasons it would be useless to ask counsel from the Bishop in a case where we must already anticipate what that counsel would be.

On the other hand, the Bishop ought to be consulted when there is question of those who have committed suicide. But if this cannot be done, the Parish Priest ought, as a general rule, to grant Ecclesiastical burial to the suicide, for the reason that his self-murder may be supposed to be the effect of insanity, of which the Parish Priest alone cannot be a competent judge. It would be the province of the Bishop to examine the case, and pronounce a safe opinion on it.

As regards public sinners—such as public blasphemers, assassins, prostitutes and the like—we must take into account whether they were of such evil repute as to be regarded by the public as unworthy of Ecclesiastical burial, so that, as Cardinal Gousset says, (tom 2, n. 636), it would be a fresh public scandal to bury them in consecrated ground. In this case the Parish Priest must deny them Ecclesiastical burial, even though he should not have an opportunity of consulting the Bishop. This rule, however, must be understood to apply to blasphemers only in case they are notoriously such, and the same is to be said of assassins. In the case of prostitutes, they should belong to the class who make a profession of immorality, or at least who are so barefaced and notorious as to rank with professional prostitutes. Of course what has been said applies to these different classes of persons only when they have given no sign of repentance, so that they have died in certain and public final impenitence.

It must likewise be remembered that, except in these cases of manifest unworthiness, the Bishop need not be consulted even when it might easily be done; because if the unworthiness were not thus manifest, the Bishop would not forbid burial in consecrated ground.

Ecclesiastical burial should be refused absolutely to those who die in the very act of committing a manifest sin, as, for example, should a murderer be killed by his intended victim at the very moment when he was attacking him.

Christian burial must likewise be denied in the case of a person who when dying had rejected with insults and blasphemies the ministrations of the priest, in presence of witnesses capable of bearing testimony to the fact. However, if such insults and blasphemies had been uttered in the presence of the priest alone, or of some intimate friend, as a brother, a son, a wife, &c., the Parish Priest ought to grant Ecclesiastical burial. He ought also to grant Ecclesiastical burial, should the bystanders testify that, though the dying man had at first refused the consolations of religion, he afterwards asked for them before death, or had given some outward sign of repentance. Cardinal Gousset teaches, moreover, that if the priest had succeeded in speaking with the dying man in private about the reception of the Sacraments (as he ought always strive to do), should there be no public scandals to be repaired, and should there exist among the people a general impression that he had made his confession, the Parish Priest ought not to deny him Ecclesiastical burial, even though in reality he had given no sign of repentance.[1]

Finally, Christian burial must be denied to those

---

[1] Si sacerdos solus testis fuerit impœnitentiæ moribundi, non est deneganda sepultura ecclesiastica, nisi aliunde ipsi denegari debeat; sed tacere debet sacerdos de impia dispositione moribundi, et sinere, ut credant, eum fuisse sacramentis rite expiatum. Debent enim vitari scandala, quantum fieri potest. Imo operæ prætium erit, ut

who are killed in a duel, even though they should have given signs of repentance, as was directed by Benedict XIV. in the Bull *Detestabilem*. Gury held at one time that if the principal in a duel had died outside the actual place of combat, and after having given signs of repentance, he might be buried in consecrated ground; but in his last edition he changed this opinion, in conformity with the Bull just quoted, which says: "*etiamsi extra locum conflictus sacramentis muniti decesserint*". Scavini remarks that this last provision is not observed in all dioceses *(de duello)*.

Let it however be held as a rule in every case that the Parish Priest, whenever he can, even at inconvenience and expense, ought to consult the Bishop before refusing Ecclesiastical burial.

sacerdos, dubius de dispositione moribundi, ipsum absque testibus alloquatur et ad confessionem inducat, ne malus ejus animus innotescat; modo tamen aliquod scandalum non sit necessario reparandum. — Ita statutum est in variis diœcesibus et id prudentia suadet. (Gury. Theol. Moral., n. 1689, edit. Ratisb.) — *Translator.*

CHAPTER III.

OF THE SACRAMENT OF PENANCE.

§ 1. OF THE STUDY OF MORAL THEOLOGY.

IN order to administer the Sacrament of Penance properly, it is necessary to attend to the study of Moral Theology, which cannot be neglected by Priests who aspire to a parochial benefice. The Concursus, or at least the Examination to which they have to submit before receiving the benefice, obliges them to this study, and it may therefore be said that when a Priest obtains a Parish he is at least sufficiently instructed to hear confessions.

But it must not be supposed that the amount of knowledge which he then possesses will remain with him for ever, so that he may thenceforward dispense with his books, and rest satisfied with what he has already studied. The human memory is liable to forget; and in the case of a science so vast, so complicated, and so full of positive legislation as is Moral Theology it is not enough to have studied it once—a Priest must study it continually.[1] It fre-

---

[1] Speaking of the necessity of constant study for those whose duty obliges them to hear Confessions, St. Liguori says:—"Non facile sibi suadeant, quod satis idoneos ad tantum munus se reddere possint sine diuturno studio scientiæ moralis; pro qua certe non

quently happens that when certain Parish Priests come to discuss some point, and that not even a very difficult one, they give evidence of having forgotten a great deal of what they must have known when they took part in the Concursus for a parish. And what wonder that they should? We allow ten and twenty years to pass by without revising our Moral Theology, and will we still presume to call ourselves well instructed? A Parish Priest, then, must never give up the study of Moral Theology.

§ 2. Of the Choice of Authors and Opinions.

The authors who within the last few centuries

sufficit aliquam percurrere summulam earum quæ circumferuntur, nec satis est generalia principia hujus facultatis scire, ut quidam, qui casuistas contemnentes litteratorum arrogant sibi nomen, autumnant" (St. Lig., lib. VI., tract 4, n. 628). And elsewhere he says: "Nullus Confessarius intermittere debet theologiæ moralis studium, quia ex tot rebus tam diversis et inter se disparibus, quæ ad hanc scientiam pertinent, multa, quamvis lecta, quia rarius accidunt, temporis progressu e mente decidunt; qua de re oportet semper frequenti studio eas in memoriam revocare". (St. Lig. Praxis Confessarii, cap. 1, § 3, in fine.)

Touching the same subject, we find the following among the Decrees of the First Council of Westminster (Decree XXIV., n. 11.) "It is expedient that all, except Missionary Rectors, should have their faculties limited as to time; so that at first they receive them for a year, and then gradually for longer periods. But let all Priests bear in mind, that the Bishops have a right, which is exercised in many places, and most highly commended by Benedict XIV., to subject Priests again to Examination, especially junior ones, before they renew their faculties. If Priests will in this way persevere in sacred studies and in reading the Word of God, they will find the wisdom that sitteth by the throne of God, meeting them in their sacred ministry, as an honourable mother."—(Eccli XV., 2.)—*Translator.*

have written on Moral Theology are exceedingly numerous, and, as is known not only to Parish Priests but even to tyros in the Sacred Science, they may be divided into two classes—those, namely, who favour opinions which lean towards rigorism, and those who adopt milder views. Now, from which class ought we to select our authors? And of these opposite systems which ought to be preferred?

Before I answer these questions, I shall state two indisputable facts. The first is, that all the ministers of God who have been men of action and of experience have invariably inclined towards the milder doctrines, leaving the more severe ones to the speculations of students and of recluses. The other fact is, that Parish Priests who dislike the milder opinions almost invariably find their confessionals deserted; so that, though they may effect some good through other means, they will be able to effect exceedingly little through the administration of the Sacrament of Penance. These are facts which cannot be disputed. I was not in the least surprised when I read once in a somewhat rigid author, that for forty years, during which he had been hearing confessions, he had never met with a case of an invalid marriage. What else could be expected when his only penitents were friars, nuns, and devotees. I have also heard of a Parish Priest, who, during the entire paschal time, had heard the confession of only one woman.

Having stated these two facts by way of preface, I will next observe that formerly this question might possibly furnish matter for a lengthened discussion; but since it pleased God to give the world a theologian like St. Alphonsus Liguori, who by his learning and sanctity has won the sympathy of almost all confessors, and since all the more modern authors of any repute aim at nothing more than to expound and comment upon his work, there seems to be no longer any necessity for treating the subject at length. Indeed it is a consolation to know that in our times there are very few Parish Priests who do not select as their text-book of Moral Theology, St. Alphonsus, or some of his commentators, such as Scavini, Neyraguet, Gury, Cardinal Gousset, &c.

It is worth remarking that Cardinal Gousset attributes religious laxity in France to an undue preference for rigid doctrines, and he adds: "the weaker the faith has become among us, the more necessary it is to deal mildly with sinners who return to God: *infirmum in fide suscipite*". (Justific. of Mor. Theol., &c., Introd. and Moral Theol., vol. 1, n. 296: vol. 2, n. 547.) I have already touched upon this point elsewhere, when speaking of preaching.

§ 3. OF ASSIDUITY IN HEARING CONFESSIONS.

The Parish Priest who is zealous for the conversion of sinners and for the salvation of souls, is assiduous in his attendance in the confessional, where he can more immediately accomplish both these objects.

The Parish Priest ought not to confine himself to discharging this duty on some fixed days; but ought

OF THE SACRAMENT OF PENANCE.   357

to be prepared to exercise this holy ministry on every day in the year, whether it be a Festival or a week day. Every day there may be in the parish a soul which has need of being reconciled with God ; and it ought be to him a matter of the greatest importance that this soul should not have to wait even for a single day without doing so. Even pious souls have sometimes urgent need of some spiritual comfort. And let a Pastor be careful, when fixing an hour for hearing confessions, to consult not his own convenience but that of his people. The only hour which can be really suitable to them must be in the early morning, when the poor and those who are constantly occupied during the day can attend at the church, before going to work or to business. Wherefore a Parish Priest ought to rise very quickly in the morning, and proceed without delay to his Confessional.

But some one may say, would not the better course be that, after rising early, he should first make his meditation, next say Mass, and then, after having made his thanksgiving, proceed to hear confessions ? This pious advice would not be excusable coming from anyone except from some person who had never filled the office of Parish Priest, and who would therefore speak according to the promptings of his piety, but without the light of experience. The remarks which we made above at page 279, and which we shall make later on when speaking of prayer, are very appropriate to this subject. It is a fact that whoever goes to his Confessional at a late hour hears but few, and these few belong to the class of rich and well-to-do persons. Methodical and precise piety does not suit Parish Priests, just as a regular and precise manner of living will not suit mothers. Mothers must eat, sleep, and take a little recreation, but they do all this in a somewhat irregular manner, and whenever the constant care of their children permits them; nevertheless, they enjoy excellent health, and to a greater degree than many other women who live strictly according to system. In like manner Parish Priests must take spiritual food and repose, which they find principally in private prayer; but they can do so only when the duties inseparable from the care of souls permit it, and often very irregularly. Nor must we suppose that they will on this account possess less spiritual strength and vigour than other Ecclesiastics who are more regular and methodical; for we must not imagine that grace will make a worse provision for the spiritual necessities of a Parish Priest, than nature makes for the corporal wants of a mother.

Let the Parish Priest then be careful to attend in his confessional at an early hour of the morning, and let there be no distinction made in this respect between town and country; for if, in country parishes, the labouring classes and their wives have to go to their work at an early hour, the poor and labouring classes in towns and cities have to do the self-same. Let him, moreover, exhort those who have leisure to attend in the church on week-days to go to confession on these days, so that there may be

OF THE SACRAMENT OF PENANCE. 359

an opportunity of hearing on Festivals those who cannot come on working days.

§ 4. OF THE CONFESSIONS OF MEN.

Later on I shall speak of the confessions of those men who make special profession of piety; for the present I shall treat exclusively of the confessions of those whose character is rather the opposite of this, but who, nevertheless, approach the Sacraments from time to time, at least at Easter; for it is well that the Parish Priest should keep some few points specially before his mind, when hearing the confessions of persons of this class.

The first point is, not to keep them waiting when they come to Confession. Wherefore a Pastor ought to show himself ready to hear them whenever they ask for Confession, even though the hour should be inconvenient or unsuitable. Should there happen to be both men and women at his confessional, let him hear the men first. As a rule, their occupations are of more importance than those of women, and moreover they are usually more impatient, so that if they be not heard quickly they go away and do not return again. Women, on the other hand, in addition to having more time at their disposal, are more patient and wait longer.

The second point to be remembered is, to receive them, not only with unvarying kindness, but even with a pleased and joyous manner, as if, in fact, the Parish Priest looked upon it as a privilege and a most delightful occupation to hear their confessions. Even though they should belong to the lowest order, he must invariably speak to them with the greatest kindness and affection; for by this means a favourable impression is made upon them, they are disposed to confess well, and to approach the Sacraments more frequently in the future. The Parish Priest ought never lose sight of this counsel, even in his ordinary conversations with men. It is a matter of the greatest importance that they should entertain feelings of affection for him, since they will thus profit the more readily by his advice, exhortations, and corrections; and just as he ought invariably to avoid everything which borders on affection in his relations with women, so he ought habitually to cultivate it in his relations with men.

A third point to be kept in view is, that the Parish Priest should guard himself against suggesting to penitents of this class rules of perfection, which would be neither appreciated nor understood by them. Let him, as a general rule, content himself with instilling into their hearts a hatred of mortal sin, and inculcating the observance of the commandments, dealing with them all the while in a frank, open, indulgent, and kind manner. It is necessary to do this in order that they may not come to regard him as a sour ascetic, and shrink from returning to his confessional.

While adopting this course, however, the Parish Priest must be guided by discretion, especially when there is question of withdrawing them from the occasions of sin; for if a Parish Priest were to be mild and indulgent in permitting to his penitents what might prove really dangerous to their souls, he should be accounted a traitor instead of a loving father. Let him then be as indulgent and mild as possible, but without ever ignoring the principles of justice, morality, charity, and the like.

§ 5. OF THE CONFESSIONS OF WOMEN.

There cannot be the slightest doubt that to hear the confessions of women is the most dangerous and fatal rock which the minister of God has to encounter in the stormy sea of this world; and therefore a Parish Priest—and still more a young Parish Priest—if he be wise and prudent, cannot possibly be without dread of this rock. But, at the same time, this very sense of dread is his best safeguard; for there is no danger that he who fears this rock will ever dash upon it.

Whoever fears it prays constantly and fervently to obtain an unfailing supply of divine grace; and when he is seated in the confessional, in the exercise of his sacred ministry, he does not omit to raise his heart frequently to God, that He may preserve him in that state of indifference and insensibility which cannot be sufficiently prized.

Whoever fears this rock keeps a guard over his eyes: he never observes who it is that may be seated at his confessional, nor does he speak with his face turned towards his penitent. Some confessors know all their penitents, even though but a short time has elapsed since they first began to confess them. Happy are they who do not know even a single one, unless, perhaps, they may have had occasion to speak with them outside the confessional! It proves that they have known how to keep a guard over their eyes, and this is a certain proof that they have also kept a perfect guard over their heart.

Whoever fears this rock never uses any expressions of friendship or familiarity, but is reserved, serious, and respectful in all his words, even though the woman who may be confessing to him is not of a rank or condition to inspire respect.

Whoever fears this rock speaks to every woman as he would speak to a spirit—that is to say, as he would speak to a soul separated from the body, seeing in them nothing but the image of God, purchased and ennobled by the blood of the Lord Jesus Christ. Woe to the man who should consider in them beauty, or vivacity, or youth, or such other vain and dangerous qualities.

Whoever fears this rock must keep his heart hermetically sealed against every sentiment of affection, even though it should owe its origin to the splendid mental gifts, or to the rare virtues which he may discern in any woman. Indeed, he must be specially watchful in this last-mentioned case of women of rare virtue; for under such circumstances the illusion is more plausible, and the Devil more easily ensnares the most enlightened, and those who have the best intentions.

Whoever fears this rock puts the fewest possible questions to his penitent when certain delicate subjects are mentioned in confession. He is satisfied with knowing the species of the sin, and he is most cautious not to enquire into those particulars which affect only the manner of committing it, and merely increase its malice. And here it will be well to remark that even the most rigid theologians, who require the "*circumstantiæ aggravantes*" to be mentioned in confession, were forced by good sense to make an exception in the case of circumstances affecting the violation of the virtue of chastity, and to admit that, in this case, the aggravating circumstances ought never to be disclosed. And assuredly good sense could never approve or tolerate the disclosure of certain filthy details which accompany sins of this kind. (See Gousset, Theol. Mor., vol. 2, p. 424.) O ye who are incautious in asking questions, respect yourselves, respect weak souls, have a reverence for the Sacrament! Of you the Angelic Doctor well says (in Summa. Verbo *Interrogationes*): *potius estis contaminatores quam confessores.*

Whoever fears this rock never contracts familiarity or friendship with his penitents, who remain perfect strangers to him after he has been hearing their confessions even for ten or twenty years. It is not a matter calculated to give edification, it does not show priestly prudence and caution, that a confessor, after having heard a woman's confession, should stay to talk with her on the street, or go to visit at her house.

A Parish Priest must use all these precautions and safeguards if he be young, because he needs them, and if he be old, in order to give good example to others, as well as because, as experience shows, though there is less danger for those advanced in years, yet even for them it is always great. By adopting the precautions here laid down, a good Parish Priest will see verified in himself a miracle which is one of the most beautiful proofs of the truth of the Catholic religion—namely, that all Priests, whether they be Parish Priests or not, who cherish the holy fear of God in their hearts, continue to hear the confessions of women for ten, twenty, thirty, forty, fifty years, and even to the last day of their lives, without having to deplore that the exercise of the sacred ministry has ever been to them the occasion of even a single sin. This is a matter which, without a special and wonderful assistance from God, would be impossible, and which the world does not wish to believe, but which is nevertheless a most certain fact for those who have experience of it.

With regard to female penitents, the Parish Priest must take care never to appear jealous when his penitents go to confession to others. In addition to the fact that this jealousy might spring from an inordinate attachment, it might also cause some of them to make bad confessions even for years, as has often happened. Sometimes a Parish Priest fancies that because he has been hearing the confessions of certain girls and women from their very infancy, they repose such entire confidence in him that they would not hesitate to confess to him any sin whatsoever. But the very opposite happens; for they feel the greatest shame and reluctance to declare to him certain weaknesses of an indelicate nature, and, in consequence, never tell them at all.

Wherefore, should any of his penitents express a desire to go to confession to any other priest, a Pastor ought to appear perfectly satisfied, unless, indeed, she might wish to confess to some one whom he knew to be very ignorant, or somewhat lax; and in this case, since the state of her soul might render a change of confessors advisable, he ought to make such arrangements that she may, at least sometimes, confess to a priest to whom she would not be personally known. Should the Parish Priest at any time suspect that one of his female penitents has been to a strange confessor, he ought not even ask her what time has elapsed since her last confession. Finally, as a general rule, the pastors of small parishes ought for this purpose to invite from time to time (as we have already observed when speaking of the sacred functions, p. 131) an extraordinary confessor, who, especially in the case of women, will find occasion for the exercise of his zeal and patience, in hearing over again more than one confession, which had been already made to the Parish Priest, or to some other local confessor.

§ 6. OF THE CONFESSIONS OF CHILDREN.

A zealous and enlightened Parish Priest pays

great attention to the confessions of the children—even of those who have not yet been admitted to Holy Communion. He takes care that even these latter go to confession from time to time, and receive the benefit of Sacramental Absolution; and he does not adopt the custom followed by some, who make them go to confession once only in the entire year, namely at Easter. Children require very special attention, in order that the first seeds of vice may be eradicated from their tender hearts, and Christian virtues planted there instead; and how could sufficient provision be made for their spiritual culture, if their confessions were heard only once a year?

Moreover, I said above that a zealous Parish Priest takes care *that, from time to time, these children receive Sacramental Absolution.* At first sight this observation might seem superfluous, from the fact that they confess their sins for the express purpose of receiving Sacramental Absolution. Nevertheless, in practice, it will be found that they do not amount to the same thing. I have heard a Parish Priest, a Doctor in Theology, boast of never having given absolution to children who had not yet made their first Communion; and precisely the same custom is observed by those who wait, one would be inclined to say as a mere matter of form, to confess them all in a helter-skelter fashion on some given day at Easter time.

Here is a specimen of the manner in which some persons hear the confessions of these children: They listen to whatever sins the child tells them, (there would not be time to question them on what they may possibly be omitting), and then they say: "*now, be a good child; be obedient to your parents; hear Mass devoutly; and say your prayers regularly. For your present penance say three Hail Marys. Benedictio Dei Omnipotentis, &c.* The confession is *finished!* Another child comes into the Confessional, and in this manner they are heard by the hundred in a short time.

Now can this be called hearing the confessions of the poor children, or is it not rather mocking them, and going through a burlesque of the Sacrament? Children of seven years are capable of sinning, and do sin; and still more is this true of children who have attained the age of eight, nine, ten, eleven, twelve, and thirteen years—an age at which some of them have not yet received the Holy Communion. And when they have sinned, and sometimes grievously, are they, on presenting themselves for Confession, to be mocked in the manner described above? Surely a simple benediction instead of Sacramental Absolution is no better than a mockery!

Wherefore, when we sit down to hear the confessions of children, we ought to have the intention of administering the Sacrament of Penance, of which absolution is an essential part; and not only when hearing them, but also when questioning them, we ought to form an estimate of the state of their consciences. Wherefore, if they still lack discretion, or if they have not sufficient matter for the Sacrament, we ought to give them a simple benediction, and dismiss them in peace. But if, on the other hand, they have the full use of reason, if they accuse themselves of grievous or notable sins, we ought to excite them to sorrow for them, we ought to endeavour to dispose them for Sacramental Absolution, and then we ought to absolve them just as we would adults.

It will sometimes happen, nevertheless, that, even after we have laboured to dispose children for absolution, we will still remain doubtful whether they are deserving, or capable of it. In such circumstances ought we to run the risk of giving absolution, and expose the Sacrament to the danger of nullity? In this case, we ought, as a general rule, to dismiss the children with a simple benediction. However, should they have committed grave and notable faults, we ought, as theologians teach, to give them conditional absolution—*si es dispositus*—and this will remove all danger of irreverence towards the Sacrament. And, indeed, even though some children should never accuse themselves of serious sins, yet we ought sometimes to give them conditional absolution, the more so, should they be rather grown, in order that, as St. Alphonsus remarks, they may not remain always deprived of the benefit of the Sacrament.

Some think that there is no necessity for giving absolution to children before they have been admitted to first Communion, precisely because they are not to communicate. Consequently, if a child of the age of eleven or twelve years, who has already made his first Communion, comes to Confession to them, they absolve him every time, because they would scruple to allow him communicate whilst stained with the sins of which he has accused himself. But if, on the other hand, the child is not to communicate, because he has not yet made his first Communion, in this case, even though he may be twelve or thirteen years old, they send him away without absolution, and so leave his soul burdened with his sins, being all the while perfectly satisfied with the course they have adopted, because, indeed, in his case there is no fear of a bad Communion. According to the manner of thinking, then, of such persons, it would seem that it is important to have one's soul free from sin when approaching the Most Holy Eucharist, but that otherwise it is of no consequence. They say in acts, if not in words: there is no fear of a sacrilegious Communion; therefore we may spare the absolution. But has Christ instituted the Sacrament of Penance that Christians may by this means recover divine grace if they have lost it, or has He instituted it solely in order that they may not make sacrilegious Communions? The unreasonableness of such a practice ought to be evident not only to confessors who have studied Theology, but even to little children who have been instructed in their Catechism.

Moreover, do not these very priests teach that children who have passed the age of seven years are bound to go to Confession, and that parents are culpable who do not see that their children fulfil this duty? What would these priests say to a father or to a mother should they accuse themselves of having children who had reached the age of eleven, twelve, or thirteen years, but who had never yet been to

Confession ? They would not hesitate to judge them guilty of mortal sin. And why should these children be obliged to confession ? Is it merely that they may get the confessor's blessing ? It would be ridiculous to oblige any one, it matters not whether he be an adult or a child, to come to confess his sins in detail, for the mere purpose of receiving a blessing, which he could receive equally well by assisting at the end of a Mass.

It is a remarkable fact that those who have a leaning towards rigorism commit a greater number of mistakes, in proportion as they wish to secure themselves against committing any at all ; and while they labour to take precautions against all possible errors, they fall into those which are most obvious. In fact, in order to avoid all risk of occasionally giving absolution when it ought to be withheld, they adopt a course which will certainly lead them to withhold all the absolutions which ought to be given. Through fear of sometimes profaning the Sacrament by giving an occasional invalid absolution, they continually profane it by designedly performing a ceremony which is but a parody of the Sacrament.

Nevertheless, in order to justify a practice so unjustifiable, they say that children who have not yet been admitted to Communion, being still but imperfectly instructed, accuse themselves of their sins in too confused a manner; that very often they have not the necessary sorrow; that sometimes they have not even a sufficient knowledge of the principal mysteries of faith; that, moreover, when one of these children presents himself for confession it cannot be discovered whether in his previous confessions he has received absolution, or only a simple benediction; and that, consequently, it is not prudent to venture on absolving these children, until they come to make a general confession preparatory to their first Communion.

Let us consider for a moment what weight ought to be attached to these objections. Children, we are told, confess their sins in too confused a manner. Here we must remind the reader of what we said above (app. i., § 2.) regarding the integrity of confession, where we stated that everyone is bound to confess his sins *in a manner proportionate to his capacity;* and that when any one makes his confession as well as his capacity allows, the confession is a good one. Consequently, a Theologian is bound to confess in a manner which might be expected from a Theologian; the man of mature years and sense is bound to confess like a man of mature years and judgment; a child is bound to confess like a child, and is bound to nothing more. Wherefore, if children confess confusedly because they do not know how to do better, they confess well, and are capable of absolution. Meanwhile, what is there to prevent the confessor from supplying for any defect there may be in the matter of integrity, by putting a few questions to his penitent?

We are next told that children confess without the necessary sorrow. Very often this is perfectly true; but does it not frequently happen that adults, as well, come to Confession without the necessary sorrow? And how does a zealous confessor act in this case? Does he dismiss them with a benediction? Certainly not: instead of doing so, he exerts himself with diligence and charity to stir up within them the necessary sentiments of repentance, and then absolves them. Well then, let the same be done with children, and they likewise can be absolved from their sins. Nay, it must be borne in mind that the hearts of children, being yet guileless and uncontrolled by passions of long standing, are far more easily moved to contrition for their sins than are the hearts of adults. We observe, in fact, that if some considerations are suggested to them regarding the malice of sin, the hatred that God bears to it, the punishment to which it exposes us, and so forth, they show themselves more easily moved than adults; and this ought to stimulate us to do all in our power to dispose them for Sacramental Absolution, and moreover encourage us to give it to them, since we have thereby good grounds for believing that its validity is sufficiently assured.

But if it is true that they easily relapse, we must not therefore conclude that they were badly disposed when they were absolved: we must rather attribute their fall to a change of will, which with them is extremely variable and inconstant. And it is for this very reason that they ought to be readily absolved again when they return to Confession; because it will be very easy to excite them once more to sorrow for their sins which will be sufficient for

OF THE SACRAMENT OF PENANCE.

justification. This, however, does not, of course, apply to cases in which these children might be in voluntary occasions of sin which they would show themselves unwilling to abandon.

Here I wish to make a most important observation, which seems to have been overlooked by many theologians, and which ought to encourage the confessors of children, and of adults as well, to give them absolution, and to permit them to approach the Holy Communion, even though they may not be as fully satisfied as they could wish of their good dispositions. This observation is, that all the Sacraments, when they are received in good faith, that is, when they are received by a Christian who believes himself well disposed for their reception, although in reality he should not be as well prepared for them as he might be, confer grace on the sinner, provided his will be not badly disposed, or, in other words, provided he have no actual attachment to sin. This doctrine is taught by St. Thomas in several places (in 4 Dist. 9 q. 1 a. 3—Tertia, p. q. 79, art. 3); but he lays it down with particular clearness (p. 3, q. 69, art. 10), where, speaking of Baptism, he says: "Quando aliquis baptizatur, accipit characterem quasi formam, et consequitur proprium effectum, qui est gratia remittens omnia peccata. Impeditur autem quandoque per *fictionem*; unde oportet quod remota ea per pœnitentiam, baptismus statim consequatur suum effectum." (art. 10 in O.). Now in the preceding article he explains what he means by "fictionem":—" Dicitur autem aliquis *fictus* per hoc quod voluntas ejus contradicit vel baptismo vel ejus effectui" (art. 9 in O.). From this we see that if one's will be not badly disposed, that is if he have not an affection to sin, there can be no impediment to grace. Even the rigorist, Collet, when explaining the words of the Council of Trent where it says that the Sacraments confer grace upon those who do not place an obstacle to it—*non ponentibus obicem*—remarks that this obstacle cannot be sin *per se*, but rather the affection to sin: " *Peccator gratiæ obicem ponit cum in peccato sibi complacere perseverat;* sed obicem per se et immediate non ponit peccatum" (De Euch. P. 1, c. 8). From this doctrine we infer that penitents who are in good faith, (and children generally belong to this class), that is who believe themselves well disposed for the reception of the Sacraments, obtain justification or sanctifying grace with the remission of all their sins, provided they have no actual attachment to sin.

Indeed, this doctrine follows from the teaching of the Church regarding the efficacy of the Sacraments, which produce grace *ex opere operato*, that is by means of the intrinsic virtue given to them by Christ. Sin, far from being *per se* an obstacle to this intrinsic power, is rather cancelled and destroyed by it; and the only thing that can prove an obstacle to its efficacy is the perverse will which continues to love sin, and with which it is impossible to combine sanctifying grace, which is the result of divine charity, or rather divine charity itself diffused in our hearts, so that it is the contradictory term of a bad will, just as good is the contradictory of evil.

Now, that it is possible for the soul to be still in a state of sin, without any longer having an attachment to sin, is evident in the case of those who repent of their sins through attrition, yet whose sins are not cancelled until they receive absolution. It is clear that these have already renounced the attachment to sin; yet, meanwhile, they continue stained with it until they receive the Sacrament of Penance. We find an illustration of the same truth in the case of those who are preparing themselves for a change of life, and for that very reason abstain from committing their former sins even before they formally repent of them. In such persons sin still dwells, but not an attachment to sin.

This doctrine ought to afford great consolation to the confessors especially of children and of ignorant persons, in whom we may more easily, nay ordinarily, find good faith. Let confessors do all in their power to dispose them well for absolution, that is to say, let them endeavour to excite them to real sorrow for their sins and to an efficacious resolution not to commit them any more, and, having done this, let them not be too nervous or too cautious about giving them absolution. Even should they not succeed in disposing them as well as they could wish, yet so long as they do not retain a perversity of will, that is, any attachment to sin, they will be justified by the efficacy of the Sacrament, the only obstacle to which is that perverse will or attachment. This is moreover the doctrine of Melchior Cano (Prælec de Pœnit), of Soto (in 4), of Card. Toleto (in Summa lib. 2 c. 4), of Navarro (in man. cap. 10, n. 4). No one will deny that these are old theologians of note, and, united with St. Thomas, their authority is so weighty, that it would not be easy to counterbalance it by greater, or even equal, authority among modern Theologians.[1]

[1] Since this is a point of great importance, I shall quote here the other passages from St. Thomas that have been merely alluded to above, and from the Theologians of his school : " Si quis ad corpus Christi accedat, aliquo peccato mortali in ipso manente, quod ejus cognitionem præterfugiat, non peccat, immo magis ex *vi Sacramenti* remissionem consequitur" (in 4 ut supra) — "Potest tamen hoc Sacramentum operari remissionem peccati. . . . . etiam perceptum ab eo qui est in peccato mortali, cujus conscientiam et affectum non habet: forte enim primo non fuit sufficienter contritus, sed devote et reverenter accedens consequetur per hoc sacramentum gratiam charitatis quæ contritionem perficiet et remissionem peccati" (D. Th. 3 P. q. 79, art. iii.)—" Si quæras quando ex attrito fiat contritus virtute Sacramenti, respondeo, id primum evenire quocumque attritionis genere homo sit attritus, si existimat se præstitisse quod necessarium erat, ignoretque invincibiliter se non habere sufficientem dispositionem ; quia is *non ponit obicem*, sed bona fide accedit ad Sacramentum ; *Sacramentum autem in non ponente obicem semper habet effectum.* Quo fit ut omnia Sacramenta ex hujusmodi attrito contritum faciant ; quod D. Thomas lucide tradit 3 P. q. 79, art. 3 ; et in comm. super illud Joan. c. 11 *solvite eum.* . . . ." (Melchior Canus in Prælect. de Pœn.)—"In Baptismo sufficit existimata contritio ; idem autem paritate rationis dicendum de Sacramento pœnitentiæ res ipsa per se clamat." (Dom. Soto in 4)—" Quando quis desiderat habere contritionem, licet vere non habet, sufficeret ad gratiam in Sacramento percipiendam si pœnitenti non constaret se non esse vere contritum " (Card. Toleto in Summa ut Supra).

Finally Navarro, recommending the confessor to exert himself to the utmost to excite his penitent to sincere contrition, says :

Another objection is that children are often ignorant of the principal mysteries. No doubt, in several places we have to deplore such ignorance in a greater or a less degree; but it is at the same time certain that where the Parish Priest takes proper care to instruct them in the Christian Doctrine, the children of such parishes are not found wanting in the knowledge of those articles of faith which are most necessary to be known. Moreover, when a Parish Priest doubts whether a child who is confessing to him possesses the requisite knowledge, it is his duty to examine him, and, should he find him ignorant, no one doubts that he is bound to instruct him, so that he may become capable of receiving the Sacraments as soon as possible. It must likewise be remarked that we must not require from children a great amount of knowledge, even with regard to the principal mysteries. A very crude kind of knowledge, proportionate to their capacity, is sufficient. (See § 4 on Matrimony).

Finally, with respect to the last difficulty put forward above, if we are unable to discover whether the children have received absolution in their pre-

---

" Quod si adhuc his omnibus ad dolorem non sufficienter eum moveri consideret, interroget an doleat quod non doleat tantum quantum deberet, et an vellet hujusmodi dolorem sufficientem concipere. Quod si annuat, satis erit," (in man. et supra).

All Theologians, ancient and modern, teach the Catholic Doctrine regarding the efficacy of the Sacraments which produce grace *ex opere operato*; nevertheless it would appear that many moderns without being aware of it, explain this doctrine in a manner which does not correspond to the force of these words.—*Author's note*.

vious confessions, we must presume that what ought to have been done was done actually. The children confessed their sins to obtain absolution; if they were disposed, they had a right to receive it, and if they were not disposed, they had a right to be reminded that they were being sent away without it. They are not obliged to confess their sins twice over. Therefore, when they now present themselves to a new confessor, if they are disposed, or capable of being disposed, they ought to be absolved, since we must presume that their former confessors acted towards them in like manner. And should it have happened that some former confessor had withheld absolution from them without reminding them of the fact, there is no doubt that these sins, even supposing them to have been mortal, would be forgiven in virtue of the absolution which they would receive from us. Neither the actual confessor, nor the child, but the confessor who had withheld absolution from his penitent without telling him so, would be accountable for the irregularity whereby the child would not be *directly* absolved from these former sins.

Wherefore, it is certain that we ought not to wait for the general confession preparatory to first Communion, in order to give absolution to children, but we ought to absolve them at once. One of the advantages to be derived from making the general confession afterwards will be that, in accusing themselves again of all their sins, they will then be absolved directly even from those from which they may have been only indirectly absolved in the past.

We see, then, clearly how frivolous are these objections; but the real strong objection, which cannot be rebutted by mere argument, is this : *we do not want to lose time with children.* To remove this objection we must beg of God to give us enlightened zeal, and, having obtained it, we will be influenced with a desire to help little children, who, if we regard them with the eye of Faith, constitute the most precious portion of the Christian flock. Then we will not believe that we are losing time if we hear their confessions patiently and carefully; we will believe, on the contrary, that it is time most wisely occupied, and spent in a most holy exercise, from which we shall ourselves afterwards derive much consolation. What husbandman has ever doubted that trees must be cared for from the time that they are but delicate shoots ? And can any Parish Priest suppose that it is not a matter of importance to train up Christians to virtue from their very childhood? This seems to prove sufficiently that the Sacrament of Penance ought to be administered to children as well as to adults, even though they should not yet have been admitted to first Communion ; and, moreover, that confessors, and especially pastors of souls, fail notably in their duty, if they omit to absolve children when they are disposed, or capable of being disposed, for Sacramental absolution.

We shall now pass on to some other observations on this subject. One of the most important of these is that the confessor should never scold a child, or reprove him harshly, while he is making his confession.

One harsh word is enough to make the child stop short: if he has other sins to accuse, he will no longer tell them: to every question put to him he will answer No; and it becomes impossible to extract the truth from him afterwards. Wherefore, we ought always to speak to children with great kindness, even though they should accuse themselves of heinous sins: nay, it is under such circumstances that we ought to give them the greatest encouragement, and even promise them expressly that we will not scold them.

Again, great diligence must be employed in finding out the occasions of their sins, namely, whether they are occasioned by the companions with whom they associate at school, at work, at play, or by their parents, &c., in order that the confessor may be in a position to suggest suitable remedies. Meanwhile, should the child be placed in the occasion of sin from any of the causes mentioned, the most opportune, and, as a rule, the necessary remedy is to induce him to make known to his parents, masters, &c., the person who is leading him into sin. It happens not unfrequently that some little boy, and especially some little girl, is tempted by coaxing or by presents to commit, or to permit some sinful action on the part of a relative or friend of the family. Sometimes children meet with such occasions of scandal at school, in business houses, or in a workshop. The confessor must be persuaded that, generally speaking, there is no other really effective means to save betrayed innocence, except by disclosing the authors of the scandal to those who are able to prevent it; and he should not be restrained from suggesting this means to his penitent, through fear that it may give rise to disputes, quarrels, or other disagreeable consequences in families—should it be even between husband and wife. Betrayed innocence deserves the first consideration; and when we do not know any other effective means to protect it, we must not pay any heed to disagreeable consequences which may follow from our action—the more so when we reflect that, sooner or later, the crime will be discovered, and that consequently, even though we were to tolerate this betrayal, yet not even so would the evil results of which we were apprehensive be avoided. But all hesitation regarding this matter must vanish, when we reflect that the confessor is bound to seek before everything else the spiritual good of his penitent, and the more so if the penitent happen to be a poor little child, who of himself is far less capable than an adult of providing for his own wants.

Another most important remark is, that the confessor should exercise the utmost discretion in questioning children on matters relating to the Sixth Commandment, so as to avoid all danger of teaching them what probably they do not already know. And let not the confessor be afraid lest the confession may thereby be defective in the matter of integrity; for the child is not bound to confess better than he knows how, nor is it lawful for the confessor to instruct him on the subject. Therefore, there can be no ground for doubting that the confession will be properly made, even though the child should not well express the species of his sins. On the other hand, it is universally admitted by Theologians that confessors ought to guard scrupulously against putting questions which might cause scandal, by imparting a knowledge of sins which previously were unknown.

I must not omit to remark, in conclusion, that when children are neither actually disposed, nor capable of being disposed, for absolution, they must never be sent away with a simple blessing, as is done by so many confessors; but they must be excited to the love of God, and to contrition for their sins, both in order to accustom them to practise acts of the love of God, and above all to provide, as best one may, for the necessities of their souls. The confessor, then, may excite the child to these acts by saying to him: *Do you know that the Lord has done and suffered so much for us that He even died upon the Cross? You know that the Lord is so good that no one can ever love Him as much as He deserves! Oh how good the Lord is! We ought to love Him more than everything—Do you love God with all your heart? Yes: and is it not true that you love Him with all your heart precisely because He is so good?* Then he may add: *Are you not sorry for having so much offended God by your sins?—Yes: repent of them with all your heart, and promise Him never more to be guilty of them, etc.* This will be found a far more advantageous method of dealing with them, than to dismiss them with a simple benediction.

Meanwhile, let it be borne in mind that not only

children, but adults likewise, when they are sent away without absolution, ought to be excited to contrition for their sins, because it may happen that their souls will thereby be freed from mortal sin. As a matter of fact, a confessor refuses absolution to a penitent either because he has not the necessary faculties to absolve him from his sins or from some censure which he may have incurred, or because he judges him to be insufficiently disposed. In the first of these cases, the penitent may be so well disposed as to recover the state of grace, although he cannot be absolved through the defect of jurisdiction in the confessor; and thus, by exciting him to contrition, he may be justified thereby. In the second case, although the confessor may judge the penitent indisposed, and although it may be true that he was really indisposed when he presented himself for confession, nevertheless, since it is always possible to err when judging of interior dispositions, it is quite possible that the confessor may have been mistaken when forming his judgment; and it is possible likewise that though the penitent may have entered the Confessional without the proper dispositions, yet in a moment he might become disposed by means of an earnest exhortation from the confessor. For the change of will always takes place in an instant, which is that indivisible point of time in which from having been bad it becomes good. Meanwhile, since this change is altogether interior, it may remain hidden from the confessor, who believes it to be his duty to dismiss the penitent without Sacramental absolution. In both these hypotheses, of which the confessor can have no certain knowledge—namely, that of a pre-existing disposition, and that of a disposition obtained during the act of confession—the penitent, even though unabsolved, would yet be justified by making an act of sincere contrition.

From what has been said we may see how important it is that the confessor should excite his penitent to contrition for his sins, when he judges it fit to dismiss him without absolution. Nay, he ought to exhort him to make many such acts until he returns to Confession; because, by making them frequently, he may the more easily succeed in eliciting at least one sincere act, which will justify him, and rescue him from the horrible state of mortal sin. I have said that "the confessor should excite his penitent"; because if he contents himself with merely saying: "Make the act of contrition," and does not endeavour to suggest to him suitable reflexions on the infinite goodness of God, it will easily happen that the penitent will merely repeat with his lips the words of the act in a mechanical manner, which will be of no service whatever.

Speaking to Parish Priests, it is unnecessary for me to remark how erroneous it would be to suppose that an act of contrition restores the soul to the grace of God only in case of necessity. This is an error condemned expressly in the case of Bains, who taught that perfect charity could exist in a soul together with mortal sin. (See prop. 32 and 70.)

The Church teaches, on the other hand, that a simple act of the love of God, provided it be perfect, cancels from the soul every sin, and any number of sins, even outside the case of necessity; though, as Theologians teach, there still remains the obligation of confessing them in due time.

§ 7. OF THE CONFESSIONS OF PIOUS PERSONS.

We have already remarked (part I., chap. II.) that good Parish Priests pride themselves in training up pious souls, who are the edification, the "good odour," the "good leaven" of their parishes. This training must be given especially in the Confessional, where we come to know the graces that God grants to those souls whom He calls to a higher grade of perfection in His service, and where we can give them that direction which is suited to each one's particular requirements. Wherefore, good Parish Priests and Directors of souls exert themselves to bring persons of this class to Confession every eight days if possible.

I would not, for many reasons, approve of their going to Confession more frequently than this. In the first place, because pious seculars must attend to the duties imposed upon them by their position in life, or by the interests of their families; and these duties might easily come to be neglected by them, were they to be found seated at the Confessional several times in the week. In the next place, because the Parish Priest who spends a good deal of time with a few pious penitents, will not be able, afterwards, to find the necessary time for the confessions of sinners, and for attending to the other affairs of his parish. In the third place, because those persons—invariably women—who would wish to go to confession every day, are generally ninnies, and the more frequently they confess the more silly do they become. The Parish Priest, likewise, who is continually listening to them, without ever growing weary of them, acquires the reputation of a silly man, and perhaps of something worse should they happen to be young and giddy. However, should he be in the habit of hearing one of this latter class several times a week, and of devoting to her on each occasion a considerable portion of his time, he must be prepared to hear his character spoken of in unfavourable terms.

I am well aware that we sometimes meet with souls who stand in need of special direction, because of the spiritual trials with which God visits them; that it is necessary to hear persons of this class frequently; and that it is not always possible to get rid of them quickly. But, on the other hand, such souls are extremely few, and, moreover, they do not belong to the class of those who give occasion for uncharitable remarks.

Wherefore, with some very rare exceptions, the Parish Priest, as a rule, ought not to hear the confessions of these devout penitents oftener than once a week; and he ought to spend very little time in doing so; in order that the confessions of persons of this class may not trespass upon the time necessary for hearing others whose necessities are greater. If he wishes to instruct them in matters appertaining to the Spiritual Life, let him recommend to them some good book which will keep them simple-minded and humble, and will inflame them with the love of God. He can find nothing better suited to this purpose than the "Practice of the love of Jesus Christ," and the "Spiritual Treatises" of St. Alphonsus Liguori. Should any of these penitents be unable to read (a case of extremely rare occurrence in our times), let him teach her the maxims of the Saint in a brief and simple style, always avoiding in the Confessional long conferences, which can never be of advantage either to the penitent or to the confessor. From these long conferences there may spring up a feeling of affection and mutual attachments, which, however innocent they may be, do not cease at the same time to be defects. It is remarkable that long conversations of this kind, which would prove very tiresome if carried on between men, become quite endurable when they take place between men and women. The fact is that, even when we do not perceive it, we always carry about with us as our inseparable companion our natural propensity to evil. Moreover, it is of the greatest importance to keep these devout penitents very simple-minded and humble, because there is no accounting for the freaks of female levity. They easily yield to temptations of vanity, suffer themselves to become the victims of delusions, and stray from the right path.

I will observe, in the next place, that though persons who are of a pious disposition ought to cultivate the virtue of prayer very much, if they wish to keep themselves on the path of Christian perfection, and to make still further progress, nevertheless we must not bind them all to the practice of meditation. We see that the great masters of prayer, such as St. John of the Cross and St. Teresa, teach that there are souls (St. Teresa says *many* souls) who cannot practise this kind of prayer.[1] Constant experience also teaches us that there are souls endowed with extraordinary virtue, and even favoured by God with special graces, who do not make mental prayer. I have known many such, and among others one whose life from infancy to extreme old age was a continual practice of perfection and of the most solid virtue, yet who on hearing the subject of meditation mentioned said, although with a laugh: "*that word fills me with terror*".

I do not make these remarks by any means to depreciate mental prayer, which has been so praised and recommended by the masters of the spiritual life; but in order that we may be on our guard against insisting on it indiscriminately in the case of all souls who are leading a spiritual life. This is done by certain indiscreet Directors, who do not guide their penitents along the road by which God calls them, but force, and almost drag them along another road of their own choosing, while the poor

---

[1] St. Teresa. "Way of Perfection," ch. 19. St. John of Cross. Tratt delle spine. Coll. viii.

souls, thus forced and dragged, suffer thereby torture and spiritual loss. These Directors ought to read the above-mentioned treatise of St. John of the Cross; and, did they do so, they would require the practice of prayer from all, but they would not require mental prayer except from those souls whom they might see disposed towards it.

It must be borne in mind, however, that I am here speaking of meditation performed in a methodical manner, divided into points, continued for a certain specified time, etc.; for simple meditation, that is to say, the simple consideration and reflection on the Eternal Maxims is necessary for all Christians in order to live well, and to save their souls. In truth, how could a person live well and work out his salvation, were he never to call to mind or reflect on Death, or Judgment, or Hell, or Heaven, or the Lord's Passion, or such like truths? Wherefore, it is unquestionably necessary for a Christian to meditate, that is to think and reflect on the truths of our Holy Religion. It is of this kind of meditation, which is suited to the capacity of all—even of rude and unintelligent persons—that we must understand those various passages of the Scriptures and of the Holy Fathers which speak of meditation as indispensable. Meanwhile, many persons make use of these passages to prove the necessity of methodical meditation, without reflecting that they are not to the purpose, and are therefore useless to prove what they would wish.

The virtue of mortification also must be practised

in a special manner by those who lead a spiritual life; but care must be taken that, in doing so, they do not overstep the bounds of moderation. We may recommend to all, and even rigorously exact from devout persons, those mortifications which far from injuring the health rather serve it; such as temperance in eating and drinking, never to eat out of the usual hours of meals, to be content with as much sleep as is necessary, and so forth. The same may be said of those mortifications which are generally harmless; such as some simple fast, to abstain from some dish or from some fruit for which we have a particular liking, to bear patiently with some trouble, under which head may be included many things which cannot injure anybody. Such mortifications as these are to be insisted upon in proportion to the spiritual progress of the penitent; but the fasts must not be permitted to anyone whose health is weak, and who has need of taking food frequently.

There are other mortifications which cannot prove hurtful if they be practised with discretion by persons who enjoy good health, such as, for example, the moderate use of the discipline, and of a light steel chain. It is true that the present age is very much opposed to this kind of mortification, and the very name of these instruments of penance almost makes people shudder; nevertheless, it is evident that one could not absolutely censure such mortifications, without at the same time censuring the practice and the universal sentiment of the saints, and of the masters of the Spiritual Life—a proceeding which would be exceedingly rash. However, chains and hair shirts which irritate the nervous system are to be specially forbidden to sickly persons, and to those whose constitution is weak.

As regards other still more severe mortifications—such as to sleep on the bare earth, or only for a few hours of the night, to perform extraordinary fasts, to take the discipline for a long time, to wear a hair shirt continually, to eat disgusting food, to become benumbed with cold through the lightness of one's clothing, and other like practices which are really hurtful to bodily health—these ought never to be permitted without having good grounds for believing that the person who practises them is called by God to a life of extraordinary penance and mortification.

It is quite true that the saints practised all these penances, and even others still more severe; but, then, the saints were moved to this by an extraordinary divine impulse, and therefore they did not prove hurtful and deadly to them, as would have been the case in the ordinary nature of things: nay even we know that, nothwithstanding the extremely austere life which they led, they endured long, incessant, and most severe labours, and many of them lived even to a very advanced age. To practise penances of this kind, without an evident divine inspiration, is simply to tempt God. But, then, it is a very difficult matter to know when any one really has this divine inspiration; and much prayer would be required, as well as counsel from very prudent and experienced persons, before anyone could persuade himself that it exists in his particular case. Let a Director not hesitate to forbid penances of this kind; because he may rest assured that when the divine inspiration to practise them does exist, God will make it clearly known to him.

It must likewise be borne in mind, with regard to the saints, that those who practised extraordinary penances also enjoyed extraordinary spiritual consolations, by which their human weakness was so wonderfully strengthened, that they received no injury from those austerities which otherwise would have proved intolerable. I was for some time directing a person who used to spend the entire day in very severe labour, and almost the entire night afterwards in prayer. Fearing lest her health might suffer from this course, I ordered her to take I forget how many hours of repose; and when, in consequence, she wished, through a spirit of obedience, to resist the spiritual impulse which was hurrying her along to contemplation, she heard a voice which asked her: "And is not this repose?" She never afterwards suffered any evil effects from the observance of her custom, and I received from this incident a little instruction.

I must remark, furthermore, that if these austerities were permitted without a divine inspiration, not only the corporal health, but also the spiritual well-being of the penitents would suffer: because, once they perceived that extraordinary penances were permitted to them, they would easily conceive a high esteem of their own perfection, and would become miserable victims of pride. This is never so when the inspiration comes from God; for He guards His own gifts, and cannot permit that His creatures should suffer on account of them.

I remember having read how St. Philip Neri used to say that it is a lesser evil that our body should have rather too much than too little vigour; for the defect of strength might be more injurious, and more difficult to remedy, than its excess. St. Francis de Sales also used to say that the absence of moderation in fasts, in the use of the discipline and hair-shirts, and in other austerities, renders the best years of the lives of many people useless for works of charity (see Gousset, Theol. Moral., vol. 2, n. 456). Wherefore, it will be necessary for the confessor to control the transports of fervour in pious souls, and not to permit them to practise external mortifications except under due restrictions. Where there is question of persons living in religious communities, where it is prescribed that the discipline be taken in common, they ought to comply exteriorly with the formality of the rule, in such manner as not to suffer from its effects. (See Mocchetti, *Discorsi Sacri*, etc., n. x.— Schram. Iustit. Theol. Myst., tom. 1, § 98, Schol. 2.)

§ 8. OF THE DIRECTION OF PERSONS WHO RECEIVE EXTRAORDINARY FAVOURS FROM GOD.

It cannot be doubted that, here and there, God has specially favoured souls, upon whom He confers extraordinary favours, in order to detach them the more effectually from the world, and unite them more intimately with Himself—souls adorned with the most rare and precious gifts of grace, and who are admitted to the secret and ineffable joys of divine contemplation. Such souls may be met with even where one would least expect to find them—where there is least instruction and training—because *spiritus ubi vult spirat*. The fact that he found some soul of this kind in almost every place on the missions in which he laboured continually for thirty years, induced Father Sacramelli to write his highly esteemed *Direttorio mistico* (see chap. i.). Wherefore, it may easily happen that a Parish Priest should find some such soul among the flock entrusted to his care, and may have to undertake to direct her, especially should the penitent live in a country district, remote from a town or city, so that no other confessor might be available except the Parish Priest.

The first remark which I shall make on this subject is, that a Parish Priest would do wrong to his priestly character and office, and would show himself extremely ignorant, were he to refuse to believe in the reality of extraordinary graces, regarding them all as impostures, or the illusions of weak minds. Such a one would set himself up for being more enlightened and unprejudiced than all the Doctors of the Church, than all the Saints and all the masters of the Spiritual life, who in every age have constantly recognised the reality of these graces. This would be incredible presumption, and almost a proof of infidelity; because such a theory would be in opposition to innumerable decrees and decisions of the Church, which recognise the existence of such graces. Moreover, their reality is a matter which has satisfactorily stood the test of scientific examination, and is a fact based on such undeniable historical evidence, that it can no longer be called in question.

Nor could a person justify himself by saying that he admits, indeed, the extraordinary favours vouchsafed to the Saints in the ages past, and treats lightly those only which are represented as happening at the present day, and which have not yet received the approval of Theologians, or of the Church. Whosoever should speak thus could not, indeed, be accused of speaking rashly or presumptuously against the authority of the Doctors of the Church; but yet his language would be manifestly absurd. As a matter of fact, there was a time when those special favours which he is prepared to recognise had not that approval to which allusion has been made above, and therefore they ought all to have been treated with contempt. The extraordinary favours granted by God to St. Brigid, to St. Gertrude, to St. Catharine of Sienna, to St. Mary Magdalen de Pazzi, to St. Teresa, to St. Peter of Alcantara, to St. John of the Cross, to St. Joseph of Cupertino, and to innumerable other servants of God, ought to have been treated with contempt, because in the lifetime of these Saints, Theologians did not write in support of these favours, nor did the Church pronounce any decision regarding them.

For the rest, there is no doubt that some of the

modern favours, which certain persons affect to despise, for the reason that they have not yet received the support of Theologians nor the approval of the Church, will receive this support and approval at some future time, namely, when the canonisation of the saints of the present century will take place. All the centuries have had their saints who were favoured with extraordinary graces; and it would be, to say the very least, foolish to pretend that the present century must have no saints. Wherefore, considering these favours on their own simple merits, we must regard as worthless the distinction which some would draw between those which happened in past ages, and these which take place in our own times.

In the next place, I will remark that it would be, on the other hand, extreme simplicity to regard as heavenly favours all the extraordinary occurrences which we sometimes meet with, especially in the case of women, when they allege that they have had visions, ecstasies, and so forth; for it is evident that many of these things are simply the offspring of imagination, and are sometimes also malicious inventions. Wherefore, a Director of souls must neither be too sceptical nor too credulous, but in forming his judgments must proceed with true christian prudence, which demands that matters of this kind be cautiously weighed, and that we should then believe or disbelieve them, according as they appear to us clearly true or the opposite. Should they seem doubtful, we must never pronounce definitely upon them.

Meanwhile, in order to proceed with due prudence, the confessor must endeavour to acquire a knowledge at least of the principles of Mystic Theology. Without such knowledge, it would be real presumption to pronounce a decision on matters of this kind, as it would be real presumption to attempt to deal with any science or profession without being acquainted with it in some degree. For this purpose, I would wish a Parish Priest to study at least the short appendix which St. Alphonsus has written upon this subject, and which may be found at the end of his Moral Theology. (Appendix I. *Quomodo se gerere debeat confessarius in dirigendis animabus spiritualibus.*) No doubt it is but an outline, and extremely brief; however the Director who is acquainted with it will not be entirely ignorant of Mystic Theology. I would wish him to read also the works of St. Teresa, from which he would receive many lights, and extraordinary spiritual nourishment for his own soul. Indeed it may be said that no one can read these works without deriving great advantage from them. How desirable it would be that they were read by every Parish Priest and confessor!

When the Parish Priest, after having thus acquired some knowledge of Mystic Theology, meets with souls that seem to be favoured with extraordinary graces and gifts, he will be able to discover prudently whether these ought to be attributed to God, or to the Devil, or to the sport of fancy, or even to imposture. Should he meet with them in a person who is possessed of profound humility and self-diffidence, of ready obedience, of dove-like simplicity, and entirely detached from the things of this world, he may conclude that these graces and gifts come from God; and, without manifesting any esteem for the soul so favoured, he ought to bestow special care on the direction of that soul, as he must invariably do when God bestows upon any person special proofs of His love. Meanwhile, he must not look for absolute immunity from every defect as a preliminary condition to pronouncing a favourable judgment upon the particular graces bestowed upon a soul; for God permits defects even in the Saints, in order to keep them humble. We should always keep before our mind that most wise remark of St. Bernard: *Sic nimirum conservandæ humilitatis gratia, divina solet pietas ordinare ut quanto quis plus proficit, eo minus se reputet profecisse. Nam et usque ad supremum exercitii spiritualis gradum, si quis eo usque pervenerit, aliquid ei de primi gradus imperfectione relinquitur, ut vix sibi primum videatur adeptus.*" (Sermone de quatuor modis orandi). The supposition that holy souls, and those highly favoured by God, ought to be free from defects, repeatedly led persons to judge that the special favours conferred by God on St. Teresa were the work of the Devil, and even her confessor was of this opinion (see her life written by herself. Chap. 23 and chap. 25).

When a Spiritual Director meets with any soul that is probably favoured by God with graces of this kind, he must direct all his efforts to keeping that soul humble, and, above all, to persuading her that virtue by no means consists in such heavenly favours, since they are often bestowed upon weak and inconstant souls, to strengthen them and preserve them from falling into grievous sins—nay, that, as St. Teresa teaches, God sometimes allows them to be tasted even by those who are in sin, in order to bring about their conversion (*Way of Perfection*, chap. 16).

He ought to add that, generally speaking, such favours are open to great suspicion, since they are often found to be mere illusions; so that, though they may appear to be the work of God, we sometimes discover that they are nothing else than frauds of the Evil One, and sports of fancy. He ought, therefore, to recommend to his penitent not to pay any attention to them, and not to speak of them to anybody except himself, as St. John of the Cross inculcates in several places. Finally, he must assure his penitent that by acting in this manner no spiritual loss will ensue, even though the supposed favours should prove to be diabolical illusions; whereas by pursuing a different course they might prove hurtful, even though they were real favours from God, since they might cause the soul to consent to some thought of vanity or self-esteem.

And here I will remark that we cannot sufficiently deplore the imprudence of certain Directors, who, when they meet with any soul that seems to enjoy extraordinary favours, immediately conclude that they have discovered another St. Teresa, or St. Catharine, and pretend to recognise in her the highest grades of contemplation. They compare what they hear from their penitent with what mystics say of the spiritual espousals; and, according to their lights, they decide that their penitent has attained to a degree of perfection as high as can be reached by any creature living in the world. They then wish to get the opinion of this penitent on their most important affairs; they seek information from her regarding things hidden or yet to come, and sometimes even they do not hesitate to order her to write her life. In this manner they persuade the poor creature that she is a Saint, and a great Saint, and it is easy to see how very dangerous this may prove, if God do not providentially assist her, or deliver her from a Director so misguided.

It is true that, from time to time, many souls enjoy, some more some less, particular favours and graces from God; but it is likewise true that the St. Teresas and the St. Catharines are extremely few. Wherefore it would be exceedingly imprudent to treat these souls in the manner in which the Saints were sometimes treated by their Directors; and to do so might prove the cause of their ruin. Whenever it appears to us certain and evident that any soul is favoured in an extraordinary manner by God, our first endeavour ought to be to keep her humble, so that she may not cease to merit a continuance of these favours should they be real. I say: *should they be real:* for in such matters it is very easy to be deceived. He must afterwards proceed with the greatest caution, and take counsel with holy men who are both enlightened and prudent.

I would also remark, with St. Teresa, that if souls are kept humble and lowly in their own esteem, extraordinary favours, even if counterfeited by the Devil, cannot injure them (*Way of Perfection*, chap. 38). It must likewise be remembered, as the same saint observes, that Directors ought to be on their guard against disturbing such souls, even though they should entertain serious doubts regarding the reality of their extraordinary gifts. Let them be kept humble and simple-minded, but let them not be frightened by being told that any extraordinary grace which they think they receive is merely an illusion of the Devil. It causes too much alarm to souls that love God to hear that their Confessor considers them, so to speak, a plaything in the hands of the infernal Enemy, who is permitted to mock and deceive them at pleasure.

Whenever the Director knows that these supposed favours are nothing else than the result of imagination and a weak mind, he ought to do all in his power to disabuse his penitents of the mistake under which they labour. He must, however, take care not to impose upon them the obligation of believing as he himself believes—that is, of persuading themselves that they have been the victims of illusions; for it would be extremely difficult to succeed in doing this, and no man of sense would attempt it. Persons of disordered imagination or of weak mind are to be pitied and treated with the greatest consideration, in order that their infirmity may not increase, and that they may not become the victims of still worse illusions.

Finally, I must remark that it is very dangerous to conceive too high esteem for those souls which appear more specially favoured by God. Those who on this ground assume that they are great saints on account of their supposed lights, revelations, &c., may adopt imprudent measures, which may be followed by lamentable consequences—such as would be, for instance, to publish their supposed favours and prophecies, which, being often found inconsistent and untrue, afford matter for mirth to unbelievers, and bring piety into discredit. Wherefore an enlightened Director will reflect, in the first place, that extraordinary graces are by no means a measure of sanctity; and that, consequently, as St. Teresa teaches, there are souls who never receive any of these extraordinary favours, and yet in God's sight are superior in virtue and merit to those who do receive them. Should the Director at any time happen to be requested by a penitent of this class to promote some good work, let him do so, provided it be something very simple, from which no harm could result even though it were suggested by the Devil, such as, for example, to give a Retreat to the people, to pray for the conversion of sinners, &c.

I shall conclude with two counsels which are well worthy of attention, and which give great light to Directors. The first is borrowed from St. Thomas of Aquin, who says that those who are endowed with a real spirit of prophecy do not always speak under the impulse of this spirit, and that consequently we can never be certain that their words will be verified. The second is from St. John of the Cross, who remarks that when the Devil knows a soul to be guided by God by extraordinary means, he makes use of the self-same means to deceive her. Wherefore, as long as the Church makes no pronouncement, we can never have absolute certainty regarding matters of this kind.

CHAPTER IV.

OF EXTREME UNCTION.

THE Parish Priest ought to keep the Holy Oil in the Church in the place set aside for this purpose. This place ought to be dry, clean, and suitably ornamented, as prescribed by the Canons, and if there be anywhere special diocesan regulations on the subject, these also ought to be observed. He must see that the Holy Oil is borne to the sick in a respectful manner, and that the burse, the surplice, and the stole are clean and decent, as befits things that are employed in the administration of a Sacrament.

It frequently happens that the Parish Priest is called to administer this Sacrament when the sick person is already in a dying condition. Under such circumstances, putting on the surplice and stole, should he have time to do so, let him take the little vessel of Holy Oil, and, omitting all the other prayers, immediately begin with anointing the eyes, pronouncing at the same time the form, and then, without delaying to wipe the oil off the parts, let him finish anointing all the other senses. He will afterwards wipe the parts anointed, and should the sick man survive he must recite the prayers that had been omitted, as prescribed by the Ritual.

If, on the other hand, the dying man should be just on the point of expiring, let the priest take the Holy Oil, without putting on the surplice or stole, and commence to anoint one eye, one ear, one nostril, the mouth, and finally one hand, if it can be done conveniently (I say: *if it can be done conveniently;* because the sense of touch being extended throughout the entire body, the anointing of the head would suffice for it), saying at the same time, *sub conditione: Per istas sanctas unctiones et suam piissimam misericordiam indulgeat tibi Dominus quidquid deliquisti per visum, auditum, odoratum, gustum, locutionem, et tactum.* St. Alphonsus remarks that it is advisable to say the word "*deliquisti*" before naming the senses; so that, should the sick man expire during the act of anointing, the form may be complete at least with respect to some one sense.

I must, however, remark that in this case there is a custom of making only one unction, namely, on the forehead, saying: *per istam sanctam unctionem et suam piissimam misericordiam, indulgeat tibi Dominus quidquid per sensus deliquisti.* Nevertheless, since grave theologians are of opinion that the unction of the five senses is necessary for the validity of the Sacrament, and since it is extremely easy to accomplish the unction of all the senses in the manner indicated above, I think that, since there is question of the matter of the Sacrament, the method which I have pointed out, of anointing all the five senses consecutively, ought to be preferred. However, should the priest judge that, absolutely, there would not be time for doing this, and should he decide to employ only a single unction, he might express the form thus: *Per istam sanctam unctionem et suam piissimam misericordiam indulgeat tibi Dominus quidquid per sensus deliquisti, nempe visum, auditum, odoratum, gustum, locutionem et tactum.* It must be observed however in such cases that should the sick person survive, all the prescribed unctions ought to be repeated immediately *sub conditione*. Further remarks regarding the administration of this Sacrament will be found above in the first appendix to the second chapter.

CHAPTER V.

OF THE SACRAMENT OF ORDERS.

§ 1. Of the Training of Young Boys who show Signs of an Ecclesiastical Vocation.

NOTHING is more desirable for the good of the Church than that she should always have a supply of worthy Ministers, in sufficient numbers for the requirements of the people. It is true that it is the duty of Bishops to make provision for this want; nevertheless, it is evident that they, as a general rule, do not come in contact with, nor are they acquainted with, the young boys of their Dioceses. As a natural consequence, they are not in a position to discover those who give good hopes of an ecclesiastical vocation, and can form no opinion of their qualifications until they are presented to them. Parish Priests, on the other hand, know the good families among whom vocations to the Priesthood are found; they know the young boys who are in the habit of frequenting the instructions, and the religious functions of the Church; they are in a position to form an estimate of their capacity; to know their inclinations and tendencies;

and so to form a well-founded opinion as to which of them would be suited for the Ecclesiastical State.

Therefore, in this matter, Parish Priests can, to a great extent, make even better provision than Bishops for the wants of the Church ; and they will confer an inestimable service on the Church, if on discovering the young boys who give good promise of a vocation, they will devote themselves to training them for the Ecclesiastical State, by forming them in a special manner to practices of piety, and by putting them to begin their studies. And in case there should not be in some parish a competent schoolmaster, and that the parents should be unable or unwilling to send the boy to a College or a Seminary, the Parish Priest will be performing a work of great charity, and one highly conducive to the glory of God, if he personally undertakes to superintend the preliminary studies of youths of this class, and to prepare them, as far as he can, to embrace the Ecclesiastical State.

There is no doubt that Bishops, especially now-a-days, when ecclesiastical vocations are becoming so rare, will do all in their power to facilitate the entry of good youths into the Sanctuary, and will therefore be disposed to avail themselves of the assistance of those zealous Parish Priests, who may interest themselves in directing their young parishioners towards this career.

Nor should good Parish Priests be deterred from acting thus, by the fact that in certain places there may exist very strict laws regarding the education of ecclesiastical aspirants. These laws depend upon the will of the Bishop, and can therefore be easily changed, especially if a change be evidently necessary. If a Parish Priest will initiate in his studies a good youth who corresponds to the care bestowed upon him, Providence will not fail to supply the means of his one day attaining to the dignity of the Priesthood. Let the Parish Priest console himself with the thought of the great good which a zealous Minister of God can effect in the midst of the Christian people, and let him reflect that his little pupil may one day become such, if he only have capacity, a good disposition, and good training.

§ 2. OF THE VIGILANCE TO BE OBSERVED WITH REGARD TO ECCLESIASTICAL ASPIRANTS, AND OF THEIR TRAINING.

Should a Parish Priest have in his parish aspirants to the Ecclesiastical State, he ought to keep a strict watch over their conduct. Should he perceive them straying away from the right path, he must give them paternal advice; and should his words prove fruitless, he must lay the case before the Bishop, both in order that he may administer a more severe admonition, and, also, that he may become acquainted with their character, before they present themselves for ordination. If a cleric gives any indication of moral depravity, or ventures to manifest unsound principles and maxims in the matter of faith or morals, and does not amend as soon as he is admonished by his Parish Priest, there is not the slightest doubt that he is already very bad, and it is evident that, if ordained, he must turn out an exceedingly bad priest. Consequently, the Parish Priest who, by making known to the Bishop the bad dispositions of a cleric, prevents his ordination, simply prevents him from receiving, to his own greater injury, a character which he would dishonour, and which would prove a torture to him throughout Eternity: he will simply be preventing many scandals, and, perhaps, the damnation of many souls. We must keep always present before our minds that well-known saying of St. Gregory the Great: that the interests of God's glory never suffer greater injury than they do from bad priests.

Should a Parish Priest have in his parish clerics boarding with some family, or with some private person, he ought to ascertain whether there might be any danger for them in these houses—such as would exist, for example, should there be living in the same house any girls or young women, even though these should be given to piety. For, the piety of such young persons would not prevent the passions of the poor young cleric from being daily stimulated, with a risk of his yielding to temptation : nay, the very fact of seeing these females well-conducted and pious, would but encourage him to converse with them with the greater confidence, in as much as he would consider that in their case there existed less danger.

Therefore, he would not be on his guard against exhibiting towards such persons those first slight tokens of affection which might be entirely innocent, or nearly so ; then, after a short while, they would begin to make an impression on his heart, and would occupy his thoughts day and night. The very least evil to be anticipated from such a state of affairs, would be the loss of the young man's vocation to the Ecclesiastical State. Whenever a Parish Priest becomes aware of a danger of this kind, he ought to suggest to the parents, directly or indirectly, to place their son to lodge elsewhere; and should this advice remain unheeded, he ought to acquaint the Bishop with the circumstances.

The Parish Priest must see also that the clerical aspirants practise teaching the Catechism to the children, in order that they may thus be preparing themselves, according to their capacity, for the exercise of the Sacred Ministry. However, he must carefully avoid employing them to teach girls who are somewhat grown, since this would expose them to great danger, as we have already remarked elsewhere. We could not expect that the youthful cleric, while teaching the Catechism to young girls, would always keep his eyes like St. Aloysius: nay, there would be reason to fear that, were he to converse with them often and at length, some one of them would make a dangerous impression upon him.

The Parish Priest must likewise exert himself to instil into clerical aspirants sentiments of true zeal, and good maxims, so as to form their characters, and to dispose them to become fervent and holy Ecclesiastics. It is necessary to inspire clerics with sentiments of true zeal, by means of which they will not only aspire to save souls without any regard to temporal recompense, or to praise or honours, but may even be prepared to undergo trials and sacrifices whenever it may be necessary. What wretched priests will not those clerics become, who aspire to the Priesthood as others aspire to some temporal office—merely to earn a livelihood; or who seek for a post of dignity through vanity, and thus grow up in absolute indifference as to whether virtue or vice is to prevail in the vineyard of the Lord! And when I say this, I must not be understood to mean that one ought to refuse the rewards, the advantages, or the dignities which may be attached to the exercise of the Ecclesiastical Ministry; but I mean simply that these things ought to be regarded merely as accessories, in the absence of which we should do good, just as well as with them.

The maxims to be principally inculcated on young clerical aspirants, are those which regard disinterestedness, charity, and thorough soundness of belief in all that relates to the doctrine of the Church:—

1. That it is very honourable in an Ecclesiastic to cherish poverty, even though he may have a large income. For, even large incomes are always insufficient, if one wishes to meet the want which daily presents itself of promoting those various good works which cannot be promoted without money.

2. That an Ecclesiastic ought to be so cautious, circumspect, and chaste in all his movements, looks, and thoughts, that one might apply to him the words which the Church sings of St. Aloysius: *Vel carnis expers Spiritus, vel angelus cum corpore.*

3. That an Ecclesiastic ought always to look to Rome, whence proceeds the true light of Christian wisdom, and that he may not depart a hair's breadth from what is there believed, and is taught from the Chair which God has there established.

Finally, the Parish Priest must endeavour to cultivate in the hearts of Ecclesiastical aspirants piety, which evidently is *ad omnia utilis, promissionem habens vitæ quæ nunc est et futuræ*, and which for this very reason is so violently combatted by the Devil and by his followers. If a Parish Priest is bound to cultivate piety among the people, surely he ought still more to promote it among those whose duty it will afterwards be to maintain and spread it among the laity. Clerics sometimes neglect to cultivate pious practices, under the pretence that they do not wish to subtract any time from their studies. Let us not give the lie to the Apostle: let us be convinced that piety is *ad omnia utilis*, and, consequently, useful also for our advancement in our studies, and notably in ecclesiastical studies.

Let the Parish Priest exert himself in a very special manner to inspire clerics with a love of frequent, nay, of very frequent, Communion. I will not repeat here, what I have already said, in an earlier part of this work, when speaking of the Holy Communion. I shall merely remark that that frequent reception of the Holy Eucharist which, according to the Council of Trent and the Roman Catechism is suitable to seculars, ought without doubt to be suitable in the case of ecclesiastics. Mgr. De Segur observes, in the little work already quoted, that "a young cleric who would not feel an attraction towards the Blessed Sacrament, could scarcely become a good Priest, and a Director who could not understand the importance, nay the necessity, of very frequent Communion for youthful aspirants to the Ministry, would evidently be an inexperienced guide of souls". What kind of Priests will certain clerics become, who almost force themselves to go to Confession once in the month : who never take up the Life of a Saint, or other spiritual book, who lose their time lounging about sacristies, without hearing a Mass on week-days, or who feel ashamed to uncover themselves in the street when they hear the sound of the *Angelus* bell ? Well indeed may the Church weep on the day on which clerics of this class will be admitted to Holy Orders.

CHAPTER VI.

OF THE SACRAMENT OF MATRIMONY.

§ 1. OF THE INTERFERENCE OF THE PARISH PRIEST IN ARRANGING MARRIAGES.

PRUDENCE requires that the Parish Priest should never interfere in arranging marriages, since the relatives are sufficiently zealous in this respect. Let him not, then, seek out or suggest alliances, but allow all marriages to be arranged without his intervention. It is not edifying to see a Parish Priest zealous in getting young girls married. It is a very superfluous kind of zeal. Nay in his case, as in the case of all other Ecclesiastics, it is an exhibition of zeal both dangerous and liable to misrepresentation; for, if the girls be poor, the evil-minded world will suspect that affection has something to do with it, and if they be rich, interest will be supposed to have influenced his action to some degree. In the arrangement of matrimonial alliances the world wishes to have its own way, and it is well that it should. Priests who do not meddle in such affairs will be acting rightly in the sight of God, and will, at the same time, merit the approval of men.

Priests ought to exert themselves in aiding young girls to abandon the world when the Spirit of God calls them to a state of continence. This is a matter in which they may laudably exercise their zeal, and, in doing so, they will be performing a very meritorious work, because young girls will have need of their comfort and assistance, to overcome the opposition which the world will infallibly offer to so holy a project.

In opposition to the views which I have put forward on this subject, some one may say: Suppose a girl have no relatives to interest themselves in settling her in the world, will not the Parish Priest be performing an act of charity in seeking out a partner for her? I reply that it is proved by experience that not even in this case does a girl, who is anxious to get married, stand in need of the intervention of the Parish Priest. These girls are not so neglectful of their own interests, or so indolent, as not to be able to make out a partner for themselves. Nay, furthermore, it must be remarked that if a girl has no relatives to watch over her, the Parish Priest ought to be doubly cautious, and ought to guard against manifesting in her case an interest which might be maliciously misconstrued by the evil-minded. And if, in some extremely rare case, the Parish Priest should judge it necessary to interest himself in getting a girl of this class married, he should do so only *indirectly*, taking care that the direct management of the affair be left in the hands of others, and that he should himself keep in the background, as though he had no interest whatever in the matter.

It would be, rather, the duty of the Parish Priest, whenever he can do so prudently, to use his influence towards preventing those marriages which, as far as one may judge, are likely to prove unfortunate. Should he see a girl anxious to marry a young libertine, an unbeliever, or a man of bad character, and that the poor creature would thus become the victim of the imprudence or caprice of her parents, he ought to interfere, to prevent such a marriage. I say this, however, with the limitation *if he can do so prudently*. Because, oftentimes, parents who are desperately anxious to have their daughters married, do not wish to receive any counsels or suggestions on the subject. Wherefore, should he anticipate that, on the one hand, his advice would prove fruitless, and, on the other hand, might draw down upon him hatred or hostility, he ought to follow the rule : *Noli effundere sermonem ubi non est auditus.*

Should a young girl happen to have been seduced, a zealous Parish Priest must not omit to do all in his power to persuade her seducer to marry her as soon as possible. Interference of this kind involves no danger, and, so far from being taken in bad part by any one, it will be commended. However, it must be carefully borne in mind that this remedy is not to be invariably put in practice. Let us suppose the case of a girl who is so immoral that we must anticipate that she will prove unfaithful to her husband, or, again, let us suppose that the seducer is a man so utterly regardless of the sanctity of the marriage-tie that, if he were to wed the girl under compulsion on the part of her relatives, or of the tribunals, he would either abandon his wife, or by ill-treatment would force her to abandon him—in such cases it would not be prudent on the part of a Parish Priest to endeavour at all hazards to bring about a marriage between the parties. The same remark applies to every other case in which there are grounds for anticipating that the marriage will prove unfortunate. In fact, to act otherwise, would be to remedy an actual dishonour, namely, the seduction of the young girl, by a permanent disgrace, which an unhappy marriage would undoubtedly prove to be. Wherefore, a prudent Parish Priest, before taking steps to bring about a marriage between the seducer and his victim, ought to reflect carefully whether such a marriage is likely to prove fortunate, and should there be no such hope, he must rather content himself with exhorting the girl to penance, and the relatives to patience.

But, it may be said, does not the law, both Ecclesiastical and Civil, require that reparation be made by marriage for the wrong done to the girl? This is undoubtedly true; but only in the hypothesis that marriage will repair the wrong without causing a greater one.

But, it may be said furthermore: will not the offspring thus remain illegitimate? I reply that it is a lesser evil that the offspring should remain in the condition in which it was born, than that it should be legitimised with the evident risk of entailing all those evil consequences which there is grave reason to anticipate from marriages contracted, so to speak, for mere form's sake, by persons who would be unwilling afterwards to recognise or respect them.

It sometimes happens that injudicious parents try to force their children to remain unmarried, either from motives of family interests, or even through caprice, and that because of this involuntary celebacy they live in a state of habitual sin. There is no doubt that a Parish Priest is bound to admonish such parents to allow their children due liberty to marry.

Finally, when the Parish Priest finds persons living in a state of concubinage, he ought to put forth all his zeal to induce them to render their union legitimate by the reception of the Sacrament of Matrimony. And here I would remark that some continue for long years in this unhappy state through pure indolence, so that, once they are exhorted by the Parish Priest to marry, they raise no objection on the point. I have many times known this to be the case.

§ 2. OF THE PUBLICATION OF THE BANNS.

The Publications of the Banns ought to take place *inter Missarum Solemnia*. This, however, is not necessary in places where the Mass is not sung, and where a different custom prevails. Wherefore in this matter one ought to attend to local custom, sanctioned by the Bishop. With us the publications are made at any of the Masses at which the Congregation may happen to be most numerous, whether that be the Parochial Mass, at which the Parish Priest explains the Gospel, or any of the later Masses. They are likewise made after the explanation of the Gospel at noon.[1]

It is necessary that the publications be made on a Festival Day; but it is disputed whether they may be made on a suppressed festival, in places where the people are accustomed to frequent the churches on these days just as on days of obligation. In practice one ought to follow in this matter the custom of the Diocese.

Parish Priests are aware of the canonical reasons for which the Bishop can dispense from the publication of the Banns. However, since it is the duty of the Parish Priest to petition for this dispensation, the question arises whether he ought to refuse to do so whenever the parties about to contract marriage do not bring forward a really canonical cause, which would justify a dispensation.

According to Canon Law, a Parish Priest ought to refuse to petition in such a case, even though there should be question of dispensing from only a single

---

[1] In Ireland, as a rule, the Banns are not published, a dispensation being obtained in almost every case from the Bishop or his Vicar. Parish Priests are, however, most strictly bound to satisfy themselves that no impediment exists which would prevent the celebration of the marriage; and, the better to secure this, there is inserted at the end of the Statutes of the Synod of Maynooth (Appendix xvi., Forma vii., p. 291) a form to be filled up by the Parish Priest when applying for a dispensation.—*Translator.*

publication. However, in places where the custom is introduced of not acting up to the strict letter of the law in granting dispensations of this kind, the Parish Priest can petition for them even where a strictly canonical cause does not exist. He must be careful, however, not to set forth in his petition any false allegation, but must state the cause put forward by the parties themselves who seek the dispensation, leaving the Bishop to decide whether it be sufficient or not. Now a Parish Priest would be making a false allegation, were he to state in his petition, in the absence of canonical causes, that the parties about to contract marriage "*petunt dignis de causis dispensationem*"; for, the canonical causes alone can be said to be *worthy* of a dispensation. In this case, suppressing the words "*dignis de causis*," he ought simply to state the reasons for which the contracting parties seek to be dispensed from the Banns.

It might be asked whether a Parish Priest ought to petition for a dispensation even when it is sought for without any reason, but solely because of the strong dislike felt by some persons to have their names published in the Church. In truth, the answer to this question ought to be a decided negative; nevertheless, if in any Diocese the rigour of the law were so unduly relaxed that a dispensation would be granted merely because it was desired by the petitioners, how ought a Parish Priest to act? Ought he to manifest his disapproval of the practice of his Ecclesiastical Superior, refuse to conform to the general custom followed by the other Parish Priests, and take the consequences of his singularity, which might sometimes prove serious? All this he ought to do if there were question of the observance of some Natural law; but he ought not to do so when there is question only of an Ecclesiastical law, which has been allowed to fall into disuse. It is the duty of Bishops to require that their priests shall observe the Ecclesiastical laws, and not *vice versa*. Consequently, the Parish Priest ought not to refuse to forward the petition in the circumstances in question.

§ 3. Of Marriages of Conscience.

Whenever necessity, or even convenience, requires that a marriage should be celebrated secretly, the Church permits it to take place without any kind of publicity, and that the record of it be omitted from the ordinary Register of marriages.[1]

Should a Parish Priest become aware of the necessity of a secret marriage, he ought, in virtue of that charity which he is bound to exhibit towards his parishioners in all their spiritual necessities, to exert himself to obtain the required permission from

---

[1] It is scarcely necessary to remark that, when the Author says that these marriages are allowed to be celebrated "without any kind of publicity," we must not suppose that the presence of the Parish Priest and two witnesses can be dispensed with in places where the law of the Council of Trent regarding Clandestinity prevails. Whoever wishes for the fullest information regarding secret marriages should read the Encyclical of Benedict XIV. "*Satis vobis compertum*," which will be found in the beginning, or at the end, of St. Liguori's Moral Theology.—*Translator.*

the Bishop, laying before him all the reasons which he may consider sufficient for the purpose. It is hardly necessary to add, however, that the Bishop alone has the right to decide as to the sufficiency of these reasons.

Regarding the celebration of a marriage of this kind *in articulo mortis*, I must refer the reader to what has been already said in the Appendix on the assistance of the Sick.

§ 4. OF THE RELIGIOUS INSTRUCTION NECESSARY FOR THOSE WHO ARE ABOUT TO CONTRACT MARRIAGE.

When a Parish Priest has reason to doubt that the parties about to contract marriage are sufficiently instructed in the truths of the Christian Doctrine, he ought, before marrying them, to question them, and to give them the necessary instruction, should he find them ignorant. This obligation, however, might pretty frequently involve the Parish Priest in difficulties, since there are very few, now-a-days, especially in cities, who would be willing to submit to an examination of this kind, which they consider fit only for children. Many persons, although ill instructed, and consequently, in need of being taught the Christian Doctrine, would become highly indignant were the Parish Priest to hint that he wished to question them regarding the truths of Faith, and would be likely to reply to him in insulting language. Wherefore, we must see how far precisely does the strict obligation of a Pastor in this matter extend. The remarks which I am about to make will serve likewise to tranquillise those Confessors who are too ready to believe that they are bound to insist on General Confessions, because of the ignorance of the mysteries of Faith which they discover in their penitents; and will convince them that the ignorance which would render the faithful incapable of receiving the Sacraments is far more rare than is supposed by very many persons.

First of all, if we consider the matter carefully, we shall find that those who are so ignorant of the primary truths of Faith, as to be incapable of being admitted to the Sacraments, are far less numerous than is supposed. As a matter of fact, it is not true that they are really ignorant of all that they seem not to know. There are many who, if questioned in the ordinary manner on the mysteries of Faith, remain confused and silent, so that one would be inclined to pronounce them hopelessly ignorant; but if we put the questions to them in a different form, they answer in such a manner that we feel quite satisfied that they know these mysteries substantially. If you ask them what is meant by *the Unity and Trinity of God, the Incarnation, the Passion and Death of Our Lord Jesus Christ*, they fail to give an adequate reply. But if, on the other hand, you ask these same persons —*Are there several Gods, or one only?* they will reply: *One only*—*Are they the Christians or the Unbelievers who adore the most Holy Trinity, the Father, the Son, and the Holy Ghost?* they will make answer: *the Christians*—*Was the Infant Saviour of the World born of the Virgin Mary, or of St. Elizabeth?* they will reply: *of the Virgin Mary—Was it on the Cross that Christ died, or in some other manner?* they will reply: *On the Cross.* From this we must conclude that they are not really ignorant of the substance of the principal mysteries of Faith.

And assuredly it would be extremely difficult to find a Christian ignorant of the Unity of God, if for no other reason than that he has never heard God spoken of in the Plural. The same must be said of the Trinity, when we reflect that he has heard it mentioned thousands of times, and has been taught to make the sign of the Cross. The self-same remark applies to the Incarnation, and to the Passion and Death of our Lord Jesus Christ. Times without number, a Catholic sees the image of Mary with the Infant in her arms, he sees Him represented as born in the stable, worshipped by the shepherds, adored by the Magi, &c.; he has repeatedly seen Him represented as scourged at the pillar, crowned with thorns, nailed to the Cross, dead in the Sepulchre, risen from the dead, &c. Therefore, it is impossible for him not to understand that Christ was born of the Blessed Virgin, that He suffered and died through love of us, that He arose again, and so on of the rest.

We must be persuaded that the external worship of our holy Religion, and in a special manner the Festivals of the church, are of themselves a great source of instruction for the people, particularly the Solemn Festivals of Christmas, the Epiphany, the Annunciation, Good Friday, Easter, Ascension Day,

Pentecost, Trinity Sunday, and *Corpus Christi*. These Festivals are a real Catechism, from which the most negligent and ignorant Christians must of necessity derive instruction in the most important truths of Faith.

Furthermore, there is a very great difference between being ignorant of these truths, and not being able to give expression to what one knows about them. In order to be admitted to the Sacraments it is necessary to know the truths in question, but it is not necessary to be able to explain them in suitable language.

These views are not merely mine, but they are those of Monsigneur Devié, Bishop of Belley, whose words are quoted and approved by Cardinal Gousset. "In a Catholic country," he says, "where the exercises of religion are publicly practised; where the sign of the Cross is continually made in the name of the Most Holy Trinity; where the august Sign of our Redemption is to be met with in the churches, in the houses, in the fields, often with the image of the expiring Saviour nailed on to it, in a manner calculated to rivet the attention; where the anniversary days of the birth, of the death, and of the resurrection of the Saviour are annually celebrated; where the image of Mary holding Jesus in her arms, and other images representing various circumstances of His life, are continually before the eyes of the Faithful; it is difficult for Catholics to be ignorant of the great mysteries of the Most Holy Trinity, and of the Incarnation, to such an extent that the absolutions given to them would be invalid (and the knowledge which suffices for Absolution is sufficient for Matrimony). It is certain that they may know and believe these mysteries, without being able to give expression to their knowledge." (Card. Gousset, Theol. Moral., v. 2, n. 573.)

But it may be advanced in opposition to this doctrine that if we are to presume that every Catholic, even though ignorant, has generally speaking a sufficient knowledge of the principal mysteries of Faith, there is no reason why the Church should direct Parish Priests to examine parties about to contract marriage regarding them, whenever they may have doubts of the sufficiency of their instruction.

But it must be borne in mind that the Church does not prescribe merely what is of absolute necessity for the valid reception of the Sacraments, but also what is becoming. Wherefore, since it is most proper that Christians should not only have a knowledge of the mysteries of Religion, but should, moreover, be instructed in such a manner as to be able to render an account of their knowledge, she justly requires that when there is reason to suspect the absence of this higher class of knowledge, they should be questioned before being admitted to the celebration of the marriage contract. And she does this all the more justly, in as much as these parties, should they have children, will be obliged to instruct them in the truths of Faith, which they will be unable to do if they themselves have merely a knowledge of the doctrine, without the faculty of giving expression to it. However, when the church requires something for the sake of propriety, even though it be a matter of grave consequence, we may omit it, if, as in the case under discussion, it cannot be accomplished, or even attempted, without exposing ourselves to affronts and insults.

Meanwhile, I have drawn attention to this doctrine, which at first sight may appear lax, in order to remove the embarrassment of poor Parish Priests who, on the one hand, find themselves obliged to assist at the marriages of certain parties, of the sufficiency of whose religious instruction they cannot help entertaining doubts, while, on the other hand, these parties would submit to any sacrifice, rather than be interrogated on the Catechism like children.

Wherefore, it would seem that we ought not to censure the conduct of a Parish Priest who (1) would exempt from the examination in question all those persons whom he can prudently judge to be sufficiently instructed; who (2) would in a considerate manner propose some questions to those of whose instruction he may have reason to doubt, provided he knows that they are likely to submit to be questioned; who (3), finally, would omit altogether to interrogate those whom he might judge likely to be so incensed by any such proposal, that he could hope for no good result from the attempt, but might even expect insulting replies. This is the course adopted now-a-days by good Parish Priests, and it does not seem prudent to aim at anything beyond it.

It may be objected that, when parents are so ignorant as not to know how to enunciate in a suit-

OF THE SACRAMENT OF MATRIMONY. 429

able manner the truths of Faith, they will not be able to teach them to their children. But it must be remembered that we do not usually find this degree of ignorance in women, especially if they have had any instruction; and it is the women, rather than the men, who are accustomed to teach the children. Moreover, if the parties go to Confession, the Confessor will lay down for them all that is necessary for the good education of their children, and, consequently, will inform them also of the amount of instruction which they themselves need in order to impart to their children a knowledge of the truths of Faith. On the other hand, who would venture to assert that a Parish Priest ought to refuse to assist at the marriage of those who, as far as he can foresee, will not train up their children properly? Were this so, it would be no exaggeration to assert that a Parish Priest could not assist at half the marriages which are celebrated in our times. Furthermore, it must be remarked that Benedict XIV. teaches (De Syn., lib. viii., cap. 14, n. 6[1]) that a Pastor is bound to assist at the marriages of those who are so stupid, and so deficient in memory, as to be unable to remember and repeat the principal truths of Faith; and yet it is certain that persons of this class will not be able afterwards to teach these truths to their children.

[1] We subjoin the passage from Benedict XIV. to which the Author alludes in the text:—"Unum tamen advertendum addimus, nimirum quandoque evenire, ut quis præcipua Fidei nostræ mysteria et sciat et credat, cætera pariter, quæ necessitate præcepti sunt addiscenda, aliquo saltem rudi modo perceperit; sed, quia hebetis est ingenii, et exilis memoriæ, post omnem adhibitam

§ 5. Of the State of Grace necessary in those who are about to contract Marriage.

A Parish Priest has a much more serious cause for anxiety, when either of the parties about to be married refuses to go to Confession before receiving the Sacrament of Matrimony; and the anxiety becomes all the greater, when the Pastor knows that the party in question is a bad Christian, who neglects Paschal Communion, eats meat on Fridays, and so forth. This is a case which occurs not unfrequently in our times.

We must observe, first of all, that if we wish to adhere rigorously to the teaching of Theology, Sacramental Confession is not necessary for one who, being in a state of mortal sin, wishes to contract marriage. If we except the Blessed Eucharist, which, as we learn from the Council of Trent, cannot be received by a person conscious of mortal sin without previous confession, all the other *Sacramenta vivorum* may be received after recovering God's grace by a simple act of contrition, which includes the resolution of going to Confession afterwards in due time. And if an exception ought to be made in favour of Extreme Unction, it is because should the sick man die, he would be unable afterwards to confess his sins, and

diligentium, illa memoria retinere et recitare non valeat: in hoc autem rerum statu, non debet perpetuo arceri a Matrimonio, quod est institutum in officium naturæ, et propterea nemini, sine propria culpa, est denegandum; sed curabit Parochus ut, qui eo memoriæ defectu laborat, frequenter audiat quæ semel crasse didicit, ne ab ejus mente penitus elabantur".—*Translator.*

on the other hand, the Sacrament of Extreme Unction is considered as the complement of the Sacrament of Penance.[1] Wherefore, Theologians commonly teach that whoever is conscious of mortal sin may receive Confirmation, Orders,[2] and Matrimony, provided he previously recovers God's grace by contrition alone.

In the first place, then, if the parties about to contract marriage should assert that their conscience did not reproach them with any mortal sin, the Parish Priest would have no right to insist on their going to Confession before receiving the Sacrament of Matrimony.

Again, should the parties say: we believe that by means of contrition we have made provision for the necessities of our consciences, and we will go to Confession afterwards in due time, the Parish Priest ought, indeed, to exhort them to go to Confession before marriage, but, should they still refuse to do so, he ought to yield, and to assist at the marriage.

[1] The Author might have added another reason for the necessity of confession (when possible) before Extreme Unction, at least in some cases. To be a fit subject for Extreme Unction, one must be *in periculo mortis*. Now, under such circumstances, there is a *Divine precept* obliging a person to go to Confession if he can. (De Lugo De Pænitentia, Disp. XV., Sec. 3., n. 37); and consequently if there were any danger of his not surviving after Extreme Unction, for a period sufficiently long to allow of his making his confession, he would be strictly bound to go to Confession first, no matter how contrite he might be.—*Translator*.

[2] Since, however, those who are ordained in Major Orders invariably communicate at the Mass at which they are ordained, it is clear that, if conscious of mortal sin, they would be bound to go to Confession before Ordination, not precisely because of the reception of the Sacrament of Orders, but because they are to receive the Blessed Eucharist.—*Translator*.

Nor ought he to be deterred from following this course, because of Synodical Laws directing the Parish Priest to require from parties about to marry certificates of having gone to Confession. For, these laws are *directive*, rather than intended to impose a new precept which *per se* does not exist.[1] Diocesan Synods wisely command Parish Priests to insist on all possible guarantees (we must understand the reservation—*where they can*) to make sure that the contracting parties will receive the Sacrament in a state of grace; but it is impossible to suppose that they can have intended to impose upon the Faithful more than was ordained by our Lord when instituting the Sacraments. Now, it is indisputable that Christ has not imposed an obligation of confessing venial sins, and, consequently, the Parish Priest could not oblige persons about to contract marriage to go to Confession, if they should affirm that they were not conscious of being in the state of mortal sin. Nor could he oblige them to Confession were they to say that they had already made provision for their spiritual necessities by an Act of Contrition; since Theologians agree in teaching that this means of

---

[1] On this subject O'Kane writes as follows *(Supplement to the Notes on the Rubrics*, n. 1095): "In some places Confession is strictly required by a special law, or custom having the force of law, and the Parish Priest should not assist at the marriage until he is satisfied that the parties have confessed. This is the case in France (Carriere, 62, 3rd ; Bouvier, c. I., art. 2, § II., Quaer. 1st). We believe the same is the case in Ireland, but there may be circumstances in which it would not be expedient to insist on it, and in these the Bishop should be consulted (Carriere, 63 ; Bouvier, loc. cit. ; Gury, II., 585)."—*Translator.*

justification is sufficient for Matrimony. Nay, we might add that particular Synods would not possess sufficient authority to order Confession in these cases, since it is not within their power to make additions to what has been ordained by Christ in this matter.

The most serious difficulty arises when the parties about to contract marriage refuse to go to Confession because they do not care to put themselves in a state of grace, and also because they do not believe either in the grace of God, or in the Sacrament of Penance, their only object in contracting marriage being respect for the Civil law, in order to place themselves under its protection, and to secure those rights which are annexed to a legal marriage.

It is certain that in such cases the Parish Priest ought to employ all his zeal to convince and persuade those careless or unbelieving persons to dispose themselves to receive the Sacrament like Christians; and should they still continue obstinate, he ought to put off the celebration of the marriage, and to consult the Bishop, who, in his prudence, will decide whether this be a case for the application of a theory recognised as true by several Theologians. The Parish Priest ought then to carry out the orders of the Bishop without any fear of doing wrong; because in these cases, which of themselves are difficult, and which may entail grave consequences of scandal, of complaints on the part of the Civil Authorities, and so forth, the Parish Priest will be entirely justified if he acts upon the orders of his Bishop.

It must be borne in mind that if parties wish to

receive the Sacrament of Matrimony in mortal sin, we cannot prevent them from committing this great crime, by compelling them to go to Confession. For, if they are unwilling to confess their sins, and yet cannot avoid going through the form of doing so, they will present themselves to a Confessor, and, while pretending to make a sincere confession, will merely tell him some invented trifles. He will then give them a certificate of Confession, and thus, by means of the sacrilegious profanation of another Sacrament, they secure the presence of the Parish Priest at their marriage. Here, then, we have *two* sacrileges instead of one.

From all that has been said, we may conclude that when the Parish Priest has not time to consult the Bishop, and fears serious consequences should he refuse to marry the parties, he would not be doing wrong in assisting at the marriage on his own authority.

For the rest, there is no doubt that, in the ordinary cases, Parish Priests ought to observe the Synodical Decrees, which direct that they should require a Certificate of Confession from parties about to enter into the marriage state, before they assist at their marriages. They would act very improperly were they to show themselves negligent in this matter; because it would thus come to pass that many, through pure indolence, would omit to go to Confession, and would contract marriage in a state of sin.[1]

---

[1] Before concluding this subject, it may not be out of place to quote the following passage from O'Kane, regarding Confession

§ 6. Of the Jurisdiction necessary for the Validity of a Marriage.

The Parish Priest ought to be most careful that one at least of the parties whom he is about to unite in marriage belongs to his own parish, since otherwise the marriage would be invalid. Sometimes Parish Priests suppose they have some reason for concluding that the parties are their parishioners, and they immediately decide to assist at their marriage; yet, nevertheless, should their fancied reason prove groundless, the marriage remains null and void. There are even some country Parish Priests who regard as their parishioners every one who was baptised in their parish, even though the families may afterwards have gone to reside elsewhere. This would be a glaring error, which would not leave the slightest doubt regarding the invalidity of a marriage at which a Parish Priest would assist on such grounds.

Wherefore, it is not enough that a Parish Priest should *suppose*, according to his own lights, that he

preparatory to Matrimony:—"It is very important that the Confession be not delayed till all things are prepared for the marriage, for it may happen that an impediment would then become known, so that it would be necessary to break off the marriage, or obtain a dispensation; and it is easy to see the embarrassment that would be caused if the Confession, in such a case, were deferred till the very day of the marriage. For the duty of the Confessor in this most perplexing case see St. Liguori, Lib. vi., De pænit., n. 613." (O'Kane, *Supplement to Notes on the Rubrics*, n. 1095.)—*Translator.*

has the right of assisting at a marriage: he must be *certain* of it; and if he cannot have this certainty, he ought to procure an unquestionable authorisation, either from the Bishop, or from the Parish Priest whose right it might be to assist. If a Parish Priest does not take these precautions, it may easily happen that the parties will be living in a state of concubinage instead of marriage; and should they one day come to discover the invalidity of their supposed marriage, incalculable evils may result, both to their families and to their offspring. All these evils might spring from the vilest cause, namely, from the fact that the Parish Priest acted precipitately and assisted at the marriage, in order not to lose the marriage fees.[1]

§ 7. OF THE CONSENT OF THE PARENTS.

Before publishing the Banns, and still more before assisting at a marriage, the Parish Priest ought to make sure of the consent of the parents, or, should these be dead, of the guardians of the parties about to marry. The Church requires of children that, as a mark of due respect, they should take counsel with their parents before marriage, and ask their consent.

[1] Wherever the Decree of the Council of Trent on Clandestine Marriages is in force (as in Ireland) few cases cause greater perplexity from time to time than those arising out of the question of *domicile* and *quasi-domicile*. The subject will be found treated at considerable length, and with his usual clearness and learning, by O'Kane, in his *Supplement to Notes on the Rubrics*, §§ 1001-1069, pp. 13-44.—*Translator*.

This mark of respect is not limited to any age, and, therefore, it is not lawful even for persons of full age to omit it, so that a Parish Priest would be wanting in his duty if he were not to require in their case also the consent of their parents.[1]

Parish Priests must be careful not to constitute themselves judges of the motives which may influence parents in preventing the marriages of their children: to decide in such matters belongs to his Ecclesiastical Superior. Wherefore, a Parish Priest must always require the parties who are about to marry to ask and obtain the consent of both their parents, or, should these be dead, of their guardians; and should they, after failing to get this consent, persist, nevertheless, in their resolution of getting married, the Parish Priest must refer the matter to the Bishop, and await his instructions.

Should the Parish Priest act otherwise, he would fail in his duty in the eyes of the Church, and he might also involve himself in difficulties with the Civil Laws.

---

[1] The Author seems to hold rather rigid views regarding the obligation of persons of full age in this matter. St. Liguori (lib. vi., n. 849) enumerates seven cases in which a person would not be bound to be guided by his parents with regard to marriage; and it may be said, in general, that when the opposition of the parents is *unjust* and *unreasonable*, a child is not bound to obey. O'Kane gives a very sound, practical advice to a priest who is called upon to marry persons whose parents do not consent to their union: "A Priest," he says, "when asked to assist at such a marriage, must carefully weigh all the circumstances, and, if possible, arrange matters so that the parents may be induced to consent, or at least may have no reason to complain of him for assisting at the marriage". (*Supplement to Notes on the Rubrics*, 995.)—*Translator*.

§ 8. OF MISTAKES OCCURRING IN THE NAMES OF THE CONTRACTING PARTIES IN DISPENSATIONS OBTAINED FROM ROME, AND IN THE PUBLICATION OF THE BANNS.

Mistakes of this kind are not always avoided even by careful Parish Priests, because an oversight in reading an extract from a Baptismal Register, or in copying a name, is a matter which may very easily occur. Should the Parish Priest detect a mistake regarding a name in a dispensation received from Rome, and should it be still possible to correct the mistake in time, he ought to consult his Ecclesiastical Superior and be guided by his decision. Should the mistake occur in a dispensation granted by the Bishop, or in the publication of the Banns, he ought to consult the Bishop, who will provide in the case as he may think fit.

On the other hand, should a mistake occurring in a dispensation received from Rome be detected only at the last moment, when the marriage is about to be celebrated, and should there be no time, without great inconvenience, to defer the ceremony for the purpose of consulting the Bishop, then, if the error be simply a clerical one—such as writing *John Smith* instead of *James Smith*—the Parish Priest could assist at the marriage on his own authority. For, although the style of the Roman Curia requires that application be made for a rectification of the error before the dispensation is put in force, yet, since it is agreed upon by Canonists and Theologians that an error of this kind cannot render the dispensation invalid, we ought to interpret the intention of the Church in favour of the immediate celebration of the marriage, whenever it could not be deferred without danger of grave spiritual or temporal loss, and also of serious troubles and disagreements in the families of the contracting parties. The Parish Priest should afterwards explain to the Bishop the course he had adopted, and await his instructions.

The Parish Priest ought to pursue the same course should the mistake occur in a dispensation asked from the Bishop, and also, as a rule, when the mistake occurs in the publication of the Banns. I say, *as a rule;* because if the mistake in the publication were calculated to lead the listeners into error— as would occur, for example, if the mistake regarded the name and surname—the publication would be null, and the Parish Priest could not assist at the marriage, inasmuch as the Banns had not yet been published. If, however, the mistake affected a name only, the publications being otherwise correct as regarded the surnames, the parents, and other particulars, those who are listening will easily be able to detect and correct the mistake themselves.

§ 9. OF INVALID MARRIAGES.

When a Parish Priest discovers that a marriage has been contracted invalidly, if the impediment which caused the invalidity is known to the supposed wedded pair, so that they are, consequently, in bad faith, since they know their union to be unlawful, he ought immediately to order them to separate; and should he be unsuccessful in inducing them to do so, he must denounce them to the Bishop.

If, on the other hand, the supposed wedded pair are in good faith, either through ignorance or inadvertence, he must say nothing of the invalidity of their marriage until he has taken counsel with some prudent persons, or, better still, with the Bishop, in order to find out what he had best do to render the marriage valid, without giving rise to scandal or to any unpleasant consequences.

Indeed it would be extremely imprudent to inform the supposed husband and wife of the nullity of their marriage, without having previously taken steps to render it valid; because, if they should continue to cohabit, those acts which, owing to good faith, were before only material sins, and, consequently, without guilt in the sight of God, would thenceforward become formal sins; and, moreover, there would be reason to fear some irremediable rupture between the parties, which would entail misery upon their families and upon their offspring. But if, on the other hand, the dispositions of the parties be carefully studied, as well as the best method to be adopted in order to render the marriage valid, the evil may be remedied prudently and successfully.

Should there be reason to foresee that irreparable mischief would follow, were they to become aware of the invalidity of their marriage, their good faith ought to remain undisturbed for ever; but in pursuing this course, a Pastor ought at the same time to take counsel with prudent persons, and especially with the Bishop.

If, however, on the other hand, the Parish Priest were convinced that the supposed wedded parties were God-fearing persons, who would fully obey his directions, so that there would be no danger of sin or of any other evil consequence, he ought to inform them immediately of the invalidity of their marriage, in order to prevent even material sin. Nevertheless, in this matter, which is so extremely delicate, and so fenced round with danger, he ought never to rely on his own judgment; for, otherwise, notwithstanding all his calculations, evil consequences might follow, especially if the parties happened to be young, or might give occasion for suspicions in their families by occupying different sleeping apartments, and so forth.

Finally, should the impediment be known to one only of the parties, and should this one be aware of the invalidity of their marriage, it is clear that on no account could the party in question discharge the duties of Matrimony until the marriage had been rendered valid. In such circumstances, the Parish Priest ought to consult Theologians, in order to remove the danger of sin as best he may, and he should have recourse immediately to the Bishop, as indeed he ought to do in every case where he discovers a marriage which requires to be rendered valid. The Bishop might happen to have extraordinary faculties to meet the wants of the case. Should he not have them, and should the impediment be public, or not arising *ex delicto*, application should be made to the Dataria; but should the impediment be secret and arising *ex delicto*, recourse should be had to the Cardinal Penitentiary.[1] The Reader will find these matters treated fully by Moral Theologians.

[1] Priests in English-speaking Countries should never apply directly to the *Dataria* or *Pœnitentiaria* for dispensations, as no notice would be taken of their letters. It is not even advisable to write directly to *Propaganda*. The easiest and safest plan is to send to their Bishop a petition for the dispensation, drawn up in proper form, with a request that he should forward it to Rome. As all the Bishops have agents at Rome, the dispensation will thus be procured more securely and more expeditiously than if a priest were to apply for it personally.—*Translator.*

PART III.

ON THE PRACTICE OF SOME OF THE VIRTUES WHICH ARE MOST NECESSARY TO A PARISH PRIEST.

CHAPTER I.

OF THE PURITY OF CONSCIENCE NECESSARY TO A PARISH PRIEST.

§ 1. OF AVOIDING MORTAL SIN.

THERE is no man more unhappy than the hypocrite, who must always be careful to exhibit exteriorly a manner of life which is ever condemning the affections and the desires of his heart. If a Parish Priest does not keep his soul free from sin, he must play the part of a consummate hypocrite; because there is no one who is so strictly bound as he is to give an example of piety, and who is at the same time compelled to pass his life so much exposed to public observation. A Parish Priest, then, whose heart is bad, must be an accomplished hypocrite, and, therefore, supremely unhappy.

Hypocrisy, it is true, may save a man's honour for a period, longer or shorter in proportion to the perfection of his cunning and to the contingencies which may arise; but it is not be hoped that it will save him for ever. Wherefore, a hypocritical Parish Priest ought to regard it as certain that one day or other his real character will be discovered, and his honour irretrievably ruined; because once he becomes known in his true colours, even though he should reform his conduct, no one will believe in the sincerity of the reformation, and, however real it might be, it would still be regarded merely as a fresh exhibition of his hypocrisy.

It must be remarked, moreover, that among Seculars we find some, who lead a pretty bad life, who fall from time to time into some sin, then amend for a while, and, should they again fall, do not abandon themselves entirely to iniquity, but rise up once more. But, on the other hand, this kind of mediocrity is rarely to be met with in priests, and especially in Parish Priests, who do not live constantly in the grace of God. In fact, the daily celebration of the Holy Mass, and the continual administration of the Sacraments places them as it were in a kind of necessity of committing sacrileges, and these sacrileges reproduce in them the effect which was produced in Judas of old: *Introivit in eum Satanas.* And once Satan has gained possession of them, he does not content himself with leaving them moderately bad, but hurls them down into the deepest depths of iniquity.

Wherefore, the condition of a Parish Priest who lives in sin makes one shudder. He begins each day with a horrible profanation of the Body and Blood of Jesus Christ, and of the very Sacrifice of Calvary, and thus each morning *judicium sibi manducat et bibit*. After years and years of such food, how glutted must he be with damnation! Every time that he administers the Body of the Lord to others, he himself commits a new sacrilege. Every time that he frees from sin the souls of others, he binds his own with a new chain. Every time that he ascends the pulpit to announce the Word of God, he hears thundering in his ears that terrible sentence: *Quare tu enarras justitias meas, et assumis testamentum meum per os tuum?* (Ps. xlix. 16.) And yet, while he thus goes on from day to day, plunging still deeper into this bottomless abyss, will you tell him to correct sinners, to prevent scandals, to promote the glory of God and the salvation of souls, to be the good shepherd of the flock of Christ? Alas! poor flock! they have a wolf for their guardian! As long as his mask of hypocrisy lasts, he will remain in the garb, indeed, of a shepherd, but carrying always in his bosom the evil disposition of a wolf. And what kind of death must follow such a life? Who will not exclaim, when this thought strikes him: *Viæ inferi domus ejus penetrantes in interiora mortis?* (Proverbs vii. 27.) Truly, the state of a Parish Priest who lives in sin is enough to make one shudder!

Wherefore, a Parish Priest, more than any other

Christian, and even more than any other priest, ought to take care to live continually in a state of grace. Consequently, if a Parish Priest should perceive that he falls into sin occasionally, though rarely, he ought never to rest until he succeeds in living perseveringly in God's grace; and this he ought to do, not only because he, like everybody else, may be surprised by Death while in a state of sin, and so be lost for ever, but also because of the risk to which he would otherwise expose himself of one day becoming a man confirmed in iniquity, and another Judas.

And here we must deplore a most disastrous opinion which is entertained by some, namely, that, considering the frailty of man, an occasional fall is inevitable. Fully persuaded of this, they become in a certain sense resigned to it. When they fall, they repent and resolve not to fall again, yet, with a certain fore-knowledge, all the while, that, sooner or later, they will fall again. In the abstract they believe that man can always avoid sin; yet they hold another practical belief, namely, that human weakness cannot succeed in avoiding it always. What a lamentable persuasion, what a horrible forecast is this—sooner or later I cannot help falling again into mortal sin! Meanwhile the mind remains, in a certain sense, disposed towards this condition of affairs as towards a kind of necessity, and by this very means a relapse is greatly facilitated.

Ah! would that there were no Ecclesiastics of this type! However, it is very easy for them to bear in mind that unless we are prepared to admit the heretical doctrine of necessary sin, we must recognise it as a dogma of Faith that every Christian can live always in a state of grace provided he wishes to do so, and that if he fall, even once in a lifetime of a hundred years, it will be because he wished to fall. Not only an Ecclesiastic, but every Catholic who is even moderately instructed must confess that human weakness is not only great but very great, so that, if we view the matter from this standpoint, to sin is the easiest thing in the world; but he must admit, at the same time, that this weakness, when strengthened by divine grace, becomes invincible, so that there is no temptation so strong that it is unable to resist it. How can we ever refuse belief to the Apostle, who assures us that: *Fidelis. . . . Deus est, qui non patietur vos tentari supra id quod potestis?* (1 Cor. x. 13.) Let us be humble, let us pray, let us avoid dangerous occasions, and let us never for a moment grow weak in the firm hope of living constantly until the hour of Death in the friendship of God, and, consequently, free from every stain of mortal sin.

§ 2. Of avoiding Venial Sin.

However, a Parish Priest must never rest satisfied with merely avoiding mortal sin: he must, also, propose to himself to avoid fully deliberate venial sin; and he is bound to take this resolution, because he himself often preaches the great truth that to fall deliberately into venial sins disposes the soul to sin mortally. He is bound, moreover, to take this resolution, because he himself rigorously insists upon it in the case of pious souls who are in the habit of frequent, and still more from those who are in the habit of daily Communion, while he celebrates the Holy Mass every day, which is even more than simply going to Communion. There is no doubt that fully deliberate venial sin can be always avoided just as well as mortal sin. And in truth, if a man adverts fully to what he is doing, why should he find it more difficult to refrain from telling an officious lie, than to refrain from swearing what is false? more difficult to refrain from stealing a penny, than to refrain from stealing a pound?

And let no one reply that this doctrine is opposed to the teaching of the Council of Trent (Sess. 6, Can. 23), where it is defined that man cannot abstain from all, even venial, sins, during the entire course of his life, without a special privilege from God; because the Council is there speaking of those sins which are committed with only *partial* advertence, and which are the result rather of human weakness than of human malice. All theologians and masters of the spiritual life are agreed on this point, and teach with St. Alphonsus De Liguori that: "All those faults which are committed with full advertence can well be avoided with the assistance of God's grace". (Practice of the love of Jesus Christ, chap. viii.)

CHAPTER II.

OF THE DESIRE OF PERFECTION NECESSARY TO A PARISH PRIEST.

§ 1. A Parish Priest ought to be a Master of Perfection.

That a Parish Priest may be really good, it is not enough that he carefully avoid everything which he knows to be an offence of God; but he must also study to enrich his soul with all those virtues which constitute positive perfection, and make a man aim at pleasing God in everything, with the self-same anxiety with which he endeavours to avoid offending Him in anything.

In fact, a Pastor ought necessarily to be a master of Christian perfection; because it is not only probable that some soul will come before him seeking to be guided in this path, but if he hears Confessions, as is his duty, he must undertake the direction of many such, since there are everywhere to be found many pious souls who aspire to perfection in the divine service. Some one may say that there is no necessity why such souls should be directed by the Parish Priest, since they may be recommended to apply to other masters of the Spiritual Life. This reason, however, will not hold good for parishes in which the Parish Priest is the only Confessor; nor for those other parishes in which there may be, indeed, another Confessor, but yet one incapable of being a good Spiritual Director. Now, parishes of this kind are very numerous. On the other hand, the parishioners, who have always the right to place their consciences under the direction of their Pastor, do not, surely, lose this right when they form the resolution of leading a spiritual life, and of striving after perfection. And yet how is it possible for a Parish Priest to be a master of perfection if he does not aspire to it himself, if he sets no value on it, or perhaps treats it with ridicule, as some are accustomed to do in order to gain the reputation of being strong-minded?

§ 2. How necessary it is that a Parish Priest should have a good Director.

It is easy to understand how reprehensible is the practice of those Parish Priests who are accustomed to go to Confession to the first priest they meet, and perhaps to the very priest whom they hold in least esteem. They will tell you openly that they go to Confession solely in order to get the benefit of Absolution, and that the Absolution is equally valid whether it be given by a learned and holy man, or by one who is ignorant and sinful. But will not every one acknowledge that these persons, who are so thoughtless, or rather so proud, as not to know that they stand in need of a guide, of a master, of a physician, to direct, enlighten, and heal their souls, are precisely the very persons who most certainly do require something more than the mere benefit of Absolution from their sins?

Even though one should be very learned and most capable of directing others, he ought never to believe himself qualified to direct his own conscience. In order to exercise us in holy humility, Divine Providence has so arranged that no one can ever be his own guide, master, and physician, but that each one of us must be dependent upon others. Whoever should be so thoughtless as to disregard this virtue, or so proud as to suppose that it did not concern him, would, for this very reason, have need of a learned and pious Confessor or Director, to enlighten him regarding the necessities of his own soul and the duties of the Sacred Ministry.

Wherefore, since a Parish Priest is bound to strive after the attainment of Christian perfection, he must seek out for himself a learned and pious Director, to whom he may entrust the guidance of his conscience. And if, as often happens, he be unable to find in the neighbourhood of his parish anyone distinguished for learning and piety, he ought to seek for him elsewhere, and to confer with him on his spiritual necessities from time to time, while for the confession of his sins he might select the best of the neighbouring priests, in order that it might be easy for him to obtain frequently the benefit of Absolution. I have said that he ought to select *the best* of the neighbouring priests; for a Confessor is always a physician, and people invariably wish to secure the services of the best physician they can find.

Moreover, it is very important that a pastor should have his ordinary Confessor near him, so that he may be able to go to him frequently. It is the custom of pious Parish Priests to confess every eight days, and we ourselves are satisfied with nothing less than this in the case of those to whom we permit daily Communion. Alas! it happens too frequently that some do not know how to require of themselves, what they know how to require in the case of others. Some priests go too seldom to Confession, and, perhaps, they are not the priests who are most diligent in preserving purity of conscience.

§ 3. How a Parish Priest ought to regulate his Exterior Life.

The perfection to which a Parish Priest must aspire ought not, as a rule, to present anything extraordinary to the eyes of the world. Among all the Ministers of God, he is in fact the one who is most brought into contact with the world, and it is necessary that the world should not find in his person anything to offend it. Wherefore, the virtues which would be proper to an Anchorite or a Cenobite would not suit a Parish Priest. The virtues of retirement, of solitude, of silence, of pronounced contempt for the things of the world and for its judgments in matters which do not involve sin, and a singular exterior austerity of life, do not suit a Parish Priest.

A Parish Priest who should give himself up to retirement and solitude could not know fully the wants of his parishioners, and would be living for himself and not for his flock. In like manner, were he to cultivate silence, and avoid conversing with his people, he would remain isolated, and would be in a great measure at a disadvantage in helping souls. Again, were he to manifest too great contempt of the world, even in matters which may be tolerated, and where it does not clash with the spirit of the Gospel—for instance, were he to wear shabby, thread-bare, or, worse still, dirty clothes, or to show himself scrupulous in innocent matters which are sanctioned by the practice of all good persons—people would hold aloof from him as an eccentric, unsociable man; his very sermons would produce no effect; and his advice would neither be sought after nor heeded.

Just as a good Anchorite or Cenobite would be a bad father of a family, so, in like manner, would he be a bad Parish Priest. And if parishes are sometimes entrusted to Cenobites to be governed by them, we find by experience that, just in proportion as they endeavour to be good Parish Priests, they cease of necessity to be good Cenobites. There are some general virtues which are necessary and useful to every Christian, such as Faith, Hope, Charity, Humility, and so forth. There are other special virtues necessary and useful only to a particular class of persons, such as solitude, silence, and a singular austerity of life; and if we should wish to impose the practice of these virtues upon all, we would obtain as the result defects instead of perfections. Wherefore, certain works on asceticism, which have been written for Religious, that is to say, the rules of perfection laid down in them, are not all suitable for Parish Priests, just as they are not suited to various other states. Such, for example, is the third part of the celebrated, and most excellent treatise of Father Rodriguez on Christian Perfection.

The Supreme Pastor of our souls, our Lord Jesus Christ, ought to be the model upon which inferior pastors would fashion their lives. His life was of necessity most holy, yet it was ordinary. He lived not in the desert, but in the cities: He used to converse with persons of every class—even with sinners, in order to convert them, and He used to sit at table with them: He did not, ordinarily, perform long fasts, nor did He require them from His Disciples. (Matt. xi. 19; ix. 14.) He used to have a little money, and allowed it to be kept in order to meet daily wants. (John iv. 8; xii. 6.)

With this ordinary rule of life He had access to all places, He could hold intercourse with persons of every class, and very easily do good to all. Let the Parish Priest endeavour to do likewise; and, if he does so, there is no doubt that the Lord will provide him with all the graces which may serve to sanctify his ordinary life. On the other hand, it would be a stupid error to suppose that extraordinary and exceptional practices are necessary to sanctity.

CHAPTER III.

OF THE PRACTICE OF HUMILITY.

A PARISH Priest must be able to say with Christ: *non quæro gloriam meam.* (John viii. 50.) If he wishes to effect any good, let him seek the glory of God alone; for the Lord does not lend the assistance of His grace to the vain desire—daughter of pride—of making a show before the world. If a Parish Priest labours solely for the glory of God, such labour is really fruitful, and cannot fail to draw down the blessings of Heaven. In the present chapter, however, I mean to speak more particularly of that humility which a Pastor ought to practise in his relations with his neighbours, in order to give good example, and to draw souls to Christ.

A Pastor, then, ought to be on his guard against boasting of his own good works, against priding himself on the success of his good projects, and, above all, against depreciating others in order to exalt himself. It is easy to understand how reprehensible is the practice of those who are always eager to bring prominently under notice the change for the better which they have introduced into the parish regarding the frequentation of the Sacraments, the abuses which they have extirpated, the improvements which they have made in the church, and so forth; and especially when, in doing so, they direct attention to the neglect or incapacity of their predecessors. If a Parish Priest does good, his parishioners have eyes to see it, and they will know how to appreciate his labours without his boasting of them.

A Parish Priest must likewise be on his guard against the weakness of letting it be perceived that he is conscious of being esteemed by his parishioners for his learning, eloquence, piety, or other good qualities; and still more must he guard against the vanity of "fishing for compliments," which might lead him to question them somewhat in this style: *What do you hear the people saying of my preaching? How did you like my catechetical discourse? Is it not a fact that my audience is growing larger each Sunday?* These and other such silly questions are set down to vain-glory even by plain, simple people.

Again, a Pastor must practise humility in the encounters which he will sometimes have with the wicked and the ignorant. Certainly a Parish Priest must not show that he is offended by the impudence which he may sometimes meet with from persons of this class; for to do so would only increase their effrontery. Therefore, he must show himself calm, indeed, and resolute, but let him take care not to enter into a dispute with such persons, returning shout for shout, and insult for insult; for, they have nothing to lose in the matter of respectability and dignity, while the Parish Priest, on the other hand, has a great deal to lose in this respect. Let him, then, be content to employ with them calm, quiet argument, which is the only means from which he can expect any good result; for, bold, impudent persons are never vanquished, but are rather made still more furious, by stinging and insulting words. It is true that oftentimes more than ordinary patience is required in order to remain calm under such circumstances; but one must ask the spirit of patience from God, and put it into practice, lest he be tempted to do worse. Should he see that persons of this class fly into a passion on purpose, he must simply take leave of them, and withdraw from their presence.

Should a Pastor have to endure any insults or wrongs, he must meekly forgive them, even though it might easily be within his power to require satisfaction from the offender. If a secular calls a person to account for an insult, everybody says: *he is right in demanding satisfaction;* but, on the contrary, everyone expects a priest to forgive, and says: *he ought to take no notice of it.* People wish that he should copy more closely the meekness of the Saviour.

A Parish Priest must be particularly careful to be humble in his dealings with the poor and lowly. To be humble with the rich and powerful is not always true virtue; for it is frequently but meanness and cowardice. It is true virtue to be humble with those who are powerless to injure us even though they might wish to do so. And let not a Parish Priest imagine that his dignity will suffer by being humble with the poor and the lowly; for, on the contrary, sensible people will thereby conceive a far greater respect for him, and even those who may have offended him, when the first impulse of passion has passed away, will acknowledge the wrong they have committed, and will be compelled to do honour to the meekness of their good Pastor.

CHAPTER IV.

OF THE PRACTICE OF FORTITUDE.

§ 1. OF THE FORTITUDE REQUIRED IN A PARISH PRIEST IN ORDER TO FULFIL HIS DUTIES, AND TO PREVENT CRIMES.

A PARISH Priest must carefully distinguish humility and meekness from weakness, which would often wish to clothe itself with the mantle of these virtues. In matters which are his absolute duty, a Pastor ought to show himself firm as a rock, and ought not to yield to the threats of any person whatsoever. This unbending firmness is the distinguishing mark of the Catholic conscience, and ought to be the first qualification of a Pastor of souls. In every age we have had brilliant examples of this courage, and our own age, also, abounds in them.

However, it is well to remark that a Pastor ought to exhibit this unyielding firmness only when there is question of an absolute duty from which he cannot by any possibility be dispensed, such as, for example, in case anyone should wish to force a Parish Priest to preach a false doctrine, to administer the Sacraments to an unworthy person, and so forth. For, the duty of preaching the truth, the duty of administering the Sacraments worthily, and other such like obligations, are duties which bind always, and in every case, no matter what the consequences may be; and if we have made an exception in a previous chapter with regard to Matrimony, it is because the Parish Priest is not the minister of this Sacrament. But if there be question of duties which are not such absolutely, but only relatively, and as circumstances permit, a Parish Priest must not always be equally unbending in discharging them. For example, the duty of correction is relative to the fruit which one may have reason to expect from it; and, consequently, should a Pastor foresee that correction, whether public or private, would prove hurtful, he not only may, but ought to omit it.

When there is question of doubtful duties, if the Parish Priest be constrained to violate them by the force of circumstances, he ought, if time permits, to take counsel with his Bishop, and to carry out whatever orders may be given by him; but if he should not have time to do this, and if the evils which threaten should happen to be serious, then the case would arise for the application of the doctrine of St. Alphonsus: *lex dubia non obligat.* If a Parish Priest were placed in such straits, it would be for him a matter of doubt whether he was forbidden to consent to a certain request made to him, and therefore it would be lawful for him to consent without committing sin. Nay, we must add that if his refusal would be likely to entail serious evil consequences, he would be bound to consent; for one ought never to provoke a certain and very grave evil, through fear of doing something which is but an uncertain evil. If he should afterwards discover, after more mature reflection or study, that he had made a concession which he ought not to have made, he could repair the scandal by declaring that, in such a pressing emergency, he did not know that he was doing a thing forbidden to him, and that, had he known it, he would have discharged his duty at any cost.

It must be remarked, however, that when there is question of yielding in a matter which is generally regarded as unlawful, a Parish Priest could not be justified in seeking out frivolous pretexts for the purpose of creating a doubt, and then flattering himself that, in virtue of the doubt thus created, he might comply with the unjust demand. For, when the act to which he is asked to consent is commonly regarded as unlawful, he ought to refuse his consent at any cost.

A Pastor must likewise take care not to allow himself to be intimidated by dangers which are imaginary rather than real, or which are of little consequence; and still less ought he to be frightened by the annoyances which he may have to endure when he resolutely pursues the path of duty. There are some Pastors of souls who, through indolence and a dislike to suffering the least annoyance, allow their parishes to become a prey to all kinds of disorders. In their parishes daring sinners can promise themselves perfect security in carrying out any evil enterprise, provided they take care to circulate a few hints of certain dangers and annoyances which may possibly be in store for the Parish Priest if he should attempt to interfere with them. When such Pastors come to hear of these threats, they immediately shelter themselves behind the bulwark of their own laziness. They act as snails do when they find on their path some obstacle over which they are unable to pass. They shut their eyes and ears, and no longer hear or see anything. As far as they are concerned, everything is going on splendidly. They think themselves extremely prudent men, and they even pride themselves on this wonderful prudence of theirs, and would wish to instil it into others. These are the men who, after they have been governing a parish for a number of years, think they are pronouncing a high eulogium on themselves by saying: *I have never had a quarrel with any one; I have always been esteemed and respected by everybody.* In truth, the reeds might boast in the same fashion that they have never struggled with the storms, and might pretend to teach their very submissive prudence to the oaks.

But, as a matter of fact, it is not true to say that such Pastors enjoy the esteem and respect of all. They are esteemed by the bad, as is natural; but, for the self-same reason, they do not enjoy the esteem of the good. That prudence of theirs is nothing else than cowardly, reprehensible weakness; and it is the cause why all moral disorders can with perfect impunity strike root, spread, and grow strong in their parishes. If a parish have the misfortune of being governed for a great number of years by one of these prudent Pastors, it remains completely ruined.

§ 2. Of Fortitude in coming to the rescue of Souls.

Above all things, a Parish Priest must be on his guard against this false prudence and most cowardly weakness, when there is question of helping some soul to escape from the bondage of sin, or of preserving an innocent soul from falling into it.

It sometimes happens that a young woman who has been seduced, becoming alive to her unhappy condition, would wish to escape from the clutch of the demon that has seized her, and, in consequence, has recourse to the Parish Priest, in the hope of being assisted by him in her necessity. Now, should he happen to be one of those prudent Pastors who never wish to come into collision with anybody, and still less, with dangerous characters, what does he do? He tells her that he is delighted to hear of her good resolution of abandoning sin; he advises her to pray to God, and that He will help her, but adds, that he is not aware how he himself can be of any possible assistance to her; that she had better see whether she may not be able to find some priest or friar, or lady to interest themselves in her case; that, as far as he is concerned, he really does not know . . . he really can't . . . and so forth. The consequence is, that the poor creature, who does not know to whom to apply, and who finds it very hard to make her case known to others, in order to receive that assistance of which she stands in need, generally despairs of finding a remedy in her distress, and so continues in her sin.

Again, it sometimes happens that a bad man, under pretence of performing some service—for example, of giving instruction in some art or other—succeeds in inducing an innocent young girl to frequent his house. The Pastor, who knows the danger, ought immediately to warn her thoughtless parents to save this innocent dove from the claws of that hawk; and should she have no parents, he ought to find some other means of rescuing her. This would be his strict duty; but if he be a Pastor of the prudent class, what does he do? He soliloquises somewhat in the following fashion: "I ought to be very cautious not to compromise myself. And, after all, *can* I prevent this evil? Will her parents co-operate with me? May not they, perhaps, be conniving at the matter? And may not the girl herself be already seduced and ruined? On the other hand, that scoundrel is capable of doing anything. If I interfere with him, I may have to pay dearly for it . . ." In this manner he completely justifies his non-interference in the matter: the hawk tranquilly holds its prey: the Parish Priest is prudent!

It is easy to understand that Pastors who look on thus with folded arms at the havoc which the wolf is making among their flocks, (of course I mean through

OF THE PRACTICE OF FORTITUDE. 465

fear of the wolf), are altogether unworthy of the name, and openly reject the example of the Good Shepherd who "*dat animam suam pro ovibus suis*".

New Parish Priests who suffer from timidity must, furthermore, bear in mind that, as experience shows, the danger of serious evil consequences in the cases to which we have alluded is far more imaginary than real. It is true that immoral men look with disfavour on a Parish Priest who allows them no peace in their evil practices and interferes with their intrigues; but it is not true that they wish to plot deadly vengeance against him, if for no other reason, for this, that since they regard their victims in no other light than simply as a means of gratifying their brutal passions, they will easily find other means of doing so, which the Parish Priest will be powerless to prevent.

All my life, I have known Parish Priests who never shrank from doing their duty when cases like those mentioned happened to turn up, and not one of them, as far as I know, ever suffered any harm in consequence of having done so. Perhaps, also, Providence affords a special protection to the Pastors of souls, in order that they may not easily be tempted to weakness, in a matter which so nearly concerns the salvation of their flocks.

Let not new Parish Priests, then, allow themselves to become the victims of vain fears; and even though they should believe that they are encountering real danger, let them be persuaded that it is actually less than they suppose. Let them place their trust in the Lord, and let them dread above everything else, the remorse which would torment their conscience, should they ever have to recall to mind that, through a cowardly sense of fear, they had abandoned to the hands of the Devil, a soul that was calling out to them for aid, or had allowed him, without a struggle, to tear a soul from the heart of Christ, and seize it as his prey.

CHAPTER V.

OF THE PRACTICE OF CHASTITY.

§ 1. OF THE SPECIAL DANGERS WHICH BESET THIS VIRTUE.

CHASTITY is a virtue which every Christian ought, one might almost say, to hold up to public view; because it is a virtue which one may never hide through humility, and which, as St. Vincent Ferreri used to preach, ought always to shine forth in the sight of the world. Now, if this is true in the case of every Christian, it applies still more to the Priest of Christ, to the Pastor of Souls.

It is not my intention to speak in this chapter of the intrinsic excellence of this virtue, but of the precautions which are necessary for a Parish Priest in order to preserve it, and to be a living model of Chastity in the midst of his people.

First of all, he ought to reflect on the special dangers to which he is exposed above other priests; for, more than other priests, he must frequently visit the houses of seculars, must converse with persons of every class, must receive them in his own house, must speak with them in private, and treat of subjects of every kind according as the necessities of their souls may require. Wherefore, if we consider the matter attentively, we must be convinced that there is no one of the Church's ministers who fills an office more dangerous than that of Parish Priest, and it follows, as a natural consequence, that a Parish Priest ought, of necessity, to be a man of well-proved chastity.

§ 2. GENERAL PRECAUTIONS.

Supposing, then, that a Parish Priest possesses the virtue of chastity, he must take every suitable precaution to preserve it. The very first of these precautions ought to have reference to hearing the confessions of women, of which we have already spoken when treating of the administration of the Sacrament of Penance (§ 5). The remarks which we there made upon the subject were brief, indeed, but yet of the greatest importance, and ought to be read over again attentively.

A Parish Priest, moreover, must adopt several precautions whenever, for any reason, he has to speak with women. The first precaution is, to avoid speaking with them in private whenever he can possibly do so; and when this is unavoidable, as often happens, let him always speak with them in some place accessible to others, such as in the sacristy, or in some corridor opening on the Church. Should it be necessary for him to speak with them in his own house, let him do so in the hall, if they be women of low condition who do not expect to be treated with much ceremony; but if they be persons whom he cannot avoid inviting into the drawing-room, let him always leave the door entirely open. These precautions ought to be all the more scrupulously observed, the younger and more attractive the women may happen to be.

Let him take care, in the second place, when conversing with females not to look them fixedly in the face, but to speak to them with his eyes modestly cast down. To act otherwise would produce a very bad impression; yet some persons, nevertheless, are accustomed, when conversing with women, to fix their eyes upon them, as if they were the most indifferent objects in the world.

Let him, in the third place, be careful not to indulge in jokes or laughter with women, but to speak 'with them respectfully, and with becoming gravity. I say *respectfully*, because a priest should respect all females, no matter how low their condition, if he wishes to respect himself as he ought; and to joke and laugh is not an indication of respect, but rather of familiarity.

Finally, let him take care, not to prolong his conversation with them more than is necessary. It must be borne in mind (and why should we delude ourselves into questioning the fact?) that so strong a bond of sympathy exists between man and woman, that merely to be in the company of one another is always a pleasure to them of which they never grow weary. Hence it happens that, without adverting to it, they prolong their interviews far beyond what is necessary; and it cannot be denied that superfluous conversation of this kind is always more or less dangerous. This precaution ought to be attended to in the Confessional likewise, as we have elsewhere remarked, because there, more easily than elsewhere, the Devil deludes the incautious.

In what has been said, however, I by no means intend to insinuate that a Parish Priest should have a scruple about speaking to women. The nature of his ministry requires that he should speak frequently with them as well as with men, and even more frequently as we know from experience, for it is the women who principally have recourse to the Parish Priest regarding matters which concern their families.

We have elsewhere said (see p. 58) that it would be a mistake to accept in the full rigour of the terms the doctrine of the *Sermo brevis et durus*. It was not reduced to practice by our Divine Lord in the case of Mary Magdalen, or of the Samaritan woman, or of the woman taken in adultery, and was employed by Him only in the case of the Cananean woman in order to try her Faith. Nor was this manner of dealing with women practised by St. Philip Neri, by St. Francis de Sales, by St. Vincent de Paul, or by other Saints. And, surely, a Parish Priest is the father of all his flock whether they be men or women; and a father who should always speak sternly and curtly to his children could not hope to win their confidence, and to bring them up well. There is a

OF THE PRACTICE OF CHASTITY. 471

wide difference, however, between speaking with women gently and charitably, as was the practice of Christ and the Saints, and keeping up with them long and idle conversations.

These precautions are of great importance not only for the Parish Priest, but also for the sake of females themselves, and, especially, of some of them who are endowed with extraordinary sensibility, and are very susceptible of dangerous impressions. They are also most important for the sake of giving edification to the people, who are always exceedingly observant of the conduct of their Parish Priest, and, where he is concerned, criticise even the most trifling particulars, which no one would think of noticing in the case of seculars.

§ 3. PRECAUTIONS TO BE OBSERVED IN THE HOUSES OF SECULARS, ESPECIALLY WHEN ENGAGED IN THE DUTIES OF THE MINISTRY WITH SICK WOMEN.

A Parish Priest ought to be particularly cautious when visiting at the houses of his parishioners, either for the purpose of blessing them, or of assisting the sick, or for any other purpose whatever. On these occasions a Parish Priest ought to be polite; but if there are women present, his conduct should also be marked by gravity, and he ought to refrain from jokes and laughter. If he will only discharge his duty with modest gravity, he will win and retain the respect of his parishioners.

On such occasions he ought to refrain from taking

hold of little girls by the arm, or patting them upon the head, and still more from catching them up in his arms, or otherwise caressing them. These are things unbecoming the gravity of a Parish Priest, and besides might not the saying: *qui tetigerit picem inquinabitur ab ea*, be verified in such cases? A little more or a little less endearment seems to me, all the while, pitch by which one may be defiled.

He must likewise be on his guard against paying useless visits, or indulging in idle conversation, where there are women. Parish Priests who labour assiduously and zealously for the salvation of souls have no time to spare for visits and idle conversations: indeed it often happens that they have not time even to discharge those obligations imposed upon them by the usages of society. How does it happen, then, that certain Pastors are always paying visits, and almost every day waste entire hours in conversation? Can we suppose that these men labour, and pray, and study, as much as they ought? We are forced to conclude that if they did they would not find so much time to squander.

However, it would not matter so very much if their visits were paid to families composed only of old ladies and men, with whom they might remain to converse for a while: but the worst feature in the case is that these visits are paid to young ladies, and that the conversation consists of chit-chat kept up with women and young girls. I may, perhaps, be told, in justification of such a course, that these are pious persons who have been well brought up. I am willing to grant it; but, all the while, these useless visits and these idle conversations carried on with such persons, will always be attended with danger.

It would be a great blessing if we were thoroughly convinced that when we visit and converse with persons of this class in the discharge of the duties of our Ministry, the Lord always shields us with His protecting hand, and that, if we employ due precautions, not even the fire of the Babylonian furnace —*Succensa nimis*—can harm a hair of ours; but that, on the other hand, when we visit and converse with such persons idly or on some silly pretext, which it is always easy to discover when we wish it, we cannot promise ourselves this protection, and a single spark, falling on us unawares, may cause us to blaze up like stubble.[1]

Whenever a Pastor, in assisting sick women, has to remain alone with them in order to hear their confessions, let him always leave the door of the apart-

---

[1] It terrifies one to recall to mind the fall, recorded by St. Cyprian, of many Ecclesiastics even of high rank, who, though endowed with such Faith as to work miracles, and with courage sufficient to withstand the torments of martyrdom, yet, on surviving, yielded miserably to the seductions of sensuality. "Mentior," says the Saint, "si non videmus exinde interitus plurimorum. . . . . post confessionum victoriarumque calcata certamina, post magnalia et signa vel mirabilia usquequaque monstrata, noscuntur cum his omnibus naufragasse, cum volunt navi fragili navigare. Quantos leones domuit una muliebris infirmitas delicata, quæ cum sit vilis et misera de magnis efficit prædam." And he makes the following noteworthy remark on those who will not learn at the expense of others : "Sed hæc est semper incredulitas humanæ duritiæ, ut non solum audiendo sed etiam videndo, non credat alios interiisse nisi et se ipsam viderit interire"—(Baronius ad an. 253) *Author's note.*

ment open, and place his seat at a suitable distance from them; and let him be still more cautious not to keep his face turned towards them. Let him adopt these precautions for his own sake and for theirs, as well as to give due edification.

Let him not perform any service for the sick woman, such as to give her a drink, to lift up her head, or, still worse, to wipe away the perspiration from her face. Let him leave these things to be performed by her attendants, and let him not presume on taking any such liberties with her, even though to do so might seem an act of charity. In like manner let him not feel her pulse, especially if she be young, unless, perhaps, it may be necessary to do so in order to ascertain the danger of her condition, for the purpose of administering Extreme Unction or of giving the Benediction *in Articulo Mortis*. As a rule, no good purpose is served by doing so, and in this matter whatever is useless ought to be avoided. We ought to except the case where the sick woman herself might ask the Parish Priest to feel her pulse, for a request so simple ought not to be denied her; and though in this case compliance would not be necessary, yet it would not be useless.

§ 4. PRECAUTIONS TO BE ADOPTED REGARDING RELATIVES WHO MAY BE LIVING WITH THE PARISH PRIEST.

A Parish Priest must be careful above all things not to keep in his house any persons whose presence might endanger his chastity, or even his good name; and he should take care likewise that no such persons frequent his house for the purpose of performing any service or labour.

A Pastor may safely keep in his house his mother and his sisters, provided they be persons of good character; for, otherwise, they would bring great disgrace upon him, and neither a feeling of filial devotion towards the one, nor of affection for the others, ought on any account to induce him to shelter them under his roof. Supposing them, however, to be persons of good moral conduct, he may have them to live with him; and to do so may oftentimes be even useful, on account of the good which they may effect among persons of their own sex. For, if they be truly pious, they can contribute very largely to the diffusion of piety among other women and young girls. He must take care, however, that women and girls be not in the habit of frequently visiting the Presbytery, even for pious purposes; and, consequently, the mother and sisters of the Parish Priest ought not to encourage such visits, but ought to have some place of meeting outside the parochial house, where they might attend to matters of piety. The danger arising from the habitual visits of women and girls to the parochial house, caused St. Augustine to express a wish that Ecclesiastics should not have even their nearest female relatives to live with them.

With the exception of his mother and sisters, or of an aunt advanced in years, let not a Parish Priest have any other female relatives living in his house, unless in case of real necessity. Sisters-in-law, cousins, and nieces are more or less dangerous to a Parish Priest, or at least to his good name, as everyone must know who has a lengthened experience of the world.

However, it may happen that, for unavoidable family reasons, a Pastor may be obliged to receive into his house some of the relatives just mentioned, and in this case several precautions must be attended to. The first of these is that the relative in question be a steady and well-conducted person; for, otherwise, no possible necessity could justify a Parish Priest in receiving her into his house. He could not justify the act by saying that he received her in order to reform her conduct, or to prevent her from becoming still worse; for, the first duty of a Parish Priest is to save himself and his own reputation. If he can contribute towards her conversion, let him do so with all possible zeal, but never by bringing down upon himself scandal and disgrace. In a case of necessity he might possibly—but barely possibly—receive her, if she had already given indisputable, public, and continued proofs of repentance, so that he would no longer have anything to fear for himself, nor would the people have any reason for being displeased at his action.

The second precaution is, that the female relative in question should lead a positively pious and devout life, so that she would prove a source of real edification to the parish. Wherefore, he should not permit her to dress in a showy style, like women of fashion:

nay, he ought to insist that she should dress plainly and modestly, that she should frequent the Sacraments, and take part in the good works and associations established in the parish. In this manner, she, too, might effect much good among the people, as has already been remarked when speaking of the mother and sisters of the Parish Priest.

The third precaution is, never to trust himself in his familiar intercourse with her, but, on the contrary, to observe all due caution, in order to prevent the development of a mutual attachment, which evidently might become dangerous. The Parish Priest ought to fear more for himself in her case than in the case of any other person; for, there is no comparison between the danger proceeding from one with whom we live continually, and that which may threaten from a person who lives apart from us.

The danger becomes extreme if the person be young, attractive, and of an amiable disposition. How fatal may not a gentle, retiring, sweet disposition prove! It may inspire the heart, only too easily, with a feeling of affection, guiltless at first, which will lead one to love the society and conversation of that person; but, later on, the heart becomes enslaved, the mind entirely engrossed with thoughts of her, and the imagination inflamed, until the poor cleric, without perceiving it, becomes miserably infatuated about her.

Should a Parish Priest, then, be compelled by circumstances to live with a relative of this kind, in order to prevent any evil consequence—and any misfortune of the kind would be irremediable—let him keep a strict watch over himself, let him keep a guard upon his eyes, let him avoid useless conversation, let him be extremely careful to shun all familiarity—in one word, let him dread that person more than any other. And he should fear her none the less because she might happen to be pious, and a person of the most rigid virtue; for, when the Devil cannot succeed in inducing us to commit wicked acts, he is content with making us yield to bad thoughts, and to effect this the co-operation of a second person is not necessary.

§ 5. Precautions to be observed regarding the Domestic and other Females connected with the Service of the Parochial House.

His female servant may prove a very dangerous rock for a Parish Priest, and the more so if he lives alone, without having in his house either a relative or another priest. Indeed, it would be desirable that Parish Priests should have in their service a man rather than a woman; but it must be confessed that, in practice, the adoption of this course would be surrounded by difficulties well nigh insuperable. Therefore, we must allow Parish Priests to have female domestics, and, indeed, such is the custom of all good Pastors—a custom which we could not presume to censure without unduly straining our zeal.

Since a Parish Priest, then, must have a female

servant, let him take care, especially if he live alone, that she be a widow, or a spinster advanced in years; and such a one as cannot prove a probable source of danger to himself, nor excite suspicions, nor give rise to any unseemly remarks among the people.

I have said: "*a widow* or *a spinster*," in order to exclude altogether any married woman, no matter whether she might happen to be living with her husband, or not. For, in the first case, there would be an evident impropriety and scandal, except, perhaps, she should be so old that there could not possibly be any ground for suspicion; and in the second case there would be the danger to fear that the husband might blacken the character of the Parish Priest. I have said, furthermore, that she should be "*advanced in years*". And, in truth, what can we think of those Parish Priests who take into their service young girls of twenty, or twenty-four years of age, not devoid of grace and beauty, and yet are not afraid to live alone with them, and even presume to hear their confessions? Would it be rash to judge badly of such men? I think it would not: because they are evidently acting contrary to the rules of christian prudence, and to the prescriptions of the sacred Canons of the Church. Wherefore, they must evidently be imprudent men, and devoid of the fear of God; and it is hard to suppose that a man who is imprudent, and has but little of the fear of the Lord, can preserve his chastity under the circumstances which we have mentioned. We, Parish Priests, invariably dissuade young girls from entering the service of an unmarried man, especially if he be still in the full vigour of his manhood. How, then, can we with propriety make an exception in our own case?

We have remarked elsewhere (p. 127) how undesirable it is that a Parish Priest should live alone with his female servant, even though she should be steady, pious, and of suitable age; but if he cannot avoid living with her, let him be extremely cautious not to stand on those intimate and familiar terms with her, which very naturally spring up when a man and a woman, who are not near relatives, live together for a long time—an intimacy and familiarity which oversteps the bounds of friendship, and which, under the plea of charity and necessity, justifies certain mutual liberties which, though not positively bad, are, nevertheless, absolutely unbecoming and disrespectful—an intimacy and familiarity, in fact, bordering to a certain degree on that which belongs to another state. Where such intimacy exists, both parties feel a certain kind of remorse, which does not leave them altogether at their ease; but from day to day they go on smothering it with the delusive thought that they are doing nothing sinful, nothing which could not be justified on the score of charity and necessity, since, being compelled to live alone in one house, they are bound to assist one another. Yet, with all this, the remorse is never entirely stifled, and it is always whispering to both, much against their will, that there is something censurable in their conduct. Therefore, let a Pastor be careful, on no account, and under no pretext, whether excusable in a greater or in a less degree, to allow a familiarity to spring up between himself and his servant, which may at any moment proceed to further lengths, and which, even though it should never proceed further, is, nevertheless, altogether unbecoming, and both destroys the spirit and dims the lustre of priestly chastity. This admonition may well be taken to heart, likewise, by those pious persons who have some confidence in their own virtue.

But, supposing that a Parish Priest has living with him some female relatives or others, so that he is not quite alone, may he then retain young girls in his service? I reply that in no case could we approve of his doing so; because, though the danger would be less in the circumstances just mentioned, yet it would not cease, all the while, to be considerable, and would, probably, give rise to unseemly remarks among the people. We have said above that in case of real necessity, and provided he adopts the precautions there laid down, a Parish Priest may permit even a young female relative to reside in his house; but what possible necessity can be imagined which could oblige him to keep in the parochial house a young female servant? The young servant can always earn her bread elsewhere, and he can always find a female servant of suitable age. Wherefore, without any exception, we must always disapprove of the conduct of a Parish Priest who retains a young female servant in his employment.

We must remark, furthermore, that the good name of the Parish Priest may suffer, if he allows his female servant to assume an air of authority in his house, or to meddle in parochial affairs; for, people might thus be led to believe that there existed between them an undue degree of familiarity, and this might lead to a further suspicion that there existed likewise between them an undue affection. Let the Parish Priest command in his own house, let him manage the affairs of his parish, and let his servant obey, and confine her attention to the kitchen and to the discharge of her household duties. Nor should a Parish Priest fear that he will in this manner sin through pride, or be wanting in charity. Humility requires a Parish Priest to be subject to his superiors, but not to his servant; and charity requires that superiors should keep their inferiors in their proper place. Human love, and above all sensual love, produces familiarity between those who love one another; charity, on the other hand, is always accompanied by respect and the observance of due decorum.

Finally, let a Parish Priest be careful not to place himself under any obligations to his servant, by not paying her her wages regularly, and promising to make her at his death heir to the entire, or to a large portion, of his property. For, should the Parish Priest die intestate, the poor creature would be left penniless; and should he make a will in her favour, both the deceased priest and his heir will come in for the curses of his relatives, and the uncharitable suspicions of the evil-minded.

Another source of danger is to be found in those women and girls who frequent the parochial house, for the purpose of assisting the priest's servant in those labours which she is unable to accomplish unaided. If these persons be giddy women or young girls, in addition to being a source of danger to the Parish Priest, they afford idle persons an opportunity for tittle-tattle, especially in country places where the conduct of a Parish Priest is more closely watched and criticised. The danger and the opportunity for criticism would be all the greater, if the Parish Priest were to indulge in pleasantries and jokes when conversing with these women. They consider themselves honoured by the familiarity with which the Parish Priest treats them, and they begin to grow vain of it: afterwards they consider themselves esteemed and even loved by him, and they take pleasure in this; later on, they conceive an affection for him, and because of it they are always looking out for opportunities of conversing with him, they vie with one another in tendering him their services, they are always speaking of him, and let it be seen that they are in love with him. This state of affairs cannot possibly exist without great danger for a Parish Priest, and especially for a silly Parish Priest—as are all those who affect to be gay and witty in the company of women—and it unquestionably supplies matter for disedifying conversations.

§ 6. Precautions regarding Alms-giving in the case of Poor Women.

If poor women, to whom a Parish Priest is bound

to give alms, happen to be young and good-looking, let him so arrange matters that it will not be necessary for them to come often to his house. Let him, by all means, assist them to the best of his power, in proportion to their needs, and even frequently; but let him contrive so, that his alms will reach them through some of their relatives or acquaintances, in order that they may have no excuse for coming to his house, at least very frequently.

Let him be particularly careful not to allow poor mothers to send their daughters to him for the purpose of soliciting alms. Sometimes mothers designedly send their daughters on such errands, both to save themselves from being reproached by the Parish Priest with their importunity or want of consideration, and also because they suppose that the Parish Priest will be more compassionate in dealing with the daughters than he would be with their mothers. Therefore, whenever the daughters come in this manner to solicit alms, the Parish Priest ought always to send them away empty-handed, telling them that if their mothers want anything they must come for it themselves.

§ 7. Precautions regarding the presence of dangerous objects of Art in the Parochial House or in the Church.

Let the Parish Priest be careful not to retain in the parochial house any picture, print, or statue which may be somewhat immodest and profane. It might appear superfluous to remind a Pastor of this; for, one might suppose it impossible that such a thing could occur, in as much as it would not only be an occasion of danger for himself and for others, but would moreover be a disgrace to a person in his position. Nevertheless, the imprudence of some Pastors is so great, that we occasionally find in the Drawing-room of the parochial house statuettes, prints, and pictures, which offend by their profanity and indecency.

And what an edifying thing it is to hear the Parish Priest attempting to justify such imprudence—to call it by no harsher name—on the plea that he has not bought these objects; that they are heir-looms, and that he keeps them because they have some artistic merit; that nobody minds them; and that worse may be found in some churches!

But how can a Parish Priest, who, when there is question of chastity, ought always to show himself more an angel than a man, who ought above all things to avoid giving the slightest indication which might lead anyone to infer that he did not hold this virtue in the very highest esteem, who, as we have remarked elsewhere, ought to a certain extent to parade this virtue before the world, letting it appear resplendent in his character, whose duty it is to inveigh unceasingly against all incentives to the vice of impurity and especially against prints, pictures, and statues, of an immodest tendency—how, I say, can a Parish Priest ever seriously put forward the above-mentioned pleas to justify his conduct in retaining such objects in his house, and even in the room set apart for the reception of visitors? Will they not be, to say the least, standing evidence to his parishioners of his imprudence, a practical refutation of his sermons, and a proof that he himself does not believe all that he preaches regarding the danger and sinfulness of immodest pictures and images?

Supposing that these things had been handed down in his family as heir-looms, he ought to have got rid of them at least when he was ordained priest. They ought to have been destroyed, and not exhibited to defile the parochial house. And even if they have some artistic merit, must that merit be respected, to the prejudice of the right which souls have not to be scandalised? And, again, if objects more or less indecent are to be met with in some churches, why should we conclude that, consequently, they ought to be tolerated elsewhere, instead of concluding rather that such objects ought to be removed from the churches?

And let it be borne in mind that, when I speak here of indecent objects, I am not speaking of figures entirely nude, or of other like glaring indecencies, but I speak of those objects which are calculated to offend the eyes of a chaste, pious, young man, and of a modest young girl. And, in truth, how could it be tolerated for a single instant, that persons of this class should find anything calculated to wound their modesty in the house of the Pastor of their souls, or in the House of God Himself.

And since it is true that the licentious artists of

past centuries have profaned even the churches by some of their productions, and that traces of this profanation still remain in our own times, a Parish Priest ought certainly to be careful that there is nothing bordering on indecency in his own church, or should there be, he ought immediately to have it removed. If there is question merely of some things which do not come much under observation, the Parish Priest can apply a remedy without attracting public attention to the matter. During the hours when the church is closed, a painter, a plasterer, a sculptor can quietly remove in a very short time whatever is indecent. And I would remark that a Parish Priest must not neglect to have this done on the plea that these objects attract little or no attention; for, since they are exposed to the gaze of all, it may happen, more frequently than we suppose, that especially little boys and little girls, who are endowed with sharp sight and unlimited curiosity, may cast their eyes upon them and be scandalised thereby. Then, again, we frequently say that a thing is not noticed, simply because the person who notices it does not announce the fact to us. But in any case, why should we tolerate indecent objects in a church, whether they be noticed or not?

I may remark, also, that although it is possible that some rather indecent object may not attract attention in a church—for example, some painting blackened by age, or some statue covered with dust and lying in an obscure corner—yet it is impossible that an immodest painting or print or statue will not challenge attention when placed in the drawing-room of the Parish Priest, where it suffers neither from age, nor from dust, nor from an obscure position.

§ 8. Precautions to be taken against Calumny.

The Pastor of Pastors never permitted the charge of incontinence to find a place among the innumerable calumnies by which His enemies sought to blacken His reputation. A Parish Priest must take care to lead a life so circumspect, that calumny, which often rests on no stronger foundation than mere trifling appearances, may never find an opportunity of injuring his good name.

However, should calumny ever charge him with this vice, and should the charge be utterly groundless, a Pastor ought to defend himself at any cost, and never to rest satisfied until his innocence be made clear as the noon-day sun; for no case can ever arise in which it would be lawful for him to renounce the honour which belongs to him through the practice of this virtue.

But if the Parish Priest had given some occasion for the calumnious remarks by acts of imprudence on his part—for instance by frequently visiting at the home of some young ladies, or by keeping in his own house some young girl or giddy servant—then, no matter how innocent he might be, he ought to remove the occasion without a moment's delay. He should never again set foot in that house, he should immediately dismiss that servant, he should prove by acts, which are the most convincing arguments, that he has no attachment to these persons. How scandalous it is to see a Parish Priest, in the face of the injurious remarks which are whispered abroad about him, still continuing to frequent that house, still retaining that girl in his service, and, perhaps, ready even to renounce his parish rather than dismiss her. The people thus become persuaded that, if their Pastor were not blinded by a terrible passion, he would never permit his reputation to be ruined for a cause so trifling ; and, consequently, even though he were in reality innocent, yet he would be chargeable with a most grievous fault in allowing himself to appear guilty.

It is most deplorable that in this respect we sometimes meet with inexplicable instances of imprudence which baffle all comprehension. We sometimes see an Ecclesiastic who is learned, zealous, a martyr, so to speak, to duty, disinterested, charitable, and held in high esteem by all for these good qualities, yet who will turn a deaf ear to the injurious remarks which are circulated about him either because of the giddiness of his servant, or because of the frequent visits which he receives from some imprudent girl, or because of the visits which he himself pays. And even though his friends and relatives should remonstrate with him, he still refuses to take any notice of the reports that are in circulation, and remains perfectly satisfied with his one stupid defence: *I am calumniated.* Meanwhile, his reputation is ruined, his zeal comes to be regarded as merely a cloak for hypocrisy, and his very learning but condemns him all the more. Discreet and charitable persons can only shrug their shoulders, meanwhile, saying with themselves: *the entire proceeding is a mystery.*

§ 9. CONCLUDING REMARKS ON THE SUBJECT OF CHASTITY.

I fancy that at this point more than one of my readers will have said: this author is, unquestionably, the most indiscreet of rigorists; he is imposing so many restrictions upon us, that he wishes to render the practice of this virtue impossible. Well, if the charge of indiscretion and rigorism be levelled at me by one who has not yet had much experience in this matter, I will bear it with the best possible grace; but were it to come from a person of experience, I would feel tempted to tell him, as the mildest thing I could say, that he is a very simple man—far more simple, indeed, than a Parish Priest ought to be.

As far as my opinion goes, I believe that we ought to apply to a chaste Parish Priest the saying of St. Philip Neri, with regard to the young: *Show me a young man who is chaste, and I will show you a saint.* The Parish Priest who has sufficient grace to overcome the most violent and seductive of all the vices, will have more than enough of grace to gain the mastery over all the others. David, who was strong enough to strangle bears and lions, had, surely, more than sufficient strength to strangle foxes and dogs.

But, then, what Parish Priests will have this abundance of grace, except those who, profoundly conscious of their own weakness, propose to themselves to lead upon earth the lives of Angels. The Fathers and Doctors of the Church, and the Masters of the Spiritual Life are unanimous in laying down that nothing less than this will suffice, if an Ecclesiastic, and especially a Pastor of souls, wishes to lead a chaste life; and even if the point were not thus established by the weight of authority, it would, nevertheless, be evident to me as the result of long and well-proved experience.

I do not know what amount of authenticity attaches to a revelation which says that there are never many priests' souls in Purgatory; because either they live in conformity with the spirit of their vocation, and take their departure to the next world pure and holy, so that they have but little time to spend in a state of purgation, or they fall into the vice of impurity, and go down into the depths of Hell. At all events, even if this revelation be nothing more than a pious illusion, it expresses, all the while, a very plausible truth.

CHAPTER VI.

OF THE PRACTICE OF MORTIFICATION.

§ 1. OF THE MORTIFICATION OF THE SENSES.

IF a Parish Priest wishes to be chaste, he must of necessity be mortified. Chastity without mortification is as impossible as whiteness without light.

And here I must remark that, as far as chastity is immediately concerned, the first of all mortifications to be practised is that of the senses; and on this point I wish to quote a passage from St. John of the Cross, which has always appeared to me very terrifying, and which merits the serious attention, especially, of priests. Speaking of *the injuries inflicted on the soul by those who place the pleasure of the will in natural goods,* the Saint mentions six such goods, the second of which he says *consists in exciting our senses to pleasure and sensual delight.* Then, continuing to treat of this subject, he says: "No pen can describe, no words can express, the greatness and extent of the evil resulting from our seeking after pleasure in the blandishments of the senses and in natural beauty. For, because of this, we daily see many men dying,

OF THE PRACTICE OF MORTIFICATION.

many reputations ruined, many properties squandered, many rivalries and disputes fomented, many adulteries and rapes committed, and so many Saints falling, who may be compared to the third part of the stars of Heaven dragged down to earth by the tail of the serpent; we see the fine gold tarnished by the mud, and the renowned and noble sons of Sion, who used to be clothed in raiment of gold, esteemed as broken earthen vessels: *Quomodo obscuratum est aurum, mutatus est color optimus, dispersi sunt lapides Sanctuarii in capite omnium platearum? Filii Sion inclyti, et amicti auro primo, quomodo reputati sunt in vasa testea, opus manuum figuli?* (Lamentations iv. 1-2.) And where is it that this deadly poison does not penetrate, and who is there that does not drink much or little of this golden cup of the scarlet woman of Babylon, mentioned in the Apocalypse: *I saw a woman sitting upon a scarlet-coloured beast, full of names of blasphemy, having seven heads and ten horns* (Apoc. xvii. 3); by which we are given to understand that there is scarcely a person, whether of high or of low degree, whether holy or sinful, to whom she does not present this cup of hers, and thereby, in some degree, gain an ascendancy over their hearts. For, as it is there written of her: "all the kings of the earth have been made drunk with the wine of her whoredom;" and she collects beneath her throne all the states of the earth, including even the most exalted and renowned one of the Priesthood, placing, as Daniel says, her abominable cup even in the holy place: *et erit in templo abominatio desolationis* (Dan. ix. 27). There is scarce a strong man whom she allows to escape without giving him to drink much or little of this cup, which is that pleasure of which we have spoken above. Therefore, it is said that all the kings of the earth have been made drunk with this wine; for there have been very few, no matter how holy, whose minds have not been clouded by this intoxicating cup of enjoyment and delight in beauty and natural charms. And remark the expression, *have been made drunk:* for when one has tasted this wine of pleasure, it immediately reaches the heart and inflames it, and destroys the reasoning powers, as ordinary wine does in the case of drunkards. This it does so effectually that, if some medicine be not immediately taken in order to eject the poison, the life of the soul is imperilled. For, once man's natural weakness is thus stimulated, the soul becomes reduced to a condition so miserable that, like Samson, after his eyes had been plucked out and his hair shorn off, it will see itself a slave at the mercy of its enemies, and afterwards will perhaps die the second death, as Samson suffered natural death with his enemies, the Philistines. All these misfortunes come to man's soul from drinking spiritually of these sensual pleasures, as Samson's misfortunes resulted from bodily drink, until, to his great confusion, his enemies may say to him, as to Samson: "Thou art he who didst break triple cords, who didst tear lions into pieces, who didst slay thousands of the Philistines, who didst tear gates from their hinges, and didst set thyself free from all thy enemies". (*Salita di M. Carm.*, lib. iii., cap. 21.)

OF THE PRACTICE OF MORTIFICATION. 495

This passage, replete with truths which are evident to any one who has experience of the world, is really calculated to inspire one with terror; but at the same time, it makes us see how careful we must be to mortify our senses, in order that, some day or other, we may not have to drink of the cup of Babylon, more deadly than any poison.

§ 2. OF THE MORTIFICATION OF THE APPETITE.

The gratification of the appetite, likewise, is very hurtful to chastity; but since enough has been said already concerning this virtue, we shall at present consider the mortification of the appetite under other respects, and first of all we shall speak of the scandal given by a Parish Priest who indulges his appetite, and of the contempt in which he is held by his flock.

Unfortunately, instances do occur from time to time of Parish Priests who are given to drink, and we may hear such remarks as the following, made about them among the people : "*there is no use in speaking with the Parish Priest after dinner*"—"*If he made that statement after dinner, you had better get some confirmation of it*"—"*when he was delivering his catechetical discourse, one might see that he did not well know what he was talking about*"—and so forth. A person once asked myself whether Baptism is valid when administered by one who is drunk ? No doubt there is usually a great deal of exaggeration in accusations of this kind; nevertheless how humiliating it is for a Parish Priest when he cannot help feeling that such remarks are made about him in his parish ! And yet he really gives occasion for such remarks, when he is seen after dinner far more hilarious than usual, indulging in silly talk and banter, and with eyes more sparkling and face more flushed than in the early part of the day.

It seems impossible that a vice which is very costly, which does not spring from any of the more violent passions, which is more usually met with among the most abandoned characters, and which of itself is so degrading, can be found among priests, and what is still worse, among the Pastors of souls, who ought to be models to their flocks! And it seems more incredible still that the Priest—or the Parish Priest—who falls a victim to this vice never succeeds, as a rule, in emancipating himself from it, but, on the contrary, abandons himself to it more and more as his years increase, and, in some cases, would even prefer to renounce his parish than to give up a habit so degrading!

I shall not now add a word more on the subject of chastity, of which I have already spoken at such length, but at the same time I would simply ask is it possible for a priest who indulges overmuch in wine to be chaste?

Again, what an exceedingly bad example does such a priest give to drunkards, who are to be met with in every parish! How can he discharge his duty towards such persons by admonishing and correcting them?

Again, consider the contempt in which a Pastor of this description is held by all his parishioners. Not even the most charitably disposed among them can feel any pity for him; because they are roused to too much indignation when they see the priestly character and the pastoral ministry so degraded, and when they reflect on the general scandal which his conduct causes to souls.

Finally, I need not mention the injury which is caused to bodily health by the abuse of spirituous drinks; for it is well-known that it brings on premature old age, and causes violent diseases and sudden deaths.

Even in the matter of meats, also, a Parish Priest can be intemperate, to the notable injury of his property, of his health, and of his character. He might become one of those *quorum Deus venter est;* who sacrifice to this idol their property, by spending more than they can afford, and sometimes by contracting debts which they are afterwards unable to pay; who sacrifice to it their health, by generating in their bodies hurtful humours, which in time produce most severe maladies and premature deaths; who sacrifice to it their character, by making themselves the table-talk of the public, and a standing joke for the parish wits.

Those Ecclesiastics, also, are held in disrepute who are always talking of good living, and who speak upon this subject with such satisfaction and evident relish, that, from listening to them, you would conclude that they supposed the topic to be one of paramount importance; and they show themselves so learned in all that appertains to the *cuisine*, that they might challenge even professional cooks to a trial of skill. The same remark applies to those clerics who speak with admiration of sumptuous dinners, and consider themselves fortunate whenever they can secure an invitation to one. Finally, those Ecclesiastics are held in low esteem who evince a preference for the friendship of those who keep a good table, and by words and deeds profess themselves their most obsequious servants. Parish Priests of this class deserve at least the pity of all men of sense; and indeed some people would not hesitate to say that they would be much more suitably placed, were they to preside over an eating house, instead of governing a parish.

§ 3. Of Mortification in the matter of Luxuries.

A Parish Priest must be careful not to seek after the luxuries of life, which are scarcely endurable in wealthy Seculars. Under this head we may class very expensive clothing, graduated to a nice scale of warmth so as to suit the varying temperature of the different seasons; artificial appliances to keep up continually a moderate temperature in their apartments; soft beds, and a late hour for rising; a fixed hour for a daily walk, regulated with such precision as never on any account to be omitted; and a vacation extending over the greater part of the autumn.

Should a Parish Priest wish to enjoy all these luxuries, and perhaps justify himself in doing so on the ground that there is nothing wrong in them, but that, on the contrary, they contribute to give him that health which is necessary for him in order to fulfil his duties and support the labours of the ministry, I reply, that he is deceived by an overdue attachment to his own comforts, and that all these matters, far from facilitating the discharge of his duty, tend only to prevent it. How could a Parish Priest who is so extremely careful about the temperature of the atmosphere remain to hear confessions in the church for long hours during the cold winter mornings? How could he pass the nights by the bedside of poor dying persons in wretched cabins, where he could hardly find a ricketty chair on which to rest? And should this delicate Parish Priest have to go out in the middle of the night to face the wind and rain and snow, how will he be able to endure these discomforts and hardships?

It is true that the only delicate Parish Priests are those whose large revenue allows them to support other priests to do all the rough work of the parish for them, while they themselves take their ease; but who will venture to say, that, in acting thus, they are discharging their duty properly? It is very proper that a Parish Priest should have a curate to assist him in discharging his pastoral duties; but to seek assistance in discharging one's duty is a very different thing from throwing over altogether upon the curate all the troublesome work of the parish. And then, again, is not the curate also a human being, who might be injured by bad weather? And must a parishioner who may fall sick in the night-time, or during bad weather, be deprived of the consolation of seeing his Parish Priest, of being comforted by him, and of making his confession to him, especially if he had been in the habit of confessing to him?

Let a Parish Priest, then, pay due consideration to his health, in proportion to what his strength and age may require, for this is both reasonable and necessary; but let him, at the same time, carefully guard against luxuries; and even though it might be in his power to enjoy them in abundance, let him abstain from indulging even in one, since, otherwise, he would render himself less effective for the work of the ministry. Moreover, whether he wishes it or not, he will be compelled from time to time to forego these comforts to which he accustoms himself, and thus his health will be affected the more easily, both because hardships press more severely on those who live delicately, and also because persons of this class are always, more or less, invalids.

With regard to walks and vacation, we certainly do not mean to condemn either the one or the other, unless a Pastor should indulge in them to excess. Walking is almost as necessary as food and sleep to a Parish Priest, who spends a good deal of time in the confessional and in reading; for a life at once laborious and sedentary is most unhealthy. However, a Parish Priest should endeavour to turn his walks to good account, by going to perform some work of charity, or to promote something useful in some quarter of the parish. But at any cost let him take exercise, even daily if he can, as it is necessary to preserve his health and strength for the discharge of the duties of his ministry.

OF THE PRACTICE OF MORTIFICATION.

I must express a different opinion regarding vacation, which, as a rule, is not necessary. Without it, in fact, a man may live even to a good old age in excellent health, as countless people do live, to whom a vacation is either impossible or inconvenient. If a Parish Priest has special need of a vacation—a real need, and not an imaginary one created in his own fancy through love of idleness and amusement—he may absent himself from his parish with the leave of his superior; and, if he require it, he may even take the full two months' vacation allowed him by the Canons. But it ought to be borne in mind that such leave of absence could not be justified on the mere plea of improving one's health; because if this plea were once admitted, it would become quite general, and would hold valid for every one; since even those who are in robust health would, in all probability, become even still more robust by enjoying every year one or two months' change of air, and entire freedom from all parochial cares.

Moreover, we cannot suppose that a good Pastor, anxious for the welfare of his flock, would wish to abandon them for a considerable period without real necessity. Just as a father, or, that still more expressive type of pastoral love, a fond mother, could find no pleasure in a long vacation which would entail a separation from their children, so a good Pastor could not really enjoy a long period of relaxation which would separate him from his flock.

Having directed attention to these few matters, it is unnecessary to descend more minutely to particulars in order to point out how a Pastor ought to reduce the virtue of mortification to practice; but it is easy to understand that he ought to practise it with the same earnestness that is manifested in this matter by all those who aspire to the attainment of christian perfection, excluding, however, those extraordinary austerities which, as a rule, are unsuited to those who are engaged in the pastoral ministry.

§ 4. Of the discretion to be observed in corporal Mortifications.

I have said in the last sentence of the preceding paragraph: "*excluding extraordinary austerities*"; because I do not suppose in a Parish Priest certain extraordinary impulses of the spirit of penance, which are, perhaps, as rare as the gift of miracles, and which, moreover, are quite unsuited to the laborious nature of his ministry, which requires not only strength of mind, but strength of body as well. In order to be able to remain seated for long hours at the Confessional during the forenoon and occasionally also after dinner, to preach morning and evening on Festivals, to assist the dying, and to perform the other duties of the pastoral office, mere strength of mind will not prove sufficient, but physical strength is also required; and unless we wish to pretend that God will bestow it upon us by a miracle, we must allow our bodies that amount of repose and nourishment which is necessary for them. And how can we presume that God will bestow strength upon us miraculously, when it lies within our own power to have and to preserve it by those natural means which He has ordained for that purpose?

Wherefore, it must be borne in mind, that a Parish Priest would be performing an act not of virtue but of imprudence, were he to deprive himself of the necessary amount of sleep, which is as indispensable to a man as food. All men require about seven hours' sleep, and a Parish Priest who should habitually subtract from this to any notable extent, would gradually undermine his health to such a degree, that he would be unable afterwards to repair the injury. And let it be remembered, that one cannot, by an after-dinner nap, compensate for want of sleep during the night-time; for, if the nap be only brief, it will be insufficient, and if it be prolonged, it will prove most unhealthy. Observe, however, that what has been said applies solely to the case of a Parish Priest who *habitually* and *notably* subtracts from the hours required for sleep; for, to curtail his sleep *occasionally*, or sometimes even to dispense with it altogether, when it may be necessary to hear confessions during a Retreat or a Mission, or to assist some dying person, could not do him any injury.

The remarks which I have made about sleep are equally applicable to food. It would be imprudent on the part of a Parish Priest to perform long fasts, or to use very coarse food which would be unsuited to his constitution. We must eat to live; but this is not enough: we must eat in order that we may be strong and vigorous to perform all the good which

God wishes to be performed by us during our lifetime.

However, enough has been already said on this subject in Part II., chap. 3, § 7; and it is the less necessary to dwell upon it at greater length, in as much as excess in the practice of mortifications and penance is not a very frequent failing in Parish Priests. Nevertheless, I have thought it advisable to say something on the subject, in order to caution some austere and rigorous Pastor who might feel inclined to go to excess in his own case, and, from doing so, might easily proceed a step further, and wish to impose his own peculiar views upon others. For, as St. John of the Cross most truly remarks, *a director always communicates his own spirit to those who are placed under his direction.*

CHAPTER VII.

OF THE PRACTICE OF DISINTERESTEDNESS.

ONE would suppose that the clergy ought to be more free from the vice of avarice than any other class of persons; for, since they never can have a family of their own, they ought not to be tempted by this passion as much as others who either actually have, or may at some future time possibly have, children to provide for. Nevertheless, in our experience of life, we do not find this to be a fact. The Devil, who by avarice tempted and overcame one of the Apostolic College, still tempts by the same vice some of the successors of the Apostles in the Priesthood, and they become his prey just as easily as seculars. Some persons, indeed, would even say that they fall more easily, but I do not believe this to be true; and though it may appear so, the reason of this is found in the fact that avarice in a priest is a more monstrous crime, and, consequently, more noticed than in the case of a layman.

However this may be, it is certain that disinterestedness is one of the virtues most necessary to a Parish Priest. Even though he may be endowed with many good and rare qualities, yet, if he is seen to be covetous of money, or of miserly habits, he is neither loved nor respected, his words carry no weight with them, and he is universally disliked. Therefore he ought to guard carefully against avarice, and against the manifold deceitful excuses which the Devil puts before us in order to make it seem justifiable in our eyes. These excuses may be reduced to the following:—

1. *The poverty of our relatives.*—Should our relatives be in *real* want, we ought to relieve them, especially if there should be question of our parents, brothers, or sisters, who might not be able to procure their necessary maintenance. It must be remarked, however, that relatives expect too much from Ecclesiastics. If they have a son or a brother who is a secular and lives apart from the family, they expect nothing from him; while, on the other hand, they expect everything from a son or a brother who may happen to be a priest. Other relatives who are not so nearly related as those just mentioned, should not be assisted on the same scale, but much more moderately, even though they should be in real want. In any case, and at all hazards, the Parish Priest must be careful never to appear greedy of money, or to be guilty of a niggardly act—matters in themselves most injurious to his good name, and which, after all, will not increase his parochial income to any notable extent.

2. The second excuse put forward is *the necessity for making provision against some unforeseen contin-*

gency, such as sickness, a deficit in the annual income, &c. Some Parish Priests avail themselves of this pretext in order to accumulate as much money as they can: consequently, they hoard up every penny they can lay hold of, they are niggardly in the matter of even the most trifling outlay, and they give the public an opportunity of seeing that they are covetous, even to meanness. Although a moderate amount of forethought for necessities which may probably arise cannot be condemned, yet we ought to leave the care of our future to God, and to guard well against placing more reliance in our own prudence than in His Infinite Providence. It is a fact well established by experience, that no good Parish Priest is ever in want of necessaries, to the extent of being reduced to straits, and of being obliged to have recourse to what is humiliating; and if any one ever is reduced to such a condition, we may rest assured that he is not a good Parish Priest. Will not the promise hold true in our case: *Quærite primum regnum Dei et justitiam ejus, et hæc omnia adjicientur vobis?*

3. The third excuse is that *it is commendable to put some money by, in order to do some good with it after death.* No doubt legacies bequeathed for good purposes are always laudable; for, what is good does not cease to be good and meritorious when performed at the point of death. But if we reflect that Parish Priests have only too many opportunities of doing good during their lifetime, we must see how proper it is that they should be on their guard against the otherwise holy desire of doing good after their death.

Experience proves that some persons, through allowing themselves to be deceived by those holy intentions which they mean to have carried into effect after death, neglect those good works which they ought to see executed during their lifetime. It is well to remember that it is quite possible for men to entertain most liberal projects to be carried into effect after their death, and yet to be the slaves of the most degrading avarice all through their lives. In truth, it is not even possible to be inordinately attached to money for the period which will come on after we shall be dead; and we know from experience that even the most notorious misers leave in their wills very large legacies for pious purposes.

It would be well, furthermore, to reflect how small must be the merit of this so-called *liberality* after death; and I advisedly use the term *so-called*, because I am forced to smile whenever in a public Charitable Institution I read on the base of a colossal marble statue, an inscription to the effect—that the deceased has bequeathed all his enormous wealth to the aforesaid Charitable Institution, and that, in consequence of this act, the Governors—*tantam animi liberalitatem admirati*—have erected this statue to his memory. Could we call a man liberal for surrendering to a highwayman everything that he possesses—even to the shirt upon his back? Certainly not: and, just in the same manner, when a man bequeaths all that he has at the point of death —that is to say, when it is no longer possible for him to retain even a farthing—it is a matter of perfect indifference, as far as the merit of the virtue of liberality is concerned, whether he leaves it to a hospital or to a theatre, or orders it to be flung into the sea. In order to perform an act of the virtue of liberality, one must have it in his power to retain what he gives away; but it is an abuse of terms to lay claim to this virtue, when he gives away something because he finds it impossible to keep it any longer.

Wherefore, a shilling given for the love of God when it is in our power to withhold it, is far more meritorious than a million forced from us by Death, more inexorable than any highwayman. At the hour of death, the only merit we can claim is that of preferring to bequeath our money for some good purpose, rather than for an object which might be either indifferent or bad; just as if we were to recommend to a robber to make good use of the money which we are compelled to leave in his hands.

4. The fourth excuse put forward is *the duty incumbent on a Pastor not to injure the parochial revenue by being too ready to forfeit his fees.* It is perfectly true that a Parish Priest ought to exact his fees from those who are able to pay them, and he would act wrongly were he too ready to renounce them; because the people would soon become accustomed to this large-handed treatment, and, as a natural result, his successor, if unable or unwilling to act in like manner towards them, would find himself placed in an extremely difficult position. Wherefore, there is no doubt that a Parish Priest who should consent to

forego his fees without just cause, would fail in his duty; but this, of course, must be understood with discretion.

I would remark that not only is a Parish Priest obliged by charity and justice to remit the payment of fees to those who, because of their poverty, are absolutely unable to pay them, but he ought also to remit them to those who, while absolutely able to pay, yet believe that they ought to be dispensed from doing so, because they likewise are very poor; for, to exact fees from such persons would give rise to scandalous disputes and contention. Moreover, should persons in easy circumstances refuse, through ignorance or unbelief, to contribute to the support of their Pastor, a Parish Priest ought to condone payment in their case also; for, should he attempt to enforce his claims, it is certain that he would gain nothing thereby except insults and abuse. Let us be persuaded that now-a-days a Parish Priest cannot exact his fees except from such as wish to pay them, and only in such amount as they are willing to give; so that if anyone should be unwilling to contribute more than half what he ought to pay, it is impossible to compel him to pay the entire. Let a Parish Priest, then, require the payment of what he is justly entitled to; but let him do so with all that moderation which is necessary in order that the sacred character with which he is invested may not be insulted, and that scandals may be avoided.

And yet, it is precisely with regard to this point that some Parish Priests show themselves covetous, and even sordid—disputing with those from whom they are certain to receive nothing, or exacting their rights to the smallest fraction, and wrangling over pence and half-pence. It would be very desirable that such Parish Priests should look up their accounts, in order to see, at the end of the year, how much they have actually gained by being so very exacting. Parish Priests will easily get their fees from honest, respectable persons, even though they be not very pious, provided, only, they be well brought up; but from the ignorant and the irreligious they have nothing to expect. A grasping disposition brings nothing to a Parish Priest except dishonour and trouble; and even though he may succeed thereby in making some trifling addition to his income, yet, if he balances his accounts accurately, he will not in the end find himself richer by a pound. This will not seem an exaggeration to any one who is experienced in these matters. A hundred acts of niggardliness, put them one with another, will not bring him on an average half-a-crown a-piece, while no amount of money will compensate for the discontent, the complaints, and the unpleasantness to which they give rise.

Again, it would be a proof of avarice and meanness in a Parish Priest to wear threadbare and patched clothes, to spend nothing on the purchase of books, to higgle a good deal about the price when making a purchase, and, still worse, not to be prompt in paying his workmen their fair wages.

From another point of view, the want of books is a

great misfortune for a Parish Priest, especially if he be young, and still capable of improving himself in his studies. A Parish Priest ought to be anxious, as far as his means will allow, to stock his library with a good supply of useful books, especially if he lives in a country place where there are no other libraries except his own. What poor, shabby things are the libraries of certain Parish Priests! They afford incontestable proof that the Pastor is very ignorant in every branch of his professional studies.

A Parish Priest must take care, likewise, not to appear anxious to get presents. He would give evidence of covetousness in this respect, by welcoming with extraordinary manifestations of joy those who come to him with presents; for, by his conduct he would say as plainly as in words: *come again, and bring more.* His covetousness would likewise be apparent, were he to manifest great cordiality towards those of his parishioners who frequently make him presents, while adopting a cold and distant manner towards those who do not.

Above all, a Parish Priest should guard against purchasing farms or estates, unless, perhaps, he might happen to be a man possessed of a private fortune. When the people see their Parish Priest, whom they know to have little or nothing of his own, making purchases of this kind after he has had charge of a parish for a few years, they understand very well that he is amassing money, and that he looks upon his Benefice as a business speculation, which, if well managed, is capable of improving the condition of his family.

In proportion as the father of a family is deserving of praise, who saves up money to purchase an estate and improve the *status* of his children, so, in the same proportion, a Parish Priest deserves to be censured, who saves money in order to enrich his relatives.

CHAPTER VIII.

OF THE PRACTICE OF PRAYER.

A PARISH PRIEST ought to be a man of prayer, and it is evident that he has very special need of prayer, in order to discharge, in a fitting manner, the duties of his ministry. But, some one may say, does not a Parish Priest pray quite enough if he celebrates Mass, and recites the Office every day? I am fully satisfied that a Parish Priest who devoutly celebrates Mass, and devoutly recites the Divine Office, prays as much as is required for his own sanctification, and for the sanctification of his people, likewise. If the holy Mass be daily celebrated with the proper dispositions, what graces ought it not to obtain, what a spirit of sanctity ought it not to infuse into a Pastor! And ought not the Office, also, recited with attention and recollection, become for the Parish Priest an inexhaustible fountain of graces and heavenly wisdom? Whoever, then, has the grace to celebrate Mass and to recite the Office with real devotion, might rest content with this much, and dispense himself from all additional prayer.

However, experience teaches that this twofold grace

is never given to those who do dispense themselves from all other prayers. Let us, for instance, observe whether among those priests and Pastors of souls who never say any other prayer except the Mass and the Office, we will find any one of whom it may be said: *He celebrates Mass very devoutly, he recites his Office with great recollection.* Why deceive ourselves? We will not find even one such; nay, more, it will be very difficult to find even one priest of this class who does not hurry through the Mass and Office in a careless, disrespectful manner.

And this will not surprise us in the least, if we reflect that one cannot succeed in celebrating Mass and in reciting the Office devoutly without a lively faith, which will keep us fully penetrated with a sense of the excellence of both the one and the other; and it is impossible to have, or, at least, to preserve this lively faith without mental prayer. If we neglect mental prayer, our faith grows so weak that the Mass and the Office become little better than two material acts, devoid of unction and fervour for the soul of the Priest, and, consequently performed without devotion—or rather more generally performed in a hurried and irreverent manner.

Wherefore, according to the teaching of all Masters of a Spiritual Life, a Parish Priest cannot dispense himself from attending to mental prayer. But, then, it may be asked whether he is to impose this obligation upon himself so strictly, as to look upon it as indispensable for every day without exception. Any one who has a practical knowledge of what it is to discharge the duties of a Parish Priest will answer, without the slightest hesitation: *No*. There are days when no one possessed of common sense would require of a Parish Priest—I mean of a Parish Priest who works hard—to make mental prayer. On Festival mornings he must go into his Confessional early, and remain there for long hours; he must celebrate Mass, and explain the gospel to his people; afterwards he must prepare for his catechetical instruction; and even though he should not have sick calls or other such matters to attend to, he will be kept busy until evening. Then, in the evening he will probably still have some portion of his Office to recite, and it would be advisable to say, in addition, Matins and Lauds for the next day. After all this has been accomplished, will any one possessed of common sense require that a Parish Priest should begin mental prayer?

So far for Festivals: but even certain week-days occasionally occur, also, when a Parish Priest is kept extremely busy from morning to night, in the duties of the ministry, and when it cannot reasonably be expected, that he should force himself to find time for this laborious kind of prayer. I use the word *laborious* advisedly, although some people think that they can show, without the least trouble, that it is the easiest thing in the world. No less an authority than the Ven. Da Ponte, who was better acquainted with this subject than most men, teaches that mental prayer is a difficult and laborious exercise (Introduction to Part I., § 6), and whoever practises it knows that this is true. Surely, then, we cannot expect a man who is already weary to begin this laborious kind of prayer. Nor can we escape from this difficulty by painting to ourselves in imagination men such as they might be—all fervour and spirit after a day of prolonged labour and occupations which are not invariably pleasant. We must take men as we find them under such circumstances, often weary and prostrated in strength, and more in need of some recreation than of a new and severe mental occupation.

On such days—whether they be Festivals or Weekdays—it will be quite enough for a Parish Priest to recite his Office and say a few customary daily prayers, to pay a short visit to the Blessed Sacrament, to raise his thoughts to God frequently during the day, and to endeavour to perform all his duties with the proper intention of promoting His glory. I remember that a Confessor, skilled in matters appertaining to the Spiritual Life, used to say: *when the Confessional deprives you of the time for meditation, it supplies the want of it.*

However, a Parish Priest ought to be careful not to dispense himself altogether from mental prayer, on the plea of severe and continual labour in the works of the ministry. To do so would be injurious alike to himself and to his parishioners, since it would be too much to expect that a Parish Priest could preserve the true Ecclesiastical Spirit, if he were so entirely occupied in his labours for others, as never to bestow a thought on the affairs of his own soul and keep his Faith alive in the midst of his labours. Wherefore he ought, if necessary, even to lessen his labours, notwithstanding that they are holy, in order to give a little time to mental prayer. And just as we must disapprove of that rigorous rule which would require a Parish Priest to make mental prayer every day without exception, so we must likewise disapprove of that unduly lax doctrine which would dispense him from the habitual practice of meditation, on the plea of the many duties which he is called upon to discharge.

Good Parish Priests make a Retreat in some religious house from time to time—at least every two years, or every third year at the very utmost. It is impossible to estimate how useful this is both for themselves and for their parishioners, since during these days they not only have time, but are as it were compelled, to reflect upon the reformation of their own lives, as well as upon the reforms which they ought to introduce into the government of their parishes.

A Parish Priest who never makes a Retreat—unless, indeed, he may happen to be scrupulous, and as such, forbidden to do so by his Director—affords grounds for suspecting that he belongs to the class of those who shrink from looking into their own consciences, because they fear to discover there what they do not wish to see—that is to say, certain matters on which they love to close their eyes when they go to Confession, and celebrate the Holy Mass. Such persons resemble children, who, when they see some object which terrifies them, try to give themselves courage by placing their hands before their eyes.

There is no doubt that priests of this class have greater need of a Spiritual Retreat than any others. Some persons lull their conscience to repose after this fashion: "that act, after all, is of no consequence, or at best it is but a trifle . . . . there was not full malice in that other act. . . . . I think I need not be much troubled about that other affair, on the ground of *parvitas materiæ*. . . . . I ought not to imperil the peace of my soul, &c." If such persons only once made a Retreat, they would see matters in a far different light. They would see that that act was of some consequence . . . . that there was full malice . . . . that there was *materia gravis;* and by remedying everything by means of a good confession, they would acquire true peace of soul, to which they are at present utter strangers.

CHAPTER IX.

OF THE PRACTICE OF ZEAL.

§ 1. THE ZEALOUS PARISH PRIEST EXERTS HIMSELF TO THE UTMOST, AND WITHOUT SPARING HIMSELF, TO PROMOTE THE GLORY OF GOD AND THE SALVATION OF SOULS.

There are some Parish Priests who greatly resemble statues fixed in a niche; and just as there are some statues which are highly valued, so among these Pastors you may find some who are praised by men. Parish Priests of this class look upon their office as an honourable and lucrative one, and they discharge the duties attached to it mechanically and by routine, taking great care never to fail in those duties which are, so to speak, material—never, for instance, omitting to preach on Festivals, never allowing the sick to die without the Sacraments, and so forth. In as much as they guard against such faults as these, they have no fear of incurring the censure of the world, and think they have a right to say: *I do not omit any of my duties; I perform everything that the Canons of the Church and custom require from a Parish Priest.* As a matter of fact, these Parish Priests do possess negative goodness, in as much as they cannot be reproached with grave neglect in the discharge of the duties of their ministry; and if, in addition to this, they are courteous and gentlemanly, if they are learned and well-read, they are highly esteemed, as a general rule, and are regarded as good and respectable Parish Priests. Nevertheless, if we reflect on their manner of administering their parishes, we are forced to call them, in a great measure, Statues—cold, lifeless statues—statues that are even an incumbrance to the unfortunate parish in which they are placed.

These Parish Priests hear Confessions, but only at hours which suit their own convenience, and only on certain fixed days. If penitents come to them who are ignorant or insufficiently disposed, they are rudely sent away. They get rid of pious penitents, telling them plainly that they are frequenting the Sacraments too often, and that it would be much better for them to look after their families, and attend to their domestic duties. The consequence is that their Confessional is all but deserted, and scarcely anybody is seen there, except, now and again, a few wealthy people.

These Parish Priests preach, but always upon general topics. They never deal with those special points which would be most necessary for the people, in view of the particular circumstances of the times or of the locality. If they be men of a literary turn, they aim at style in their sermons in order to please the educated, while the poor people, meanwhile, understand but little of their discourse, and derive scarcely any advantage from it.

Should there be disorders and scandals in the parish, these Pastors, with a prudence all their own, shut their eyes to the fact. They see nothing wrong, and they take no precautionary measures against evil-doers. If any of their parishioners wish to be good, they may be good; if they wish to be bad—why, let them. It would seem as though the salvation or damnation of souls were a matter which did not in the least concern these good, easy-going Pastors.

There might be an immense amount of good to be done in the parish in promoting the frequentation of the Sacraments, the instruction of youth, and many pious practices among the people, but these Parish Priests never bestow a thought on such matters. As long as they continue to govern the parish, everything must go on precisely as it has always gone on in the past. They will not tolerate the introduction of new practices: the very fact that a practice is new is for them a conclusive proof that it must be bad.[1]

[1] It would be desirable that those indiscreet opponents of everything in the shape of novelty should read a beautiful passage from the letter of St. Bernard *ad fratres de Monte Dei*, from which we extract the following words: "Cum manifestum lumen veritatis obnubilare non queunt, de solo novitatis nomine cavillantur, veteres ipsi, et in veteri monte nescientes nova meditari, utres veteres non capientes vinum novum, quod si eis infunderetur, rumperentur. Sileant ergo qui in tenebris de luce judicantes, vos arguunt novitatis ex abundantia malæ voluntatis, ipsi potius arguendi vetustatis et vanitatis."—*Author's note*.

Not only are these Pastors inactive themselves, but, moreover, if they have in the parish any zealous priest who is anxious to do good, they grow jealous of him, and instead of encouraging and helping him, they leave nothing undone to discourage and oppose him, in order that he may not disturb that happy repose in which the parish is slumbering. In a quiet, good-humoured way, they turn him into ridicule before seculars, they assail his arguments with smart remarks, and in the end this good priest is forced either to resign, or be content to lead a miserable existence.

Then it is that the parish feels the full weight of that cold statue which it has got in the person of its Parish Priest—a weight which crushes every tender bud of devotion and piety. But precisely because this statue does not disturb the bad, looks with favour upon the indifferent, and offers opposition only to the good whom he forces to suffer in silence, the statue is applauded, and the world says: *he is a good Parish Priest*.

But, in saying this, the world lies. The good Parish Priest is he who is zealous for the glory of God and the salvation of souls; who promotes both the one and the other as far as his ability, his position, and his purse will allow; who, in a word, acts in a manner diametrically opposite to the course pursued by the statue described above. It is another characteristic of the good Parish Priest who is zealous for the interests of his sacred ministry never to calculate the precise amount of work to which he may be strictly bound in duty, but only what the love of

God ought to prompt him to do. How utterly mean it is, to wish to give to God barely what we are bound to give Him by positive precept!

He who aims so low as this will surely strike far below the mark, and will, therefore, fail even in discharging that strict duty in regard of which he thinks he would not wish to fail. Let a Pastor of souls reflect whether our Lord Jesus Christ, the Pastor of Pastors, spared Himself in any respect when there was question of promoting the glory of His Divine Father, and of effecting the salvation of souls!

§ 2. A ZEALOUS PARISH PRIEST WILL AVAIL HIMSELF OF THE ASSISTANCE OF THOSE PRIESTS WHOM HE HAS IN HIS PARISH, AND WILL FOSTER THE PROPER SPIRIT IN THEM BY MEANS OF ECCLESIASTICAL CONFERENCES.

Since a good Pastor is resolved to perform, for the glory of God and the salvation of souls, not only all that he is bound to do, but all that he can, the natural consequence is that, in a certain sense, he multiplies himself, and labours for his flock with the aid of every suitable instrument which he can find to hand.

He calculates, first of all, to what extent he can count on the priests who are resident in his parish; and, as far as each one's capacity allows, he makes them all co-operate with him in working out this great end. He strives to secure their good-will, by giving them proofs of his esteem and regard whenever an opportunity of doing so may arise; so that they may be induced to assist cheerfully in all the works of the ministry, whenever they may be requested to do so. If these priests entertain a kindly feeling for their Parish Priest, they prove a great help to him whenever he may need their assistance, nor will they refuse to do at his request what otherwise they would not be bound to do.

Above all, a Parish Priest must endeavour to gather these priests round him for the purpose of occasionally holding a conference with them on Ecclesiastical subjects. By this means he becomes better acquainted with their spirit, he is enabled to correct any erroneous habits of thought which may have been growing upon them, he is in a position to instil into them safe principles and sounder maxims, and, should their principles and maxims be already sound, he has an opportunity of strengthening their growth.

It is difficult to realise all the good that is effected by conferences of this kind between zealous Pastors and their priests. They create and foster that oneness of thought and action, which is the mainspring of harmony between priests in the exercise of the sacred ministry—a harmony which edifies the people, encourages the good, and is a source of terror to evil doers. In these conferences projects are formed for promoting good works, and the plans are discussed for carrying them successfully into execution. In these conferences all the priests are encouraged by their Pastor to labour in the vineyard of the Lord, each according to his ability—one by preaching, another by hearing Confessions, another by instructing the children, another by interesting himself in the confraternities and other pious congregations which may be already existing in the parish, or which it might be advisable to establish there. In this manner the Parish Priest works through them all; and with their co-operation accomplishes in a very short time an amount of good, which, unassisted, he would not be able to accomplish even in the space of several years.

These conferences have always been encouraged, and sometimes ordered by zealous Bishops, and have been always adopted in practice by Parish Priests endowed with a true Ecclesiastical spirit. If a new Parish Priest should find them already established in his parish, he should not allow them to fall into disuse, or to be held too rarely, but should be careful to maintain them in full vigour, and to hold them frequently. Should they never have been introduced into the parish, let him make a beginning, even though he should have only a few priests in the place. Nay, though the curate should be the only other priest in the parish, yet, even so, let him hold conferences with the curate; since there is nothing in the world to prevent even two priests from holding conference together to their own great advantage.

The chief subject of discussion at these conferences ought to be Moral Theology—a study which is so necessary to Confessors, and which will prove extremely useful to the Parish Priest himself, even though he may already be well read in the subject;

for it embraces an extent of matter so wide and varied, that it includes almost everything relating to the guidance of souls.

Should there be good Parish Priests in the neighbourhood, a zealous Pastor might likewise contrive to bring them, also, together to an occasional conference; in order that all may mutually improve one another, and discuss the good which it may be in their power to effect among their people. These conferences are even of greater importance than the others, since their influence is more widely felt.

§ 3. A ZEALOUS PARISH PRIEST AVAILS HIMSELF OF THE ASSISTANCE OF PIOUS SECULARS.

In every parish, no matter how small, we may always find a number of persons who are more or less inflamed with the love of God; and there is no doubt that all of these may be made very useful to a good Parish Priest. For no one can be inflamed with the love of God without zeal for His honour, and, indeed, what else is zeal, according to the teaching of the Angelic Doctor, but the product of the fervour of charity? (1-2, q. 28, a. 4, O.)

Wherefore, such persons of both sexes are very capable of helping the Parish Priest, and they are, moreover, very anxious to do so. A Pastor may find persons of this class among those pious old men who, having learned the vanity of the world, are leading lives of holiness; he may find them among those good youths endowed with a naturally virtuous disposition, who have been given to the practice of piety from their very infancy; he will find some pious widows of this class; he will find, also, some good young girls similarly disposed, especially if they have already formed the great resolution of persevering in the state of holy virginity—a resolution which more than any other conduces to a life of perfection, and even inspires persons with an Apostolic spirit for the furtherance of every good project.

These devout souls will form the nucleus of pious Congregations and Unions, and will prove the mainstay of the good institutions established in the parish. By their exertions and zeal they will win over the negligent to frequent the Sacraments and the preaching of God's Word, they will persuade them to sanctify the Festivals, to join in the performance of works of Mercy, and to lead for the future an edifying life.

However, the greatest service of all in work of this kind can be rendered, as experience shows, by pious widows and girls, who take it upon themselves to look after female children neglected by their parents, and young women who are wavering between a worldly and a pious life. They will direct many of the former into the good path of Christian virtue, and will rescue many of the latter from those first snares which the world lays for the inexperienced—nay, they will induce them to lead a spiritual life, and to become the means of winning others over from the world, instead of themselves becoming its prey.

And it must be remembered that without such

help as this, a Parish Priest could not possibly attempt much of the good which might be accomplished for women. How could he possibly collect together young girls between the ages of twelve and twenty years, and spend his recreation hours familiarly with them, telling them edifying stories, and exhorting them to devout practices, to detachment from the world, and to the love of God? Woe to the Parish Priest who should attempt a mission of this kind, which, though holy in itself, would quickly become in his case a scandal, and a cause for reproach! And still worse, what would be said if he were to hunt up those girls in houses not favourable to piety, as, for instance, in factories, in shops, in public taverns, where, however, zealous women may go in search of them without any risk of scandal, or of uncharitable remarks?

To accomplish work of this kind, some Pious Unions of women have been formed, which cannot be too highly commended. Of these I would mention specially that of *St. Raphael and St. Dorothy*, and, in the next place, the two *Pious Unions of the Sons and of the Daughters of Mary Immaculate*. The members of these two last mentioned sodalities, though living in the world, propose to themselves to aspire to Christian perfection, not only by the exact fulfilment of the Divine law, but also by the perpetual observance of perfect chastity, and by cultivating in a special manner the virtues of obedience and of poverty of spirit. They propose to themselves, furthermore, to labour as far as they can for the sanctification of their neighbour.[1]

§ 4. A ZEALOUS PARISH PRIEST IS VERY MODERATE IN HIS AMUSEMENTS.

I do not mean to be so rigid as to hold a Parish Priest guilty of a fault because he occasionally indulges in the chase—provided, however, it be not *clamorosa*—or spends an occasional hour in playing some legitimate game. This is not forbidden by the Canons, nor do I mean to forbid it, and I would scruple to judge ill of a man for indulging moderately in these recreations. However, since I am dealing exclusively with practice, I may be permitted to say that the passions of the chase and of gambling are very injurious to the spirit of a Parish Priest, and very detrimental to the interests of his flock. They are two passions by which a good deal of a Parish Priest's precious time is quickly squandered, and by which he is easily brought to neglect his duties.

If a Parish Priest allows himself to be enslaved by a love for the chase, many a morning he will ab-

---

[1] The pious association of *St. Raphael and St. Dorothy* may be found described in a work published at Genoa (Tipografia della Gioventù), in 1863, and entitled "*Rules of the Congregations of the Children of our Lady of Dolours*". The same publishers brought out, in 1864, the "*Rule of the New Ursulines, Daughters of Mary Immaculate,*" a pious association which flourishes in Rome and the suburban Dioceses, and is spread throughout all Italy. "*The Pious Association of the Sons of Mary Immaculate*" is more recent. Their rule also was printed at Genoa (Tipografia della Gioventù), in 1866.—*Author's Note.*

sent himself from his Confessional, contenting himself with merely celebrating the Holy Mass in a hurried fashion, and sometimes, perhaps, omitting to do even this. Priests who are fond of the chase do not like to be bound down to the work of the Confessional every day, especially at certain seasons. Then, again, how can they attend to mental prayer? Even they themselves can hardly be offended if we suppose them no more accustomed to it than David was to the coat of mail with which Saul invested him, and which he put aside saying, *usum non habeo*. These, again, are the priests who are remarkable for rushing through the Divine Office, and who rarely say it at the proper time.

The passion for play is even still more injurious to a priest, since it makes him lose not only the evening and a good part of the night, but the morning also; for, if he sacrifices his sleep in the night, he must make good the loss by staying in bed in the morning. Moreover, it is not a rare occurrence to see Ecclesiastics giving evidence of covetousness and impatience at play, and squandering foolishly at the gaming table money of which they are bound to make a good use.

It must be remarked in general that a special virtue is required in order to preserve due moderation in these amusements. Many, indeed, would wish to preserve this moderation, yet they complain, nevertheless, that they do not know how to do so.

It is, furthermore, worthy of remark that very zealous Parish Priests can never find time either for the chase or for play. Pastors of this class are, thank God, numerous, and they are all perfectly content to live in ignorance of the rules of the chase and of the gaming table.[1]

§ 5. A ZEALOUS PARISH PRIEST PROMOTES EVERY WORK OF CHRISTIAN PIETY.

Just as a person may take pride in having his garden rich in every variety of beautiful flowers, so in like manner a zealous Parish Priest prides himself in having his parish rich in all the works of Christian piety, which are the flowers that adorn the garden of the church. Now, this rich variety in spiritual matters is highly conducive to the sanctification of souls; for, in spiritual, as in corporal matters, tastes

---

[1] In the Synod of Maynooth (Decretum xviii. *De vita et honestate clericorum*) we find the following decrees relating to amusements forbidden to priests:—

118—"A publicis equorum cursibus, a venatione quæ fit cum magno clamore, equis et canibus, et a theatrorum publicorum quorumcumque spectaculis, etiam iis quæ nuncupantur *opera* scenica et *circus* equestris, prorsus abstineant. Si quis vero clericus sive sæcularis sive regularis hanc legem violaverit, suspensionem ipso facto incurrat."

119—"Cum in chartis lusoriis haud modicum aliquando tempus teratur et desidia turpiter foveatur, caute admodum adversus hujusmodi lusum se munire debet sacerdos præsertim ubi da pecunia agitur, ne aleatoris illi nota inuratur."

120—"Conviviorum festivitatem ad intempestam noctem producere viro Ecclesiastico omnino indignum judicamus: nec cum debitâ ad orationem attentione, nec cum decenti ac devota sacrorum mysteriorum celebratione ullo modo conciliandum: et districte prohibemus ne sacerdos aliquis chartarum vel alios hujusmodi lusus ad multam noctem protrahat."—*Translator.*

differ, and the greater is the abundance of devout practices in a parish, the greater will be the variety of spiritual food for the members of the flock, so that many who would feel a dislike for a particular devotion, and would, consequently, abstain from practising it, will feel a relish for another, and will adopt it.

It is not my present intention to enter into particulars regarding this subject, because, here and there throughout the preceding pages, I have already alluded to the various works of Christian piety which ought to be promoted by a Pastor; I shall merely remark that we cannot reckon among zealous Parish Priests those who scoff at many pious practices which are classed by some under the head of *Jesuitism*—a term which in our times is only too significant.

CHAPTER X.

OF THE PRACTICE OF OBEDIENCE.

A Parish Priest must, above all things, be obedient to the Church; and, therefore, he ought to observe scrupulously that Canon Law which has really emanated from the Church, and has received her sanction. Those persons are both foolish and wicked who follow a Canon Law which the Church has condemned, or who intepret the Canons in a manner different from that in which they are understood by the Church. A Canon Law which the Church rejects, or which is interpreted otherwise than as the Church interprets it, cannot have any authority. It involves a contradiction in terms, being at one and the same time canonical and uncanonical. It is a bastard Canon Law, the offspring of the Church's enemies, and utterly repudiated by the Church herself. Now, it is evident that the Church speaks through the Sovereign Pontiff, and through the authorities constituted by him. Let a Parish Priest, therefore, always, and in all circumstances, obey the voice of the Church.

In doubtful matters, and in everything which comes within the sphere of Episcopal jurisdiction, let him obey his Bishop. I have said in *doubtful matters;* because, in some circumstances, doubts may

OF THE PRACTICE OF OBEDIENCE.

now and again arise as to what really is the wish of the Church. If, in cases of this kind, the Bishop speaks, he must be obeyed, and he will afterwards be responsible before God and the Church for his decision. A Parish Priest must obey the Bishop fully and cordially, even though it might be possible to disobey him with impunity; for, though a Bishop, especially in large dioceses, cannot come to discover all the violations of the law of which Parish Priests may be guilty, yet they are all known to God.

We ought to reflect that, as I have elsewhere remarked, the happy issue and efficacy of orders emanating from the Bishop depends upon us, Parish Priests. Those who are placed by the Holy Ghost to govern particular churches, which under the jurisdiction of the Supreme Pontiff constitute the Holy Catholic Church, being animated by the same Divine Spirit, publish those regulations which they judge most opportune for the religious instruction of the people, for the more becoming administration of the Sacraments, for the conversion of sinners, for the encouragement of the good, for the extirpation of vice, and for the secure establishment of piety. Now, if Parish Priests, with that holy earnestness which springs from a humble and good disposition, correspond to the zeal of the Bishops, these latter can console themselves with the thought that their regulations will prove most beneficial to the flock of Christ; because when they have the support by word and act of all their Parish Priests, the zeal of the Bishop becomes multiplied, and permeates every corner of the Diocese. But if, on the other hand, the Parish Priests do not co-operate with their Bishops, all Episcopal regulations will become a dead letter, or nearly so, since it is extremely difficult for Bishops personally to exhort and persuade the Faithful. Wherefore, Parish Priests ought to reflect upon this great responsibility with which they are charged, that, namely, of rendering the zeal of the chief Pastors either fruitful or inoperative.

Let them remember, furthermore, that the Bishop is not only their superior, but also their father, master, and counsellor, assigned to them as such by God; and therefore their relations towards him ought to be regulated by filial reverence, by entire docility, and by continual dependence upon him in all that they may propose to themselves to do.

Filial reverence requires that a Pastor should not offer any opposition to his Bishop; and indeed it would be well that a Parish Priest should never oppose his Ordinary, even when he might have just cause for doing so. Disputes between a Parish Priest and his Bishop are like disputes between children and their father: they look badly in the eyes of the world, and, as a rule, they end unfortunately.

Now and again, a Bishop, misled by false reports from persons whom he judges trustworthy, may entertain an unfavourable opinion of some one of his Parish Priests, and influenced by this opinion may grow cold towards him, may reprimand him undeservedly, and may even take measures somewhat prejudicial to him. Should the Parish Priest be in a position to establish his innocence before his Superior, let him do so, in order that he may come to know the true state of the case; but if the Parish Priest have no evidence to put forward in his own justification, or if the Bishop be unwilling to receive the evidence, his best course will be to accept this trial in a spirit of perfect resignation, as coming, for his greater good, from the hand of God. And let him be assured that the trial does come from God; for, as experience itself shows, God really does ordain all trials for our greater good.

There are two cases, however, in which this spirit of resignation would be out of place, that is, when calumnious charges are made affecting the chastity or the honesty of a Parish Priest; for, the vices of impurity and dishonesty bring with them so much infamy that no priest, and especially no Parish Priest, could afford to allow any imputation of this kind to rest upon his character. Wherefore a Parish Priest, while observing all due reverence towards his Superior, would be bound to leave nothing undone towards clearing himself of charges of this kind. This, in fact, would be a case when a Parish Priest, conscious of his innocence and able to prove it, would be bound to demand a strict judicial investigation at the hands of the proper authorities. In a matter so delicate and so vitally affecting his character, no one could blame a Parish Priest for challenging the unfounded prejudices of his Bishop; and there is reason to suppose that God would allow the innocence of His

Minister to be established to the great consolation of the Bishop himself, to whom nothing could be more pleasing than to be convinced that in a matter of this kind he had been deceived.

The entire docility which a Parish Priest ought to manifest towards his Bishop, requires that in all disputes which he may have with his Church Committee, with the Confraternity established in his parish, with the local Authorities, and so forth, the Parish Priest should be prepared to submit cheerfully to any counsels which he may receive from the Bishop. It is to be presumed that the Bishop is more prudent than he, or that he is at least less influenced by passion and prejudice; for when a person is not deciding in his own cause, he is the better able to weigh the arguments for and against, and to estimate the consequences which may follow from conceding or withholding a certain right. Moreover, when a Parish Priest leaves a case entirely in the hands of the Bishop, he cannot by any possibility be blamed, no matter how the affair may eventually be decided. There are some Parish Priests who bring upon themselves a world of trouble and annoyance, and who pass their lives in interminable disputes, simply because they do not know how to yield full obedience to the counsels of their Bishop.

Finally, a Parish Priest ought to be continually dependent on his Bishop, that is to say, he ought not to take up good projects on the impulse of his own individual whims, but ought to submit them to the judgment of his Bishop, in order to avoid the risk of acting imprudently.

In saying this, I by no means wish to insinuate that a Parish Priest ought to have recourse to the Bishop and seek his approbation and permission for every good work which has to be done in the parish. When the good which he proposes to do is purely good, and involves no risk—such as, for instance, to promote the frequentation of the Sacraments, to establish pious Congregations approved by the Church, and the like—it would be doing the Bishop a wrong to suppose for a moment that he could oppose it. Nor could there be any reason for supposing that he would be unwilling to see such good works carried out without his express permission, which indeed it would not be lawful for him to refuse. The dependence on the Bishop of which I am speaking is to be practised with regard to all those matters, which, however good and holy they may be in themselves, might involve risk because of some special circumstances of the times, or of persons whom they might affect; such as, for example, the risk of law-suits, the risk of disagreements with the Church Committee, with the local Authorities, or the like. If Parish Priests were not always to rely on their own judgment, but were on the contrary to take counsel with their Bishops on all matters of importance, or which might involve risk, the prudence of the Bishop would save them from many mistakes, and the good which they would effect would not be occasionally marred by evil consequences, as has sometimes happened.

Everything may be easily and successfully accomplished if we will only bear in mind that *Spiritus Sanctus posuit Episcopos regere Ecclesiam Dei.*

CONCLUSION.

HAVING now finished this work, which I undertook for the benefit of New Parish Priests, there are two matters for which I would apologise and crave their pardon, namely, for the imperfections of my style, and for the freedom of language which I have employed in treating my subject. I am not a *littérateur*, and therefore I do not know how to write with terseness and elegance; while, as regards the second point, speaking as an elder brother to his juniors, I considered myself privileged to employ the most frank and plain language, just such as one member of a family might employ towards another. This same feeling of seniority has emboldened me to dispense with all ceremony, and to speak out the truth plainly, such as I knew it. This course may often have appeared presumptuous in a writer possessing no authority from his position, or his talents, or his learning; however, since my book must now go before my brethren such as it is, I venture to hope that their good nature will make allowance for its defects, and will pardon my freedom of speech. But, notwithstanding its defects, I find comfort in the thought that this work of mine must be substantially good,[1] because, in addition to being the result of experience—that best of teachers—it has also received the approbation of those who are qualified to pronounce judgment upon its merits. Let my readers, then, attend to the substance of what I have written, and pass over whatever appertains merely to the manner in which I have set it down.

In my concluding remarks I shall waive all compliments and ceremony. To you, New Parish Priests, it is a matter of paramount importance that you reflect upon the immense good which you can effect among the flock of Christ, if you commence your pastoral career burning with zeal for the glory of the Good Shepherd, and for the salvation of those souls which were dearer to Him than His very life.

You can do immense good, if you reflect that to you it belongs to break to the flock of Christ the bread of the Word of God—that Word which is powerful enough to eradicate from all hearts every vice, and to plant there every virtue, by teaching them the great truths of Religion, in comparison with which every light of human wisdom is but darkness—that Word which produces Saints, and, if need

---

[1] That the Author did not deceive himself in forming this estimate of the value of his work, is proved by the fact that it has already run through *nine* editions in Italy. This fact speaks for itself; but the Reader will find, moreover, in the Translator's Preface, prefixed to this volume, the opinion of the celebrated Jesuit Theologian, Fr. Ballerini, regarding the merits of Frassinetti's "Manual"—an opinion, expressed in language so strong, that we might almost be inclined to suspect it of exaggeration. —*Translator.*

be, Martyrs—that Word which made the Pagan world Christian, and by which we must prevent the world from again relapsing into Paganism, as the folly of our age would seem to desire.

You can do immense good, if you reflect that you are the Ministers of the Sacraments, those fountains of salvation and of eternal life whence sinners receive justification, the good, perfection, and the Church of God her brightest lustre; and above all, that you are the Ministers of the Most Adorable Eucharist, wherein is perpetuated the Priesthood of Christ, and in which the Church here on earth possesses all that is best and most beautiful in Heaven.

To you, also, is assigned the task of correcting the erring, of counselling the doubtful, of encouraging the timid, of checking the imprudent, and of coming to the relief of all the necessities of your people, whose fathers you are.

Mere philanthropy has never ventured even to pretend to the vast field for labour which charity opens up to you for the performance of every good work, both spiritual and temporal; so that, as the experience of all centuries proves, and as the most enlightened statesmen admit, it is on you that even Civil Society rests its hopes, since it recognises its surest foundation and its main support in that Religion which you teach, and the practice of which you inculcate upon the people.

You can do immense good, if you reflect, that, being now in the flower of your age, your physical and mental powers are at their best, and that you can promise yourselves very many years of incessant labour. Oh, how much good cannot you perform, which has become impossible for us who already feel the weight of years!

It is true, your lot has fallen upon evil days, whereas ours was cast in happier times. Nevertheless, since the times are liable to change, and good and evil days come by turns in this poor world of ours, a brighter future is in store for you when we, old men, shall be in our graves. Meanwhile, console yourselves with the thought that in periods of affliction the virtue both of Pastors and of their flocks is refined and purified. It is a very debateable question, whether greater good is done in the Church of God in time of peace or in time of persecution; and I would not venture to decide whether, all things being considered, Religion has been more flourishing in the prosperous days that have gone by than it now is in this hour of trial. The words of our Redeemer must be verified: *in mundo pressuram habebitis sed confidite, ego vici mundum* (John xvi. 33). In the eyes of God, the world, at the very moment when it rages most fiercely against the Disciples of Christ, is no better than a crushed and vanquished foe.

Courage, then, my brothers. Be not intimidated by the hostility of the times in which you live; but begin and continue your pastoral career, burning with zeal for the glory of the Good Shepherd, and for the salvation of those souls which, as I said before, were dearer to Him than His very life. If you do so, immense will be the good which you will accomplish in the Church of God, in defiance of the times, be they ever so hostile.

The Church expects this immense good at your hands just now, when the times are for her so sad and bitter. This afflicted Spouse of Christ, rendered more beautiful and noble by her sufferings, expects it from you. Her present troubles are unique in her long history; but they only make her all the more noble and beautiful, as Esther of old, when she swooned away through fright, appeared more beautiful than ever in the eyes of Assuerus.

The time is not far distant, let us hope, when her Spouse will stretch forth to her His Sceptre to make her strong again, for He loves her with an exceeding great love. And will not we, also, love this Church which merits the immense love of Christ? Nay, will not each one of us, in a transport of love, exclaim with St. John Chrysostom: "I love her, I love her, I am infatuated with love of her"? And will not each one of us exert himself to the very utmost to achieve all that she desires and expects from him? Yes, this shall be our firm resolve, for it is thus only we can prove the love which we entertain for her.

APPENDIX.

ON THE PERPETUAL ADORATION OF THE MOST HOLY SACRAMENT FOR THE EXALTATION OF HOLY CHURCH.

(See p. 156, *Supra*.)

THE more we cause the incense of prayer to ascend to the throne of God, the more copiously do we draw down His mercies upon men. Therefore, whoever labours to promote the Spirit of prayer in the Church not only promotes thereby the glory of God, but contributes also to the Salvation of Souls, who will be saved in greater numbers in proportion as Heaven showers down upon them more abundant graces.

The pious practices of "perpetual worship" which have long been established in the Church, and have been favoured by the Saints, contribute largely to promote this spirit of prayer. The prayer promoted by associations of this kind is so much additional prayer which would not be said otherwise. It is not interfered with by our ordinary devotions, nor does it interfere with them. It is suited to almost all classes of persons: many persons are willing to take part in it: and few of those who join the association neglect it. I have said that it is suited to almost all class of persons, because, not being obligatory every day, it does not become troublesome, and, moreover, because it may be said in any place, and under any circumstances that are not absolutely incompatible with prayer. I have said also that many persons are willing to take part in it; for it is a most beautiful practice which pleases many persons much more than several other devotional exercises. And, in truth, what practice can be more consoling than that several persons should unite to form, as it were, a choir, for the purpose of sending up to God, all the year round, a song of uninterrupted praise? What else is this but to imitate on earth what the Saints are doing in Heaven? The Saints, entirely absorbed in God, never cease to bless His Infinite Majesty. This is throughout Eternity the occupation of all of them collectively and of each individually; for since they have laid aside the weakness and misery of the flesh, they know no other want except to enjoy their Union with God. But since it is impossible for us to do this individually, we endeavour to accomplish it by uniting together in large numbers. Finally, I have said that few of those who join the association neglect to perform their portion of prayer: because though they are aware that they are not bound to do so by any conscientious obligation, yet it would pain them to think that, through any neglect on their part, the perpetual worship should be interrupted; and hence they are accustomed to withdraw from the association rather than remain members of it while neglecting their allotted portion of prayer.

The foregoing remarks go to prove how effectively these associations of perpetual worship promote the spirit of prayer in the Church, and they prove also that whosoever endeavours to spread such associations among the people, is performing an act of zeal which tends very distinctly to the glory of God. What has been said up to the present is intended to encourage pious souls to promote the spread of these associations; I shall now set down the motives which they may put forward, in order to induce such of the Faithful as are piously disposed to become members of them. The following motives will serve for this purpose.

1. Unbelievers and bad christians in vast numbers are continually insulting God by their sins, and this perpetual outrage is never interrupted by day or night. How pleasing, then, must it be to God to see a number of pious souls forming themselves into an association to make atonement to His Eternal love by an uninterrupted offering of praise! It is in this manner that the incessant hosannas of the Angels in Heaven make reparation for the continual blasphemies of the demons in Hell.

It would fill us with horror to imagine a number of wicked men banding themselves together, and apportioning the days and hours between them, so that no moment might pass without finding some one of them engaged in blaspheming God. Who could ever fully realise the enormity of such guilt? And who, then, on the other hand, can calculate the immense merit of those pious souls who form themselves into an association for the purpose of offering to their God an unceasing tribute of praise?

2. Whoever becomes a member of an association for perpetual worship, acquires, in a certain manner, the full merit of the entire year's prayer. By this I mean that in virtue of the efficacious co-operation of all the associates in keeping up an unbroken prayer all the year round, each individual associate, by merely performing his own allotted portion of, let us say for example, twenty-four hours' prayer in the twelve months, will have at the end of the year the merit of 8,760 hours' prayer, that being the number of hours in the entire year.

Having said this much by way of preface, I would now bring under the notice of my readers the practice of the perpetual worship of the Most Adorable Sacrament, for the Exaltation of Holy Church. It is impossible to imagine any nobler object of worship than this, which is no other than the perpetual pledge of God's love for souls. Nor can we think of any more suitable application of our prayers than to offer them for the Spouse of Jesus Christ and our own dear Mother, whose many necessities are known to us.

This adoration is carried on all through the day and night, but somewhat differently during the more difficult hours of the night. From 4 A.M. to 11 P.M. each associate has assigned to him half an hour's prayer in the week; but those associates whose time for prayer is fixed for the hours between 11 P.M. and 4 A.M., take only one hour's prayer each month. In this manner 266 associates would be required for the easy hours (*i.e.*, from 4 A.M. to 11 P.M.), and 150 for the more difficult hours (*i.e.*, from 11 P.M. to 4 A.M.), making in all, 416 associates. In order to make provision for those months which have thirty-one days, an additional hour in each month should be assigned to seven of the most fervent associates.

Two separate lists must be prepared. One of these, intended for associates who make only half-an-hour's prayer, must be divided into seven columns, corresponding to the seven days of the week, and each column must contain the names of 38 associates. The second list, intended for those who make one hour's prayer in the month, between 11 P.M. and 4 A.M., must be divided into 30 columns, each column containing the names of five associates. Each associate will then receive a card on which will be written his name, his surname, and the hour assigned to him for prayer.

Should the number of those seeking admission into the association be in excess of what would be required, several associates might be appointed for prayer at each hour, both of the day and of the night; taking care, however, to distribute them equally over all the days and all the hours, with the exception of the more difficult hours of the night, when we ought to be content with a smaller number.

Such is the method which I propose, and which, if not absolutely the best, will, at all events, be found suitable, as a rule, for all places. It will even suit country parishes; for if they be large, each parish will be able to have its own association; while, if

they be small, two or three of them can unite to form
an association between them. Moreover, this method
which I have sketched will be found easy; because
half-an-hour's prayer in the week cannot prove
wearisome to devout persons, nor will one hour's
prayer every month be too much for fervent souls,
even though they should have to interrupt their
night's rest to make it. Finally, this method will
be sure to be carried out in practice; both because it
is simple, and also because the day and hour for
prayer being fixed, and recurring at regular short
intervals, they are not likely to be forgotten, as might
otherwise easily happen.

During the hour or the half-hour appointed for
prayer, each associate will recite the Acts of Faith,
Hope, Charity, and Contrition, adding three *Paters*,
Aves, and *Glorias* for the living and the deceased
members of the Association. He may employ the
remainder of the time in mental or in vocal prayer, as
he pleases, either in the Church or in his own house,
having previously formed the intention, however, of
honouring the Most Holy Sacrament by this prayer,
and applying it, as has been said, for the Exaltation
of our Holy Mother the Church.

Before concluding, I must not omit to notice two
objections which are usually put forward by some
who are in the habit of raising difficulties in the
case of every good work. The first objection is, that
those who get up during the night to make the
prayer assigned to them will injure their health, and,
especially in winter, will be sure to bring on them-

selves an attack of sickness. But any one can see that this danger is very remote, indeed. As a general rule, Religious do not suffer in their health, though they not only get up in the night time, but leave their cells and go down into the church to chant the Office. How much more unlikely is it, then, that a person will contract an illness from merely getting out of bed for an hour once, or, at most, twice in the month, without for an instant leaving his bed-room. Oh! how many persons leave their beds and their houses in the dead of night to attend to their temporal affairs, and do so oftener than twice in the month! Why, then, are we to be so extremely careful of our health only when there is question of works of piety?

The second objection is, that this perpetual adoration will often be interrupted during the night time, because the Associates will not awake at the appointed hour, and it will often be interrupted during the day as well, because of the interference of other business incompatible with prayer. I reply that these interruptions during the night will not occur as frequently as may be supposed; for, when a person makes up his mind to awake at a certain hour, he generally succeeds in doing so. Nor will interruptions occur frequently in the day time; because, when a person knows the day and the hour assigned to him for prayer, he can easily make such arrangements beforehand, as will prevent the interference of any other business at that particular hour. In any case, even though interruptions should occur, the principal point is to make the prayer as soon as one can. Those accidental and involuntary interruptions do not destroy the substantial continuity of the worship, and both the glory given to God, and the advantages reaped from it by souls, are just as great as if these interruptions had never occurred.

To all the other objections that may be raised, the following general reply may be given, namely, that whatever succeeds, and injures nobody, cannot be either impossible or hurtful. Now, the pious association of the Perpetual Adoration does succeed, and does not injure anybody, as experience proves in those places where it has been established; and, consequently, we may conclude that it is neither impossible nor hurtful. I might reply, furthermore, that it is far easier to raise difficulties against good works than to promote them; but that much greater credit is due to those who promote them by their exertions, than to those who hinder them by raising difficulties.

www.ingramcontent.com/pod-product-compliance
Lightning Source LLC
Chambersburg PA
CBHW031938290426
44108CB00011B/603